Adventures in the Archaic

the
LIFE
OF
IDEAS

SERIES EDITOR
Darrin McMahon, *Dartmouth College*

After a period of some eclipse, the study of intellectual history has enjoyed a broad resurgence in recent years. The Life of Ideas contributes to this revitalization through the study of ideas as they are produced, disseminated, received, and practiced in different historical contexts. The series aims to embed ideas—those that endured, and those once persuasive but now forgotten—in rich and readable cultural histories. Books in this series draw on the latest methods and theories of intellectual history while being written with elegance and élan for a broad audience of readers.

Adventures in the Archaic

Primitivism, Degrowth, and the
French Social Sciences, 1945–1975

RYAN L. ALLEN

The University of Chicago Press
Chicago and London

The University of Chicago Press, Chicago 60637
The University of Chicago Press, Ltd., London
© 2026 by The University of Chicago
All rights reserved. No part of this book may be used or reproduced in any manner whatsoever without written permission, except in the case of brief quotations in critical articles and reviews. For more information, contact the University of Chicago Press, 1427 E. 60th St., Chicago, IL 60637.
Published 2026
Printed in the United States of America

35 34 33 32 31 30 29 28 27 26   1 2 3 4 5

ISBN-13: 978-0-226-84634-7 (cloth)
ISBN-13: 978-0-226-84636-1 (paper)
ISBN-13: 978-0-226-84635-4 (ebook)
DOI: https://doi.org/10.7208/chicago/9780226846354.001.0001

Library of Congress Cataloging-in-Publication Data

Names: Allen, Ryan L., author.
Title: Adventures in the archaic : primitivism, degrowth, and the French social sciences, 1945–1975 / Ryan L. Allen.
Other titles: Life of ideas.
Description: Chicago : The University of Chicago Press, 2026. | Series: The life of ideas | Includes bibliographical references and index.
Identifiers: LCCN 2025020901 | ISBN 9780226846347 (cloth) | ISBN 9780226846361 (paperback) | ISBN 9780226846354 (ebook)
Subjects: LCSH: Primitivism. | Social sciences—France. | Anthropology—France.
Classification: LCC GN345 .A443 2026 | DDC 300.1—dc23/eng/20250602
LC record available at https://lccn.loc.gov/2025020901

♾ This paper meets the requirements of ANSI/NISO Z39.48-1992 (Permanence of Paper)

Authorized Representative for EU General Product Safety Regulation (GPSR) queries: **Easy Access System Europe**—Mustamäe tee 50, 10621 Tallinn, Estonia, gpsr.requests@easproject.com
Any other queries: https://press.uchicago.edu/press/contact.html

*For my parents,
Stephen and Janice Allen,
and sister,
Brianna Allen*

In order to speculate safely on an inhabitable future, perhaps we would do well to find a rock crevice and go backward. In order to find our roots, perhaps we should look for them where roots are usually found.
    URSULA K. LE GUIN, *Dancing at the Edge of the World*

Contents

Preface ix

Introduction: The Promise of a Certain Primitivism 1
1 Archaic Religion in a New Key: Georges Bataille at Lascaux 17
2 The Work of Nostalgia: Henri Lefebvre's New Theory of Survivals 59
3 Georges Devereux: Mohave Shamanism and
  the Future of Ethnopsychiatry 99
4 Mircea Eliade and Neopaganism as Postcolonial Critique 141
Epilogue: Primitivism in Our Time 178

Acknowledgments 189
Notes 191
Archives Consulted 229
Index 231

Preface

The consequences of climate change are set to be the most gripping drama of the twenty-first century. The Anthropocene, or the "age of man," is one name for the unfolding ecological crisis. It is also the name given to the current geological epoch, in which humanity has become the main driver of planetary change. Since the Second World War, we have altered the Earth's ecosystems and atmosphere so profoundly that we are now a geological force in our own right. As a species, we openly flout the backpacker's motto to "leave no trace," carving proof of our productivity so deeply into the geological record that it will be visible for millennia to come. And we seem obstinately committed to doing so. There was a time when such human signatures adorned only the surface of subterranean rock walls; now the cumulative impact of modern man has left unsightly scars on the planet's lithosphere.

It is generally agreed that if we continue our current course of unabated growth, we may face the sixth mass extinction in Earth's history and the first caused by humanity. Once it was meteorites, mega-volcanoes, and plate tectonics that brought on extinction events; these days the cataclysm is us. There we have it: mankind's ascent from animal origins to ecological disaster. Even in the short term, the consequences of the Anthropocene—droughts and desertification, megafires and extended fire seasons, sea-level rise and flooding—threaten the quality of our lives and the continuity of our communities. Of course, anthropogenic climate change is not the only legacy of postwar Western society, but if the frenetic pace continues, it might be the only one that matters. Is it any wonder, then, that we look back nostalgically on the days when we lived on less and enjoyed some sense of balance? Whether the past, especially the deep past, can offer pointers to our response to the climate crisis is the crucial question I address in this book.

Adventures in the Archaic is about four French-based intellectuals who had their own feeling that the whole of civilization was on a precipice. Sometimes in concert, more often at a distance, Georges Bataille, Henri Lefebvre, Georges Devereux, and Mircea Eliade advanced a primitivist critique of the dramatic upswing in growth after the Second World War. In this turbulent landscape of scorched-earth economies and intensified globalization—which started with the victory over fascism in 1945 and continued until the international stagnation of the 1970s—these thinkers pined for the primitive, though in quite different ways. They saw age-old folkways as useful guides precisely because they ran so counter to the ever-accelerating age. They extolled so-called archaic cultures as carriers of cultural and ecological wisdom, and thus as partial cures to the ills of postwar society. These would-be reformers were torn between renewing and returning; at times they tried to fashion the age-old anew, at other times they spoke of restoring an earlier state—which explains their use of all those verbs starting with the prefix *re-*, recover, revive, rediscover, resurrect, resuscitate, rejuvenate, reawaken. In an age obsessed with the onrushing present, these intellectuals reached backward in order to move forward. Future primitive, I argue, was their unspoken motto.

The work of these four intellectuals was marked by a shared antipathy toward modernization and a reverence for what they called "survivals"—traditions that they believed could bridge the gap between an archaic past and a more sustainable future. The reason they championed certain survivals was simple: They thought primitive cultures cultivated less alienating, more intimate, and more enduring ways of life. It is in this sense, and in this sense only, that they were primitivists. Distressed about razed landscapes, riotous new cities and looming nuclear apocalypse, they turned to the vivid remains of Paleolithic painters, the seasonal rhythms of rural France, and the ancestral traditions of Indigenous peoples.

While varying in doctrine and discipline, the thinkers in this book were united by a single temporal orientation. In what follows I preserve the differences between the four intellectuals, yet I speak throughout of the postwar primitivists, and call their ideas collectively "postwar primitivism." By doing so, I offer an original reassessment of four oeuvres influential in and beyond the French social sciences. In the years immediately after 1945, the postwar primitivists argued that what had survived the long passage of time mattered more than ever. Yet they were discerning, selective *archaïstes* as they knocked the word "archaic" out of its semantic inertia. Theirs is a story, then, of a primitivism of a certain kind.

Research for this book began in Normandy in November 2018, at the precise moment the *gilets jaunes* first took to the streets. Like everyone else, I was

PREFACE   xi

struck by how the movement, named for the high-visibility yellow vests protesters wore, stymied neat categorization. Left, right, progressive, reactionary—none of the standard labels seemed quite right. What was happening out there on the provincial roundabouts, the emblematic site of yellow-vest protest? A harbinger of a new French far right? Or a collective discontent driven less by xenophobia and more by contempt for urban elites and the global systems that enrich them? I now know what I suspected at the time: The sense of things being all mixed up spoke less to the inconsistencies of the movement I was observing than to the shortcomings of dividing people into partisans of progress or resentful reactionaries.

The largest and longest French protest since May 1968 may have started as a backlash against a diesel tax meant to curb fossil fuel consumption, but it quickly became something else. Unfettered by any one trade union or political party, the *gilets jaunes* agreed on one thing: They were adamantly opposed to President Emmanuel Macron's plan to turn France into a "start-up nation." That much was clear. As the months wore on, and as one weekend protest bled into the next, there appeared anticonsumerist critiques, ecological considerations, talk of a postcapitalist commons, and even calls to restore the moral economies that had regulated preindustrial societies—the months-long movement had come a long way from demands for unregulated petrol. Quite naturally I found myself wondering whether there lurked at every occupied roundabout a critique of the present state of society based on something older, more natural, and more sustainable.

In this book I report on a remarkable outpouring of primitivism at the very start of what many economists and climate scientists now call the Great Acceleration. Since the "economic miracle" that remade the West after 1945, intellectual historians and scholars of literature and the arts have either erected primitivism as a model or sought to bury it for good. Beginning in the 1980s, primitivism was held responsible for racism, empire and war, and positive assessments of it drew only derision or disbelief. Such polemical attacks and out-of-hand dismissals seem unsatisfactory today, when, in the crucible of the Anthropocene, everything is (or should be) on the table. The vicissitudes of modern history once more call for revision. Should some lowly archaism be the foundation for every new adventure? Yes and no, I will argue. At any rate, we're going to have to live differently, perhaps for a very long time. And if nothing else the postwar primitivists have the merit of rejecting a Pollyanna-ish faith in business as usual.

In what follows I reveal the how and why as well as the times and places of the postwar primitivists. I read their mid-twentieth-century oeuvres as thought experiments in the art of reviving time-tested alternatives. My point is not that they were prophets of our time or that they always provided a fully fleshed out program for reform—they weren't, and they didn't. Instead, I argue that these untimely thinkers show that if primitivism is to have a place in the intellectual life of the next mid-century, it must be more discerning, more selective, and more closely tied to the social sciences than is typically the case. No small task, but it has been done before. Seventy years ago, the primitive was good to think with. Might it be time to once again venture in the archaic?

INTRODUCTION

The Promise of a Certain Primitivism

> There is nothing more naïve, or more indicative of a failure to learn one of the real lessons of the history of thought, than the tendency of some, even among philosophers, to take the bare fact that a way of thinking is now *démodé* as indicative either that it is false or that it will not come back.
> ARTHUR O. LOVEJOY, "Reflections on the History of Ideas"

In a passage in the provocative *Diary of a Bad Year*, J. M. Coetzee observed that "the argument that the past was better than the present cannot be won, but at least it can be bravely put."[1] We should not be surprised that the Nobel laureate, who is himself prone to nostalgia, spoke of the past in this way. It isn't very easy to determine whether the backward-looking view is a noble longing or a vain conceit; whether we would do well to search for roots where roots are usually found, as the epigraph to this book suggests, or whether waxing nostalgic is simply an excuse for everything from exclusion to misogyny and myopia. In short, Coetzee simplified things somewhat.

This book reinterprets the work of Georges Bataille, a specialist in prehistory; Henri Lefebvre, a philosopher turned rural sociologist; Georges Devereux, an ethnographer and psychiatrist; and Mircea Eliade, a historian of religion, in the postwar period. I take account of each of them in the succeeding chapters. But I want to say now, summarily, that they were a quartet who made a concerted movement toward a new primitivism. As different as they were, they gave rise to a style of thinking rooted in the revival of times past. They bravely argued that certain customs of the past were indeed better than those which appeared in the present.

The curious interrelations of these four intellectuals have allowed me to sketch the main coordinates of what I am calling postwar primitivism. Archaic was these thinkers' preferred replacement for primitive, although that didn't stop them from using the word *primitif*. For three decades after 1945, these terms grew into capacious concepts around which critics of grow-or-die modernity coalesced. Why this acute interest in the *archaïque* after the first half of the twentieth century? Two historical developments spurred this intellectual effusion: the end of European empires and the remaking of Western societies after the Second World War. Taking their cues from the French anthropologist Marcel Mauss, the postwar primitivists sought alternatives to societies that put little stock in local community or cultural continuity—that is, they sought alternatives to societies that quashed the so-called archaisms that are my subject.

Bataille (1897–1962), Lefebvre (1901–1991), Devereux (1908–1985), and Eliade (1907–1986) were children of the twentieth century. Born within a decade of one another, they reached maturity between the two world wars and experienced the same events at about the same age. This rough unity of generational experience shaped their sensibilities without fully determining them. It is no coincidence, then, that their major primitivist works appeared in the late 1940s and '50s when they were middle-aged men. Historians know that the "economic miracle" that remade Western societies after the Second World War was extraordinary; but most scientists now tell us that the massive overhaul was in fact epoch-making. It is not clear when historians will start calling the economic miracle by a different name, but some already call this new age in the history of the carbon economy the Great Acceleration, an appellation tinged with disapproval. From our present-day vantage point of carbon emissions and climate change, the Great Acceleration looks like a one-way road to disaster, which effectively closed the book on an entire geological era.

In this book I defend three claims: First, the postwar primitivists linked the Great Acceleration's emphasis on growth with the ravages of industrialization, imperialism, and world war. These social thinkers did not wait for signs of a slowdown to advance a trenchant critique of growth. Second, I show that for three decades after 1945 primitivism found a home outside the transformative capacities of art and in the concrete inquiries of the social sciences. This corner of the French social sciences proved to be a handmaiden not to war and empire but to a certain primitivism. Third, *Adventures in the Archaic* reveals for the first time a countervailing strand of postwar French thought rooted in the selective revival of times past. Archaic, nostalgic, shamanic: All the problems considered here are located in temporality. To tell the history of how four early proponents of degrowth used the French social sciences to salvage what had survived—that is this book's raison d'être.

The critique of growth is ongoing and ever-urgent, but it is not new. It began sometime in the eighteenth century and runs, I contend, through postwar primitivism to today's degrowth movement. Seven decades ago, the postwar primitivists asserted that the central problem of capitalist societies is the problem of growth. Their curse (and ours) was a fixation on growth and a perverse confidence in its capacity to right the wrongs it creates. All this came at the expense of intimacy, continuity, stability, and sustainability.

Primitive cultures, however, took precautions against accumulation and demanded expenditures of wealth in festivals and creative works. It was only with the end of these ancient interdictions that history was identified with growth and progress largely coincided with history. How and why archaic practices came to be regarded as an antidote to the ills of rampant growth is the stuff of *Adventures in the Archaic*. That the postwar primitivists were early and exemplary degrowth theorists is the first of three central claims I make.

The reason these intellectuals embraced the prehistoric, provincial, and primitive lies in the distinctive nature of the French social sciences after the Second World War. Thanks to the ascendancy of the human and social sciences in the first half of the twentieth century, primitivism could turn scientific and flourish beyond the friendly confines of avant-garde literature and the arts. The postwar primitivists imagined alternatives, but they didn't conjure them out of thin air or discover them in the unconscious. This second claim foregrounds the postwar-primitivism-contra-surrealism argument that runs throughout the book and sets *Adventures* apart from studies of primitivism in popular culture and the arts.[2] Each chapter that follows details the developments and debates of a different French social science. To be clear, *Adventures* is not an institutional history of, say, the social sciences section of the École pratique des hautes études. Rather, I situate the thought of each postwar primitivist within the fields of prehistory, ethnopsychiatry, rural sociology, and the history of religions.

The fact is that the real subject of this book is not generational experience or limitless growth or even the French social sciences. *Adventures in the Archaic* is a book about time, about the relation between past, present, and future, realized as such. What was peculiar about the postwar primitivists, I argue, was their particular handling of time. What was most important to the ideas of Bataille, Lefebvre, Devereux, and Eliade after 1945 was their shared nostalgia, their laments over what had been lost, the way they looked backward in order to move forward. Their fundamental outlook was not political and negative (antigrowth, anticapitalism, etc.); it was temporal and positive (pro–durable communities, pro–cultural continuities, etc.). They cared little that anyone who questions progress is immediately branded old fashioned, out of touch, not with it, and not to be trusted. Postwar primitivism was at once a reactionary and a radical phenomenon, which cannot be separated from a selective revival of times past. This is a story of how four thinkers rescued the past as something living, instead of deeming it the dead material of progress.

Needless to say, the postwar primitivists were not entirely alike. Nonetheless, Bataille, Lefebvre, Devereux, and Eliade arrived at three strikingly similar themes: a conviction that tradition was a mixed bag, a sense that cultural pessimism could be creative, and a tendency to assert that the archaic was both stubborn and persistent and about to disappear.

First, and critically, the postwar primitivists asserted the continued relevance of long-held customs. They were willfully and at times stubbornly anachronistic. Calling cultural survivals precious was one thing, declaring them pertinent was quite another. In an era when it was fashionable to celebrate novelty and adolescence, they chose the customary and the time-tested; when everyone else leaned into the promise of hypermodernization, they took the side of what was primitive, although not unreservedly so. Their embrace of *certain* archaic arts of living was a rejection of the climate of the times and the all-or-nothing approach. The very old is a mixed bag, so it was important to pick through it with discernment. The postwar primitivists often spoke of the archaic in glowing terms, without insisting on the less favorable aspects of the past.[3] They believed that the cultural cachet tradition offered was too fertile to dismiss. While this book is a history of mores and morals rather than of politics, it demonstrates that cultural stewardship was not the privileged preserve of one political party. In the struggle against the capitalist present, stories of past greatness have not always been dismissed as the reactionary ravings of a shipwrecked mind.

Cultural pessimism played a crucial role in the second theme common to Bataille, Lefebvre, Devereux, and Eliade. Unlike their contemporaries, they remained skeptical of modernization's mobility and progress. But their skepticism didn't morph into resentment, cynicism, or nihilism, as it did for some of their more literary-minded predecessors. In the right hands, it seems, nostalgia need not be noxious. My analysis reveals a clear correlation between cultural pessimism and the search for time-tested alternatives. It was thanks to their pessimism, not despite it, that their criticisms became creative. Discontent with contemporary society, these primitivists prove, need not foster resentment; rather, it can be a spark to reform society. Primitivism was for them a reformer's science. And these would-be reformers understood that tearing down is an easier, speedier process than restoring—as anyone who has ever swung a sledgehammer knows. As a consequence, they were committed to reviving cultural survivals and not content with criticism alone. It came to this: the promise of a certain primitivism. Certain cultures encouraged more or less creative, communal, healthy, and sustainable ways of living. These were the simple criteria by which these primitivists compared far-flung cultures. If the first theme examines their attraction to archaic traditions, then the second explains how it was that cultural pessimism went hand in hand with an optimistic belief that those traditions could be revived for redemptive ends. Cultural pessimism was for them a beginning, never an end.

Finally, each postwar primitivist advanced a somewhat paradoxical position. This book's third theme shows how contradictory ideas coexist in the work of even the most astute intellectuals. In a world bent on change, the problem of persistence was paramount. The thinkers I write about argued that when it came to culture, well-worn paths tended to stay that way. Cultural survivals naturally resisted decay; they may not be eternal, but they had survived hundreds of vicissitudes and could endure a hundred more. All the same, each intellectual decried the imminent disappearance of these same survivals. Wave after wave of change meant the cultural disinheritance of entire generations. Driven by a sense of impending loss, these adventures therefore have a tragic aspect. The new, all-consuming agora of global capitalism that had inaugurated the Great Acceleration would eliminate all that had hitherto survived.[4] Bataille, Lefebvre, Devereux, and Eliade repeated this mantra of loss until a paradoxical position eventually emerged. The paradox of the postwar primitivists can be broken down into two propositions: first an assertion of inevitable persistence and then a recognition of imminent disappearance. The former was a reason to remain confident, the latter a cause for alarm.

To be clear, the postwar primitivists were paradoxical not because they lacked clarity or were enamored with ambiguity. Obscurantism—so often paired with paradox in postwar French thought—did not figure in their writings. Their thinking was genuinely paradoxical for no other reason than that they celebrated persistence while at the same time decrying disappearance. In the chapters that follow I remain attentive to the presence of this contradiction in their shared project of salvaging what had survived. When looked at from a less propositional angle, however, it is possible that this paradox merely expressed a historical reality: Cultural elements that were once thought timeless could, in an age of unprecedented change, suddenly reveal themselves to be the most fragile of things. So, regardless of its logical contradiction, the primitivists' paradox often appeared well-founded.

Years before the postwar primitivists took the stage, two French social scientists, Émile Durkheim and Marcel Mauss, were attuned to the rapid changes wrought by large-scale industry and invisible-hand capitalism. Behind their jaundiced view lay a stark reality: Modern Western societies had turned man into an economic animal. In a world in which everything was categorized in terms of buying and selling, the cold calculations of *Homo economicus* had become society's guiding principle. The most serious consequence of the new merchant morality was in social relations. Immoderate competition, in which one party gets the lion's share and the other a pittance, had led to a state of permanent hostility between capital and labor, an antagonism which is "absolutely peculiar to the industrial world," Durkheim wrote in *The Division of Labor in Society* (1893). There seemed to be little more to life, Mauss lamented, than "the skimpy life that is given through the daily wages doled out by employers."[5]

What did they think was the proper response to the ills of modern society? In societies like ours, Durkheim argued, a spontaneous unfolding of the division of labor was the solution to the problem of social disintegration. Contra the postwar primitivists, he thought that the remedy was "not to seek to revive traditions and practices that no longer correspond to present-day social conditions." Tradition had lost its sway, the yoke of primitive practices had been thrown off; nothing to do about it save change, go forward, and specialize, for when specialization meets good management, the individual stands a chance. Nor is this all: Specialization brings in its train more autonomy, more activity, more flexibility, and more geographic and social mobility. A roving nexus of individualism and interdependence—how novel! At any rate, society must go forward; it cannot go back. And it cannot be otherwise: "It is because society changes that we must change."[6] If there seems to be something naive in Durkheim's faith in progress, it is worth remembering that the founder of French sociology was a true believer not in the unfettered market but in measured government regulation and relative social equality.

Nothing so progressive can be found in his nephew's *The Gift: The Form and Reason for Exchange in Archaic Societies* (1925). Thirty years after Durkheim's *Division of Labor*, Mauss sought to recover older customs far removed from modern commercial practices. His was a backward-looking view that set the stage for the postwar primitivists. In particular, the solemn rite of gift exchange was a once-dominant custom too long forgotten. Reciprocal generosity was a natural way of interacting, a human way. Fortunately, this age-old tradition was not lost but still alive, the French anthropologist tells us. Here's Mauss: "A considerable part of our morality and our lives themselves are still permeated with this same atmosphere of the gift, where obligation and liberty intermingle." Although the past was imperfect, so-called archaic societies knew a thing or two about how to slow down and sit down around the common store of wealth. Hence, Mauss's own postwar (post–First World War) imperative: "We can and must return to archaic society and to elements in it."[7] Turning back the clock—how quaint! To many moderns, nothing could be more retrograde and therefore more contemptible. To the postwar primitivists, however, no sentence was so crucial.

Primitivism is a strange and capacious category. The classic work on the subject is *Primitivism and Related Ideas in Antiquity* (1935). Written by the American intellectual historian Arthur O. Lovejoy and his Johns Hopkins colleague George Boas, the book was the first of a planned four-volume series. Lovejoy's introduction to the first volume, "Prolegomena to the History of Primitivism," remains essential. Primitivism is indeed enigmatic, but it is also what Lovejoy called a unit-idea, a perennial theme in the history of ideas which has long preoccupied the best of minds.[8] Primitivism is not a modern invention; it was not invented by Rousseau. Even prehistoric cave paintings express a desire to return to our animal origins. From the mists of antiquity to the fog of modernity, primitivism is one of the most potent tendencies in human thought.[9]

Skepticism plays a key role in primitivistic thinking, and nothing draws doubt out of a primitivist better than the idea of progress. Misgivings about what we call the progress of civilization are at the core of primitivism. Today, the ideology of inevitable and unending growth, which has played so great a part in the history of the last two hundred years, has found new life in the convergence of quick techno-fixes and a starry-eyed optimism. There is a long record, however—the whole of the primitivist tradition—that vehemently questions such unquestioning faith in progress. It has long been suspected that the human animal, Lovejoy once wrote, "would have been less harmful to himself and his fellows if he had never gained the powers which technological progress has put in his hands."[10] First apprehension, then skepticism, and finally a feeling of intense dissatisfaction have accompanied many of the outcomes of modernization thus far. Given how central misgivings are to primitivism, is it any wonder that we arrive at cultural pessimism?

Soon fierce criticism of the historical process that goes by the name progress appeared. But there was a positive side to primitivism, so pessimism and critique do not explain it all. Intense dissatisfaction, it turns out, is something to which the intellect responds. After all the doubt, some primitivists remained prudent, drawing inspiration from pasts once lived, not merely imagined. The primitivists in these pages, for example, maintained that from what we know from anthropologists, prehistorians, rural sociologists, and historians of religion, it is not the case that we can expect nothing better than a technological enhancement of contemporary life. Rather, they believed in a creative combination of progress and the primitive. Some advances and novelties are or can be bad. So, too, are some things that come from the deep past obviously bad. Therefore we should not hesitate to say that tradition, like progress, is a mixed bag. These two movements, intense dissatisfaction and selective revival, combined to create the primitivism I call postwar primitivism.

The other foundational work alongside *Primitivism and Related Ideas* is Robert Goldwater's *Primitivism in Modern Painting* (1938).[11] Like modern thought, primitivism is one of the most recurring tendencies in modern painting. In one way or another, all modern art is infused with the primitive, the art historian tells us. To what does primitivism in modern painting refer? In the main, it denotes not real-world referents but the techniques and inspirations of European painters. "Simplicity of technique, spontaneity of inspiration" was the primitivist's motto. One need only think of the naive techniques of art brut or the role of the unconscious in surrealism. That Goldwater could survey almost a century of painting and find a pining for the primitive speaks to how consistently we have longed for something different. In overripe civilizations, amid the clutter of congested cities and abstract modes of belonging, primitivistic expression flourished. Yet it is only narrowly correct that spontaneity and simplicity capture the essence of primitivism. A different picture emerges when one shifts the frame from twentieth-century art to the mid-century social sciences.

As Goldwater shows, primitivistic attitudes first seized European artists roughly between 1890 and 1910. Hence, the high point of artistic primitivism arrived just at the time when colonial destruction was most keenly felt. A new, more invasive imperialism, in other words, was a necessary condition for aesthetic innovations of the primitivistic type. One of the lessons of this era of colonization is that wherever one encounters disappearance, there primitivism will be too. Like its colonial counterpart, an omnivorous primitivism soon swallowed up everything erstwhile and elsewhere, as the word primitive came to describe exotic curiosities from the tropics, the art of peasants and proletarians, and the traces left behind by Paleolithic hunters. In a pattern that will soon become familiar, modernists triangulated the primitive, the provincial, and the prehistoric. A nexus therefore emerged that mentally brought together Indigenous tribes, rural pastoralists, and Paleolithic peoples. But whether the meaning of primitivism is located in colonial conquest or in a desire for something other than the civilizations that were responsible for imperialism remains an open question.

Primitivism has long been a subject of debate, in and outside the academy. Do primitivists really want to return to some supposed state of nature? Lovejoy thought they did. For him, primitivism amounted to an assertion of the superiority of the state of nature.[12] But there's a catch. Lovejoy did not pretend that the state of nature was a simple, single state. On the contrary, he was well aware that nature has meant a great many things to a great many primitivists—which is why, for the student of intellectual history, nothing is more needed than an understanding of the sacred name of nature. In his essay

"'Nature' as Aesthetic Norm," Lovejoy identified no fewer than eighteen separate meanings of the term nature; the desire to get back to something more natural, then, can mean many things.[13] As a consequence, just as there are various misgivings about the present, so too are there a variety of primitivisms. For his part, Lovejoy distinguished between chronological and cultural primitivisms as well as hard and soft primitivisms. One is earlier, the other is elsewhere; one is all aggression, savagery and violence, the other all sweetness, sensuality and calm.

It is easy enough to dismiss those who are fond of the primitive. Primitivism is politically fraught, awfully masculine, and easy to mock. Primitivists, detractors declare, are at best naive daydreamers and more often racists who should know better. What is less easy to brush aside is the inherent value of certain age-old customs now that a sense of general crisis dominates our thinking. One has only to think of the manifold challenges of anthropogenic climate change to realize that we are in an all-hands-on-deck situation. "We are all agreed," Lovejoy once said, "that the world is a ghastly mess, and that it is a man-made mess." Yet there are primitive possibilities out there for a life richer and more intricately human than our own; that is primitivism's steadfast presumption. There have been other ways of living on this Earth that attract curiosity, arouse admiration, and demand our attention, ways of living that can nourish us as well as the planet on which our lives depend.[14] It is counterintuitive, to be sure, to think that there are archaic solutions to modern problems. But that is just what primitivists think. The meanings of "archaic" and "primitive" changed across the twentieth century, and they can change again. In our accelerated age, the way back just might be the way out. Or, better still, a selective revival of more primitive ways of life might be part of the way out. As we race to ruin, what better time than now to be out of step with the times?

But it is to the realities of the past, not the problems of the present, that the historian must attend. I gladly accept that the proper temperament of an intellectual historian is a degree of cool detachment toward the present and a burning interest in the past.[15] The four primitivists I write about in this book were would-be reformers who wanted to ameliorate man's postwar estate. For these primitivists, the way to improve society and avoid catastrophe was not to continue the current course, but to undo the work of history and "scrape off from human life the accretions which had grown upon it."[16] No doubt they overstated their case. Yet, in doing so, they redefined ideas of the archaic and the primitive between 1945 and 1975. What is very old is hard to imagine. But one can try, and it helps to have a good guide. The four intellectuals I call postwar primitivists are good guides. They prove that in the 1950s, '60s, and '70s one of the most potent traditions in the history of ideas was not yet relegated to the attics of time. Writing during the decades of decolonization and hypermodernization, they insisted on anticolonialism and anticapitalism as the politics of a proper primitivism.

The year 1983, however, was a bad one for primitivism. Criticism closed in from the Right and the Left. In *The Tears of the White Man*, the French philosopher Pascal Bruckner denounced solidarity with primitive peoples and the third world as a dangerous fashion. As he saw it, the fad for the primitive was not enlightened—it was reckless and illiberal. Bruckner's stated aim? To expose the "militant self-denunciations" made by the "self-appointed partisans of the Third World."[17] He accused the French Left of a having a gnawing self-hatred, a festering *haine de soi*. Primitivists tell us that "we are the worst, in contrast to the people of the Third World who are the purest," Bruckner wrote. Far from being creative, primitivists were racked with guilt and debilitated by despair. They believed that the new white man's burden was to denounce the West and show solidarity with the Global South. Devaluing Europe became a surefire way to obtain an intellectual passport into the leftist intelligentsia. You gained admittance in three simple steps: First, side with the downtrodden and identify the other as the model of natural goodness; next, accuse and berate oneself and one's colonizing country; and finally, exhibit your heartfelt remorse for all to see. Western thought had thus become stilted, crushed under the solemn shame of its colonial past.[18]

Time and the Other, by the German anthropologist Johannes Fabian, also came out in 1983 and was a pivotal critique of primitivism.[19] But, unlike Bruckner's *Tears*, this critique came from the Left. Fabian is especially good at explaining how the temporal assumptions of anthropology perpetuated racism and empire. For decades there existed in anthropology an unexamined distinction between ahistorical primitive peoples and everyone else. The living Earth was thus divided: on one side, a pure slice of the past; on the other, an ever-advancing present. This Manichean distinction was the necessary lie of every successful anthropology. Primitivism too feeds on temporal distancing—without it, it is impoverished and unremarkable. When we say that some far-flung place offers a glimpse into the past, we repeat the primitivist's reduction of time to space. Indeed, a reliable indicator that an intellectual is a primitivist is this very folding of time into space.[20] The subtitle of *Time and the Other* is *How Anthropology Makes Its Object*. Objectification, domination, and destruction have always been part of anthropology, Fabian argues. The science of primitive societies did not just emerge alongside colonialism; it was part of the colonizing process. Or, more dramatically, anthropologists didn't just document dying societies; they helped put them in the grave.[21] It was time to see primitivists for who they really were. Together *Tears* and *Time* sought to close the book on any primitivism that took itself seriously. There was no question about it: Primitivism was one unit-idea about which nothing more should be said.

Because the Bruckner-Fabian interpretation has found broad acceptance, we must take a closer look at how the end of empire brought an end to postwar primitivism. One could do no better than to turn to James Clifford's *The Predicament of Culture* (1988), a powerful account of primitivism's postcolonial crisis. We are in a predicament, Clifford tells us: We can't in good conscience celebrate the cultures responsible for colonialism, nor can we leave home and hope to find something radically new. Thus, a new kind of "ethnographic surrealism" is needed. And ethnographic surrealism, Clifford knew, had found an early and exemplary expression in Paris in the 1920s and '30s. The avant-garde journal *Documents*, the writings of Michel Leiris and Aimé Césaire, and the Collège de sociologie exemplified how primitivism could be an aesthetic project. Unnerving images, ambiguous arguments, displaced narratives, hybridity, fragmentation, defamiliarization—this was the only way to speak of the primitive. Clifford thus formulated a poststructuralist solution to the problem of postcolonial primitivism, advocating subversion and a breakup of authority.[22] Hence, as the twentieth century came to a close, the only acceptable primitivism was a tongue-in-cheek, self-referential primitivism; the only acceptable uses of the word *primitive* or *archaic* were those laced with irony.

Recent work has taken up the matter of primitivism's demise: what happened and why it happened. By 2000 primitivism had had its day; that much was clear. Racist, rooted in imperialism, encouraging acts of appropriation—primitivism was by definition "problematic." Primitivism is a briar patch, to be sure. No matter how deftly you move about, you are bound to hit a snag and draw severe reaction. That's progress, people will say.[23] And it's true that in the first decades of the twenty-first century most people welcomed primitivism's demise. Their calculation was simple: Since there is no politically correct primitivism, we must put primitivism to rest once and for all. Since then, it has been difficult to write about primitivism, that thorniest of traditions in the history of ideas. Yet there is some solace to be had: After so many postmortems, after countless pronouncements that primitivism is dead and buried, the idea keeps climbing out of the grave. After the requiem, resurrection.

It's an odd thing to consider the resurgence of primitivism after decades of ill repute. There are fresh signs, however, that as the crises of fast capitalism and anthropogenic climate change alter our valuation of nearly everything, we are beginning to reassess what was once deemed archaic. The desire for a habitable climate future seems to have reawakened what is archaic in us; for better or worse, old forms of stability stir. "Suddenly we've changed back into what we had never ceased to be: primitives," writes the French philosopher Michel Serres.[24]

Two recent books by Victor Li and Ben Etherington challenge the negative assumptions that have surrounded primitivism for decades. Primitivists such as Jean Baudrillard, Aimé Césaire, D. H. Lawrence, and Marshall Sahlins were not, they argue, closet imperialists; rather, they undermined the status quo of Euro-American society and sought alternatives to it. Li and Etherington recuperate the primitive in two ways: First, they argue that primitivism is an indispensable mode of cultural comparison and critique. A "primitive" is required to question the West's sense of superiority and its faith in progress. "Theorizing always needs a savage," Li concludes in *The Neo-Primitivist Turn* (2006).[25] Etherington adds to this an important revision. In *Literary Primitivism* (2018), he shows that primitivism was not an exclusively Western tendency; it had a "decolonial horizon."[26] Francophone intellectuals such as Césaire, Frantz Fanon, Léon-Gontran Damas, and Léopold Sédar Senghor vindicated the "savage" and repurposed primitivist tropes. These two books are better than their predecessors. Shunning contemporary wisdom, they reveal the cul-de-sac we find ourselves in without the prism of primitivism.[27] Without visions of origins and elsewheres, how can we contemplate alternatives to the capitalist world system? It's all proof of my contention, which was first Lovejoy's contention, that primitivism is indeed a unit-idea—by definition hardy, persistent, and adaptable. We would do well to recall his warning that "there is nothing more naïve, or more indicative of a failure to learn one of the real lessons of the history of thought, than the tendency of some, even among philosophers, to take the bare fact that a way of thinking is now *démodé* as indicative either that it is false or that it will not come back."[28]

Adventures in the Archaic contributes to a new corpus of intellectual history attuned to cultural and ecological sustainability. The postwar primitivists contended with some of the most contentious rifts in their society and ours. *Make it new! Remake it as it was. Change life! The more things change, the more they remain the same. No time like the present. The good old days. Glorify progress. Cling to the past.* Enigmatic as it was, primitivism was one way to confront the rise of global capitalism and the Great Acceleration. Of course, it remains to be seen whether the archaic still has inherent value in an age of anthropogenic climate change. But this is a history of four intellectuals who took responsibility for keeping alive alternative ways of living and relating.

All this keeping alive required discarding the imperatives of modern time, replacing them not with irony but with revival. Such temporal heresy was characteristic of the postwar primitivists and their truest strength. The past cannot walk into the future when history is synonymous with novelty; the past has no future when history is something to be "made," they argued. The postwar period, however, was defined by the continual production of the new—new looks, new digs, new values, one new wave after another. It was a regime of the unrepeatable, in which time seemed out of joint and everything seemed out of nature. It was a temporal regime that needed to be resisted.[29]

In the tradition of works by H. Stuart Hughes and Carl Schorske, *Adventures in the Archaic* follows the intellectual lives of four leading voices in the fields of prehistory, ethnopsychiatry, rural sociology, and the history of religion. The story of the postwar primitivists reveals a particularly rich sensibility that flourished in the first years of the Great Acceleration and helps paint a complex portrait of French intellectual life after 1945.[30] Keeping a primitivist sensibility as my guiding thread led me to unexpected connections between two of the usual suspects in twentieth-century French thought (Bataille and Lefebvre) and two lesser-known Franco-Balkan intellectuals (Devereux and Eliade). Sharing no single discipline, institution, or political passion, these intellectuals look like an unlikely quartet, at least at first glance. What they did share was a passion for what had survived the long passage of time. To a man, they were also committed to careful observation and rigorous analysis. Objectivity and objective reasoning mattered, and these primitivists grounded their postwar oeuvres in the methods and evidence of the human and social sciences. By the middle of the 1970s, they had transformed many ideas without changing most minds. With an eye on this century's obstinate rush toward ecological disaster, I suggest why these mid-twentieth-century reformers compel a broader reevaluation of the history of primitivism in modern European thought.

The human and social sciences are more or less what the historian H. Stuart Hughes meant by *social thought*. Beginning with *Consciousness and Society* (1958), Hughes identified social thought as an indispensable category in the history of modern ideas. He believed that intellectual historians should examine a small number of broad-based social thinkers whose ideas eventually took hold. The postwar primitivists fit the bill. Each one formulated a pathbreaking body of work that shaped their preferred scholarly discipline: Bataille anticipated the passions that continue to shape the study of parietal art; Lefebvre gained a reputation as an urban sociologist of the first order; Devereux moved comfortably between ethnography and psychiatry and altered the course of each; and Eliade was a founding figure in the academic study of religion. According to Hughes's model, historians should study the ideas of influential innovators in their pristine state. So, in addition to published writings, my sources include manuscripts, field notes, journals, and letters. It is in these published and archival sources that historians walk "the *via regia* of intellectual history."[31]

What follows is an intellectual history written with the conviction that ideas have their own reason for being. The real drama of this book then is in the making sense of seventy-year-old ideas about archaic rites, primitive cultures, and cultural survivals. Each chapter analyzes a wide range of one intellectual's writings in roughly chronological order from the early 1930s to the early 1970s. As I profile four men with ties to the French social sciences, I dedicate the most space to rigorously reconstructing their ideas. But since intellectuals don't live in a vacuum and ideas never walk alone, I set these four biographies against the backdrop of French reconstruction and, to a lesser extent, the end of European empire—the tumultuous climate in which the *archaïque* caught fire.[32] Historical contexts are thus not entirely sidelined, but neither are they given sweeping priority. Complicating the matter is the lingering sway of the social history of ideas and the study of discursive formations and scholarly networks. The historian Robert Darnton once cautioned that "to pull some Voltaire from the shelf is not to come into contact with a representative slice of intellectual life from the eighteenth century."[33] But my concern is not with a *representative* slice of French intellectual life after 1945; rather, I tell the story of four unorthodox thinkers whose ideas stood apart from the main currents of their day. Some ideas are worth revisiting quite apart from whether or not they aligned with prevailing mentalities or were widely circulated and consumed.

There remains the question of temporal scale. Following appearances of the archaic across the French social sciences, I realized that the idea blossomed in a relatively short period. The evidence itself therefore imposed a rather narrow time frame of three decades, as did my desire to reach across several branches of knowledge. But the problem of temporal scale is more complicated than that. On the one hand, the postwar primitivists were exceptional. No longer were literature and the arts the principal vehicles to rescue the past as something living. On the other hand, there was a precedent in the social sciences for paying attention to archaisms, and a French precedent no less. If the postwar primitivists had a progenitor, it was Marcel Mauss. But a truly satisfactory answer to the question of their exceptionality requires tracing primitivism over a much larger timescale than I have set out here. And there is nothing quite like the *longue durée* to drive home the point that nothing is ever entirely new in the history of ideas. Primitivism—one of the grand traditions in modern European intellectual history—is no exception to this rule.[34]

What follows is a specialized study devoted to the work of four intellectuals and four main subjects (sacrifice, survivals, shamanism, and cyclical notions of time) in the space of three decades. The first chapter, "Archaic Religion in a New Key," enters directly into the depths of the archaic world by examining the painted cave at Lascaux, in southwestern France. It became Georges Bataille's favorite subject shortly after its discovery in 1940. As the author of one of the first illustrated books on Lascaux, Bataille had special access to the cave. His unusual experience there honed his understanding of sacrifice and his critique of capitalist accumulation. The chapter first establishes Bataille's credentials as a theorist of archaic religions and then examines the special character of French prehistory in his thought. A theme eventually emerges from Bataille's celebration of the most primitive of religious rites: the desire to rediscover a lost intimacy with the animal world.

Chapter 2, on the rural sociologist Henri Lefebvre, plunges further into the archaic traditions of southwestern France. "The Work of Nostalgia" is essentially an episode in the fate of rural France after the Second World War. I show how Lefebvre channeled his nostalgia for the old French Southwest into a provocative new theory of survivals. Special attention is paid to the influence of his former student and chief collaborator, Charlotte Delbo. A holistic analysis of Lefebvre's writings in rural sociology reveals that his influential insights into the urban environment owed a great deal to the backward practices and indispensable survivals of Pyrenean peasant communities.

Georges Devereux may be less well-known than his fellow postwar primitivists, but he was no less an apprentice in the archaic. Chapter 3 concentrates on the ethnographer's formative experience in the American Southwest. Embedded among the Mohave of Arizona and California, Devereux was immersed in a culture well-versed in dream interpretation and psychosomatic healing. The chapter revives the contentious debates surrounding the mental and social status of shamans that raged in the 1950s. On reflection, it's clear that Devereux used his knowledge of primitive psychotherapy to lay the foundations for a new kind of psychiatry—ethnopsychiatry.

"Mircea Eliade and Neopaganism as Postcolonial Critique" turns to Eliade's unrivaled role in writing archaic religions into the history of religions. The fourth chapter examines the ecstatic experiences and cyclical notions of time that the historian believed were common to archaic religions the world over. Eliade argued that the oldest of religious tenets provided a much-needed bulwark against planetary crisis. I take pains to show that Eliade's passage from neopaganism to postcolonialism after 1945 was much smoother than one might imagine. The chapter concludes by looking forward to Eliade's tenure at the University of Chicago and his insistence that a pagan ideal be at the center of social thought.

In the epilogue, "Primitivism in Our Time," I sketch three recent developments in primitivism and bring the story of the postwar primitivists up to date. The chapter concludes, perhaps predictably, that last century's adventurers in the archaic were on to something. Seventy years ago Bataille was "simply struck by the fact that light is being shed on our birth at the very moment when the notion of our death appears to us."[35] Today we face a new possibility of planetary disaster. There is a growing literature on the Earth's biophysical processes and cycles and their incompatibility with unending growth. While many still struggle to come to terms with the impasse, the intellectuals of *Adventures in the Archaic* understood the need to envisage futures which from the viewpoint of the industrial model might look primitive. Decades ago, they met the need, our need, to think in long timescales and yet act with urgency. Had they known about the idea of the Anthropocene, they would have used it.

Primitivism found its voice in the middle of the last century. The question now is whether primitivist reforms should inform this century's search for viable alternatives to the present state of society. "History is our handiest counterfactual," writes David Wallace-Wells in a 2022 article, "however poor a standard it sets for a world that could have been much better still."[36] It is an uncomfortable fact, but a fact nonetheless: The primitive is good to think with.

1

Archaic Religion in a New Key

Georges Bataille at Lascaux

On February 12, 1957, Georges Bataille (1897–1962) stood before the Cercle ouvert, a Parisian literary and intellectual circle that met each month for a public-facing lecture. Living southwest of Paris in Orléans since 1951, Bataille traveled to the capital only occasionally, mostly for talks such as these. On this evening he would speak of eroticism, that strange force animating life until death. Given the topic, dozens of university students had come full of interest to the Cercle's lecture hall on the rue de Rennes in Saint-Germain-des-Prés. They would have the good fortune of hearing one of the great critics of postwar society, which led many to assume that Bataille would argue in favor of sexual liberation. "We would very much like to see someone finally sweep all the old constraints away," their looks seemed to say. The sight of André Breton and André Masson in attendance, surrealists well-known for their own sexual provocations, must have heightened the students' anticipation and perhaps quickened their pulse. To impress his audience, Bataille need only praise the free play of the passions and assail religious and moral conventions, those outdated obstacles to change. After all, lines drawn millennia ago were meant to be erased, were they not? Settling behind the lectern, Bataille unfolded eight folio sheets and began to speak. The crowd was soon surprised, and frankly put out.

"I am not among those who see the removal of sexual prohibitions as a solution," Bataille said earnestly. "I would even go so far as to say that human potential depends on these prohibitions." The crowd grumbled; recognizing the stir of dissatisfaction, Bataille pressed on. He spoke of the fact that in all times and in all places eroticism was animated by standing taboos and seasonal transgressions. Who are we to think it could be otherwise? It was neither possible nor desirable to abolish all constraint—in fact, pleasure being intimately bound to the injunctions that prohibit it, such a radical abolition would be the death of desire itself. It sounded like something out of the Paleolithic. By this point, the scorn on the faces of those thirty years his junior was unmistakable. Bataille's biographer, Michel Surya, describes those who expected Bataille to say that eroticism is free and easy and innocent (or at least that it should be) as "bewildered to hear him gravely assert that, on the contrary, eroticism is, essentially and by its very nature, accursed, accursed to a terrifying degree."[1] The crowd understood Bataille well enough; they just didn't like what he had to say. Nothing he said that day was comforting or fashionable, and the crowd found no ally in this champion of cultural survivals. Bataille was guided by a desire—born of his experience in the painted caves of Lascaux—to adopt a standpoint in harmony with archaic religions. And so, he tied the knot and constrained the will. His primitivism may have been macabre at times, but it wasn't morose or coal black; instead, his vision of the archaic burned bright. Afterward, the would-be primitivist reformer hurried to the door so as not to waste time with fawning admirers or, worse, acknowledge the lack thereof.

Bataille is widely known as a surrealist writer of pornographic fiction who rejected systematic science. Books such as *Story of the Eye* (1928) opposed order and exalted the abject, an infectious double commitment that shaped the tone and tenor of his early work. Philippe Sollers captures this side of Bataille's oeuvre when he suggests that "one day, one hopes it will be realized that it was Georges Bataille who had been the truly explosive center of twentieth-century thought."[2] But Bataille was also an avid reader in anthropology, sociology, psychology, and political economy. Intent on denaturalizing modern Western societies, Bataille eagerly followed French ethnographers such as Émile Durkheim, Henri Hubert, Marcel Mauss, Alfred Métraux, and Michel Leiris.[3] As general secretary of *Documents* between 1929 and 1931, Bataille effectively ran the pathbreaking journal, which brought together anthropology, art, archaeology, literature, and Durkheimian sociology. Across fifteen issues, many of the essays he selected and edited affirmed the enduring value of primitive and Indigenous cultures. From Bataille's first publication, "Vanished America" (1928), to his monumental *The Accursed Share* (1949), his passion for the religious rites of archaic societies remained unabated. Bataille was eccentric, but he wasn't singular, nor was the radical nature of his thought indebted to surrealism.

Most of this is familiar territory for students of Bataille. What is less well-known is Bataille's attachment to the French provinces, his erudite vocation, and his repeated efforts to distance himself from anything that smacked of surrealism. Bataille's interpretation of his roots was straightforward enough: His family was of "peasant stock" from the Ariège, a land of meandering hills and painted prehistoric caves in the southwestern part of France. But it was only after the Second World War, in his writings on Lascaux, that Bataille brought together for the first time his sworn peasant roots, his fascination with primitive culture, and his fondness for religious rituals.[4] Bataille's training at the reputable École nationale des chartes, moreover, was a solid foundation for someone who would eventually turn his archivist's eye toward prehistoric science. His work at the Bibliothèque nationale in Paris and later at the Bibliothèque municipale in Orléans was not anathema to his thinking, as is often supposed; rather, his daily labors were part and parcel of his scientific pretensions and his grand syntheses of ethnography, prehistory, and the history of religions. What's more, Bataille was no surrealist after 1945. The mutual hostility between Bataille and Breton is well-documented, and in this chapter I will show how they clashed in the field of prehistory in the early 1950s. The image of Bataille I offer, then, is one not of a subversive surrealist slouching in the gutters of Paris, but of an upright and erudite primitivist slowly pacing the painted caverns of Lascaux (fig. 1.1). Admittedly, such a reimagining will make Bataille a less elusive figure in twentieth-century thought—but perhaps that's more or less the point of an intellectual history that strives for clarity and exegesis.[5]

Bataille's life and work can be divided into three periods: the ethnographic surrealist, to borrow James Clifford's handy phrase, who wrote about primitive art in the early 1930s and directed the Collège de sociologie between 1937 and 1939; the solitary mystic who plumbed the depths of inner experience during the Second World War; and the committed comparatist who edited the journal *Critique* and wrote several syntheses of history and the social sciences after 1945.[6] The culmination of Bataille's first period was the Collège de sociologie, a study group and quasi-secret society that liked to gather around trees which bore marks of having been struck by lightning. Founded in March 1937, the Collège met every Tuesday evening at 9:30; attendees included Walter Benjamin, Roger Caillois, Pierre Klossowski, Michel Leiris, Claude Lévi-Strauss, Anatole Lewitsky, and Alfred Métraux. The Collège's aspirations were Nietzschean, anticapitalist, and undeniably heterodox. Its stated purpose: to rejuvenate older, degraded forms of the sacred.[7] After this, Bataille painstakingly explored "inner experience" for more than five years in Vézelay, a commune just outside the Île-de-France. He documented these years of tormented preparation in the three-volume *Atheological Summa* (1943–45). In Nietzschean fashion, Bataille eventually emerged from illness and isolation with the great organizing idea that would guide his postwar pursuits.[8]

The posthumously published and underappreciated *Theory of Religion* (1948) inaugurated Bataille's final period, characterized by works of mature

FIGURE 1.1. Georges Bataille in the Lascaux cave, Montignac, in the Vézère Valley of the Dordogne. Uncredited photograph circa 1954.

synthesis of prehistory, the social sciences, and the history of religion. These were the years during which Bataille collected material and cultivated a keen eye for real-world examples. It is difficult to overstate the importance of *Critique*, which Bataille founded in 1946 and edited for fifteen years, to his intellectual development after 1945. A perusal of any one of its volumes will show the prominent place Bataille accorded to his two main intellectual passions, the social sciences and the history of religions. No one, of course, was more influenced by the journal than the editor who labored over its every page. If his wartime study of Friedrich Nietzsche had prepared him psychologically for the work that lay ahead, it was *Critique* that prepared the ground for Bataille's next mature synthesis, *The Accursed Share*.[9] But it was only at Lascaux that Bataille, a book-bound scholar, acquired the kind of intimate, firsthand knowledge that shaped the work of his fellow postwar primitivists Devereux and Lefebvre.

No two of his colleagues bore witness to Bataille's sensibility better than a pair of preeminent French ethnographers, Métraux and Leiris. Ever since they first met as classmates at the École nationale des chartes, Bataille and Métraux were inseparable. Métraux recognized that while ethnography exercised a kind of fascination on Bataille, his intense curiosity couldn't hide his "visible naïveté." Nevertheless, Métraux admitted that by the late 1930s Bataille had managed not only to educate himself in ethnography but to direct it. "By a sort of curious intuition," Métraux wrote, Bataille became a "precursor to a whole school of ethnologists who sought to define a civilization's *ethos*— that is, the hierarchy of social values that give each civilization its proper value." For his part, Leiris admired the breadth of Bataille's knowledge. This "stubborn peasant," as Leiris called his friend, could hold forth on any subject under the sun, from the most elevated to the most debased. Leiris didn't focus on Bataille's alleged ties to surrealism. Rather, what he admired was his friend's Janus-faced nature: how Bataille managed to balance a vast erudition with a savage romanticism, which burned just beneath his judicious exterior. This hybrid approach, combining passion and objectivity, reached full maturity after the war, when Bataille left behind "the iconoclastic rage of his youthful revolts" and "the foot-stamping *No!* of the child's temper tantrum."[10]

After the unprecedented violence of the Second World War, Bataille changed course. He believed that something essential was missing from postwar society. The evidence of Lascaux, painted in the Upper Paleolithic period roughly seventeen thousand years ago, taught him that there was a marvelous past out there, an age when the quest for a lost intimacy flourished. As grandiose and anachronistic as it may sound, Bataille sought to build a more sustainable future by resurrecting much older mores and morals. Age-old traditions, which were not devoid of a certain violence, stood as precious bulwarks against the advance of modern technology and military might— just as the charred ancestral oak of Guernica, that stubborn symbol of Basque resistance, stood in defiance of German aerial bombardments.[11] The great organizing idea of Bataille's baroque writings—an idea that appeared in bright daylight only after 1945—was to revive archaic expenditures and counter the cold, calculating heart of the modern world. This was his challenge to capitalism; it was also the way he introduced the need for degrowth into the

French social sciences. It would only bolster his postwar project that so many so-called archaic societies in what would come to be called the third world claimed one victory after another in their own struggle against capitalism and colonization.[12] What follows reveals what the most archaic art, that of Lascaux, meant to Bataille and what it might mean to us. But first I need to establish Bataille's credentials as a theorist of religion and a lay prehistorian.

Studies in the History of Religion

After 1945 morality, like Europe itself, lay in ruins. The moral crisis of postwar Europe was no more gripping than crises of the past, but with a difference: In the wake of Auschwitz and Hiroshima, the consequences of moral faltering were amplified. And the morality promoted to defeat fascism was not reassuring. Yes, the Allies had produced a great military success, but at what cost? On every front, individuals were caught in the dynamism of productivity and accumulation. Decades earlier, Durkheim had called the alienating moral instability "anomie"; after the war, Albert Camus called it "exile," Simone Weil preferred "uprootedness"—each was a diagnostic label for the social crises of modern Europe. Anomie, it seems, had become Europe's default setting.

It was in this context that Bataille turned to the history of religion. *Theory of Religion*, completed in 1948 and published posthumously in 1973, was the first major expression of how Bataille would use the prehistory of religion to challenge the postwar order. Something so seemingly archaic and immaterial as prehistoric religion became the vehicle through which Bataille criticized the moral and material trajectory of modern society and the compound alienations it engendered.[13] The cultures that Bataille would give the name *archaïque* were a locus of resistance, a springboard from which to critique modernity's economic order, and an alternative sociocultural style which prioritized unproductive expenditure (*dépense*) over perpetual production. Bataille's appeal to the history of religion proved lasting. Although he himself had no definite religious belief outside a vague mysticism, he became a bona fide historian of religion.[14]

It was in *Theory* that Bataille stated in a memorable sentence that "for anyone to whom human life is an experience to be carried as far as possible, the *universal sum* is necessarily that of the religious sensibility in time."[15] The desire to recover a lost intimacy is the essence of religion, he maintained. For all the attention paid to sacrifice, transgression, and expenditure, it is intimacy that was the cornerstone of Bataille's social thought after 1945. Sacrifices and seasonal transgressions mattered because they were paths to the restoration of an intimacy that had been "strangely lost."[16] Beginning with *Theory of*

Religion, Bataille used "continuity," "immanence," and even "immanent immensity" interchangeably with "intimacy." But regardless of which word he used, they all denoted the same ecstatic state—the burning presence (one of Bataille's favorite phrases) of momentarily being in a world without division, and thus in a world without loss. At any rate, intimacy was the archivist's special term for the "manifestations of religious feeling" that once existed in archaic societies and might one day be revived.[17]

With *Theory of Religion*, we find a comparatist in the history of religion in the making. In the late 1940s Bataille began to build the theoretical ground for the restoration of intimacy-inducing societies. Once the savage artist, now the disciplined savant: "The work of the mason who assembles is the work that matters." It's probably the sentence that most unsettles decades of insisting that Bataille was an antiarchitectural thinker and the philosophical forerunner of deconstructionists like Jacques Derrida.[18] Nothing mattered more to Bataille after 1945, I argue, than the experience of intimacy and the durable cultural styles that beget it. It's time that we see Bataille as the constructive social thinker that he was. To this end I examine two of his actual interlocuters in the immediate postwar period, not his alleged affinities with the poststructuralists. It was during these years, when he was completing *Theory of Religion*, that Bataille's thought was shaped by two encounters, one with Simone Weil, the other with Mircea Eliade.

There are a number of striking similarities between Bataille, the confirmed Nietzschean, and Weil, the aspiring saint. They shared a fondness for Provençal troubadours and a southern way of thinking, *la pensée de Midi*. Each admired an old-fashioned mystic and a good religious heresy. But, above all, they believed they were living in a deeply dehumanizing age—although they had different ideas about how that might be remedied, to be sure. They shared an uncompromising cultural pessimism. But they were adamant that nostalgia could be creative, and so they channeled their dissatisfaction into reviving older moral foundations.[19]

Weil was an activist and militant, the epitome of a Gramscian intellectual. Despite poor health, she worked in a factory for a year, toiled on an agricultural field in the South of France, and even lived among the unemployed for a time. During the Spanish Civil War she fought against Francisco Franco in Barcelona. Exiled in London during the Second World War, she was attached to Charles de Gaulle's Free French Forces and served as an editor for France libre. It was during these years that she wrote what became her most famous book, *The Need for Roots*. Published posthumously in 1949 (Weil died of tuberculosis and heart failure in England in 1943), the book was an ethical guide to rebuilding France after the defeat of fascism. Responses to her meandering treatise ran the gamut from scorn to praise. The Romanian writer Emil Cioran, a friend of Mircea Eliade and the author of *A Short History of Decay* (1949), saw an underlying anti-Semitism in *The Need for Roots*, observing that Weil, who was Jewish, had as much "energy, will, and restlessness as Hitler." By contrast, Camus called Weil a martyr and an intellectual of the first rank—"the only great mind of our times," he called her in his preface to *The Need for Roots*. When it came to the moral rebirth of Europe after 1945, wrote the author of *The Plague* (1947), one could do no better than read Weil.[20]

When Bataille met Weil in 1931, he was intrigued by the young woman who wore only black and parted her hair down the middle. Though she embodied an asceticism Bataille disdained, he was drawn to her courage in following her convictions. They were both active in Boris Souvarine's heterodox Cercle communiste démocratique and contributed to *La critique sociale*, the journal that published Bataille's essay "The Notion of Expenditure" in 1933.[21] Souvarine described Weil as "the only brain the working-class movement has produced in years." Bataille wasn't so generous; he remembered having an unshakable feeling that despite her outward comportment, Weil was *plus fêlée*—basically, "crazy." Four years later, in *Blue of Noon* (1935), a surrealist roman à clef, Bataille included a Weil-like character named Louise Lazare. Draped in black, uncompromising and severe with herself, Lazare was a rather obvious portrayal of Weil. The fictional Louise, like the real-life Simone, dressed up rigid conformity as revolutionary action, and her self-sacrifices were more mechanical than spirited. In short, Lazare-Weil embodied for Bataille the impasse of seeing sacrifice as the duty of individuals.

Most writers who take up Weil today focus on her difficult life or her captivating prose. What is less often discussed, and what most interested Bataille, were her moral judgments. Accompanying Weil's passion was a sense of incontestable moral authority—although perhaps it is impossible to have one without the other; zeal doesn't exactly lend itself to nuance. In a lengthy review of Weil's *The Need for Roots*, "Military Victory and the Moral Bankruptcy That Confounds It" (1949), Bataille argued that postwar France needed to be rebuilt on a more solid moral foundation.[22] (There's that figure of the mason who builds again.) Weil agreed, and *The Need for Roots* emphasized individual obligation and personal sacrifice as the way out of Europe's moral impasse. But Bataille read *The Need for Roots* from the perspective of the French social sciences and found it wanting. He criticized Weil's lack of regard for social facts. Her ideas were no more than moralizing slogans: If the vigor of her expression veiled this fact, it did so only for an instant, Bataille wrote.[23] What separated his recently published *The Accursed Share* from *The Need for Roots*, he claimed, was that the former was full of concrete examples taken from ethnography, the history of religions, and the postwar present, whereas the latter was crammed with tired slogans and ideas not altogether different from those promoted by Vichy moralists.

Bataille and Weil agreed that rootedness, that decidedly unmodern quality, was moral and redemptive and a necessary corrective to the turbulent age in which they lived. "To take root once more is today a moral of the utmost importance," Bataille declared. Perhaps this shared conviction is what made *The Need for Roots* all the more disappointing for Bataille.[24] In it, Weil argued that personal sacrifice was the gold standard of moral conduct. Her fundamental principle was not, in fact, rootedness but duty. It was the individual, in her account, who needed to sacrifice, turning his suffering body into a useful tool, just as she had done. Bataille saw sacrifice differently. It was the community that needed to periodically sacrifice in order to cultivate intimacy through unproductive expenditure. For Weil, rootedness meant something like the nourishment one feels when one is a self-sacrificing, duty-bound individual. Bataille's idea of rootedness was far more primitive. He knew that the long history of religion testified to a communal warmth that burned brighter and was far less utilitarian than Weil would ever admit. Bataille recoiled from Weil's understanding of sacrifice because he believed that collective sacrificial rites, not acts of self-sacrifice, offered the best chance to remake Europe after the Second World War.

But to appreciate how Bataille's work in the history of religion set the stage for his Lascaux writings, it is necessary to go back a little earlier, to just before the completion of *Theory of Religion*. On Thursday, February 26, 1948, Bataille read a paper titled "Outline for a History of Religions" that would prove critical to his understanding of archaic religion.[25] The occasion was a two-day conference in Saint-Germain-des-Prés at the Collège philosophique, a philosophical colloquium founded by Jean Wahl in 1947. Bataille began his lecture by tracing forms of sacrifice as they unfolded in time. He insisted that you could search and search for a utilitarian character in primitive sacrifice, but you weren't going to find one. Rather, as he would argue in *Theory*, the point of these age-old sacrificial rites was to reestablish a lost intimacy. If sacrifice had a "usefulness," that was it. Sacrifice had, of course, evolved to mean many things over the centuries. But the French comparatist suggested that primitive forms of sacrifice, the heart of archaic religions, had all but disappeared. Over time, sacrifice had become tied to productivity, sovereignty, military might, and imperial growth. In the course of his two-day lecture, Bataille was unequivocal: What was called sacrifice today was in fact the antithesis of archaic sacrifice. Instead of a great cathartic collective expenditure, modern societies demanded that individuals sacrifice *themselves* so that violence could be directed to the *outside* for productive purposes.

Bataille's paper triggered an encounter, unexamined until now, that would prove indispensable to his intellectual development. After his lecture, the French comparatist received a pointed question from a then little-known historian of religion, Mircea Eliade. Was Bataille aware that many primitive cultures knew nothing of totemism and did not practice totemic rites? Bataille had argued, much as Sigmund Freud had in *Totem and Taboo*, that the most primitive of religious rites involved the sacrifice of totemic animals. Eliade told Bataille that recent ethnographic findings had shown that totemism was no longer a sufficient starting point in the history of religions. Eliade maintained that it was not totemic animals but supreme beings that were the inaugural development in the history of religion. Totemism came after, if it came at all. As the discussion came to an end, Bataille and Eliade agreed that both the desire for union with supreme beings and the sacrifice of totemic animals revealed that there was a land rich in meaning beyond the sphere of work and production. Call it a desire for union or call it intimacy, archaic religions bore witness to the fact that humans the world over desperately wanted to get out from under the thumb of useful activity, even if only for a moment.

Bataille seems to have welcomed this gentle and seemingly insignificant correction by a specialist in the field. He admitted that his schema had followed the model of cultural succession established by Edward Burnett Tylor, James G. Frazer, and Freud. "Your information is certainly better than mine," Bataille conceded. The next morning, Eliade's comments compelled Bataille to compose fourteen handwritten pages that he titled "On Eliade's Question." These pages, which are available for view only at the Bibliothèque nationale, show that when confronted with new evidence, Bataille changed his mind. If there remained any doubt, these pages make plain that Bataille's commitment to basing his work on the facts of history and the social sciences was stronger than any impulse to defend what he had said the day before.[26] In the lines you can see Bataille straining to contend with historical specificity while trying to capture religious sentiments in their totality. And it was precisely this movement—from historical realities to transhistorical mentalities and back again—that was the most fertile tension in Bataille's thought for the next fifteen years. To put archaic religions in sharper relief, he needed to commit himself to the historical record.

Bataille and Eliade quickly discovered that they had a lot in common. Both were unapologetic comparatists in the history of religion; both were keen on bringing together history and the social sciences; and both were drawn to the seasonal rites of archaic societies, especially the initiation rites of shamans. Perhaps more important, both regarded the history of religion as a story of how past societies periodically abolished the imperatives of growth to momentarily recreate a more sacred realm. Primitive cultures, Eliade said after Bataille's second lecture, were preoccupied with annually abolishing the world in order to remake it. Archaic religion rarely strayed from these cyclical rites. Eliade was in effect linking the thesis of his forthcoming book, *The Myth of the Eternal Return* (1949), with Bataille's notion of unproductive expenditure. Here were the shared elements in the symphony of their works. When Bataille played his chorus of intimacy achieved by unproductive expenditure, Eliade heard the rites of eternal return that rang out across the archaic world. It seems the neophyte and the specialist had hit on the same essential ingredient in the primitive style: the cyclical ceremonies whereby life is once again made sacred. And since this was how primitive cultures had remade themselves for millennia, perhaps there was a valuable lesson or two for Europe's own attempt to remake itself after the Second World War.

Bataille was one of the first French intellectuals to recognize the significance of Eliade's work. On March 4, 1948, a few days after their meeting at the Collège philosophique, Bataille visited Eliade at his Paris home. They met several more times that summer. Recalling one of those summer days, Eliade wrote, "Georges Bataille, just back from England, comes to see me, and we talk for two hours." Eliade believed that he and Bataille helped each other to "see problems and solutions more clearly."[27] It was not long afterward that Bataille invited Eliade to contribute to *Critique*. Between their first meeting in 1948 and when Eliade departed Paris in 1956, Bataille asked Eliade to write on all manner of subjects, from the esoteric to the ethnographic; Eliade would eventually contribute seven times to *Critique*'s pages. The subjects of these contributions are revealing; they include symbolism, primitive mythology, and the sociology of religion. It is unsurprising, then, that it was Eliade and Eliade alone whom Bataille acknowledged by name in *Theory of Religion*: "I am happy to cite as an example the friendly interventions of Mircea Eliade."[28]

Eliade showed Bataille that even in an arena as remote as archaic religion, it was necessary to be precise. But this would take some time. When another attendee at the Collège philosophique asked Bataille to provide an example of an expenditure that surpassed all utility, Bataille, tellingly, faltered. In late February 1948, with the future of postwar society ostensibly at stake, Bataille's example of unproductive expenditure was the excessive consumption of alcohol. Of course, it was an utterly unsatisfying example—the audience knew it, and Bataille knew it. Even if intoxication was akin to sacrifice (it's not), it was an individual experience, and Bataille had devoted his two-day lecture to collective acts of expenditure. It took mere seconds for members of the audience to point out the discrepancy. What's more, for a writer who wanted to move away from surrealist provocations and find a more stable ground on which to build his ensemble, this was shaky ground indeed. Old habits die hard, and the image of a headless body spewing forth its contents from an open orifice was hard to shake.

Bataille's notions of sacrifice and unproductive expenditure were in need of a definite foundation. And over the next decade, Bataille would establish it, first in the domain of ethnography and then in the depths of prehistory. The next year saw the publication of *The Accursed Share*—a strange, anticolonial work of political economy—and already Bataille's examples of sacrifice and profitless expenditure had multiplied, becoming less individualistic and more firmly rooted in the collective expenditures that encouraged intimacy and reaffirmed the social order. This is the book that announced Bataille's Copernican revolution in political economy: instead of continually circling around deprivation and production, he zeroed in on how a society expends its social surplus. For some, *The Accursed Share* was just as audacious and unsatisfying, but even its critics had to admit that something had changed.[29]

Bataille's final remarks at the Collège philosophique are important for any holistic understanding of his postwar oeuvre. In Bataille's eyes, and not in his alone, the twentieth century's great acceleration of growth had led to moral vacuity and mass violence. Bataille could not have known, of course, about how the logic of infinite expansion and accumulation would lead to our current climate crisis; but he knew the unsustainable ethos that drove it. Should we continue our present course, the world will quickly become uninhabitable, he said in 1948—"unless," that is, "we rediscover what the primitives possessed, the possibility of the gift."[30] As expected, someone from the audience shouted, "Why should we turn back the clock and recover the mindset of primitives?" Bataille clarified that he was not calling for a regression; what he meant by *revenir en arrière* had a specific sense: "I don't think I have fallen into a regression; rather, I have tried to provide answers to the most current and urgent problems." The world today, he added, is far from having taken the "decisive steps necessary to survive its present conditions."[31] Those decisive steps were for Bataille found in the cultural styles of humanity's deep past. More than anyone else, he set age-old religious rituals against postwar society's commitment to a single monetary metric (growth). In the face of what would come to be called the Anthropocene, Bataille envisaged a more ethical and sustainable community rooted in certain aspects of archaic religion. Taking up residence in primitive cultures after 1945, he never lost sight of the culture of mass production in which he lived. His writings on Lascaux had the express purpose of reviving much older, more durable pastimes.

An Affair and an Apprenticeship

In the early 1950s Bataille immersed himself in a subject that until then had been an intellectual hobby of only secondary interest: French prehistory. He read the *Bulletin de la Société préhistorique française*; he attended lectures at the Sorbonne and the Musée de l'Homme; and he quickly became knowledgeable in the scientific study of our most ancient vestiges.[32] Naturally, he was not the only one to develop a passion for prehistory after the discovery of Lascaux. During the postwar period, prehistoric cave art became a widely felt fascination, an irresistible objet d'art. And while many attributed to Paleolithic cultures all the mystery and drama that accompany the unknown, we misunderstand prehistoric art's effect on the French social sciences when we see it as only a distant echo of modernist or surrealist impulses (which was essentially the thesis of the Centre Pompidou's exhibition on prehistory in 2019). Instead, for primitivists like Bataille, the painted bestiaries uncovered in *la France profonde* expressed something hardy and permanent and decidedly unmodern. The Lascaux moment had arrived, and the presence of all those bison, ibexes, and horses was felt both in and beyond the French social sciences. What set Bataille apart from the curious crowds, however, was his long apprenticeship in French prehistory.

The ascendancy of prehistory was one of the major developments in the French social sciences in the twentieth century, a development that changed the valuation of primitive cultures for good. Beginning in the late nineteenth century, prehistorians like Henri Bégouën and Henri Breuil labored mightily to turn amateur archaeology and speleology into a veritable field of study. All that was very old, they maintained, could be known by the crisp methods of scientific inquiry. Founded on January 17, 1904, the Société préhistorique française paved the way for prehistory to become a well-established discipline by the time Bataille devoted himself to the subject in 1950. Prehistorians uncovered the most archaic expressions of human culture enshrined in caves such as Altamira, Niaux, Lascaux, Pech-Merle, Trois Frères, and Font-de-Gaume. Thanks to them, what was once unknown and inaccessible was now on full display. And after the Second World War, tourists flocked, publications exploded, and light was shed on the most primitive cultures of the Franco-Cantabrian region. Should it come as any great shock that the subterranean sanctuaries of the French Southwest reached the height of their influence in the rocketing years of *les trente glorieuses*?

For over half a century, Abbé Breuil was prehistory's most important emissary. The French scholar-priest was the "pope of prehistory," the field's uncontested *maître*.[33] Though Breuil first studied painted caves in the French

Pyrenees, he made his name examining and eventual verifying the authenticity of the prehistoric art at Altamira in northern Spain. Breuil's defense of Altamira marked a turning point for prehistoric art and for the discipline of prehistory itself. Thanks to him, prehistoric art was exonerated by science and introduced into the horizon of every educated Frenchmen. Not one to be shut up in an ivory tower, Breuil's trips through arroyos to reach out-of-the-way animal sanctuaries seem torn from the pages of *Don Quixote*. But for all his adventurousness, the author of *Four Hundred Centuries of Cave Art* (1952) insisted that disciplinary specialization was the road to scientific progress. The field's proper domain may have been the crystallized deposits of times past, but Breuil also encouraged drawing parallels between scant prehistoric evidence and living "primitive" cultures. By all accounts, the pope of prehistory was the kind of mason who reached for any available stone to build an edifice.

From its inception, then, French prehistory was no isolated academic pursuit. From the start, it straddled the porous divide between the natural and social sciences. In the first half of the twentieth century, prehistorians like Breuil moved easily between archaeology, ethnology, art history, and the history of religion.[34] The pioneers of prehistory had few qualms about linking present-day "primitives" to the ancient past. Thus, the customs and cultures of Indigenous peoples reappeared in the artistic expressions left behind in prehistoric grottoes. By making the Paleolithic correspond to the ethnographic and the provincial, the stage was set to unite all three. This tendency to think the "premodern" together only encouraged Bataille to join the ethnographic evidence that had dominated the pages of *The Accursed Share* with the facts of French prehistory. In a short time, the theorist of religion became an unabashed partisan of the Upper Paleolithic. Bataille now looked for alternatives to the spirit of capitalism not in the sultry tropics, but in the damp caverns of southwestern France. What's remarkable about Bataille's turn to prehistory, in light of his alleged aversion to "systematic science," is that he committed himself to a social science that modeled itself on the natural sciences and strove to be one of their number. Before long Bataille had discovered in French prehistory a wellspring of alternatives much closer to home, and by 1953 he was ready to say so in print.[35]

There came a point when the grandeur of prehistoric art was so widely felt that the time was ripe for a good old-fashioned scandal.[36] The affair arrived in 1952 with André Breton's smear test at the Grotte du Pech-Merle. For many, the ensuing affair and the eventual trial were just one more passing spectacle. But for Bataille something important was at stake: the reputation of French prehistory and the preservation of precious cultural survivals. From one angle, then, the whole affair was no more than a scandal tailor-made for publicity and the press. But from a different angle (and this is the one that interests me and that prompted Bataille to intervene), the story of Breton in Pech-Merle in 1952 is an allegory about the struggle of cultural stewardship against contact, contagion, and loss. Everything that evolved from Breton's infamous smear test is an object lesson in Bataille's shifting attitudes and allegiances after the Second World War. It thus bears retelling at length.

Beneath a hillside west of Cabrerets lay a frank revelation. There spotted horses, woolly mammoths, and other painted animals were discovered in 1922 in the Grotte du Pech-Merle. Pech-Merle soon became hallowed ground for prehistorians, and after Lascaux opened to the public in 1948 it became a stop on travelers' grand tour of prehistoric cave art. One of the few painted prehistoric caves still open to the public, Pech-Merle, with paintings that date to over 25,000 years ago, remains a tourist's delight. Visitors are struck by the way Paleolithic artists integrated the recesses of cave walls into their design and superimposed their drawings and engravings—there's an array of woolly mammoths, for example, that are impossibly intertwined. It's not uncommon to feel transfixed beneath these archaic animals. The father of surrealism, however, felt differently. Thanks to him, Pech-Merle has another, more scandalous history.

The caverns of Pech-Merle are near the picturesque hilltop commune of Saint-Cirq-Lapopie, and it was there that Breton bought a vacation home in 1951. The poet spent summers in this quiet and enchanting place overlooking the River Lot. On Thursday, July 24, 1952, just after noon, Breton, accompanied by his wife, Elisa, and fellow surrealist Adrien Dax, visited the Grotte du Pech-Merle for the first time.[37] Minutes after entering the painted cave, Breton reached out and touched one of the fine black lines depicting the trunk of a woolly mammoth. The tour guide promptly reminded him that touching the paintings was prohibited and that he needed to keep his hands to himself. Thumbing his nose at the guide, Breton swiped his thumb across the mammoth's trunk, removing three centimeters of black limestone chalk. In one fell swoop, the surrealist had defaced a painting preserved since time immemorial. The guide quickly rapped Breton's outstretched hand with his walking stick. "Do you know who I am?" Breton retorted. The guide, not to be upstaged, replied, "I don't care if you're the king of Spain." While insisting that he was allowed to test the authenticity of the prehistoric art, Breton called the guide a liar, a forger, and an *épicier*—the last of these insults connoting a vulgar shopkeeper and a narrow-minded country bumpkin. An altercation ensued that was violent enough to scare the schoolchildren who were among the thirty visitors to the cave. The gendarmes were called, and as the furious

Breton was escorted off the prehistoric grounds, he demanded he be reimbursed for his entrance fee.

Breton's deposition, recorded in Saint-Cirq-Lapopie four days after the incident, makes for fascinating reading. There's no denying the fifty-six-year-old surrealist's instinct for publicity. Breton stated that the guide had dealt him a severe blow before he had even stated the rules of the cave. "Naturally," he told the police, "I protested his violence, and said to the guide that it seemed to me a return to the customs of the Nazis, and that I thought those days were over." The temper of the baton-wielding guide apparently knew no bounds. As Breton passed through the wrought-iron door to leave the cave, the guide called him a coward. All told, Breton's deposition reads like the protestations of a mischievous schoolboy: I hadn't been told that I couldn't touch the art; I was the one who was wronged; after being called a coward, I had no choice but to confront him; and so on.[38]

But what had possessed Breton to damage the prehistoric art at Pech-Merle? His actions, he claimed, were a test. He wanted only to verify the antiquity of the painted woolly mammoths: "One has the urge to touch, in order to really see," he said. And sure enough, what Breton saw on his thumb was a black residue resembling charcoal. After so many years, he cried, the paint at Pech-Merle wasn't even dry! "Which shocked me," he continued, "since these lines were presumably traced thirty thousand years ago." Breton believed he had uncovered a fraud. But in reality, all this residue really proved, as Bataille and the prehistorians later made clear, was Breton's ignorance of the particulars of parietal art.

Yet the surrealist's indignation was unyielding. As the weeks went on, an incredulous Breton questioned not only the painting's purported authenticity but the authority of prehistorians like Breuil. It mattered little to Breton that Breuil had visited Pech-Merle in 1923 when the paintings were first discovered and verified the site's authenticity. Breton's strategy was to dispute both what had happened on that fateful day and the authority of prehistoric science itself. But to "win" what was now being called the Cabrerets affair, he needed a new audience; he needed to try his case in a more metropolitan court of public opinion—one less connected to prehistory and the provinces. Predictably, Breton, who was at the peak of his public powers, turned to the Parisian press. All the big dailies, including *Le Monde* and *France-Soir*, and even some serious journals like *Combat* and *Figaro littéraire*, took up the affair. As one, they defended Breton and his smear test. Article after article ridiculed the guide, minimized the damage, and described Pech-Merle as a moneymaking scheme. The dailies cast the affair as a crusade against backward provincialism by a cosmopolitan progressive who wanted to transform Saint-Cirq-Lapopie into a multicultural mecca, where artists and writers from around the world would gather.[39]

Reading these articles today, one is struck by their vitriol. The manager of Pech-Merle, Abel Bessac, for instance, was decried as a narrow-minded provincial, a mere mechanic. The journal *Arts*, a mouthpiece for the father of surrealism, hurled insults at Bessac and questioned the discipline of prehistory itself. Full of rhetorical gambits to win support for Breton, the Parisian press was unrelenting. They even asked: "André Breton, is he being hounded for having broken the law or for having involuntarily shed light on a forgery that was destined to remain in the shadows?"[40] For his part, Breton declared that prehistoric caves such as Pech-Merle were being used to promote antiquated religious beliefs and a Vichyite provincialism. *Arts* added a final touch. Above the entry to Pech-Merle, the journal informed its readers, there was a large sign that read: "For millennia, primitive man came here to sacrifice according to the laws of his religion." It was a fascinating observation. Essentially, *Arts* was wielding against prehistory and Pech-Merle the very sacrificial rites that had drawn Bataille to Lascaux: the birth of art from the belly of religious sacrifice.

Breton's press blitz did not go unchallenged. In November 1953—only three months after Bataille had published his first article on Lascaux in *Arts*—some of France's most prominent intellectuals, including Gaston Bachelard, Albert Camus, Claude Lévi-Strauss, André Malraux, François Mauriac, Jean Paulhan, Raymond Queneau, Paul Rivet, and Jean Wahl, publicly denounced both Breton's actions and the charges brought against him. Published in *France-Tireur* on November 10, 1953, their open letter began: "We learn with emotion that following a polemical incident that arose in the prehistoric cave of Cabrerets, criminal proceedings are currently engaged against André Breton, under the charge of the degradation of public monuments."[41] The intellectuals reminded readers of Breton's eminent contribution to poetry and his promotion of primitive and prehistoric arts. Nevertheless, with trepidation, the signatories censured his destructive smear test. But they also denounced—and with a little more vigor, it must be said—his upcoming trial. Breton's degradation, they believed, was the fruit of a misunderstanding, and it would be in everyone's best interest if the whole affair just went away.

More unequivocal were the protests of prehistorians. In a session held in the amphitheater of Paris's Galerie de Paléontologie et d'Anatomie comparée on the afternoon of October 23, 1952, Breuil addressed the ongoing affair. "An absurd campaign has been started against the authenticity of Pech-Merle's frescoes by people who are more excited than informed," Breuil began. Breton's destructive actions had been "wholly infantile and entirely blameworthy."

We are forever grateful, the abbé added, that the teenagers who discovered Lascaux in 1940 were not as juvenile as the father of surrealism.[42] On November 20, 1953, *Le Monde* published a letter by the prehistorian François Bordes concerning the incident at Pech-Merle. Bordes stated his surprise that throughout the yearlong affair no one seemed interested in what the experts had to say. He reminded the readers of *Le Monde* that there was an established discipline tasked with adjudicating such issues as authenticity and provenance. Breton may be an artist of the first rank, but he was no expert in prehistoric cave art. "Just because he's a well-known surrealist poet," Bordes asked, "does he have the right to degrade a historical monument to satisfy an infantile curiosity?" Breton was allowed to be ignorant of parietal art; what he wasn't allowed to do was to desecrate prehistoric works of art under the pretext of personal authentication. Should we be allowed to go to the Palace of Versailles armed with a hammer just to check for ourselves whether the windows really are trompe l'oeil? "There are laws protecting these monuments and Monsieur Breton, no more than anyone else, has no right to break them." The persistence of what had taken millennia to crystallize depended on it.[43]

Breton's trial was held in November 1953, fifteen months after the incident. The local court found the surrealist guilty of degrading a historical monument. Breton was fined 25,002 francs: one franc for damages to the state, another for damages to the commune of Cabrerets, five thousand francs for Pech-Merle, and twenty thousand francs to Bessac. The real story, of course, lies not in the final judgment but in the arguments made in the process. In a sense, the cause célèbre pitted French prehistory against surrealism and put both on trial. And the proceedings offer this novel insight: Surrealism and the French social sciences—whose union was so fertile in the 1930s—had a more adversarial relationship after 1945 than is generally presumed. In the court transcript we find Breton's lawyers chipping away at the authenticity of prehistoric paintings and the provincials who profited from them. Breton was depicted, in turn, as "an anarchist of the salon" who was drunk the afternoon he visited Pech-Merle. With the judgment finally handed down, it was hoped the affair would finally be laid to rest. But in the days after the decision, a petition circulated among the Parisian literati to form a commission to look into the authenticity of Pech-Merle's paintings. And who did this commission propose lead the investigation? None other than André Breton himself.

How did Bataille respond to Breton's smear test and the Cabrerets affair? The first clue comes on page 15 of the manuscript of Bataille's *Lascaux or the Birth of Art* (1955). Bataille concluded that Breton's antics were naive tomfoolery and his press campaign a vain conceit. The humidity of the caves, which had been sealed for millennia, explained the freshness of the archaic lines. Bataille condemned Breton's actions and dismissed his doubts about Pech-Merle's authenticity. The surrealist had no right to emblazon the rock wall with his own mark. For Bataille, the student of prehistory and the good apprentice, it was the assessment of specialists in the field that mattered. He went on, echoing Bordes: "To test the quality of a prehistoric painting by passing one's finger over it shows one's complete ignorance in all matters of parietal art."[44] What Breton needed to do was not to unleash a press campaign, but to open Breuil's meticulous and magisterial *Four Hundred Centuries of Cave Art*, published a few months earlier in April 1952. At the heart of the matter was the fact that Bataille was drawn to what Breton despised: Deep in the painted caves of southwestern France, one could momentarily cross an abyss of time and catch sight of the sacrificial rites of an archaic religion.

The Cabrerets affair forces us to rethink many things, including Bataille's notion of transgression. Just as there was a real divergence between Bataille's long apprenticeship and Breton's scandalous affair, there was a big difference between Breton's surrealist subversions and Bataille's transgressive expenditures: one was provocative and could be accomplished with a quick swipe of the hand; the other was a ritual trespass of a long-standing prohibition, which induced intimacy and ultimately reinforced the law. In "Surrealism Day by Day," Bataille made plain that he was not interested in easy degradations. Subversion was one response to postwar society; but it wasn't Bataille's. Surrealists, Bataille noted, sought alternatives to postwar life not by looking to the deep past, but by destabilizing the accelerating present. Bataille, however, demanded rigorous principles that were "commensurate with the tensions of the world today." "I advance nothing by chance," he added.[45] By the mid-1950s, Bataille's notions of transgression and expenditure were firmly grounded in what he had learned from prehistory, the social sciences, and the history of religion.

Twenty years earlier Bataille had equated primitive art with randomness, the irrational, and the formless. Wandering thoughts, bizarre lines, muddled scribbles, and deformed compositions—the pictorial art of primitives, like the doodles of children, was unencumbered by tradition. Bataille formulated his idea of formlessness in "Primitive Art" (1930), a speculative essay that was ostensibly a review of Georges-Henri Luquet's *Primitive Art* (1930).[46] Naturally, Bataille's penchant for seeing the formless in the highly stylized tells us more about his own thinking in the 1930s than it does about the cultures of so-called primitives. His insistence on formlessness between the two world wars points to two supposedly prominent features of primitive culture: spontaneity and absolute freedom. It remains a seductive interpretation, especially for those eager to merge the modernist with the primitive and the prehistoric.

But, as Bataille would later learn, it was just not borne out by the overwhelming evidence of prehistory. Formlessness, it turns out, was a stillbirth of an idea, which had little place in Bataille's Lascaux writings.[47] What kind of primitivist emerges when we separate the postwar apprentice in French prehistory from the interwar provocateur?

Breuil offered Bataille a different explanation of the enduring enigma of prehistoric cave art (fig. 1.2). The matter of why Paleolithic hunters went to such lengths to paint animal figures deep inside caves was a thoroughgoing *problématique*. Why did the vast majority of cave paintings depict animals? Why were animals art's first subject matter? Breuil thought that any answer to the problem must begin with hunger, the base appetite and principal anxiety of Paleolithic peoples. One question dominated the thinking of seminomadic hunters: Would they find enough game to survive the coming season? The meaning of prehistoric cave art, Breuil argued, flowed from there. It was hunger, then, and a deeply held belief in sympathetic magic that spurred prehistoric cave painters to depict animal figures. They would try anything to increase their yield. Breuil's interpretation of Paleolithic cave paintings was derived from the first volume of Frazer's *The Golden Bough* (1890). There the author had argued that the belief that "like produces like" dominated the mental ideation of primitive peoples. And if like produces like, then painting a faithful likeness of an animal underground would influence its appearance aboveground.

Bataille learned from Breuil that as *Homo sapiens* struggled to survive in a hostile land of scarcity, man manipulated nature and multiplied his share by painting animals' likenesses on cave walls. No dearth, no need for hunting magic, and therefore no cave art. What we see today at the Grotte du Pech-Merle was thus one more tool in the hunter's arsenal and one of several instruments intended to influence the course of daily life. Imitation was profitable, and Breuil offered the example of hunters using a stag's horns to attract deer during the rutting season. Imitative magic and the mimetic faculties of prehistoric peoples also explained the symbolic arrows that were painted on an ibex in Niaux and on some horses in Lascaux (a view that has since been debunked). An art that was wholly useful, accumulation in an age of scarcity—this is the essence of what Breuil saw when he looked at the crystallized marks of times past. Man, a resourceful carnivore, extending his empire over animal life. *Homo imperius*.

Breuil's *Four Hundred Centuries of Cave Art* was a grand tour of some ninety caves, from Altamira in northern Spain through France's Vézère Valley. "A true summa," Bataille called it.[48] With over three hundred photographs by Fernand Windels and twenty sketches by Breuil himself, this doorstop of

FIGURE 1.2. Abbé Henri Breuil, prehistorian, priest, and the most quotable advocate of the "hunting magic" interpretation of Paleolithic art. Here, at the mouth of Lascaux, he discovers no doubt another animal subdued by representation. (Wellcome Collection, CC BY 4.0).

a volume cemented Breuil's hunting-magic interpretation of prehistoric cave art. Hunting magic, Breuil wrote, held "the greatest place" in the minds of prehistoric painters. By the early 1950s Breuil's interpretation had crystallized into dogma.[49] Sympathetic magic certainly explained the Paleolithic artists' penchant for naturalism. The painters of Pech-Merle and Lascaux didn't draw nonhuman animals abstractly; they drew them true to life—the better the likeness, the more efficacious the magic. The belief was that by faithfully rendering a fully fleshed out animal, they gained a certain power over it. And Paleolithic peoples, who moved alongside the animal world, had an intimate knowledge of the animals they hunted. It was a useful technique, to be sure, even if their power over the other animals was only psychological. In this view, prehistoric art was of a decidedly productive bent. Breuil's interpretation must have struck his mid-century readers as quite familiar. One imagines the first visitors to Lascaux channeling their bewilderment into an impulse modern onlookers knew all too well: the desire to accumulate things. Like us, everything they did was in the interest of profitability. Faced with the foreign and ineffable, it is tempting to see the familiar. In this view, a prehistoric cave painting was less a creative work of art than the cunning art of work. Bataille, however, thought that Breuil's explanation left out something essential, something more human than exploiting every possible resource. Soon Bataille would arrive at a different interpretation, one less suffused with utility.

By the end of 1953 Bataille was convinced that there was another explanation of the art left behind by long-vanished cultures. In the depths of Lascaux, one was in the presence of the magico-religious, not the magico-utilitarian. Primitive thought was not exhausted by imitative magic, and Breuil had been too fixated on the hunt above the ground to grasp the depth of meaning in the rites below it. Bataille's departure from Breuil stemmed from the belief that primitive cultures should not be reduced to the core values of modern Western culture: acquisition, accumulation, and sordid self-interest. To suppose that animals first entered the human mind as meat, as labor, as *things* was to carry a modern prejudice back across millennia.[50] Prehistoric painters weren't driven by a desire to grow their share or increase their power over nature—in fact, just the opposite. The artists of Lascaux wanted to restore a lost intimacy with the animal world. They were driven by an unshakable nostalgia for our animal past and an age-old belief in our kinship with the other animals. Why else would our ancestors surround themselves with these animals if they did not want to be their intimates once more? In 1953 Bataille was only a few short steps away from enlisting the Upper Paleolithic in his critique of postwar growth.[51] But Bataille and Breuil agreed on one thing: You needed to visit Lascaux and see for yourself—although you didn't need to touch in order to see. As I said, the Lascaux moment had arrived, and it marks a fascinating episode in the history of twentieth-century primitivism.

The Ciphers of Lascaux

On September 12, 1940, four teenagers climbing a hill near the village of Montignac in the Vézère Valley discovered an entry into an underground cave. After a steep descent they saw animal paintings that no one had laid eyes on for over seventeen thousand years. They had stumbled by chance on the most vibrant prehistoric tableaux anyone had ever seen. What they saw was special: the sheer number of paintings, the size of the painted animals, their vivid polychromatic style and, above all, their excellent preservation under a layer of crystal calcite—the archaic remains near Montignac, painted in the Upper Paleolithic period, were truly one of a kind. At last French prehistory had its crown jewel, its capital treasure in troubling times. The teenagers had unwittingly discovered pristine traces of a most distant humanity that were close enough to touch (if only illicitly). Eight years later, on July 14, 1948, Henri Breuil opened Lascaux to the public. A steady stream of visitors soon passed through Lascaux's door. Breuil recorded that in 1950 Lascaux had fifteen hundred visitors per day.[52] Enthusiasm for the subterranean site was widely felt, and tourists flocked to the cold, once silent grotto. From one end of history to the other, it seems, Lascaux knew how to attract a crowd. Bataille thought that modern onlookers were attracted by the idea that they might find something immemorial and enchanting at Lascaux, the reverse of the unpredictable and disenchanted world in which they lived. Whatever the case may be, the Lascaux moment had arrived.

The history of Lascaux after 1948 is a story of the presence of the very old in an age that celebrated the new. In the end, it is a cautionary tale about the devastation wrought by the ceaseless circulations and emissions of modern humanity. But for a time, Lascaux was a place where one could encounter the "richest, most moving echo" of the primitive world. At Lascaux, Bataille believed he had finally made contact with anterior reality and returned to "the old human house."[53] He wasn't the only one to find in this subterranean corner of the Vézère Valley a genuine staging of the archaic. For many, Lascaux was a testament to the riches of former times and an example of what had been lost. "No one would have guessed the astounding antiquity of those paintings chance had uncovered," wrote Bataille.[54] And while parietal art quickly became a popular fascination, measuring the extent of Lascaux's influence is not enough. It is the site's ability to defamiliarize the all-too-familiar arrow of historical progress that needs attending to. It took no great imagination to see in the majesty of the great Hall of Bulls (fig. 1.3), the fury of the Crossed Bison, the sprightliness of the Swimming Stags, or the ridiculousness of the Upside-Down Horse evidence of humanity's early heights. "They've invented everything," Pablo Picasso reportedly said to his guide while visiting Lascaux for the first time. We have added little to the cultural inheritance left us by our distant ancestors, Bataille added. Lascaux exploded the idea that the oldest was the simplest and confirmed what most primitivists already believed: Nothing supports the contention that we are greater than they. The defamiliarization Bataille experienced at Lascaux was more than a vague awakening; it sparked a desire to preserve primitive cultures, to reevaluate them, and, not least, to revive certain aspects of them.

Bataille believed that humanity had first flowered at Lascaux. He was drawn to Lascaux not only because of its proximity, but because its antiquity was lost in the darkness of time (fig. 1.4). It was in this very cave, on the glacial fringe of Pleistocene Europe, he opined, that art and religion first sprang forth. What was fortuitously discovered in 1940, just a few months after France's military collapse, was a distant and glorious heritage, a sanctuary of noble proportions. The uninhabitable caverns, the darkness of the cave, the glow of the torches all inspired a sense of the sacred. When Bataille called the Upper Paleolithic cave the "holy of holies," he was not deviating from a temporal sense of the sacred. The drama of Lascaux's Hall of Bulls, often called the Sistine Chapel of prehistory, was quite different from that depicted on the ceiling of our modern apostolic palace. Bathed not in everlasting light but in everlasting midnight, Lascaux's august paintings were a portal into our animal ancestry rather than a window on the hands of the creator. Such were the primitivist's blandishments. Without any embellishment, however, it is safe to say that Lascaux added a primeval fuel to Bataille's ongoing struggle against postwar modernization. Lascaux was proof that there were luminous remains right underneath his feet. There, in the French countryside, were well-preserved traces of the dawn of art, religion, and unproductive expenditure.[55]

Bataille's experience at Lascaux thus sealed his preference for a domain more homegrown than the one he had discovered in French ethnography. In the 1950s he visited Lascaux numerous times. It was a fairly easy trip from his residence in Orléans to Montignac. And since he was hard at work on one of the first illustrated books on Lascaux, Bataille was granted special access to the cave. In short order, the author of the wide-ranging *Accursed Share* came to see the valley of Vézère as the ground he had been searching for all along. He no longer needed to mine far afield for viable alternatives; they persisted right underfoot, deep in French soil. My point is that place mattered. It mattered to Bataille, and it didn't escape the general public either. By dint of its location, deep in the provinces, Lascaux was linked to the wholesome but not innocent French countryside. Not long ago the mere thought of these rural environs had aroused disgust. During the dark days of the Occupation, the French countryside was a synecdoche for capitulation and collaboration, a land stained by Vichy's blood-and-soil nationalism. In the din of postwar modernization, however, the picture of this picturesque corner of provincial France was beginning to change.

With his sympathies laid bare, the Vézère Valley became the sacred ground on which Bataille based his thought. Lascaux taught him the importance of encountering the archaic in person, which he had yet to experience until then. His face-to-face encounters with some of the earliest and most vibrant artifacts of human culture were a rather delightful change from being hunched over travelers' reports and anthropological essays. Bataille began to

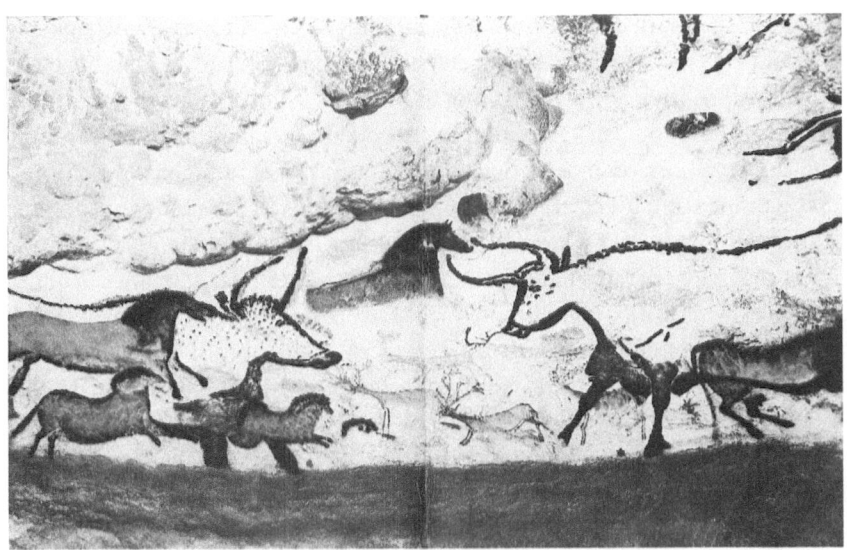

FIGURE 1.3. Hall of Bulls, Lascaux, c. 15,000 BCE. Iron and manganese oxides and charcoal on rock, 6.5 × 19 m. A long frieze of bulls, horses, and deer greeted our Paleolithic ancestors. The scene in the main hall must have only been accentuated when torchlit. Acoustics also played a role in choosing this underground location. Sound, light, and a great animal dance—the dramatic properties of rites repeated throughout the Upper Paleolithic. Published in Fernand Windels, *The Lascaux Cave Paintings* (Faber & Faber, 1949). (Wellcome Collection, CC BY 4.0).

FIGURE 1.4. Bataille with time enough to sit and take notes—words that, he must have thought, were sanctified by the subterranean environment and imbued with power by their proximity to the paintings. Uncredited photograph c. 1954.

speak in earnest of a "fieldwork" he could finally call his own. Slowly pacing the cold cavern floor in a long overcoat, his hands clasped behind his back, Bataille quite literally walked among the archaic. Thanks to his special access, the primitivist could take the time he needed to feel the touch of deep time and the burning presence of the "most ancient traces of archaic man"—and not without a shudder.[56] Bataille brought a primitivist sensibility to Lascaux: "Little would it matter what our dead ancestors bequeathed to posterity were it not that we hoped to make them, if for only a fleeting instant, live again in ourselves."[57] With its vibrant remains, Lascaux lent itself to the primitivist's championing of cultural survivals. The recently discovered cave epitomized the will to preserve and the assurance of cultural patrimony, habits Bataille knew well by training and vocation. He had become a troglodyte, in both senses of the word: a man of the prehistoric caves and one who cherishes being deliberately old-fashioned.

Bataille's fieldwork took place against the backdrop of *les trente glorieuses*. Lascaux was fated to reappear in the age that would come to be called the Great Acceleration, when bustling humanity accelerated the carbon economy and rapidly altered everything it came into contact with. When Bataille set to work on Lascaux in the early 1950s, he had before him an unmistakable difference between the glacial pace of humanity's distant past and the rapid circulations of the postwar present. He often contrasted the predictable rhythms of the Paleolithic past, when ways of living remained unchanged for millennia, with the jump cuts of the postwar present, when calls to "Change life!" could be heard on every street corner. The culture that created Lascaux "knew no swift evolution comparable to the one that today unceasingly affects every fiber of our being, every facet of our life." "Doubtless," he added, "the Reindeer Age was not an age of rapid change."[58] The constant flux of postwar society raised intractable questions about its ability to preserve. Lascaux itself soon became a prescient object lesson in loss: Not long after the cave was opened to the public, its paintings began to show signs of irreversible degradation. In just a few short years, the carbon dioxide in the labored breath of thousands of circulating tourists had upset the fragile equilibrium of the subterranean climate; if there's a better microcosm of our planet's current predicament, I'm not aware of it. Like uncorked wine turned to vinegar, the prehistoric site suffered so much in so little time.[59]

Before long (and before it was too late), Bataille was ready to break new interpretative ground. He didn't so much care about undoing Breuil's interpretation of parietal art as going beyond it. There had to be a reason most of the animals drawn were not those that Paleolithic people hunted but those that transported the imagination. In the mid-1950s Bataille argued that the deeper meaning of prehistoric cave art lay not in magical calculations but in religious sentiments, not in utility and the hunt but in expenditure and the festival. In other words, he reinscribed the archaic animals within the realm of the sacred. He refused to reduce the rich, affective origins of human culture to practical pursuits. The admirable paintings of Lascaux could not be explained by "the calculative simplicity of magic." He thought Breuil had turned Paleolithic artists into industrious bipeds whose paintings were merely one more tool sharpened in the interest of increased production—although Bataille, the good apprentice, didn't say so in such stark words. He gently admonished prehistorians to stop confusing production with expenditure, *Homo faber* with *Homo religiosus*, the profane with the sacred, sympathetic magic with archaic religion, pursuits aboveground with the passions permitted below ground.[60]

Already polished in the history of religion, Bataille brought his impressive powers of synthesis to bear on Lascaux. Published in 1955 by Albert Skira, Bataille's monograph on Lascaux was the first book to include large color photographs of the paintings. A decade and a half after the cave's rediscovery, the time was right for a synthesis of all that had been written about Lascaux's parietal art. The task Bataille set himself was immense: to both guide his readers through Lascaux's caverns (the color photos helped) and to offer a groundbreaking interpretation rooted in the laborious findings of prehistorians. So, in addition to his fieldwork, he consulted with experts and read any specialized monograph on prehistoric art he could get his hands on. He plunged into prehistory with the same enthusiasm he had the history of religion. *Lascaux or the Birth of Art* was as scholarly as it was strikingly beautiful. Combining archaeological evidence and documentary material, it was the culmination of Bataille's long apprenticeship in prehistorical scholarship.[61] And while *Lascaux* was a work of great synoptic energy, it was more than a scholarly survey. Bataille, as was his wont, dug beneath the surface of facts to get at deeper desires. At this point it won't surprise you to learn that his interpretation was primitivist, poetic even. But for all that, *Lascaux* was built on a clear and systematic exposition of the facts of prehistory. While maintaining a strict fidelity to prehistoric science, he declared that he had discovered the "general disposition" of Paleolithic peoples. And he called their ethos *archaïque*.

Bataille's ability to toggle between felicity and originality after 1945 is evident in his description of one of Lascaux's strangest paintings, commonly called "the Unicorn" (fig. 1.5). The Unicorn is a composite figure with a heavy cow's body that is dotted with feline spots and features a stubby rhinoceros's tail and an undersized head with two uncanny horns. The common view is that this particular "unicorn" (with two long horns rather than one) depicts a disguised hunter. The Unicorn was thus commonly linked to sympathetic magic and the productive principle that "like produces like." For the librarian from Orléans, however, the Unicorn was all animal. Bataille thought so not because he ignored the evidence of prehistorians, but because he knew it all too well. If there was indeed a human hiding there behind animal skeins, you would know it. According to the conventions of parietal art, what was human was not drawn naturalistically but with stiff, childish lines. Yet the Unicorn in Lascaux's Hall of Bulls was robust and naturalistic. "The impulse behind the Unicorn is not solely the desire of a successful hunt," Bataille wrote. This spellbinding behemoth—an amalgamation of the bovine, the feline, and the horned—was born of "religious imagination," not sympathetic magic. The Unicorn belonged to "the sphere of fantasy and dreams, which are controlled by neither hunger nor the real world."[62]

Any close study of Lascaux leaves the impression that the prominent hill near present-day Montignac was a gathering place for seminomadic groups following migrations of large game across the steppes of Western Europe. Lascaux was located at a natural choke point on the banks of the Vézère, an ideal location for intercepting herds of reindeer in their seasonal migrations.

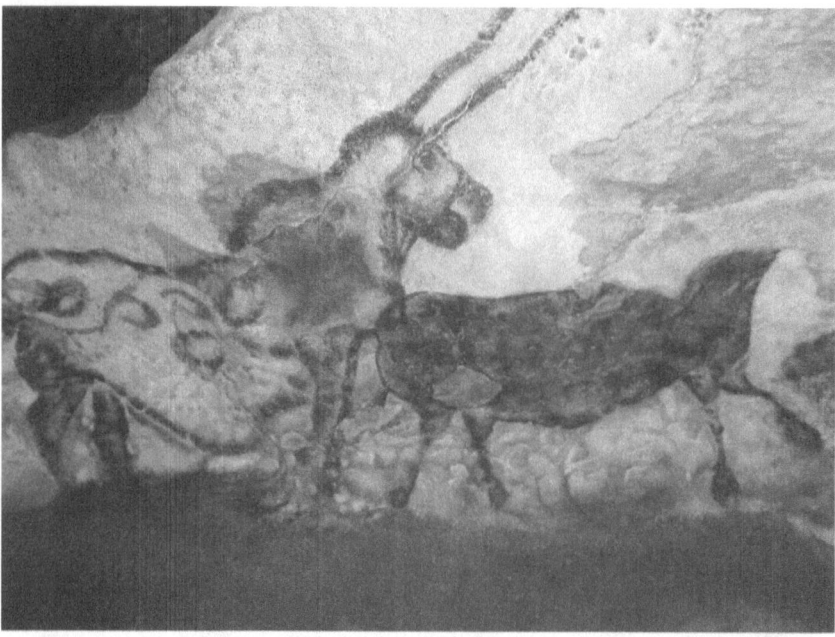

FIGURE 1.5. The Unicorn; detail from Lascaux's Hall of Bulls. A characteristically robust painting of a large bovine with two exuberant horns. This work belongs to a time when such art was tied, in the artists' minds, to nostalgic feelings. An archaic *nostalgie de la boue*, if you like, a longing for the home world, for an animal underworld.

Bataille was convinced, in the absence of evidence to the contrary, that Lascaux was no ordinary dwelling place. It was a sanctuary, a sacred site for heightened levels of artistic and ritual activity during seasonal gatherings. The Hall of Bulls, for example, with its thickly painted frescoes and its vast elongated corridor with room for some one hundred persons, is reminiscent of a *sanctum sanctorum*. It was unimaginable, Bataille thought, that such a creative work of art could have been made independent of the impulses that engendered festivals. Lascaux "still has about it something that seizes, spellbinds the visitor, quickens his pulse." "These caverns," he continued, "cause an inner distress not at all unlike the anguish connected with sacred rites."[63] He believed that certain caverns across the Franco-Cantabrian region provided the setting for the deliberate enjoyment of what is expended without utility—dark reprieves from the daily weight of restless calculation. The idea is not as far-fetched as it sounds; spacious caverns such as Lascaux's Hall of Bulls or Niaux's Salle Noir still elicit religious feeling. These acoustic enclosures, in the darkest recesses of the caves (where all parietal art is found and where no one lived), impressed on Bataille that "the drawing of a figure probably didn't alone constitute a ceremony, but it was part of larger religious or magical operation." Before religious rites were wedded to temples and cathedrals, they took place in ambiguous spaces—underground chambers, dark cells, painted caverns, and other interstitial spaces that in *The Production of Space* Henri Lefebvre called "differential."[64] In the end, Bataille declared Lascaux a world-historical moment, when the unproductive expenditures of religious festivals first appeared.

Bataille soon arrived at what he called the delicate equilibrium of archaic societies. Back then humanity was headed in a very different direction. Lascaux's paintings suggested that there once existed festivals whose expenditures deliberately thwarted the daily demands of production. These periodic festivals, which summoned all the community's reserves, were a collective defiance of "the principles presiding over the disciplined regularity of work." "Everywhere, and at every time," he continued, "the feast day denoted the moment when the rules ordinarily put up with were abruptly laid to rest." While life depended, then just as now, on the workaday world, "no one can imagine a world where burning passion would definitively cease to trouble us." The desire to exponentially increase is not the only human desire, nor has it always been the most deeply felt: "The chief concern in the earliest days was—as it still is in archaic societies—to bring work and play, prohibition and transgression, the profane season and the riot of the festival into a kind of delicate equilibrium within which contraries blend, play takes on the guise of work and transgression contributes to affirming prohibition." To be clear, primitive rites didn't interrupt some stolid serenity. In fact, the evidence points in the opposite direction: The virtue of these seasonally sanctioned transgressions was in the way they interrupted the restlessness of everyday life. Prehistoric cave art was a vestige, then, of the prodigious rites that punctuated the Upper Paleolithic. If the remains at Lascaux are to be trusted, Paleolithic peoples possessed a ballast to the demands of continual growth. And with their commitment to maintain a delicate equilibrium between production and expenditure, the gulf between primitive and modern societies grew even wider. Their chief ambition was restoring a lost intimacy with the natural world; ours, yet more economic growth—"We are poorer for our devotion to calculation and profitability."[65] It was in his Lascaux writings that Bataille's critique of our growth-based imaginary was at its most biting, and its most articulate. Walking among the archaic animals, he appears not as a forerunner to poststructuralism but as a foundational figure of the degrowth movement.

Just past Lascaux's Hall of Bulls are two bison done in dark brown (fig. 1.6). Like all prehistoric animals, they are rendered naturalistically. Although these bison don't loom as large as the bulls in the corridor, they are just as imposing. Their fur bristles, their eyes search furiously, their sexual organs are erect, their bodies strain under their brute power. "This painting," Bataille wrote, "is the most tumultuous the Reindeer Age has left us."[66] The two animals' hindquarters are joined, and gaps above their back legs suggest movement. The combined effect is that the bison appear to be feverishly circling each other. This painting, which is commonly called the Crossed Bison, was the Paleolithic painters' boldest expression of animal fury. But more important than any animal violence are the tableau's themes of fertility and recurrence. The painting's cyclical nature is often overlooked by visitors who are (understandably) unfamiliar with bison mating rituals. For the hunters of Upper Paleolithic Europe, however, the painting's subject must have been obvious: Two male bison are circling and challenging each other during the annual mating season. But then, against every expectation, it turns out that this painting was not entirely naturalistic. In reality these bison could never circle each other because one has a winter coat and the other, with a streak of red splashed across his back, has a summer coat. Thus, there was a symbolic-religious dimension to the Crossed Bison: an expression of nature's cyclical reliability and a reminder of the rites that commemorate life's fertile returns. For Paleolithic peoples, time was not unidirectional, as it is for us. More proof that Lascaux's paintings were not the product of a culture of progressive acquisition; they were carefully crafted symbols linked to the religious rites that took place underneath them.

FIGURE 1.6. "Unsurpassed power . . . bewildered, erotic, and blind."

There is little evidence that the animal art of the Upper Paleolithic was the result of "free spontaneity." Yet there it is: An odd passage in *Lascaux* in which Bataille suggested that Paleolithic artists were unencumbered by aesthetic conventions or compositional rules. Perplexingly, he concluded that the hands of prehistoric painters were "guided" by spontaneity, incertitude, and free movement.[67] Convention, it seems, mattered little in the dark recesses of the caves. But Bataille's passing suggestion was an echo of the formlessness he was so fond of in the 1930s and out of step with the general tenor of his Lascaux writings. The fact remains that Lascaux's animal art participated in a tradition twenty-five millennia in the making. Neither free spontaneity nor the idiosyncratic visions of intoxicated individuals explain the artistic style that spread across the Franco-Cantabrian region seventeen thousand years ago.[68] Elsewhere in *Lascaux* Bataille acknowledged that prehistoric painters were disciplined draftsmen who rendered animals in profile (often in a way that suggested movement); who preferred certain animals over others (bison, ibexes, and horses—the holy trinity of parietal art); who never depicted flora or landscapes or even the ground itself (letting the contours of the cave do the work for them); who painted with bold, confident brushstrokes (which suggests that they practiced their craft elsewhere, likely outside the caves); and who never signed their works of art (preferring a collective palimpsest to individual attribution). These were the contours of history's most durable aesthetic tradition, a craft passed down from generation to generation for many millennia. The culture that created it must therefore have been incredibly stable and deeply satisfying.[69]

The most ponderous rule of prehistoric art is surely the boundary between the human and the animal. Though the primary subject matter of parietal art was nonhuman animals, the painters of the Upper Paleolithic sometimes broke the taboo and depicted their own kind. And on the rare occasion when they did, they deformed the human animal with crude, childish strokes and banished their own image to the deepest, darkest, most inaccessible parts of the cave. "An extreme effacement of man before the animal" is how Bataille described what went on in the womb of the world.[70] More remarkable still was prehistoric painters' disdain for the human face. When human beings were drawn, their faces were concealed under animal masks. Bataille saw in these animal-human hybrids more evidence that Lascaux was a reconciliation with the animal realm and a momentary reprieve from the profane realities of human life. To secure a sacred realm below ground, the most primitive art had to let go of the anthropocentrism that reigned aboveground. Thus, Bataille argued, primitive cultures knew very well how to acknowledge the sovereignty and sanctity that belonged to the animal. Most Paleolithic cultures seem to have included a deep and active regard for their fellow animals. To say that prehistoric peoples perceived animals as their equals isn't the half of it; for our distant ancestors, "the animal towered above scurrying, bustling humanity."[71] A piece of prelapsarian wistfulness? Perhaps. And yet, reviving this animistic aspect of the archaic may well be a necessity if we are to develop a healthier and more ethical relationship to our fellow creatures—or, at the very least, to stop devastating and devouring them at such a cataclysmic rate. Animism is easy to criticize, even in the midst of Earth's sixth mass extinction event. But when all is said and done, there remains something attractive on an ethical level about looking at animals the way Paleolithic hunters used to.[72]

One way to get at the meaning that the paintings might have had for those who painted them is to examine "the attitudes and behavior that certain tribes of hunters, living today, observe toward animality."[73] Like Breuil before him, Bataille used Indigenous cultures to better understand Paleolithic ones. For many so-called primitives, animals are reminders of origins: The Lascaux painters had "scarcely emerged from the dark conditions of what is animal," Bataille believed. "Animals," John Berger wrote in *About Looking*, "intercede between man and their origin because they are both like and unlike man."[74] Writing well before Berger, Bataille was fond of citing *Hunting Rituals Among Siberian Peoples* (1953) by Éveline Lot-Falck, an ethnographer and the reigning expert on Siberian shamanism after the execution of the Russian émigré Anatole Lewitsky by the Germans in 1942. " 'Wild game is like man, only more godlike,' says the Navaho, and the phrase would not be out of place on a Siberian's lips," wrote Lot-Falck. Soon Bataille was writing that animality is akin to divinity. He learned from the French ethnographer how to orient the archaic idea of animality by triangulating Siberia, the American Southwest, and the ancient French Southwest. In fact, by mixing the ethnographic and prehistoric—by asserting the striking similarities between the ritual practices of Siberian tribes, American Indians, and the prehistoric peoples of Europe— Lot-Falck had articulated an indispensable idea. With the aid of far-flung parallels, she showed how shamanic cultures periodically crossed the permeable divide that separates humans from the other animals.[75]

Bataille's analysis of Lascaux's Well Scene helps explain this admittedly indefinite idea of animality. The most-discussed painting in all Lascaux, the Well Scene is an enigmatic drama passed down from prehistory. As you might imagine, it is not easy to get to Lascaux's well. It requires climbing down a narrow, almost inaccessible twenty-six-foot crevice. But once you are down in the shaman's part of the cave you will find a stick-figure man with a head resembling that of a beaked bird, the only representation of a human in Lascaux's hundreds of paintings and engravings (fig. 1.7). Unlike the bold, monumental style of the Crossed Bison or the Hall of Bulls, this bird-human hybrid is drawn simply, with stiff, immature lines. He appears to be falling down. Except for his erect penis, he is prostrate and seems to be dead or dying. To the man's right is a wounded bison, his entrails spilling out of his heavy body. As I said, it's an enigmatic scene. But one thing is certain: There is an undeniable difference between how Paleolithic painters drew human and nonhuman animals. Whereas all of Lascaux's nonhuman animals are naturalistic and alive, even when they are wounded or upside down, this solitary stick figure is stretched out and inert, and his face is hidden behind an animal mask.[76]

The first of several shifting interpretations of this enigmatic scene came in *Lascaux or the Birth of Art*. The unsteady man with the bird mask, Bataille explained, was a shaman who lay prostrate because he was in the throes of an ecstatic ascension. This interpretation is supported by the presence of another bird perched atop a rod like a weathercock near the masked man. In this view, the Well Scene is a story of shamanistic ascension that Bataille construed as a desire to overcome the renunciation of animality that was required of the earliest human beings.[77] Two years later, in *Eroticism* (1957), ecstatic experience became mournful expiation. The Well Scene now depicted a shaman in full atonement rather than in the throes of ecstasy. Hunting cultures, Bataille noted, often atone for the killing of animals in religious rites—which explains why man, that carnivorous biped, lay prostrate before

FIGURE 1.7. An anomaly in Paleolithic parietal art: In the well of Lascaux, in the most remote region of the cave, one finds a man, not altogether human. The scene's meaning is difficult to grasp, but take note of the bird theme, which appears twice—once in the man with a bird head, and again in the bird perched on a rod—and which belies any simple "hunting accident" interpretation.

a disemboweled bison.[78] Bataille then went on to declare in *The Tears of Eros* (1961) that we cannot ignore that the painted man is an ithyphallic figure. The shaman's marked sex—that is, his erect penis—surely gives the scene an erotic character. By turning to sexual excitation, Bataille connected this enigmatic prehistoric drama with his ongoing work on eroticism.[79]

One response to these shifting interpretations is to say that Bataille saw in Lascaux's Well Scene what he wanted to see. Over the years, Lascaux has meant a great many things to a great many people, and what we say about the paintings reveals far more about us than it does about them.[80] But it is important to recognize that as Bataille walked his tightrope from ecstasy to expiation to eroticism, he remained committed to the evidence of prehistory, to the importance of human-animal relations, and to the sacred significance of what is expended without utility. Whether the masked man was ecstatic, expiating, or aroused, the scene had the virtue of depicting an act that went well beyond utilitarian interests. Each of Bataille's interpretations refused to reduce primitive dramas to productive pursuits. The efficacious magic of "like produces like" did not explain what had gone on at Lascaux; the principle of utility was not the key to unlocking these archaic depths. Ecstasy, expiation, sexual excitation, and unproductive expenditure were all part of the great animal dance that marked the upper reaches of the Upper Paleolithic. Lascaux was hence a reminder of humanity's enduring search for a lost intimacy with the animal world. This was the chief virtue Bataille discovered in the cave near

Montignac. To recover a lost intimacy was the crux of Lascaux and the ultimate aim of all sacrifice, transgression, and expenditure.[81]

Writing the History of Humankind

Shortly before dusk, Bataille paused from the slow pace of writing to pace the polished floor of the library. For several days he had been holed up in his apartment adjacent to the Bibliothèque municipale d'Orléans working on the outline of a sweeping history of humanity, which he tentatively titled *Universal History, or the Bottle in the Sea: From Origins to the Eve of Eventual Disaster*. Perhaps it did not matter much what a man of sixty-plus wrote, especially since he wrote it with a prodigious élan and a propensity for the tragic. In any case, almost everything had been said—almost. He closed his eyes and foresaw a terrible reckoning. But he wasn't seeing clearly, and hadn't been for the last seven months now. Wherever he looked, or tried to look, he stared human extinction squarely in the face. But then, into his mind's eye came the creativity and durability enshrined in humanity's deep past: Painted bulls and bison came to life, other animal images poured in. He knew it was no coincidence that light had been shed on humanity's birth at the moment when the notion of our death appeared to us. Time left to cast one last message into a rising and indifferent sea—the rising sea being a metaphor for the regular excesses of grow-or-die modernity. Anyway, he was writing normally again, putting the final touches on his last will and testament, a history of humankind that ended not with a bang but with a cyclical return. The archivist-turned-primitivist pictured the day when a brilliant sun would rise over a temperate sea. But it was getting late. Before retiring, he added to his outline these final words: "Archaic civilizations, their persistence."

A sweeping historical vision shaped the mature phase of Bataille's intellectual life. His major works of the postwar period were guided by a single organizing principle: to write the history of our species, from our most archaic religious sentiments to the cataclysmic potential of postwar growth. Between 1945 and 1962 Bataille did not so much as succumb to the temptation to write a history of humankind as eagerly set out to do so. His mature works, both published and planned, were unapologetically universal; he was an unabashed, not an unwitting, historian of the *longue durée*.[82] *Theory of Religion*, *The Accursed Share*, *Lascaux*, *Eroticism*, and *The Tears of Eros* used the evidence of history and the social sciences to formulate a general interpretation of human history. The bedrock of these books was the transhistorical distinction, by now familiar, between the profane sphere of growth and the sacred realm of unproductive expenditure. While attentive to particulars, Bataille's histories covered multitudes of centuries in a flash. Each included an extensive study of prehistory and ethnography, an account of how the archaic was made modern, and a critique of postwar society. The hour of synthesis had arrived, and Bataille's desire to explain the whole of human history was no passing whim, written only for the drawer. Rather, the whole of his postwar oeuvre stands under its sign.[83]

In the late 1950s Bataille wrote several outlines for a magnum opus that would bring together much of his published and unpublished work. One outline, dated July 27, 1959, is a single handwritten page; others are considerably longer. Bataille gave one of these outlines the working title "Universal History, or the Bottle in the Sea: From Origins to the Eve of Eventual Disaster."[84] Anyone who has an eye for ingrained habits will recognize in these outlines the erudition to which Bataille dedicated his life. Despite decades of suggestions to the contrary, Bataille's training at the École nationale des chartes and his work at the Bibliothèque municipale d'Orléans were not anathema to his postwar pursuits. He knew the historical record, he gathered together the discoveries of social scientists, and he remained true to the empirical foundations on which any history of humankind must rest. Without the specialist, the comparatist is nothing, he opined. In this way (though not only in this way) Bataille was a bit like Frazer. We can imagine him, when he wasn't pacing the cavern floors of Lascaux, hunched over a desk in his office adjacent to the Bibliothèque municipale d'Orléans.

Today we would call Bataille's approach, with its narrative arc reaching back to distant human origins and culminating in a coming planetary crisis, "the history of humankind." But Bataille wasn't satisfied with summarizing the evidence of specialists. A good history of humankind was no arid compendium of facts, so he wrote with an eye toward the general meaning of human existence. The knowledge I create, Bataille wrote, is "never concerned only with details." His aim was universal, not encyclopedic: "The history of humankind cannot limit itself to a scientific repertoire of facts."[85] To be sure, Bataille possessed an intellect more open to the continuity of all previous movements as well as those to come than one finds in macrohistories such as *Sapiens: A Brief History of Humankind* (2015) and *The Dawn of Everything: A New History of Humankind* (2021).

Bataille's postwar histories were beyond the stamp of any one time and place; they were instead grounded in a transhistorical opposition between the profane sphere of growth and sacred acts of expenditure, as I've said. In the crucible of primitive cultures, a distinctive and almost unlimited tension was established between growth and the periodic transgressions that thwarted it. It was Bataille's transhistorical opposition that made the audacious act of writing the history of humankind a little less audacious. He lacked the hesitancy before the universal and the uniquely human that was characteristic of the poststructuralists of whom he is supposedly a forerunner. Bataille located human exceptionalism—the dignity of man, he called it—in magico-religious sentiments, the source of every rich, unproductive aspect of human life. "Man alone is susceptible to religion" is how he put it in "Prehistoric Religion" (1959).[86] According to Bataille, not only *were* we religious—we *remain* religious. Archaic religions have been degraded for millennia, but from one end of the Earth to the other there exists "a sovereign element" that responds to higher values and is not subordinate to calculation. Despite the centuries-long disdain, the desire to escape the imperatives of utility and growth lives on.

We have, then, a transhistorical principle, a definition of what is uniquely human, and an insistence on cultural persistence. If Bataille's turn to macrohistory was anything, it was a search for stable ground. There was an archaic bedrock beneath the currents and convulsions of human history, and Bataille was intent on chipping away at history's accretions to uncover it. For those who belonged to this turbulent generation, the regularity of primitive cultures offered more than relief. I understand that it is strange to speak of Bataille's transhistorical values and his search for stability, and that it will take some time to see a French intellectual so often associated with formlessness and subversion anew. But this is precisely what Bataille's postwar histories demand.

It should come as no surprise that prehistoric cultures contributed most vividly to Bataille's history of humankind. He didn't just include prehistory in his planned volume of macrohistory, he made it its cornerstone. Prehistory, the author of *Lascaux* wrote in two memorable phrases, was "ultimately *the* key to history" and "universal history par excellence."[87] Hence, the path to a veritable history of humankind started with archaic religions. Conveniently, the very subject that Bataille had spent the last decade studying was deemed decisive. By the summer of 1959 he had his opening chapter: an unpublished article on the valley that he called the cradle of humanity.[88] Bataille's conviction that origins were more important than anything else aligns with what I have argued in this chapter in three ways: *Lascaux* expressed the true kernel of Bataille's postwar thought; he maintained that primitive cultures were enduring sources of meaning; and his preferred domain was not the transient passions of present-day politics but the ritual sacrifices of times past.[89]

Sacrifice has consistently occupied the minds of modern European intellectuals. In 1898 Hubert and Mauss declared sacrifice the fundamental rite of archaic religions the world over. Sacrifice is an essentially religious act, one of religion's original elements. Nowhere was the role of sacrifice so great as in the act of zealously preserving the sublime idea of the animal. Moreover, sacrifice once played an outsized role in binding communities together. Durkheim, Hubert, and Mauss believed that certain sacrifices were intimacy-inducing and overcame the depletion of the social. One imagines the annual visit to Lascaux during the Upper Paleolithic as a hiatus, a season when time ground to a halt and tribes wove themselves together for the winter to come. Since the 1930s and the Collège de sociologie, Bataille had yearned for a different kind of community, one that did not disavow the affective bonds of the sacred.[90] And sacrifice was in the business of production, but it produced sacred objects well outside the humdrum chain of acquisitive activity. Again it was Mauss who led the way. Animal sacrifices, he wrote in *A General Theory of Magic* (1902–1903), must be explained "through a logical application of the idea of the sacred."[91]

Sublime, social, and sacred, then—Bataille, who had read widely on the subject, reminds us of how central sacrifice once was to notions of animality, community, and religiosity. He based his understanding of prehistory on what he knew about archaic sacrifice. One can't help feeling that he was rather too fond of seeing sacrifice in the depths of Lascaux: "What we know of animal sacrifice opens a way to an understanding of the painted caves, and the painted caves help us to understand animal sacrifice," he wrote in *Eroticism*.[92] But just as Bataille's *Lascaux* shouldn't be confused with his interwar writings on primitive art, neither should his fondness for sacrifice be subordinated to what came before. Bataille had come a long way from the years when sacrifice was synonymous with inner ravishment and intoxication. He had learned from reading Mauss and Weil that the unproductive expenditures of primitive cultures mattered more than ever—which is what led him to support the Marshall Plan, the four-year aid initiative launched in 1948 that (Bataille hoped) would voluntarily sacrifice America's social surplus in intentionally profitless expenditures. In the 1950s Bataille went to great lengths to show that collective sacrificial rites, not transactional acts of self-sacrifice, were the most radical contestation of the primacy of growth. Sacrifice itself was never the aim; intimacy was: "Sacrifice brings into a world founded on discontinuity, all the continuity such as a world can sustain."[93] If I am right, then Bataille's enduring nostalgia for archaic sacrifice was rooted in his belief that there was and always has been an alternative to lives dedicated to ever-calculating acquisitiveness. Once again we are confronted with the idea that the essence of archaic religions was a sort of creative nostalgia, a longing to return to the natural world. Nostalgia, it turns out, burned brightest in the remote past.[94]

The first grand movement in Bataille's macrohistory was a move away from archaic origins and toward slavery and war. The appearance of slavery and war is of course difficult to date, but Bataille stated with some certainty that slavery was a result of the expansionist monarchical state. He linked this new demand for accumulation, which included the accumulation of enslaved persons, to a major change in the history of religion. There was a causal relationship, he argued, between the decline of archaic religions and the rise of sovereign power and empire. There was more than a hint of Nietzsche's *Genealogy of Morals* in this, as well as a heavy dose of Frazer's eloquent writings on kingship. In any event, primitive cultures, which disdained accumulation, gave way to cultures that granted expansion the highest value. In time, war and imperial expansion supplanted sacrifice and tribal festivals. An insatiable thirst for slaves, empire, and political power put an end to humanity's archaic age.

But perhaps you think that violence was never so horrible and life never so brutish as in our prehistory. In the neo-Hobbesian view popularized by Steven Pinker, the further one goes back in time, the more violence one finds. Pinker's Whiggish *The Better Angels of Our Nature* (2011) decries prehistory as a blood-soaked age of irrational violence.[95] As Pinker would have it, the abolishment of archaic sacrifice has led to a more peaceable world. And yet, the relationship between violence and sacrifice has never been that simple. In one way or another, primitive cultures used religious rites to keep violence contained within the sacred circle of seasonal sacrifices. "How was it," Bataille asked, "that men everywhere found themselves, with no prior mutual agreement, in accord on this enigmatic act?" One reason is that sacrifice was inextricably intertwined with the curses primitive cultures laid on violence. Seasonal sacrifices suspended the otherwise inflexible taboos surrounding violence, death, and unproductive expenditure—in other words, no standing taboo, no seasonal transgression. Which means, among a host of other things, that there was nothing irrational or prelogical about archaic sacrifice.

The second seismic shift in Bataille's macrohistory, the spirit of capitalism, also originated in the history of religion. Bataille identified a world-historical shift from societies founded on religious sentiments to societies fixated on production. If the development of sovereign states was a decisive victory for accumulation and expanse, the rise of instrumental reason was an undeniable triumph for productivity and growth. A break had occurred, and what was considered valuable and virtuous was changing fast. An onslaught of modern developments flowed from the decline of rustic hospitality and aristocratic immoderation—reformations, revolutions, and the wedding of a certain religious ethic to the spirit of capitalism. Material growth had become the sacred objective of modern societies, and an antisacrificial attitude became sacrosanct. In Bataille's account there was no one moment when things went terribly wrong, when Western societies took a dire, apocalyptic turn. Instead, he wrote of an indeterminate fall into a daily diet of accumulation and into a world in which everything—humans, animals, you name it—was reduced to a thing.

The final chapter of Bataille's history of humankind was no less than the end of humanity. The dramatic finale is captured in the subtitle of one of his outlines, "From Origins to the Eve of Eventual Disaster." For him, the postwar period marked a new era of displacement, rapid movement, mass production, and nuclear proliferation—all of which would lead to eventual disaster. So, while he was obsessed with what was most ancient, he was not silent about the problems of the present. A handwritten note attached to one of his outlines read: *At the center of fascism, two world wars, and nuclear proliferation were the calculative productions of modern man.* The twentieth century was what you got when human industry went unchecked. Continuing a critique he first made in *The Accursed Share*, Bataille's denunciation was leveled against the Soviet Union as much as the capitalist West, for it too was obsessed with growth and dependent on fossil resources. Needless to say, Bataille did not regard history from the point of view of progress. Everywhere, it seemed, the arc of human history was bending toward a world driven by the regular compulsions of grow-or-die modernity. Had Bataille known about the arguments for the existence of the Anthropocene, he would have recognized them; for he believed that the second half of the twentieth century was marked above all else by the disastrous triumph of *Homo economicus*. He lived in a world that no longer crawled but ran toward universal death.

Bataille's insight into our rapidly approaching demise was not intended to bring relief. To say that Bataille's apocalyptic vision was monstrous or dizzying, or that it dwelled at the limits, as has been said a hundred times, distracts from how the accursed share of history offers an alternative to the chain of rampant production and accumulation. It is true that the cataclysmic possibilities introduced at Hiroshima demanded a new way of thinking. The arrival of the atomic age in 1945 demanded more than anodyne reportage, and Bataille often spoke of having the audacity to look human extinction squarely in the face. The fact of so many deaths in a single flash was charged with meaning, Bataille wrote in 1947.[96] And like so many others, Bataille watched in horror as the unimaginable accumulation combined with geopolitical polarization. It was an age unlike any other, and it compelled intellectuals like Bataille to dwell on the possibility that something decisive had changed. The accursed share had taken many different forms over the years, but had we reached an era when sacred acts of expenditure had finally been eliminated? Had the rapidly advancing present driven an insurmountable wedge between the deep past and the near future? At times Bataille stated that the world we live in remains, in its depths, permeated by the sacred. The poetic animality found in the caves undoubtedly endures in us; therefore, to reflect on Lascaux is to reflect on "what we still are." At other times, he suggested that it had all vanished like the images on an exposed filmstrip. Exposed to the dazzling light of modern progress, the archaic was forever lost. "We cannot even for a moment dream of recovering the richness which has been lost," he sometimes lamented.[97]

"The Eve of Eventual Disaster" has an unmistakable contemporary ring. But could humanity change course and avoid the coming cataclysm? "On all sides and in every way," Bataille had written, "a world in motion wants to be changed."[98] The author of *The Accursed Share* argued that such a change required rediscovering a much older path, one that had been buried for millennia. His universal history ended therefore not with a bang but with a cyclical return. One need only catch a glimpse of the creativity and durability enshrined at Lascaux to see why humanity might be tantalized by such a return.[99] Distant cultures knew very well how to improve the lot of the human animal. On the one hand, the world of Lascaux was a world ordered by a sentiment of prohibition. "It is forbidden" is the first rule in the preservation of times past. On the other hand, the world of Lascaux was punctuated by potlatch-like expenditures, where the pleasure of unproductive consumption was shared by the community. Bataille marveled at the warmth of these archaic ceremonies, especially when he compared them to the cold, bloodless language of economists.

Bataille reassured his readers that archaic remnants—like the animism described in the last section and the expenditures I've been explaining—lay scattered all around. You only needed to know where to look. Like his fellow adventurers in the archaic, he insisted that the lessons of primitive cultures were neither inaccessible nor destined to disappear. He thought he had quite literally read the writing on the wall and that Lascaux had taught him the durable lessons of the deep past. This was the positive side to Bataille's universal history, the subterranean Yes that replaced his foot-stamping No. Interpreters of Bataille tend to pay more attention to his transgressive subversions than to his regenerative intimacies. Yet for all his images of perversion and death, subversion and loss were not the only cards (or even the main cards) Bataille had to play. Bataille had another set of images: a brilliant sun rising over a temperate sea, a subterranean promise springing from the reservoir of the deep past. In the dark of Lascaux, Bataille had been illuminated. And so, he looked to the Upper Paleolithic, the most outdated of eras, to discover what was essential for human survival.

All was not lost. Although degraded, elements of primitive cultures lingered on. In his outlines, not two pages pass without him jotting down and often underlining—so as not to forget—*survivance*, survival. Amid the grand movements of human history, archaic manifestations of religious feeling held pride of place. We should not be surprised, then, that "mature capitalism" still harbors traces of the glorious expenditures of earlier social formations.[100] Tellingly, Bataille concluded "Universal History, or the Bottle in the Sea" with these words: "Archaic civilizations, their persistence." It was as though, teetering on the edge of disaster, Bataille had cast four hopeful words into a rising and rollicking ocean. Faced with planetary disaster, *survivance* was Bataille's final word, which he set adrift on indifferent waters. It is a stark reminder of just how fervently primitivists believe that a more sustainable future rests on the remnants of supposedly outdated societies.

Restoring the ancient quest for a lost intimacy—the thread running through Bataille's postwar oeuvre—would not come easily. The accelerating present could not be willed away by resurrecting some old sublime idea of the animal. And so, Bataille foresaw a terrible reckoning. He did not envy those who would have the misfortune of living after him. "The world is against the wall," he wrote. And whether we like it or not, we are in for "a sudden metamorphosis."[101] Though he had nuclear disaster in mind, his alarmist projections are easily applied to the present. Fully aware that our drive for more and more has become more and more disastrous, we must decide, just as we did in 1945, whether we will pass our own point of no return. Bataille's postwar oeuvre suggests that it is precisely in a partial return that we will revive more viable ways of living. Resurrecting a ballast of degrowth against the tide of productive activity is a first step to rediscovering alternatives to a world that has accelerated global warming. Grow-or-die modernity is not destiny; it is a historical anomaly. No longer certain that the planet would remain a habitable place for man, by 1961 Bataille had helped the *archaïque* put down roots in French thought. One year later, however, Bataille had died, and Lascaux, that painted hall of unproductive expenditure, had been sealed shut, likely for good.

2

The Work of Nostalgia

Henri Lefebvre's New Theory of Survivals

Between 1945 and 1975, Henri Lefebvre (1901–1991) wrestled with a problem that still bedevils critics of our growth-driven epoch: Is nostalgia a fertile first step on the way to more sustainable ways of living? Can living anachronisms be wellsprings of disalienation in the age of the Great Acceleration? Of course, Lefebvre didn't pose the questions in quite those terms. He was aware of the "diktat of acceleration" that seized Western societies after the Second World War, but he didn't call it the Great Acceleration.[1] Nevertheless, across three decades of unprecedented economic growth, which the French call *les trente glorieuses*, Lefebvre argued that what had survived the passage of time mattered more than ever. His work was marked by a suspicion of modernity and a reevaluation of what sociologists called "survivals"—traditions that he believed could provide a living link to more sustainable ways of life. It is not difficult to understand why Lefebvre, a preeminent leftist and a native of rural France, took up such a position. What needs explaining is where Lefebvre's new theory of survivals came from and why it might still matter. After exploring Lefebvre's experience among Pyrenean communities, this chapter tells an urban history of a new town in the French Southwest, and then gives an intellectual history of Charlotte Delbo's unique contribution to Lefebvre's theory of survivals. After narrating the main contexts in which Lefebvre formulated his theory, I suggest some of the possibilities inherent in the study of cultural survivals, a field that has lain fallow for too long.

Between 1945 and 1975 France underwent a startling transformation. Fossil capitalism—shorthand for capitalist modes of production powered by burning fossil fuels such as coal, oil, and gas—fueled an unprecedented dynamism that allowed France to enjoy the most rapid period of growth in its history. Today this period is called the Great Acceleration. In the course of a single generation, an economically backward territory became a predominantly urban and primarily industrial country. Thousands upon thousands of buildings were constructed where none had stood before. A big part of the relentless drive to modernize was a cultural disinheritance: a rupture with France's rural past, a break with encrusted traditions that had survived for generations. It was an era of two Frances—one under construction, the other making way and being demolished. The Great Acceleration's degradation of rural life put Lefebvre on notice. He grasped the dramatic changes of the period (it was hard not to) and turned his attention not to politics or state power but to mores and everyday life. Before it became popular to do so, Lefebvre preached rural values and celebrated village communities.[2] What he longed for was less a return to the past than the revival of certain age-old customs. As he saw it, the French countryside lay somewhere between the old and the new, between the distant past and the near future, between habit and happiness.

The writer Charlotte Delbo's association with Lefebvre is sometimes acknowledged, but, as Michael Rothberg has noted, "no one has yet attempted to make sense of that connection."[3] Delbo became Lefebvre's administrative assistant in 1961, but she was much more than that title implies. As Lefebvre's principal interlocuter for nearly two decades, Delbo shaped the direction and general tenor of his work. Yet her influence has yet to be entered into the historical record—this despite Lefebvre himself stating on several occasions how indispensable his first-rate collaborator was. In what follows, I show exactly how Delbo reoriented Lefebvre's thought in the early 1960s. Her influence, unseen until now, followed three main lines: She questioned Lefebvre's preoccupation with rural communities, demanded he revise Marxist thought rather than recuperate it, and pushed the sociologist to confront the postwar city. More precisely, Delbo challenged Lefebvre's unbounded faith in the past and questioned whether a revival of days gone by was still possible. Her second contribution was derived from the first: It was not enough to recover the authentic Marx; Marxism needed to be reinterpreted in the light of the postwar present. Only by stretching Marx's concepts beyond their original intentions could new vistas be opened onto present-day practice. This brings us to the third of Delbo's reorientations: After a decade and a half of *les trente glorieuses*, she demanded Lefebvre turn his critical acumen from nostalgic visions of the French Southwest to the sprawling streets of the postwar city. She insisted that village communities, attractive as they were, stood not at the center of France's future, but at its receding periphery.

While Lefebvre duly followed Delbo into the postwar present, he continued to peer into the past to envisage a more durable future. Peasants, workers on the land, he maintained, have things to teach us. The danger, obviously, was that their time-honored folkways would vanish in a world bent on novelty and growth. So Lefebvre urgently contemplated the clamor of his day with the eyes of an earlier age. He lionized rural villages for the fraternity, the continuity, and the quality of life he found there. "I once got to know some archaic ways of life, or the last traces of them, in a peripheral area of provincial France," he wrote. "And that is something I will never forget. It taught me a lot . . . I still refer back to it."[4] He was guided by the conviction that not all earlier ages eagerly awaited our own. And he was sure he had found in southwestern France a coherent alternative to contemporary cultures of competition, conquest, and unending acquisition. His point wasn't that the culture of the future needed to imitate some imagined pastoral utopia. Rather, the future ought to selectively root itself in cultures that had stood the test of time. It was in this way, Lefebvre believed, that we will discover a more temperate future in our past.

Born beneath the western Pyrenees in 1901, Lefebvre lived in Navarrenx until the age of thirteen. He described his parents as polar opposites and linked their personalities, in a very French way, to regional stereotypes: His Béarnaise mother was austere and reserved her fervor for religion; his Breton father was stocky and Rabelaisian. As a reprieve from his mother's Jansenist morality—and from his aunts, whom he described as scolding and sanctimonious—young Henri often wandered the well-worn paths around Navarrenx. Following the transhumant trails of shepherds, the boy lamented his rural upbringing.[5] His distaste for French provincial life did not abate when he attended the reputable Lycée Louis-le-Grand in Paris or when he studied philosophy under Léon Brunschvicg at the Sorbonne. In the late 1920s, when he and Norbert Guterman translated Karl Marx's *Economic and Philosophical Manuscripts* (1844) and introduced the concepts of alienation and overcoming into French Marxism, neither achievement rendered rural life any less backward or banal (fig. 2.1).[6]

It was only in the late 1930s and '40s, when Lefebvre immersed himself in Nietzsche's southern esprit and in the Pyrenean communities of the Campan Valley, that the budding sociologist began to see French rural life anew. By the close of the Second World War, the reversal was complete—loathing had become reverence. No longer only worn or passé, provincial pathways transformed before his eyes. As for the old stone ramparts of Navarrenx, the fortified hometown of his mother, they no longer stood for a suffocating confinement but suggested a stubborn persistence. Lefebvre's about-face toward so-called archaic societies reveals a moment at mid-century when the adjectives *archaïque* and *primitif* took on a sense "rather less pejorative than the meaning one generally attributes to them."[7] There was reason for him to be

FIGURE 2.1. The young Marxists Norbert Guterman and Henri Lefebvre set out in the early 1920s. Guterman, who served in the Polish army after the First World War and studied at the Sorbonne, moved to the United States in 1933. Despite the distance, the two men remained close. A writer and translator, Guterman translated Lefebvre's *Sociologie de Marx* (1966) into English. Uncredited and undated photograph, Norbert Guterman Papers, Rare Book & Manuscript Library, Columbia University in the City of New York.

distraught by how postwar progress was remaking the French countryside. Wherever he turned there seemed to be yet another ruin that evoked a past moment. But the dialectical nature of Lefebvre's thinking meant that wistful longing for the past only crystallized his critique of the present and his exploration of the possible. After 1945 Lefebvre grounded the French romance with radical social alternatives (traceable to Denis Diderot and Jean-Jacques Rousseau) in a robust sociology of a southwestern *terroir* that had become terribly important to him.[8]

Lefebvre's intellectual journey took him from Marx and philosophy to Nietzsche and the Pyrenees—the last of these leading to the most influential of his pursuits, the critique of everyday life in the modern world. Along the way, Lefebvre became knowledgeable in a staggering range of topics, eventually authoring a monumental oeuvre of more than sixty books on sociology, philosophy, literature, and the history of ideas. Scholars agree that Lefebvre's views were heterodox. Some attribute his unorthodox ideas to Hegelian and existentialist influences; others see a heretical oeuvre reliant on utopian impulses and surrealist subversions.[9] But the source of his heterodoxy resides elsewhere. Lefebvre's iconoclasm, I argue, lay in an adventure in the archaic that he identified with and promoted. It is this peculiar primitivist sensibility that repeatedly rears its head and upsets attempts to square Lefebvre with existentialism, surrealism, structuralism, poststructuralism, or any other movement commonly used to make sense of postwar French thought.[10] To grasp the primitivism that crystallized in Lefebvre's thinking after the Second World War, close attention must be paid to his two decades as a rural sociologist. His towering oeuvre, highly theoretical and difficult to approach, more easily yields its riches when we recognize his experience of southwestern France for what it was: an enduring influence that shaped Lefebvre's better-known tomes.

In today's interdisciplinary climate, there is a tendency to depict Lefebvre—a philosopher, sociologist, historian, literary critic, poet, and playwright—as flitting from subject to subject. Did Lefebvre really have no consistency? We need only read him to know that the whole of his thought bears the indelible mark of Marx's analysis of alienated labor in the *Economic and Philosophical Manuscripts*. Like Marx, Lefebvre meant by alienation not a vague feeling of separation but a concrete and compound product of the capitalist mode of production. Marx, who did not conceal his disdain for abstraction, insisted that alienation was a lived reality in bourgeois society. It was one of Lefebvre's great contributions to Marxist thought to widen the notion of alienation to the whole of social life and to shift the accent from production and possession to creativity and community. From the start, he understood that Marx himself had searched for an art of living that would multiply creativity and social fulfillment without separating either from labor, as the bourgeoisie did.[11] Lefebvre's critique of contemporary life was therefore built on a historical understanding of human estrangement, on the one hand, and on the real possibilities of human flourishing, on the other. There were times when creativity and community were wonderfully mingled together; *les trente glorieuses*, however, was not one of those times.

In 1939 Lefebvre published what many took to be his philosophical summa, a tight volume entitled *Dialectical Materialism*. Of all his writings before the Second World War, *Dialectical Materialism* continues to hold a favorable place among commentators, and for good reason. By helping readers see the unity of Marx's humanism and his critique of political economy, Lefebvre paved the way for what Maurice Merleau-Ponty would come to call Western Marxism.[12] That Lefebvre foregrounded the concept of alienation and "critical-practical activity" is well-known. What remains lesser known is the book's defense of certain traditions that come to us from the deep past. Lefebvre believed that dialectical materialism included a diligent tacking back and forth between a modern life that was always on the move and the countless traditions that survived this constant flux. This was the method whereby nostalgic dissatisfaction became creative. But appeals to creativity do little to clarify the kind of customs and communities Lefebvre had in mind, and *Dialectical Materialism* was reluctant to spell out specific examples of creative activity or authentic community. Perhaps this is because these were details Lefebvre could provide only after the Second World War, after he had merged Marxist thought with his sociological research in southwestern France.

Twenty years later, in the confessional mode characteristic of his two-volume autobiography, *La somme et le reste* (1959), Lefebvre admitted what he had long held to be true: In the pursuit of a sociology of everyday life, Nietzsche's insights could be fruitfully joined to Marx's. What led a Marxist on the verge of publishing *Dialectical Materialism*, his most important book to date, to turn to Nietzsche with such enthusiasm? Curiously, Lefebvre turned to Nietzsche to augment Marx and to discover more disalienated ways of living. "Under the guise of talking about Nietzsche, I spoke of other things," Lefebvre remembered.[13] Written on the eve of the Second World War, *Nietzsche* (1939) was a critical step toward a sociology of everyday life that combined Nietzsche's vision of human flourishing with Marx's concept of disalienation.[14] Lefebvre remained Marxist in orientation, but henceforth his sociology had a genuinely Nietzschean dimension. Accustomed as intellectual historians are to twentieth-century French Nietzscheanism, it must be said that Lefebvre's Nietzsche was more regionally grounded than culturally relative, more committed to human flourishing than to closing the book on humanism. In *L'existentialisme* (1946) Lefebvre put it simply: Nietzsche "never lost confidence in the human." Misappropriated by Hitlerian fascists, misunderstood by his contemporaries, the German philosopher who celebrated the untimely seemed to Lefebvre more timely than ever.[15]

Lefebvre's encounter with Nietzsche was essential to reevaluating a rural life he had once loathed. With one root reaching back to Navarrenx and the other reaching for Nietzsche, a new kind of provincialism had dawned. The author of *Dialectical Materialism* took his stand beneath the Pyrenees rather than on the banks of the Seine. And he thought that Nietzsche had gotten the South right: Southern cultures were a living bulwark against capitalism and the modern state, that "coldest of cold monsters." The provincial South—or the Midi, as it is called in France—provided first Nietzsche and then Lefebvre with a vision of moral communities before and beyond the expansionist state. Century after century the Midi resisted intrusion. Nietzsche made it his particular mission to pay tribute to those who had vigorously guarded their Provençal culture against northern incursions.[16] Centuries earlier it was northern seigneurs who tried to dismantle this "brilliant southern civilization"; soon it would be technocratic elites who would uproot all that was stable in southwestern France. With envious eyes on what was well established, Nietzsche had posed the most essential of modern problems: how to secure a more life-affirming table of values in an age of abrupt endings and new beginnings. The lessons of Nietzsche now securely joined to those of Marx, Lefebvre set out to restore "a more natural community and an outdated style of life."[17]

From Nostalgic Paeans to Indispensable Survivals

The secret to Lefebvre's theory of survivals lies in his idiosyncratic understanding of uneven development. French sociologists have a word for the cultural survivals that progress leaves in its wake: *survivances*. But Lefebvre didn't employ *survivance* in the sense commonly used in the social sciences: "To this vague idea of survivals, we would prefer the much more concrete idea of *uneven development*," he wrote in 1961. His two decades as a rural sociologist forced him to rethink Marx's underdeveloped idea of underdevelopment. Unlike sociology's standard definition of uneven development, Lefebvre's theory of survivals critiqued progressivist patterns and emphasized "an almost unlimited range of human (social) situations."[18] The problem was that the idea of uneven development was itself inadequately explained and in need of revision. Among Marxists, uneven development identified those unfortunate areas left behind by capitalism's uneven, unequal advance. In Lefebvre's hands, however, the idea of uneven development no longer bemoaned what was left behind, what anthropologists called "cultural lag" and sociologists called "survivals." In fact, just the opposite: When uneven development was *elective* and *selective*, lagging behind could be a fertile source of disalienation. In this way, Lefebvre's theory of survivals turned an outdated nineteenth-century doctrine into a window on our most basic values, a benchmark for the good life, and an indispensable element in the critique of everyday life.[19]

By the late 1960s, Lefebvre had grown fond of the verb *sou-vivre*, which doesn't exist in French. The word for the verb "to survive" is *survivre*, but the French sociologist preferred the prefix *sou* to *sur*, "under" instead of "over." *Sou-vivre*, then—it was a meaningful play on words and a glimpse of the overlap between underdevelopment and his new theory of survivals. "Underliving"—it is a word that plucks the heartstrings of our suspicion that there is something noble, or at least more ethical and sustainable, in the primitive and the homespun. At any rate, in the first years of the Great Acceleration, Lefebvre already understood that an art of underliving was essential to matters of survival. During *les trente glorieuses* he had seen enough overliving. To survive, to ride out the storm and surmount the present crisis, required reviving older arts of living that flourished on no more, and no less, than a vital minimum. It was an idea Lefebvre had been circling around for two decades. Convinced that unbridled development was not synonymous with social progress, he believed it was high time to revive what had withstood the test of time. He encouraged his readers to look toward communities whose levels of consumption were well below the Western average. How did the peasants of *la France profonde* survive? How did the inhabitants of Mexican *campamentos* live? What mores were found along the rivers of northeastern Brazil? Was Lefebvre's revivalist sensibility utopian? Certainly. He would be the last one to deny that. After all, utopian thinking is primarily concerned with what's possible and what's not. Hence, he concluded, "all thinking that has to do with action has a utopian element."[20]

It was several years earlier, in "Notes Written One Sunday in the French Countryside," that Lefebvre had struck the first chord of his revival of certain cultural survivals. Impassioned and eloquent, this chapter of the first volume of *Critique of Everyday Life* was not shy about embracing the pagan symbols, ancestral rites, and rural communities that persisted in the Basque and Béarn countryside. Lefebvre wasn't drawn to the rarefied air or the healing waters of this upland Arcadia; he was attracted to the region's special manner of living. "Rural" meant much more than agricultural; it implied a whole way of life. "Notes Written One Sunday" wasn't a timid first step toward reconsidering survivals but a paean to a once-vibrant communal life and a full-throated reply to those who deemed age-old folkways passé. Reflecting on vestiges, the meandering essay made plain how important it was to recover some of what went on in those "quiet little towns and villages which sit at the crossroads of ancient paths that have crisscrossed the French countryside for millennia."[21] The picturesque valleys of the western Pyrenees, in other words, were not just beautiful—they were full of rituals of communion, oases of quality time, and other timely lessons. But these communities in the southwestern part of France were a reality too long ignored, especially by Marxist sociologists. So Lefebvre, who had a more intimate knowledge of this mountainous borderland than any historian can hope to acquire, devoted two decades and two theses to the so-called peasant problem.[22] If peasant experience was a matter only for travelers fascinated by the unfamiliar or nationalists obsessed with ethnic purity, then the lessons of primitive cultures would surely be lost. Among the postwar primitivists, Lefebvre was somewhat unique—his "primitive" reference point was entirely European and contemporary, though that didn't stop him from linking the French peasantry to formerly colonized peoples.

Given Lefebvre's attraction to precapitalist formations, some suspected him of a secret vice: ethnographic romanticism. "And why shouldn't I try to revive certain characteristics of pre-capitalist societies?" he responded to his critics. "Wasn't one of Marx's great ideas that communism ought to take up primitive communism, but on a higher level?"[23] Here we arrive at the influence of decolonization, one of two major frames of analysis I established in the introduction. But did Lefebvre actually believe that the third world, as it was then called, could save Western society? What did he expect from the era's new nations, the "emerging" nations? Like others on the left, Lefebvre initially had high hopes for what liberation might bring both abroad and at home. But by the early 1960s what he saw was, generally speaking, unfortunate. The problem was simple: The new nations were going in a direction Europe knew all too well, burning too many of the things they loved in the interest of shooting ahead fast. In other words, they were assimilating (and, to be fair, they often had to assimilate to survive) the very things that yesterday were instrumental in their servitude. The great promise of decolonization—that once formerly colonized people achieved national independence, they would be free—was at best a half-truth. And so Lefebvre, the rural sociologist, returned his attention to a peripheral region of France, which had itself undergone something akin to colonization. For peasants and shopkeepers and rural sociologists who believed that they too had been colonized, the slogan of their third-worldism was *la même lutte*—the same struggle, which they shared with formerly colonized peoples.

Rural sociology was an ideal field for rethinking the cultural remnants that sociologists called survivals. And the Hautes-Pyrénées was a region rich with memento, teeming with survivals that had invariably left their mark. As Lefebvre saw it, leftists needed to recognize that survivals were neither dead forms nor historical conjectures. The most archaic survivals persisted alongside the most modern developments—a fact that is probably true everywhere but was particularly evident in the French countryside after 1945. Most sociologists, however, discovered only a petrified antiquity in provincial France. Lefebvre criticized rural sociologists such as Gaston Roupnel who took as natural "social facts that had been profoundly reworked by history." Stendhal, Lefebvre's favorite nineteenth-century Romantic, has a wonderful line about this tendency to naturalize what is actually historical: "A Parisian who used to go gaping round the gardens of Versailles concluded from what he saw that all trees grow clipped." Lefebvre might have idealized Pyrenean communities, but the would-be primitivist reformer didn't portray them as timeless.[24] Fine—rural communities weren't frozen in time; but were they merely stepping stones on the road to a more accelerated future? Lefebvre was intent on showing that the well-trodden paths of southern culture were much more than that. While born of wistful longing, his unflinching embrace of slower, more durable styles of life was not relegated to it. For Lefebvre, the problem wasn't to make a sterile attempt to repeat the past. It wasn't a dead society he wanted to revive. Rather, it was a new society that must be created, a society rich with the ingenuity of modern times yet warm with the fraternity of olden days.[25] As I've said, what looks like nostalgia for a bygone world was in fact the flowering of a renewed critique of capitalism, that rapacious engine of progress. Thus, on the heels of a new theory of survivals came a new watchword: revival.

Rural sociology, however, faced a sober reality after the Second World War. Lefebvre's chosen terrain, which had received so much support during the war, was in a real predicament. Caught between the tarnished legacy of Vichy's promotion of provincial life and modernization's relentless assault on village communities, pressure mounted on all sides.[26] Little indicated that rural life would survive the second half of the twentieth century. Degraded, diminished, and on the verge of disappearing—that was how folkways die. In this context, not everyone relished the peasant way of life as Lefebvre did. But thanks to his meticulous research in the French Southwest, he could appeal to the highest disciplinary standards. In fact, his doctoral theses, "Pyrenean Peasant Communities" and "The Campan Valley," epitomized the conventions of a scientific monograph to a surprising degree. They also served notice that the French social sciences had a new and original voice after 1945. His theses, which he defended at the Sorbonne in 1954, drew freely on history, prehistory, ethnography, linguistics, semiology, geography, and political economy. More to the point, however, his theses couldn't hide, and didn't feel the need to hide, his ruling passions for the *longue durée* and for a certain cultural continuity: "My interest in Campan, or any other such Pyrenean village, rests in its proximity to the distant past."[27] Cultural continuity may seem a strange theme to ascribe to the future author of *The Explosion: Marxism and the French Upheaval* (1968). But the soil, symbols, cycles, and solidarity of the French Southwest bore witness to a different way of experiencing time and space; they bore witness to a time not too long ago when the Earth and the home were still sacred entities; they bore witness to a region that, having struggled against intrusions for centuries, continued to struggle against the upheavals of tourism, state technocracy, and fossil capitalism.[28]

Since 1947 the Centre national de la recherche scientifique (CNRS) had provided Lefebvre invaluable financial and administrative assistance as he wrote about the French Pyrenees. But while on holiday in the summer of 1953, he received a curt letter from the director informing him that he was being dismissed from the institution. After five years as a CNRS researcher, Lefebvre was told on July 27, 1953, to clean out his office by the end of September. He had two months to give up his post—far less time than was typically afforded research fellows. Lefebvre admitted to his colleagues that the unexpected expulsion had thrown him into a "disastrous material situation." For someone so new to the social sciences, the abrupt dismissal must have come as a shock. Especially troubling was the way it was described as a disciplinary measure. But Lefebvre was the first to see it for what it was: a "philosophical discrimination." Tellingly, the commission that evaluated CNRS researchers had not even been consulted when the director used article 102 to justify his decision.[29]

Lefebvre's colleagues quickly came to his defense. They testified to the scientific rigor of his rural sociology and to his theoretical contributions to French social thought. Lefebvre's colleagues agreed: The philosopher-turned-sociologist was a first-rate intellectual who had mastered the minutiae of rural communities while advancing the methods by which contemporary society was understood. Letters sent to the CNRS on Lefebvre's behalf referenced his teaching record, his forthcoming theses, and his methodological contributions in journals such as *Cahiers internationaux de sociologie*. Henri Lévy-Bruhl expressed shock at Lefebvre's dismissal and hoped that the decision had been an administrative error. But like Lefebvre, Lévy-Bruhl suspected a "moral prejudice" lay behind the decision. Georges Gurvitch, professor of sociology at the Sorbonne, was even more perplexed. Gurvitch had taken part in a meeting held on June 16, 1953, where it had unanimously been agreed to extend Lefebvre's association with the CNRS and recommended his promotion to senior research fellow once he submitted his doctoral theses. Gurvitch assured Lefebvre that "the measure taken against you appears to me contrary to all existing practice at the CNRS."[30] A Marxist, a rural sociologist, and a primitivist, Lefebvre was singularly unfit for the technocratic future coming to postwar France.

In 1956, two years after defending his doctoral theses and being reinstated at the CNRS, Lefebvre gave a much-anticipated lecture on the village community. After the lecture Maxime Rodinson, the respected Marxist sociologist, wondered if there was a link between village communities and socialist societies. He asked Lefebvre if it was possible for an archaic community to become a socialist society without passing through a lengthy period of capitalist growth. It was a timely question. Was capitalistic growth indeed absolutely necessary? Could fossil capitalism be avoided? And what about the grow-at-all-cost mentality that undergirds it? A century earlier Marx had suggested that the primitive communism of rural communities might morph into socialist societies. But for most of his life Marx dismissed the idea, and in 1956 Lefebvre slammed the door on this time-traveling fantasy. "After the experience of the Russian Revolution," Lefebvre said, "it seems that bypassing capitalism is impossible."[31] When it came to culture, however, things were different. Lefebvre reasoned that any socialist society would depend on certain cultural elements held over from village communities. The door, then, to the deep past wasn't completely closed. It's unclear whether Rodinson was convinced by Lefebvre's distinction. But what is clear is that Lefebvre's vision of a genuinely socialist society was one that selectively revived the remains of so-called primitive cultures. It was a fresh argument borne of a new theory of survivals.

Driven by a sense of impending loss, Lefebvre remembered several indispensable survivals from his days in the French Southwest. All around, if one knew where to look, were long-standing arts of living that had endured time's radically accelerated passage. One need only take up a new perspective and nostalgic ruminations revealed living anachronisms.[32] If nostalgia was a seed of hope, then survivals were the bedrock from which utopian experiments would grow. With hindsight, it's obvious that Lefebvre posited survivals as a counterweight to modern technology, the society of the spectacle, the lifestyles of the rich, and the like. But his primitivist sensibility did not come all at once; his wistful longing was cultivated and pruned over two decades. It would be a mistake, therefore, to treat his theory of survivals as a passing phase, a whimsical wish to make an idealized past present. Lefebvre maintained that the secret to countering France's myopic emphasis on growth was to unveil "some of the well-hidden secrets of bygone societies."[33] It was incumbent on social scientists then to salvage what was valid from the wreckage. Lefebvre's new theory of survivals came at a critical moment in modern history: the onset of the Great Acceleration. But that was then and this is now, you might say. The thing is that as the years of warming wear on, primitivist sensibilities may find new life in the fires of +2°C.

In search of specific survivals, Lefebvre turned to the Basque and Béarn part of France. The Southwest of France historically symbolized backward France, and the Basque and Béarnais were often disparaged as the "Indians" of France. "You don't need to go to America to see savages," wrote the nineteenth-century novelist Émile Souvestre. "Here, in southwestern France, are the Redskins of Fenimore Cooper."[34] But Lefebvre saw in indigenous France a way forward, a way out, or at least a step along the way. A son of the Midi, he celebrated the Basque and Béarn tradition of worker-owned cooperatives. The region's ancient *auto-gestion* and its precapitalist gift economy, which could be traced to before recorded history, were models to be adopted.

They were more charitable and more humane modes of political economy than the technocratic solutions of state capitalism could ever offer. There is something a little disheartening about finding hope for the future in the curious spectacle of a gift economy from the distant past. It feels like a retreat, and it is easy enough to disparage forays into Stone Age economics. Yet, there is no denying the durability and benevolence of the political economy made possible by the unique ancestral culture that stretched from the Dordogne to the Pyrenees.[35] As a sociologist of France's rural Southwest, Lefebvre made his abiding achievement his idiosyncratic understanding of uneven development, on which he deliberately based his endorsement of workplace democracy and worker-owned cooperatives.

But the territory where Lefebvre comes to life is the spring festival, which appears time and again in his rural sociology. He revered the month of May, and he remembered the spring festivals of his youth when peasants ate, drank, danced, masqueraded, and made love—the old peasant lifeblood, the old Dionysian springtime, a struggle between the sacred and the profane, between liberated libidos and long-standing taboos. He was of course overdramatizing. Lefebvre's views on the archaic country festival were rarely reserved, always romanticized, and often radical. Modern country festivals, by contrast, were chaste, controlled, and drained of Dionysian joy. Over the years, the craze for pagan springtime had been consecrated to virginity (May was the month of Mary in the Catholic South) and channeled into the work-discipline of industrial capitalism. Lefebvre's chronicle of the decline of Maytime is at the same time elegiac and aspirational: elegiac because modern rediscoveries of spring were ludicrous degradations, and aspirational because spring might once again be ruled by the cycle of the seasons. From the beginning, the ancient springtime festival reaffirmed collective life in the countryside and renewed man's relationship with nature. Communal solidarity and communion with nature thus go hand in hand. Is this not what Marx meant by nature coming into being socially?

But archaic spring festivals were above all "periodic bouts of self-destruction." During festive days, Pyrenean communities "devoured all the provisions and stockpiles it had taken them months to accumulate." Doubtless these expenditures were a risk, but the real bargain of the wager was the social solidarity and relative stability of no-growth societies.[36] The idea that archaic festivals were driven by a desire to periodically expend—an idea that Lefebvre owed to Bataille—keeps coming back in Lefebvre's rural sociology. Stories of spring country festivals were not just anecdotal evidence from the early stages of his attempt to come to terms with the postwar present. Rather, what we see here became a major preoccupation for Lefebvre, one he shared with other primitivist reformers: the importance of collective expenditures that come round regularly.

Lefebvre was at the peak of his creative dissatisfaction in the early 1960s. And that dissatisfaction took the noble form of nostalgia. In his hands, nostalgia was a dress rehearsal in the art of utopian thinking—just as his rural sociology had been a dress rehearsal in urban revolution. Recounting the old ways was one way to contemplate the city of the future. Nostalgia, however, is most often seen as an unreflective and reactionary obsession, one befitting ardent ethnonationalists and religious fundamentalists, not committed leftists. This definitive condemnation of nostalgia is so typical of the Left. Atavistic, debilitating, entailing no practice, incapable of sparking creative action—nostalgia, progressives maintain, has a well-deserved bad reputation. If utopia was a dangerous hankering after the impossible, then nostalgia was a numb fixation on what had been lost.[37] Yet, to make an obvious but important point, not all cultural pessimisms are the same. Nostalgia is neither despair nor melancholy. Nostalgia is not a matter of standing on the sidelines, clutching the dead hand of the past and from time to time sighing a fine note of Byronic melancholy. The prism of nostalgia need not be debilitating; it can be so much more than a hankering after the impossible. Go anywhere near the sentiments aroused by nostalgia and you are immersed in the mysteries of creation. In the absence of a viable present (or recent past, for that matter), Lefebvre valorized the distant past. Dissatisfied with being perpetually propelled forward, he turned backward. A more useful way to think about nostalgia is as a bridge across an insupportable present to a more sustainable future. Dismissing nostalgia out of hand works like a broom to sweep all this away.[38]

Climate change and the coming ecological crisis compel a turn to the study of survivals. For those familiar with the word, it brings to mind the Victorian anthropologist Edward Burnett Tylor and Whiggish ideas of progress. When Tylor established the "noble science" of anthropology at Oxford in the late nineteenth century, he made a particular notion of survivals central to it. A steadfast believer in progress and in the certainty of its empire, Tylor defined survivals as the simple keeping up of ancient habits: "When a custom, an art, or an opinion is fairly started in the world, disturbing influences may long affect it so slightly that it may keep its course from generation to generation, as a stream once settled in its bed will flow on for ages."[39] His doctrine of survivals was intended to secure proof of progress despite the disconcerting realities of uneven development. Survivals were what was "dead among us," and Tylor marked them out for removal—like weeds, they needed to be pulled up root and branch. He concluded that it was "the office of ethnography to expose the remains of crude old culture which have passed into harmful superstition and to mark these out for destruction."[40]

Recently the idea of survivals has reappeared in the work of the literary theorist Gerald Vizenor. A scholar of American Indian literatures, Vizenor noticed in Native stories the incontrovertible presence of former times. In American Indian culture there exists what Vizenor calls a "heritable right of succession," or what others might call cultural patrimony. Erasure is a colonial myth, and Vizenor maintains that survivance (his anglicized term) is much more than a narrative alternative to histories of dominance. Survivance is a thoroughgoing practice, a strategy for resisting cultural degradation. Lefebvre, were he alive, would no doubt agree.[41]

But *survivances*, the French word for survivals, had already undergone a radical refashioning in the middle of the twentieth century, and Lefebvre, a son of Navarrenx, was one of the most important voices rethinking the notion of survivals. He stands tall among a growing pantheon of writers who have taken up the mantle of looking backward into the future. A disposition, a practice, and an idea, Lefebvre's theory of survivals can be applied in and beyond the social sciences. As an untapped field of research, the study of cultural survivals reveals the ties of custom and the bonds of tradition that have made up the texture of communal living since the Neolithic village. As a wellspring of sustainable mores, the possibilities borne of survivals are fertile enough to transform contemporary life, which is one of several steps necessary to avoid environmental disaster. In either case, Lefebvre's prescient theory of survivals finds its natural reverberation in today's degrowth and ecosocialist movements. There's a need today, perhaps as never before, to slow down, to stand still, and to root ourselves in certain sustainable elements of the past. And survivals are, by any definition, sustainable. Thus, survivals might be a way out of our pathological presentism, or at least a reliable deviation from the course set by the Great Acceleration.

The Seductive City

Ten miles from the rural commune of Navarrenx, Mourenx arose out of nothing. Lefebvre watched season by season, sometimes day by day, as the new town emerged ex nihilo. From the surveyors' initial measurements to the first bites of the bulldozers, he witnessed the sudden transformation of this remote corner of southwestern France. When the dust had settled, it was clear that the Société nationale des pétroles d'Aquitaine (SNPA) was building a brand-new town to house laborers working at its nearby Lacq industrial complex. Since 1949, when a deposit of natural gas was discovered in Lacq, the SNPA had built several petrochemical factories that seemed torn from the pages of science fiction. It turns out there was more than painted caves under this southwestern *terroir*. The Texas oil boom had arrived in Béarn, or so the speculators hoped (fig. 2.2). But the fossil-extracting enterprise needed a shiny new housing estate for the seven thousand employees who turned the dials, monitored the screens, and managed the machines. Enter the French dirigiste economy and the architect Jean-Benjamin Maneval, a disciple of Le Corbusier's architectural futurism.[42] Soon curious locals, including Lefebvre,

FIGURE 2.2. R. A. Drouot, *Butalacq* (1955), advertisement. Though otherwise undistinguished, a curious attempt by the SNPA to persuade consumers that butane is of a prolific self-generating nature, here rapidly to the whole of France. The message was that there was no shortage of saturated hydrocarbons. Image from the Bibliothèque patrimoniale de Pau.

FIGURE 2.3. Radical modernism in architecture, or social housing at its least shabby. The new town of Mourenx was a technical success, especially if an apartment was "a machine for living in," as Le Corbusier would have it. The brand-new housing complex dominates the center of the photograph, but note the industrial complex in the background. July 1, 1960. Credit: Keystone-France/Getty Images.

saw concrete pillars and sprawling cement slabs. Where once there had been twisted oaks and uncultivated uplands, there now stood tower blocks and the straight lines of a brand-new town (fig. 2.3). The sheer uniformity of Mourenx's boxes-for-living-in allowed it to be built in no time at all. In the summer of 1957, the machinery of state capitalism was running at full power.

Lefebvre saw in Mourenx *le visage de l'avenir*, the face of the future. The new town near Lacq was an example of what architects, town planners, and freshly minted technocrats from the grand polytechnic *écoles* could accomplish, a brave new world of urban space designed by a generation of experts who believed in year zeros and tabulae rasae. Lefebvre had to admit that Mourenx was one of the better products of state-directed capitalist modernization. Driven by a commitment to rapid development, postwar reconstruction was remaking much of France. Streets with traffic signals, technological efficiency, linked networks, well-apportioned and programmable lives—Mourenx was indisputably modern.[43] If the new Citroën DS was, as Lefebvre's friend Roland Barthes thought, the modern equivalent of a Gothic cathedral, then newly built housing projects such as Mourenx were the cloistered abbeys of postwar reconstruction. What's more, with its towering apartments and row after row of low-rise housing units, the new town resembled the kind of architecture one could find in the socialist states of Eastern Europe, as any photograph will show. Today it is perhaps unsurprising that the infrastructure of fossil capitalism mirrored that of a socialism built on burning the same fossil fuels, but in the late 1950s the similarity gave Lefebvre pause. At any rate, for the cadre of experts that designed Mourenx, the image of rising tower blocks had been spiritualized. The reality, however, was anything but celestial, and no one called Mourenx their spiritual home.[44]

Lefebvre lamented this urban foothold in the rural landscape—and why not? He was a throwback. As a young man he wandered Béarn's winding paths, and as an older man he returned to this part of the French countryside every summer, eventually retiring behind the rustic shutters and majestic oak door of his mother's house in Navarrenx. With its old bastide and bucolic environs, Navarrenx was for him a site of reflection and a source of inspiration. After all, it was in this country of the sun that he had converted from philosophy to rural sociology. Thus, it was his native land that Mourenx was transforming. The new town was quite literally too close to home, and it gnawed at him. He flinched as the former stillness of this Pyrenean valley was broken by the sound of the first drilled holes; he cringed at the contrast between the sky of brilliant blue above and the urban whiteness below; he trembled before Mourenx's machines-for-living-in. Tower blocks and parking lots; boxes for living in and boxes for making a living. It was only a matter of time before the upright peasant was brought to his knees by the dizzying transformations of the postwar drive to modernize. To be sure, Lefebvre had discovered the "peasant problem" at the moment when the French peasantry and their rites, traditions, and beliefs were fading into memory.[45] He saw no reason to hide his indignation, nor his wistful longing.

Mourenx eventually brought together seven thousand inhabitants, but did it foster that essential yet elusive entity that we call "community"? Lefebvre concluded from the surveys and in-depth interviews he conducted that the new town valorized individual life at the expense of community-building. He advanced this thesis in several ways. Some of the residents complained about the acoustics in the high-rise towers. Individual apartments with big bedrooms and bathrooms may foster private life, but the towers' walls and ceilings made actual privacy practically impossible. It seems Mourenx's architectural futurism was as sturdy as Lacq's mineral deposits were deep. And while the acoustics left much to be desired, boredom was public enemy number one. Monotony reigned in this Radiant City, one respondent said—much to Lefebvre's delight, I imagine.[46] New towns like Mourenx may appear to offer a diversity of entertainment and engagement, but what residents found was the empty and irreversible time of postwar modernity. How could it have been otherwise? A *cité* without a past is a city without pastimes. And Mourenx was in every sense a town without a past. Residents felt stranded, homeless at home—a rather cruel twist on the old sense of nostalgia.[47] While Lefebvre relished reading the centuries in Navarrenx, like a botanist who can tell the age of a tree by the number of rings in its trunk, he couldn't find a single trace of the past in Mourenx.

Still others claimed that commuting was the biggest challenge to social life. Several residents whom Lefebvre interviewed stated that after driving to work all week, they left Mourenx every weekend to escape the ennui of the new town. What was intended to be a paved paradise turned out to be a way station, a site of continual circulation where residents ground out a daily existence of *auto-bulot-dodo* (commuting-working-sleeping). Here, as everywhere else, the automobile was the vehicle for a floating population and a townless new town. Traffic arteries multiplied at the expense of sound community-building. The sociologist listened to his informants dutifully and concluded that Mourenx was neither a neighborhood nor a community. Rather, it was a sort of ghetto—a cloistered abbey of the postwar variety, a middle-of-the-road suburb where contemplation and community yielded to that quintessentially modern duet, leisure and loneliness. You might well earn a living in Mourenx, but what kind of life did you earn? Lefebvre knew that, despite its deprivations, there was still room for happiness in his native Navarrenx. In Mourenx, he wasn't sure.

Even if the new town overcame these obstacles and cobbled together a community, it wouldn't last long. "What can life really be like for the couples who live in this town," Lefebvre asked, "knowing that it cannot last more than twenty years, since its energy sources are dwindling?" Today Mourenx is a typical postindustrial town. The natural gas deposit has been bled dry, the tower blocks are crumbling, and it seems that nothing can stem the demographic decline (fig. 2.4). Like so many other new towns, Mourenx began to decay in 1973 with the first oil crisis. *Les trente glorieuses* was over, and by the late 1970s Mourenx had lost three thousand residents, roughly half its population, as the factories in Lacq began to close. The engines of fossil capitalism are short-lived, as we obstinately refuse to learn. And while the cold logic of

FIGURE 2.4. A different side of life—entirely predictable. Untitled photograph of a girl doing the shopping in the village of Lacq, France, September 12, 1960. Sandwiched between bread and wine, the uninhabitable future had arrived sooner than expected, courtesy of the lethal gas emanating from the nearby petrochemical works. Credit: Bridgeman Images.

capitalism is always icy, it is by no means always logical.[48] But, then again, the story of Mourenx is so familiar it hardly needs repeating here.

If there is any truth in Lefebvre's judgment, it will be found not in paper-thin walls or empty parking lots, but in the heart of the new town. The center of Mourenx may not have resembled the heart of ancient towns—there was no church, no cemetery, no promenade—but that didn't mean it couldn't foster a sense of community. The question remained: What pulsed through the heart of Mourenx? If a neighborhood can be known by the sounds that fill its squares, then the sounds of the new town were quintessentially modern: the drone of televisions and vacuum cleaners and, above all, the rumble of automobiles surging forward in consensual lockstep. Residents conformed to the machines around them, and not the other way around. The sounds of Mourenx bespoke the rhythms dictated by technological objects—the family fixated in front of the television, the drive to the self-service supermarket. Thoroughfares and supermarkets, however rational and functional they may be, were no substitute for cafés and market squares. And yet there were almost no cafés in Mourenx, because the technocrats forgot that the primary purpose of brasseries is not to intoxicate but to facilitate festive and amicable encounters.[49] What was a neighborhood without shopkeepers or artisans? To speak of community in a place like Mourenx was an absurdity. Put simply, Mourenx's analog was the factory. The new town wasn't built just to staff the industrial complex; it was meant to replicate it. Lefebvre somewhat ponderously concluded that France was becoming one enormous, sterilized factory. Needless to say, his picture of the new town was bitter and pessimistic.

But perhaps you are of the opposite camp and maintain that what mattered most is what the inhabitants of Mourenx weren't talking about: the general rise in living standards. It was true, postwar growth *had* changed a great many things, and proponents of modernization enthusiastically pointed to the objective proof: Look at how many people were participating in a petty-bourgeois ownership that extended from the parking lot to the kitchen and included cars, televisions, flush toilets, and household appliances such as refrigerators, washers, and dryers.[50] Residents of the new town may complain, but at no point did they return to the slums whence they came. Sure, Mourenx did not arouse unanimous enthusiasm, but what living arrangement does? And since, as everyone knows, you can't make an omelet without breaking a few eggs, the phenomenal rise in the standard of living during the 1950s and '60s required tearing down more than one encrusted tradition. There was too much progress at stake to worry about a few anachronistic shells that had accreted over millennia.

What the apologists of state capitalism wouldn't admit, however, was that there was more at stake in these transformations than material well-being. As Lefebvre knew from countless historical examples, while concrete democracy and cultural continuity can exist at every standard of living, neither could persist without community. More precisely, in the absence of a thriving city center, an organic culture is forced to modify its customs and thereby undermine its deepest values and its most stable habits. Hence, Lefebvre wanted to know what type of urban space fostered the kind of community formation that would buttress genuine democracy and cultural continuity. On what, materially and spatially, is a durable social fabric based? In 1961 Lefebvre didn't pretend to have the answer, but he knew the answer would be found in *styles* of living, not *standards* of living. His urban sociology, then, would strive to understand the relationship between everyday life in the city and the livelihood of democracy and culture. The sociologist essentially said that if you care about morality and democracy, then you'd better pay attention to the relationship between built environments and run-of-the-mill mores.

Lefebvre's work on Mourenx, collected in "Notes on the New Town" (1962), was a first step toward an urban sociology, but it was mostly a celebration of Lefebvre's hometown. Unlike Mourenx, Navarrenx was ancestral in every sense of the word. Built over millennia by peasants pursuing ancestral tasks under the sun of the Midi, Navarrenx was a tight little community, a sleepy old village where "life was lived in slow motion." It exemplified the unique, precapitalist culture of the French Southwest: the southern sun, a rich alluvial valley, a warm and demanding community, small farms worked by their owners, Saturday markets uniting nearby communes. Here one lived in touch with the Earth and in accordance with seasonal and diurnal rhythms. In this distant corner of France, "passions and rhythms, cycles in time and space—all was in harmony." Mourenx had changed all that; the new town was like a brand-new knife, glinting as it pierced the ancient soil. Like so many other ancestral villages across France, Lefebvre's hometown was on the verge of being cut up and swept away by postwar reconstruction. If Navarrenx managed to keep its "aroma of things gone by," it was only because the old town had been built and rebuilt according to the organic needs and desires of a centuries-old community. "Notes," it goes without saying, was ripe with nostalgia. Lefebvre gives us a marvelous picture of the provincial French Southwest, but it's a picture straight out of another century.[51]

Lefebvre was slowly beginning to realize that the solution lie not in a return to ancient communes but in an admixture of the old and the new. In other words, two worlds that now stood right next to each other and gladly ignored each other needed to learn from each other. So, too, with Lefebvre's new sociology: By the end of the early 1960s, thanks to the influence of Delbo, he was determined to root his urban sociology in the lessons of rural sociology. Lefebvre was no neo-Luddite. Machines didn't need to be smashed—they needed to be subordinated to genuine social needs. So he channeled his nostalgia and began to think of new towns as social laboratories—places where, under the right conditions, life might become a little less lonely and a lot more meaningful. Though his disdain for Mourenx remained undiminished, he aptly called these social laboratories "utopian experiments," describing these experiments as "explorations into the human possible." "With the aid of images and the imagination," he continued, these experiments would be accompanied "by incessant critique as well as unceasing reference to the given problems of the 'real.'" No, Lefebvre stated simply, we will not find a style for our age in a town like Mourenx. But neither could we return to a bygone rural life. Clearly, Lefebvre had entered new terrain. And his footing was insecure, as is apparent in his early writings in urban sociology.[52] But he steadied himself on the symbols, rhythms, and collective life of the Basque and Béarn part of France.

The predicament of what persists. On the one hand, a big part of France being remade after 1945 was the unmaking of rural life. And while the breakup of village communities was nothing new, the speed of their demise during France's reconstruction was novel and disconcerting. The sudden presence of Mourenx ineluctably entailed a new way of living, a new way of being in time and space, and a new way of seeing the past and the future.[53] By 1960 the villages of Béarn were the most instructive victims of the imperative of growth—peasants were displaced by mechanization, chemical fertilizers, land accumulation, capital intensification, spiraling commercialization, petrochemical production, and modern scientific farming. The list goes on, and it spelled the death of rural France. On the other hand, despite the onslaught, the most archaic remnants persisted alongside the most modern developments in this contested borderland. Navarrenx and its environs, Lefebvre recalled, remained "a region particularly rich in traditions dating back to ancient times."[54] *Plus ça change*. This distant corner of France was a veritable museum, a permanent exhibit of sociological fossils. And in an age motoring headlong into the future, Lefebvre cherished his native land as a reliable reservoir of times past. It was a prime example of the paradox of the postwar primitivists: If these peasant traditions could be "reborn today," he concluded, "nothing would be more interesting than this Renaissance"; such a revival would bring "a whole new meaning to the expression the Promised Land."[55] It is a prime example of how nostalgic dissatisfaction with the present can be channeled into a creative resurrection of times past.

It is central to my argument that Lefebvre's turn to urban sociology was not an about-face. He proceeded carefully: There was nothing more hackneyed than a middle-aged philosopher making a so-called epistemological break. Lefebvre thus struggled to reconcile his paeans to France's extreme Southwest with his new urbanism. It was work that amounted to creative nostalgia. The example of rural life remained indispensable. And so, the symbols, cyclical rhythms, and communal life of the French Southwest— that is, the very same elements of rural life he had spent the last two decades championing—reappeared in a new light. Symbols were neither outdated nor empty; they were affective, and they expressed a certain image of the world. Mourenx didn't have any, which made Lefebvre wonder all the more what kind of symbols and monuments might be reinvented in the city of the future. Symbols and monuments were also the sites around which Lefebvre's second major paean revolved: the cyclical rhythms of peasants that encouraged participation and fostered community formation. Tied to the country calendar, these rhythms and periodic festivals were one more way rural communities worked with, not against, the forces of nature.[56] Lefebvre never grew tired of saying that cyclical rhythms would never disappear completely, not even in the middle of new towns like Mourenx. Thus, we find the rural triumvirate of symbol-cycle-community at the center of Lefebvre's new sociological adventure. His exaltations may not have been new, but they broke the chain of nostalgic paeans.

In the mid-1960s Lefebvre began in earnest the urban project to which he would dedicate the final decades of his intellectual life. In just a few short years he had grown flexible enough to look ahead while lingering on the past—a sixty-year-old contortionist, juggling utopian aspirations and a reassuring past, which until now had been within easy reach. It was hard enough to preserve what deserved preserving in the old town; now he had to figure out how to inject it into the new. But you may ask, must we find our future in the past? Well, yes, at least in part. If Mourenx, for example, was to have a future, it would be found in the daily rhythms of the peasants who came to sell their produce there—the same peasants who prioritized quality, protected the soil and water table, and produced and consumed locally. If, on the other hand, the future of Mourenx was tied not to Béarn's immense cultural patrimony but to the mineral deposits at Lacq, Lefebvre knew that life in the new town had at most twenty more years. The point is that the elements of rural life Lefebvre championed were not merely archaic remnants waiting to be eliminated by the postwar machine; rather, they were long-standing arts of living crucial to countering the reigning emphasis on unending growth. The second point is that to understand the distinctive radicalness of Lefebvre's theory of survivals, you need to recognize his amalgam of utopian urbanism and rural life. And to understand that, you have to try to reconstruct Delbo's unique contribution to his thought.

Between Delbo and Lefebvre

Charlotte Delbo reconnected with Lefebvre in the winter of 1959–60. Delbo, who had been Lefebvre's student at the Lycée de Montargis in the early 1930s, was returning to Paris and hoped to earn a living by working for her old teacher. She remembered her intellectual formation fondly: "I have not undertaken 'official' studies, and I don't have a diploma to attest to my knowledge. But I did study philosophy with Henri Lefebvre from 1930 to 1934."[57] In what must have seemed like a stroke of luck, Lefebvre had recently been promoted to director of research at the CNRS. Unfortunately, he was still in no position to hire his former student. But the more senior CNRS sociologist Jean Stoetzel was. And so, a few months later, on Monday, January 16, 1961, Delbo started working for the CNRS. Though she was officially in the employ of Stoetzel, in reality it was the beginning of her seventeen-year tenure as Lefebvre's administrative assistant.[58] The tacit arrangement was made official in 1964 when Lefebvre secured his own sociological research laboratory. "My boss," Delbo called Lefebvre with a touch of irony and a good deal of affection. She moved into a lovely little apartment behind the Panthéon near the Place Monge. Her CNRS work paid her a modest salary every month, on which she was dependent. Delbo's work for Lefebvre, her biographer Ghislaine Dunant writes, "gave structure to her life as a single woman, while still allowing her considerable flexibility in terms of her hours."[59] In any case, Delbo's association with Lefebvre was far more important than the title "administrative assistant" would tend to imply. Reuniting with her old mentor, she quickly became Lefebvre's chief collaborator.

Soon after Delbo joined Lefebvre at the CNRS, he was appointed chair of sociology at the University of Strasbourg. As his assistant, Delbo met with his students, organized his syllabi, and helped prepare his seminars. She also accompanied him on his weekly trips from Paris, where they both lived, to Strasbourg, 280 miles away. They spent the long train ride discussing his upcoming seminars, for Lefebvre liked to prepare his lectures the same way he conceived his books, in and through dialogue. So, on their way to Strasbourg, they talked and talked, paused, and talked some more. They spoke of Marx, of urban development, of uneven development, of the nature of time. And on the way home they thought of the future and spoke of the past. No imagined dialogue has given me so much pleasure as these weekly discussions between two intellectual luminaries of the Left on their way to and from the Street City. There were four years of these intellectually stimulating trips, until Lefebvre was named professor of urban sociology at the new University of Paris in Nanterre in July 1965.

As an editor, Delbo acquiesced to neither Lefebvre's erratic style nor his primitivist sensibility. On more than one occasion Lefebvre found her assessment in his mailbox: "This is bad." These blunt summations were followed by clear-eyed critique. With her raised head and straight back, Delbo personified unbending lucidity.[60] She demanded not one extra word and encouraged Lefebvre to write more like her—spare and bare-bones, a bit like Samuel Beckett and a lot like the seventeenth-century French moralists Jean de La Bruyère and François de La Rochefoucauld. In August 1963 Lefebvre sent Delbo the manuscript for what would become *Metaphilosophy* (1965). A few weeks later, in a letter dated September 13, 1963, she expressed her "growing irritation"

FIGURE 2.5. Charlotte Delbo (1913–1985) at her secondary residence in Breteau, France. The writer's posture—ideal and unbending—is much in evidence. Photograph by Eric Schwab, Charlotte Delbo Papers, Département des Arts du spectacle, Bibliothèque nationale de France.

while reading him. She likened his manuscript to a harlequin coat. Out of two hundred meandering pages, he might keep fifty. And everything he had written about urban sociology, well, it should be set aside for another book—and thus was born *The Production of Space*, that veritable tour de force of utopian urbanism. After casting a final wry glance over his unstitched manuscript, she wrote at the bottom of the page, "I won't have people telling me my boss is going soft, and that I should pack up! If any of your students read this manuscript—Jean Baudrillard, for instance—they'd be dismayed."[61] Reading Lefebvre's manuscripts from the 1960s, edited in Delbo's hand, it's not hard to see why he called her a "meticulous and unconventional" assistant. She was so straightforward, so free from the fuzzy flattery of the hypersensitive scholar, that she quickly made herself indispensable. So sure-footed was she that Lefebvre got in the habit of waiting for Delbo's remarks before moving forward with his manuscripts.

Born near Paris on August 10, 1913, Delbo (fig. 2.5) is known today for her literary investigations of life in the Nazi concentration camps. Delbo and her husband, Georges Dudach, were arrested by the Gestapo in Paris on March 2, 1942, for their clandestine activities. Delbo helped type the anti-Nazi pamphlets *La pensée libre* and *Lettres françaises*, while her husband distributed them. After their arrest, Dudach was executed by the Germans at Mont-Valérien on May 23, 1942, and Delbo was deported to Auschwitz several days later. It is a tribute to Delbo's powers of description that she could convey, with clear-eyed concentration, the unspeakable horror she experienced at Auschwitz and Ravensbrück. Her widely read *Auschwitz and After*, which she published in three volumes between 1965 and 1971, is a testament to her powers of expression and personal resolve. Permanently marked by her wartime experience—including by a tattooed 31661, a subdermal dog tag and "a good number," she tells us, "since it can still be read on my left arm"—Delbo was one of the last century's most important conjunctions of lucid resilience and poetic expression.

But the whole of Delbo's life and writing is too easily subsumed under her horrific wartime experience. Because of this, her postwar writings at the crossroads of Marxism and urban sociology remain woefully unknown. Moreover, Delbo's immense influence on Lefebvre, one of the century's most important urban sociologists, has gone unexamined until now. Delbo's papers, housed in the Arts du spectacle department of the Bibliothèque nationale de France, show that Lefebvre's decisive turn from rural to urban sociology didn't just coincide with Delbo's assistantship, it was compelled by it. Taking nothing away from Delbo's legacy or literary oeuvre—which presents itself most forcefully in her three-volume account of her more than two-year confinement in Auschwitz—there is another story to tell.

At the same time Delbo assisted Lefebvre and edited his manuscripts, she was honing her own urban sociology. It took shape in ten reviews and one long article published between March 1961 and March 1965 in Stoetzel's *Revue française de sociologie*. And although the extent of Delbo's urban sociology cannot be told in detail here, three signposts are essential. Delbo expressed admiration for sociologists who knew how to evoke—and she practiced what she praised. Each of Delbo's reviews included memorable lines that captured her own thoughts and the essence of the book under review. When it came to Lewis Mumford's *The City in History* (1961), Delbo sympathized with the American sociologist's conclusion that "the poorest men of the Stone Age" were not so unfortunate as today's city dwellers. But this demanded a follow-up question, which Delbo delivered on cue: "And now what? What will become of social life in our huge 'savage' cities?"[62] What's more, she thought the study of urban life should be placed not only in historical perspective but in comparative perspective as well. "Contemporary world conditions" was her repeated refrain. An aptitude for languages, which Delbo had in spades, was crucial to this. She read English and Russian with ease, making her one of the few contributors to the *Revue* who could review the books on urban life pouring in from the United States and the Soviet Union. Finally, it is remarkable how much of a city girl Delbo was. She loved urban life and wasn't afraid to cite Oswald Spengler in its defense: "All great cultures are born of the city," the author of *The Decline of the West* had written. For Delbo, cities were "crucibles for fomenting ideas and art."[63] Nature, for her, had lost its charm. "I no longer love nature except in intermezzo," she wrote from the Swiss countryside not long after her release from Ravensbrück. This made for a stark contrast with her new boss, who continued to make so much of Pyrenean rural life.

There were few matters more important to Delbo and Lefebvre than the nature of the past. Beginning in 1960 Delbo, a self-proclaimed Proustian, ceaselessly enriched Lefebvre's thought on several subjects, none more so than the intricacies of time. Cleverly, almost instinctively, she fell on his desire to revive what been degraded by the passage of time. Here lies Delbo's first contribution to Lefebvre's thought: It was foolhardy to have an idée fixe only on what remains. There's a fine moment in Delbo's essay "February" where she comments on one of Lefebvre's recently published reviews. Likely referring to his "What Is the Historical Past?" published in *Les temps modernes* in 1959, she calls Lefebvre's review "remarkably concise and thought-provoking," adding that it "could become the subject of a thesis."[64] Lefebvre argued that the past was a wellspring of future possibilities.[65] The possible is never sui generis; it often emerges from some subtle revival of past possibilities. His point was simple: Understanding what was *once* possible sheds light on what might *one day* become possible. "*The past*," Lefebvre stressed, "*becomes present (or is renewed) as a function of the realization of the possibilities objectively implied in this past*."[66] Delbo didn't object to Lefebvre's emphasis on involution, but she recoiled from the idea that reviving an ancient style of living was the great imperative of the postwar period. Instead, she contended, more forcefully than Lefebvre ever did, that there were now entire groups of people who could no longer find any redemption in the centuries-old peasant past of Europe. Concentrated in cities and thrown into a perpetually advancing present not of their own making, they had no claim on what was timeworn. From the start, Delbo resisted Lefebvre's pining for a past era of rural well-being. "To live in the past is not to live," she wrote in *Auschwitz and After*, "It is to cut oneself off from the living."⁶⁷ I need hardly add that both Delbo's life and her oeuvre attest to how difficult it is for survivals to regain their former radiance. In her trademark style, at once literary and direct, she cautioned Lefebvre to recognize the sharp difference between what came before and what comes after.

Delbo and Lefebvre therefore represent two schools of thought regarding the nature of the past: Lefebvre saw a perennial past—a thread bound to the loom of time; Delbo, on the other hand, was more inclined to see the past as something that withers away—a thread bound to come undone. With a different temporal register, Delbo put forward a most significant contrast between remembrances, which meaningfully interrupt the passage of time, and reassuring parodies of the past, which offer only fleeting consolation for what has been lost. Those who knew Delbo best often found her torn between the inaccessibility of the past and the impossibility of forgetting it. And while it is true that you can find Lefebvre-like statements in her writings ("We had our entire past, all our memories. We armed ourselves with this past for protection, erecting it between us and horror in order to stay whole"), it is not long before we learn that the weight of the past—the whole lot of remembrances—can, in fact, be stripped away ("You might say that one can take everything away from a human being except this one faculty: memory. Not so. First, human beings are stripped of what makes them human, then their memory leaves them. Memory peels off like tatters, tatters of burned skin").⁶⁸ Delbo's declaration that sometimes "nothing remains of what was before" is thus in every respect the opposite of Lefebvre's emphasis on the persistence of archaic remnants. There are times, Delbo corrected her former teacher, when nothing can bridge the immense gulf between what came before and what comes after.

When it came to Marxism, then, it was only natural that Delbo, so attuned to what had passed away, should have questioned whether Marx's thought was *à bout de souffle*, out of breath. Although Lefebvre's association with the French Communist Party had ended in 1958, he remained as committed as ever to the humanist Marx beloved by so many Western Marxists. Here Delbo and Lefebvre agreed: Marxism was integral not only to understanding but also to transforming everything from morality to everyday life. Neither materialist nor metaphysical interpretations did justice to Marx's thinking. "Pitiful," Delbo wrote, "the tendency to translate Marx's thought into the 'highest' philosophical language."⁶⁹ She and Lefebvre never tired of searching for concrete alternatives to the production models of General Motors and the accumulations of the Banque de Paris. But while Lefebvre wanted to recuperate the authentic thought of Marx, Delbo's ambitions were different. How could Lefebvre build a meaningful Marxist sociology if he remained a prisoner to the past? And by "prisoner to the past" Delbo had in mind his being chained to both the primitive past and the authentic Marx.

That Marxism might be passé fifteen years into France's reconstruction was hardly surprising. Postwar France was a period of unprecedented change. Capitalism might be an idol with feet of clay, as Delbo argued, but its Achilles' heel wasn't moving too slowly or getting stuck in the mud. Delbo was surely right when she told Lefebvre on March 3, 1963, that trying to recuperate an authentic Marx was kind of like if during the fin de siècle "people had referred to Rousseau in order to make the Revolution of 1905, under the pretext that Rousseau's ideas had been effective in 1789." She encouraged her former teacher to turn a corner, to worry less about reclaiming the original Marx and concern himself instead with how Marx might be made applicable to the second half of the twentieth century: "How can Marx serve us today?" And if he can't, his administrative assistant added, then we can "grind Marx up and leave him in 1844 . . . because, ultimately, time passes."[70]

By 1960 such attitudes were everywhere on the French Left. Some pious soul, familiar with defeat, would remember the dates of what might have been: 1848, 1871, 1905, 1917. Lefebvre himself recalled that in 1945, at the end of the Second World War, "the left had great hope, but within a few years that hope had collapsed."[71] Everywhere you looked the past seemed littered with the wreckage of unfulfilled aspirations. The twentieth century wasn't the end of history, but it sure felt like it. The historian Enzo Traverso calls this tradition of mourning by Western Marxists "left-wing melancholia."[72] But was Lefebvre's rural sociology one more instance of the Left's culture of defeat? Could he afford to be so pessimistic? It seems he could. In fact, he is a sublime example of just how creative cultural pessimism can be. Not only could Lefebvre afford to mourn; he was demonstrably compelled by lamenting the impending loss of peasant culture. Mourning can be a source of stubborn resistance, a hard kernel of hope. There was nothing debilitating about Lefebvre's nostalgic paeans. Mourning and nostalgia, which are not synonymous with resignation or guilt, retain their creative power, even in the land of the vanquished and in the light of all that has been left behind.

Nostalgia: Lefebvre was waiting for the word. It rang out with such certainty and disdain. For all the ink that has been spilled over nostalgia in the last two decades, the noble sentiment is still seen as a paralyzing indulgence, something one regrettably succumbs to. But nostalgia is a strange, Janus-faced sentiment. Thus, Lefebvre didn't feel slighted when he was accused of nostalgia—on the contrary, he felt quite sure of himself. Thanks to Delbo, on whom mere nostalgia was wasted, Lefebvre didn't seek refuge in the past. He understood that nostalgia was only a first step on the way to securing more sustainable ways of living. So Lefebvre gratefully took his marching orders, and eventually his new imperative came straight out of Delbo's mouth: "In order to understand the modern world, it is necessary not only to retain some of Marx's essential concepts but also to add new ones: the everyday, the urban, social time and space."[73]

As Delbo saw it, Lefebvre was unduly concerned with recovery, be it recovering Marx's authentic thought or the traditions of southwestern France. The problem with Lefebvre's sensibility wasn't the influence of Tristan Tzara and the surrealists or Guy Debord and the situationists. As Lefebvre's intimate interlocutor, Delbo knew how negligible these influences were. Rather, the problem lay in his nostalgic paeans for a rural life that was on the verge of disappearing. Imagining that a peasant mentality might one day replace an urban mentality was a fantasy that simply would not do. All that Lefebvre had praised for the last two decades had to come across such an immense distance, while urban developments were right there, staring them both in the face. In a three-page letter dated March 1960, Delbo pushed back. As the world was being transformed all around them, she asked her soon-to-be boss: "Is this really what you want to do?" She insisted that in these turbulent times their motto must be "in our time," not "once upon a time." She told Lefebvre that his fascination with meridional cultures, crucified suns, and southern winds had little practical value.[74] And she was right, I suppose; after all, in 1960 it wasn't yet hot enough for northern cities to be ripe for southern winds. With her sleeves rolled up and her Auschwitz number in plain sight, she added, "Ce qui est mort est mort, même si cà n'aurait pas dû mourir" (What's dead is dead, even if it shouldn't have died).[75] It's a hugely revealing phrase. In essence, Delbo demanded that Lefebvre turn from persistences of the past to the tremors of the present. New towns, urban life, technological progress, the structure of modern capital—it was high time to "do for our time what Marx did for his."

Unveiling the Delbo-Lefebvre collaboration has its uses, one of them being a corrective to the view that it was the encounter between Lefebvre and situationists such as Debord that shaped Lefebvre's urban sociology. Weighing scales of influence is always a tricky matter, but with greater hindsight the evidence falls more on the side of Lefebvre's daily interactions with his assistant than on his fleeting engagements with situationists. Leftists have for too long paid too much attention to Lefebvre's situationist students and not enough to his steady collaborator. Delbo's archives show that we've had our eyes on the wrong student.[76] There was another student—a student who was under Lefebvre's tutelage in the 1930s—whose influence proved truly indispensable. Beginning in the early 1960s, Delbo challenged Lefebvre to speak clearly about the present state of postwar society. In the age after, when so much had been uprooted and grown foreign, one must be clear about what remained and what was no longer. "And now what?" she liked to ask Lefebvre. It was often the case, she seemed to say, that when he tried to resurrect some archaic survival, he simply couldn't—no matter how deft his touch or dexterous his theory. Her emphasis on "our days" instead of on "days gone by" seems to have filled a need of which Lefebvre himself had become acutely aware. It was time to turn from the archaic past to the urban present.

Lefebvre took Delbo's words to heart. The early 1960s were a turning point, the dawn of a new intellectual passion. The path was now clear for Lefebvre's urban sociology, which he inaugurated a few weeks later when he compiled his notes on Mourenx. And while there aren't two names on the pages of Lefebvre's late sociology, his and hers, side by side, Delbo nevertheless coauthored his work on urban space. But it wasn't a matter of Delbo talking him into it, wearing him down. Lefebvre was too much of a leftist for that, too committed to his ideals to shirk the responsibility of responding to the postwar present. What looks like an about-face was actually a reorientation. When Lefebvre came to speak of the coming urban revolution and "the right to the city," it wasn't a renunciation of Pyrenean rural communities or their archaic arts of living.[77] The lessons of rural sociology were brought to bear on the present; they were not abandoned. And so it was a genuinely Lefebvrian claim that there remained living anachronisms, indispensable survivals that could sustain the present.

Following Lefebvre along the same dusty paths he wandered in his youth, we inevitably come upon Mourenx—an abrupt cement island that had sprung up practically overnight in the summer of 1957. After a decade Lefebvre was still as horrified as ever at the sight of tower blocks rising where oaks and vineyards once stood. Despite a feeling bordering on physical revulsion, the sixty-eight-year-old sociologist climbed a small hill to survey the new town. He felt perfectly ridiculous: a gray-haired philosopher sitting alone on a hilltop waiting for voices from a bygone past to speak to him before he went home to jot down a few more lines about urban space. Vain, conceited, misguided! How fortunate that no one saw. Yet he kept gazing out over Mourenx, forcing a prolonged exposure. Nothing he saw had developed organically; all the qualities common to ancestral villages were missing. Mourenx was a fastidious place without a past, its main street a signaled thoroughfare that never looked backward. City planners hadn't needed to liquidate survivals to make room for modern developments because the new town didn't have any in the first place. "No," he muttered to himself, "we will not find a style for our age in a place like this." Lefebvre kept company with the old, but the past wasn't the only company he kept. As the Pyrenean sun stabbed him like needles, his own voice soon mingled with Delbo's: "What's dead is dead, even if it shouldn't have died." After rehearsing his litany of grievances, Lefebvre eventually stood up, reeling like a drunk. He had such a burning look in his eyes that had anyone seen him they would have no doubt what this theorist of survivals thought of this supposed city of the future.

The End of Accumulation Without End

"It is a very strange phenomenon," Lefebvre reflected in 1973, "that every politically active person in every regime should declare themselves to be for growth."[78] Everyone, it seemed, regardless of political stripe, seemed willing to go right to the end to maintain economic growth. Today, this is perhaps beginning to change. But in 1973, the year of the first oil shock and the start of the general crisis that is our own, Lefebvre was struck by the stickiness of the ideology of unending growth. The slowdown had started, and the urban sociologist sprang into action. He found that over the course of two centuries, growth had gone from a slogan to an essence, from an expression of value to the only value. In the twentieth century, growth was more than an economic measure; it was a veritable ideology. And it proclaimed that unlimited increase was *the* desirable thing, not just the means to desirable things. Accumulation without end, in other words, was an end in itself. Hence Lefebvre needed to first solve the problem of the ideology of growth and then show how a certain underdevelopment (selective and elective) might foster richer (more metabolic) interactions between man and nature.[79]

Ideologies of incessant growth were modern, but they were not new. Lefebvre divided the modern growth-mindset into three stages: the blind-thrust growth of the late nineteenth and early twentieth centuries, the euphoric growth of the decades after 1945, and the growth skepticism that arrived in earnest in 1973. In the late nineteenth century, a pervasive optimism congealed around the idea that economic growth could and should be unending. Buttressed by quasi-mathematical models, the image of growth grew into an exponential curve, blindly climbing up and up, year after year, quarter after quarter: more cars, more barrels of oil, more tons of cement. Whether you call the reigning ideology productivism, economism, industrial rationalism, or technological futurism, the pitiless mechanisms of production held sway over social and political life. In search of more and more resources and ever-extending markets, capitalist production had a conquering mind. A great deal has been said about the brutal combination of capitalist accumulation and imperial expansion in the late nineteenth and early twentieth centuries. And having said as much himself, Lefebvre hastened to add that nothing lasts forever—not the immense current of growth nor the ideologies that insist on it. For primitivists such as Lefebvre, unending growth was an idol and an illusion—and an impossibility.

Anyone who has read Lefebvre will know of his contempt for the period collectively called the economic miracle and known in France as *les trente glorieuses*. The nearly thirty years after 1945 were "an idyllic period for the whole of capitalism," Lefebvre wrote.[80] "Idyllic" here signifies both more and less than usual. It means a province of peace and a time of trouble, a place of greater abundance and an age that was more turbulent than quaint. It therefore meant something different from the halcyon character Lefebvre had attributed to the village of Navarrenx years earlier. At any rate, at some point in the 1950s, the ship of blind-thrust capitalism found new captains and a new fixed course. In the postwar era of French dirigiste capitalism, technocrats and technicians were the new guardians of perpetual growth.[81] Then, just as now, the new captains of industry subordinated everything to growth. Things didn't begin to change until around 1973, when some started coming around to Lefebvre's decades-old skepticism. Only after the fragility of growth could no longer be ignored did people wake up to the reality that perpetual growth was an illusion, likely impossible, and maybe even a pernicious idol. That realization soon spread like rust and ate away at growth's ideological foundations. But in reality, the reaction was worse than that: "The situation is now bleaker than ever," remarked Lefebvre.[82] A new millenarianism had crept into Western societies. With a collective sigh, many wondered if humanity would survive beyond the year 2000. This was, in a word, catastrophism. How quickly conquering minds metastasize into apocalyptic minds, and this not because of nuclear proliferation and two world wars but because of something even more dreadful: stagnation.

Part of the reason for the malaise surrounding the slowdown was how hard it had become to ignore the ecological devastation of growth. Lefebvre saw this clearly enough, and he deplored the environmental destruction produced by industrial civilization. Wherever humans live, they turn nature into a *thing*. Human beings' Promethean ambitions and their mastery of nature were ubiquitous themes in a society committed to unprecedented production for production's sake. The peasant way of understanding the Earth was a thing of the past; gone were the days of direct relations between people and nature, the source of so much vitality. The new era's willful curtailing of the lifespan of objects came in for particular scorn. That destruction itself was built into production was just one more way that the extraordinary developments of postwar society seemed bent on destroying the planet. All he could say, with a slight sense of helplessness, was that that was what capitalism did. It isolated, appropriated, and free-rode on nature.[83] At the same time, it separated human beings from the time of the seasons, the time of the commune, and the time of the body. The point was that the processes necessary for continual economic expansion ravaged everything that stood in their way, including nature and the human body. Lefebvre's reflections on the garish urban planning at Mourenx had already led him deep into the territory of devastated landscapes and razed villages. His nascent political ecology came out of the conviction, which grew stronger as his revolutionary romanticism matured, that nature was more than a costless input and a benign sink.[84]

Despite his nostalgia—or because of it—Lefebvre refused to attribute to the new industrial civilization a coherence that it lacked. Unlike Marxists such as Herbert Marcuse, Lefebvre maintained that state-managed capitalism was neither omnipotent nor omnipresent.[85] This kind of rebuttal, grounded in the social sciences, was characteristic Lefebvre. Mastery is forever thwarted: Just as nature is never in a pure state, humanity is never able to separate itself entirely from nature. No matter how mechanized it may be, labor cannot cut the human off from nature. In other words, we are immersed in the very nature we seek to control. As early as 1960, in his essay "Nature and Nature Conquered," it is clear just how much Lefebvre had incorporated ecological thinking into his critique of capitalism. Without meaning to, he had anticipated several aspects of contemporary environmentalist thought, declaring roundly: "What is known as pollution or the problem of the environment is only an ideological mask. In particular, the term 'environment' has no precise meaning; it is everything and nothing, it can mean nature as a whole or it can mean the suburbs. Pollution and the crisis of the environment are simply the surface of deeper phenomena, one of which is the uncontrolled technology that has been unleashed."[86] One may venture to guess what his critique might have been had he known of the ways anthropogenic climate change was degrading our common home. I suspect he would not have been surprised by the growing literature on Earth's regulatory systems, its biophysical cycles, and their incompatibility with the insatiable interests of economic growth.

"We humans," wrote Lefebvre, "have never managed to get over our nostalgia for this 'being': mother, earth. And perhaps it is best not to get over it, even if nostalgia may play dirty tricks. We live in hope that history will come full circle and bring back the distant past of cosmic innocence, resurrecting that lost forgotten world within us."[87] It is surely a statement that simultaneously revels in nostalgia's creative power, recalls Bataille's desire to rediscover a lost intimacy, and clamors for Delbo's injunction: What's dead is dead, even if it shouldn't have died. Lefebvre's portrait of returning to the countryside and reimagining urban space was highly romanticized. Even the motif of putting down roots, the emblematic act of the primitive peasant, was present. But Lefebvre didn't romanticize nature the way many did. Naturists and nudists, who found a new lease on life in the 1960s, prettified and trivialized nature, turning it into a cliché. While philosophers like Pierre Teilhard de Chardin transfigured nature into a vitalist ontology, Lefebvre was as unmoved by obscure ontologies as he was by simple nudity. In contrast, he stood for the happiness that flowed from rich relationships with nature. That so-called archaic societies had retained a happiness Western societies had lost was one reason he criticized the demands of limitless growth.

Much of our apprehension today issues from a lack of certainty that the Earth will remain a suitable place for humankind. Finding a way of channeling this uncertainty into a critique of capitalist-driven climate change will be one of the tasks of the years ahead. Against all odds, the revival of nature remains an arena pregnant with possibility. We now approach the real question prompted by Lefebvre's critique of growth: Can nostalgia for the past be projected toward a postcapitalist future? When does nostalgia end and despair begin?[88]

To avoid succumbing to the new malaise, so as not to feel good about how profoundly bad he felt, Lefebvre turned to the Left. If for the last three decades he had looked backward while the world rushed forward, he now looked to the Left as the world stalled. How had leftists responded to the sudden slowdown? Unfortunately, what he found was not encouraging. He grouped leftist responses to the crisis into two camps. First, there were "progressives," who maintained the ideology of indefinite growth. Whether social democrats, democratic socialists, or communists, these partisans of progress essentially picked up the baton of the bourgeoisie. But a socialist grow-or-die modernity was still a ravaging, ecologically unsustainable modernity. Lefebvre's harshest invective was reserved for those who spoke of today's technologies as if they were the divinities of yesterday. Then there were "regressives," who were eager to smash the idol of growth. Guided by some vague promise of returning to something better, these early degrowthers looked to the past and to the periphery. But such a movement would persuade no more than a handful of people already inclined to see the promised land as the land of less and less. Needless to say, Lefebvre was suspicious of both camps, calling progressives "bourgeois-successors" and regressives "so-called leftists."[89] Deeply concerned but not disconsolate, Lefebvre continued to articulate an alternative to growth without end—no small task, and one he carried out less than satisfactorily, in my opinion. Nevertheless, his inquiry came to life only when he started sketching a much-needed third way.

Well and fine, you may say: neither a return to the archaic nor a reveling in the status quo. But what then? Hadn't the twentieth century demonstrated that the idea of indefinite progress was here to stay, regardless of the cataclysms it drew down? While the capitalist may well proclaim "Après moi, le déluge," the twentieth century solidified the obdurate mantra of growth—after the deluge, yet more progress. Lefebvre's meditation on the differences between progressives and regressives may evade this rather obvious point. But it is fair to say that his foray into the origins of the degrowth movement was no humdrum academic inquiry. "In the post-agrarian society initiated by *les trente glorieuses* the rural could become a harbinger of future possibilities," the historian Sarah Farmer writes. In *Into Their Labours*, John Berger appreciates that today "the remarkable continuity of peasant experience and the peasant view of the world acquires, as it is threatened with extinction, an unprecedented and unexpected urgency."[90] The declarations, which Berger and Farmer vividly defend, could well have come from Lefebvre's lips.

They could also have come from the mouth of Marx himself, we have come to learn. After completing the first volume of *Capital* in 1867, Marx read extensively on indigenous America. He also taught himself Russian so that he could study agricultural communes in Russia. Marx realized late in life that one should not be frightened by the word "archaic," Kohei Saito tells us.[91] Marx's new relationship to time was rooted in what he learned about Indigenous communities and the rural commons. Late in life he concluded that what was needed was a return to the modes of production and forms of communal property typically found in precapitalist societies.[92] Lefebvre was aware of this, as one would expect from France's most sophisticated interpreter of Marx. In *Introduction to Modernity*, he wrote, "Marx thought that one day men will live out their everyday lives practically, rediscovering in the process something which perhaps had been accomplished by some societies now lost."[93] We need not turn our backs on technological and scientific progress, but we ought to have the humility to learn about social stability, cultural continuity, and environmental sustainability from archaic and Indigenous societies. More communal work, less overall work, an economy in which use-values predominate and workers have power over production—these are some of the lessons that accrue to those familiar with precapitalist traditions. So-called archaic societies were not driven by the logic of capital; they did not speed up production and consumption to achieve a shorter circuit of capital creation. Instead, they went slowly, produced collectively, distributed use-values directly, and maintained a healthy relationship with the natural world.

As a guide to Lefebvre's search for a leftist alternative, we can do no better than turn to the last chapter of his book *The Survival of Capitalism* (1973). Just as the first cracks in the myth of unending growth were beginning to show, Lefebvre sprang from criticizing the sordid exigencies of growth to championing an older ethos. The noncumulative customs of archaic societies forced their way once more into Lefebvre's thought. His leftist alternative was as "primitivist" as anything produced by Bataille, to whom Lefebvre was much closer in thought and feeling than is generally recognized. Rooted in the survival of antiquated modes of production and archaic styles of expenditure, Lefebvre's alternative bore all the marks of a certain primitivism.[94] Not all that is old is necessarily outdated, just as not all that is new is necessary. He knew the huge resistance to digging around in the past to find answers to the future; he had read the preface to the first volume of *Capital* and was well aware of Marx's declaration that we suffer the inherited evils of the past as well as those of the present. *Le mort saisit le vif!*[95] But for the would-be primitivist reformer, as for Marx toward the end of his life, there was more to the past, especially the deep past, than an evil inheritance. While the concepts of everyday life and the right to the city—Lefebvre's signature imprints on Marxist thought—continue to garner attention, it is arguably his attention to self-management and archaic expenditures that may be more infectious today. Without being aware, of course, of the depth and seriousness of anthropogenic climate change, Lefebvre brought the matter of durability to the fore.

Self-management provided the first positive pillar of Lefebvre's leftist alternative. Lefebvre promoted a social order in which workers decided what to produce, how much to produce, how to produce it, and how to organize the consumption of what they produced—"for without self-management, participation has no meaning."[96] And there it was—a quaint nostalgia for a bygone age when participation flourished and community mattered. Why is it that words like "participation" and "community" continue to resonate in our world today? Is it because they evoke a formerly hallowed ground that has been hollowed out? Here Lefebvre was going back over familiar ground. His ambitious aim was no less than a reconstitution of society. He believed that "the social" would expand once the shackles of present-day politics and capitalist political economy were thrown off. More democracy, more workplace democracy, more worker participation, more cooperative ownership, greater priority of the local—it would not be wrong to say that Lefebvre, guided by his revolutionary romantic perspective, had excessive confidence in the healing powers of society. But he insisted that self-management was no panacea.

It was quite easy, in fact, to co-opt the idea of cooperatives to corporate interests and market demands. Self-management thus had nothing magical about it: "Life cannot be changed by magic or by a poetic act, as the surrealists used to believe."[97]

Lefebvre began with self-management, but expropriating the expropriators wasn't enough. It was necessary to step out of the hidden abode of production and into the radiant light of unproductive expenditure, the second positive pillar of Lefebvre's leftist alternative. What was needed was a Left willing to interrupt economic growth. Lefebvre criticized those on the left who wanted to continue doing what governments had done for decades—namely, promote higher and higher rates of growth. Needless to say, these were not soothing words to those who wanted to be reassured that they were on the right path. The stakes of the class struggle were not confined to wages, the workday, or ownership of the means of production. There was also the matter of the social surplus product. The question was not: How will society's surplus be invested? But rather: How will the social surplus product be expended? The use that we put social surpluses to need not be confined to ever-greater productivity. Perhaps we touch on the fundamental problem by asking, as Lefebvre did: What, given our current predicament, do we want to do with our social surplus product? How much of it should we have, and how should we expend it?

As Lefebvre saw it, "Only one very remarkable thinker, Georges Bataille, had taken up the analysis of the social surplus product."[98] Bataille was the first thinker to turn Mauss's essay on the gift into a political economy worth fighting for. No one had espoused in such full measure the need to go beyond the productive power of labor. While most Marxists condemned Bataille's economy of excess as aberrant or abject or both, Lefebvre testified eloquently to the importance of Bataille's rethinking of social surplus. By "social surplus product," Bataille and Lefebvre meant the accumulated energies that cannot be absorbed by productive forces and must eventually explode. Nancy Fraser neatly defines such surpluses as "the collective fund of social energies exceeding those required to reproduce a given form of life and to replenish what is used up in the course of living it."[99] Rustic hospitality and sacrifice were once the names for the times and places that these excess energies, desirous of discharge, were dissipated.

It wasn't just that the productive forces of primitive peoples were relatively weak and worker-owned; it was that archaic societies knew how to expend in a manner that gave them profound meaning, social solidarity, and relative stability. Perhaps ahead of his time, and definitely against his age, Lefebvre recognized that the sagacity of archaic societies lay in their durability. He had learned from Mauss and Bataille that primitive economies moved in circles, and the more things circulated, the less—not the more—they accumulated. Festivals, feasts, initiation rites, religious sacrifices, and monumental works of art were all occasions for redistributing the social surplus product, enjoying excess in acts other than productive consumption and thwarting acquisitive impulses in the process. Therefore, calling the cyclical customs of archaic societies "survivals" didn't capture the half of it. The idea of it, cloaked in the savage colors of primitive culture, must have taken some getting used to.

The real stakes in the class struggle, then, were ownership of the means of production and control over the social surplus product. Lefebvre had finally come around to Bataille's position. Disenchanting times call for creative thinking. And Lefebvre understood that nothing so pointedly raises questions about how people want to live than the expenditure of surplus. Much was at stake: "Where we choose to invest our collective energies, how we propose to balance 'productive work' vis-à-vis family life, leisure and other activities—as well as how we aspire to relate to non-human nature and what we want to leave to future generations."[100] Such decisions are ripe for selectively uneven development; instead, they are left to market forces. Year after year we let a system designed to maximize shareholder value, not human flourishing, dictate the most precious parts of life. What Bataille and Lefebvre called unproductive expenditure is the source of all that is good, agreeable, rich, and pleasurable in life; all else is "the hard life of productive labor."[101] And so it was that what came before—a wise concoction of weak productive forces and cyclical social practices that collectively expended excess—might well come after.

3

Georges Devereux

Mohave Shamanism and the Future of Ethnopsychiatry

In 1951 Georges Devereux (1908–1985), a Hungarian-born anthropologist trained in France, attended a funeral in California's Mohave Valley. In the middle of the proceedings, he saw a car stop nearby and a man get out with camera in hand. Devereux, who had returned to the American Southwest for a sixth field season, knew immediately what it was. He had heard that there had been attempts by whites to exploit the Mohave's fear of being photographed. Photographers would descend on early morning rites such as this, sound their metallic shutters, and refuse to leave until they had been sufficiently bribed to go away. As Devereux saw it, these photographers embodied Western modernity—the spirit of capitalism; the love of money and its prolific, generative nature; and so on and so forth. The Mohave, he knew, interpreted wealth not as a sign of success or sanity, but as a character flaw and a cultural derangement. A small tribe of around one thousand, the Mohave lived where the Colorado River straddles the Arizona-California border. A people who traditionally destroyed private property at death, the Mohave thwarted accumulation and had no real symbols of wealth. Innate acquisitiveness was further dulled by an almost unlimited demand for generosity toward all and sundry. Only a week earlier Devereux had heard one of his informants shout at a neighbor, "You are rich!" She meant it as an insult, and it was taken as one.

At any rate, there was the photographer intent on interrupting a rite that had been handed down from generation to generation. By the middle of the twentieth century the Mohave's habits and fears were well-known, and some outsiders were eager to exploit these Indigenous "survivals." The best thing might have been for the Mohave to put up with the interloper and say nothing, but heartfelt culture doesn't work that way.[1] So, without much choice, a mourner broke from the group to pay the photographer off. With a haughty smile, the photographer paused, and then raised his camera and threatened to carry on. The whole scene distilled Devereux's complaints against capitalist societies. "Nothing could be more emblematic of modern times than this eager early-morning entrepreneur," he thought. These intrusions did much more than mar the authenticity of the anthropologist's experience (though they certainly did that)—they chipped away at an age-old culture already on the verge of disappearing. Cultivated in an arid desert, Mohave customs had opposed accumulation since time immemorial. Sickened by what he saw, Devereux, a man of forty-three whose primitivist sensibility had not been dulled by experience, told the photographer never to return. Yet Devereux himself was not immune to the West's acquisitive mores. Multiple times in his published writings he fondly refers to and even reproduces a photograph given to him by his friend and Mohave informant Hama Utce. She had violated the taboo against being photographed so that Devereux wouldn't forget her. To him, her cultural deviation was not a character flaw but a way of letting him know that he belonged.

A distinguished if somewhat overlooked anthropologist, Devereux began formal training in psychoanalysis in 1947. On scholarship at the Menninger School of Psychiatry from 1947 to 1952, he took up temporary residence in Topeka, Kansas. There Devereux lectured on psychoanalytic anthropology and treated hospitalized Plains Indians at the Menninger Clinic, a psychiatric facility connected with Winter Veterans Affairs Hospital. According to the historian Lawrence Friedman, Menninger was "the largest and best psychiatric training, treatment, and educational center in the world."[2] Karl A. Menninger, director of the Menninger School of Psychiatry, was the guiding influence during Devereux's Topeka years. Driven by a humane interest in Indigenous peoples, Menninger established a treatment program in which patients interacted with a whole psychoanalytic community rather than working one-on-one with a single psychiatrist, making Topeka one of the liveliest places in the world for creative explorations in psychoanalysis. And, in part, this was true: When it came to multidisciplinary research, the Menninger School shone. But an orthodox Freudianism pervaded its halls and left some, including Devereux and his successor Henri Ellenberger, feeling at times more lifeless than lively.[3] Even so, Devereux completed his training in November 1952 and became a member of the Topeka Psychoanalytic Society. One year later and he was in the front rank of researchers formulating a new social science at the nexus of anthropology and psychology: ethnopsychiatry. He wanted to firmly establish what Freud had first suggested in *Totem and Taboo* (1912–13) and Géza Róheim had later explored in publications such as *Psychoanalysis and the Social Sciences* (1947): the complementary nature of two great systems of thought, ethnography and psychoanalysis. Devereux believed that ethnopsychiatry may soon prove to be as integral to psychiatry "as anatomy is for surgery, or biochemistry is for internal medicine."[4] After 1945 he was on his way to becoming one of the great figures of the twentieth-century social sciences and the ranking world authority on ethnopsychiatry.

But, as I will show, the roots of Devereux's ethnopsychiatry lay earlier and elsewhere—not with Menninger and not in the American heartland, but with Mohave shamans and in the American Southwest (fig. 3.1). It was his fieldwork, his on-the-ground research, his years spent *sur le terrain*, that was the real germ of his ethnopsychiatry. Devereux was a master eye-opener, and his own eyes were opened when he experienced "the special tinge of an archaic culture."[5] During six field seasons between 1932 and 1951, he encountered a Native psychiatry among the Indigenous community gathered along the banks of the Lower Colorado. The sense of belonging he felt among the Mohave reminded him of the word "gemeinschaft," the sociological idea of a genuine community. He admittedly had a preference for life far from the city. This chapter locates the origin of Devereux's ethnopsychiatry in the psychotherapeutic beliefs and practices of a Native tribe in the American Southwest. A small and largely unknown culture, the Mohave played an oversized role in the history of twentieth-century ideas. As aforesaid, it was neither in Topeka nor in Freud that Devereux first crossed paths with the conjunction of cultural anthropology and psychotherapy; it was in and around Parker, Arizona. Just as Freud first learned psychoanalysis by listening to his patients, the Mohave first taught Devereux. The founder of French ethnopsychiatry maintained that it was shamans, the psychiatric healers of times past, who "spoon-fed" him Freud and turned him on to psychoanalysis. Thus, long before his formal training at Menninger, Devereux's first school in the interplay of social, cultural, and psychological factors was a Native one. After observing Mohave shamans such as Hivsu Tupoma, he knew that the diagnosis and treatment of patients must account for their cultural backgrounds.

Primitive psychiatric practice was integral to Devereux's thought, and his peculiar primitivism must be reckoned with in any comprehensive account of his oeuvre. Unfortunately, derision often still inflects descriptions of archaic psychotherapy. Primitive psychiatry has been reduced to some strange simplifications, but nothing could be further from the truth than the idea that archaic psychotherapy is no more than the savage devices of quack medicine men. Against these dismissals, and despite the fear of being seen as "going native," Devereux inaugurated a careful reevaluation of age-old psychiatric ideas and practices. In the process he revised long-standing prejudices about

FIGURE 3.1. Georges Devereux in the Mojave Desert—a straightforward image of an anthropologist on the ground and an unwitting testament to ethnopsychiatry's desert years. Undated photograph, courtesy of Georges Devereux Archives/IMEC.

shamans as wild analysts. C. N. Rudkin wrote of Devereux in the *Los Angeles Corral*, "An intelligent student of the American aborigines cannot read him without finding that his ideas about 'noble red men,' 'wild savages,' and 'quack medicine men' will have to undergo a great deal of careful revision."[6] Devereux boldly asserted that over the centuries the Mohave had developed an elaborate set of beliefs and practices concerning mental illness—which is why Mohave shamans such as Tupoma held pride of place in Devereux's ethnopsychiatry. Well before Freud, Róheim, or Menninger, Tupoma taught Devereux the importance of social and cultural factors in the etiology, symptomatology, and treatment of mental illness. So closely did Mohave dream culture correspond to psychoanalytic ideas that Devereux discovered that it was Freud who was in accordance with the shamanic folkways of the Mohave, and not the other way around. Psychiatry—real psychiatry, dynamic psychiatry—began with shamans, died with Hippocrates, and was revived twenty-five hundred years later by Freud and Jean-Martin Charcot.[7]

In eleven books and nearly two hundred articles, but especially in his masterwork *Mohave Ethnopsychiatry and Suicide* (1961), Devereux arguably did more than any other single individual to expand our knowledge of so-called primitive psychiatry. He gave to modern science a deeper, more archaic foundation than it was commonly granted and elevated shamanism's place in the prehistory of psychiatry. But he did much more: He argued that Mohave psychiatric ideas and practices could stimulate a rethinking of modern psychiatry, providing the impetus for a most extraordinary revival. Charting the future of ethnopsychiatry, in other words, required revisiting and selectively reviving psychiatry's distant past. He was not alone in saying so, but he was arguably the most inventive spokesman for the primitivist orientation of ethnopsychiatry. Not only has the significance of Mohave shamanism been overlooked in the formation of ethnopsychiatry, but so has the importance of their unique culture. Devereux employed everything from Mohave sexual mores to its shamanic style to critique Western society after the Second World War. He was a cultural pessimist who believed that most modern Western societies were dereistic societies—that is, their beliefs and practices were not in accordance with the facts of reality. As we continue to willfully disconnect decades of hypermodernization and economic growth from their catastrophic effects, it's hard to argue with his assessment. Seventy years ago Devereux saw in Mohave culture a viable alternative to the cultures of rapid change and rampant growth that have defined the era we now call the Great Acceleration. This chapter is an intellectual history that traces the histories of ethnopsychiatry, sexuality, and indigeneity between Paris, France and Parker, Arizona.

From Paris to Parker

Gheorghé E. Dobó was born on September 13, 1908, in Lugoj, Hungary, a small town in the historic Banat region. The youngest of three children, Gheorghé was the son of Eugen Dobó and Margareta Deutsch. His father was a Jewish lawyer who by all accounts had a steady practice and a good reputation. After graduating from Lugoj's Coriolan Brediceanu Gymnasium, where he received exemplary marks in French and mathematics, Gheorghé moved to Paris in June 1926 to study mathematical physics. He studied in that lively city of lights and letters between 1926 and 1933. A talented pianist and composer, Gheorghé frequented Parisian literary circles, wrote a novel, published several poems, and became friends with Jean Paulhan, a future member of the Académie Française.[8] He also worked for three years as a reader in a French publishing house, Compagnie française de traduction. In other words, from the start he was a man of letters. It was in April 1933 that a twenty-five-year-old Gheorghé Dobó officially changed his name to Georges Devereux, the name by which he had gone exclusively since his arrival in Paris seven years earlier. That same year Devereux left Paris on a two-year ethnological mission to French Indochina. Except for a few visits to the French capital and a brief stint at the Musée de l'Homme in 1946, Devereux wouldn't return "home" until 1963.

In addition to Devereux's broad cultural background, special mention must be made of his erudition. After only a few years in Paris, Devereux turned from literary pursuits to what he would later call the "reality principle."[9] His attraction to the concrete soon led him to anthropology, sociology, and the French sciences of man (the rising status of anthropologists and sociologists across the first half of the twentieth century couldn't have hurt either). Devereux's intellectual formation was truly remarkable—you would be hard-pressed to find a twentieth-century intellectual as extensively and expertly trained. He was a polymath in the older, more premodern sense of the word: "An ambulatory reference library," his colleagues called him.[10] His vast erudition is well illustrated by the letters of recommendation written on his behalf, which are available for view at the Institut Mémoires de l'édition contemporaine. Attesting to Devereux's wide-ranging learning are none other than Marie Curie, Alfred Kroeber, Lucien Lévy-Bruhl, Robert Lowie, Bronisław Malinowski, Thomas Mann, Marcel Mauss, Karl Menninger, Talcott Parsons, Paul Rivet, and Pitirim Sorokin—and that's only a partial list. Here's Malinowski on Devereux, written in 1941: "I have read practically everything he has written, and I regard him as one of the most original, creative, and constructive thinkers of his generation. To be quite frank and outspoken, as one has to be in such cases, the greatest drawback in Devereux's career has been the fact that he is, in my opinion, somewhat of a genius, and certainly he has made for himself and was given that reputation by his friends."[11] An impressive imprimatur. An apprenticeship under any one of these towering figures of twentieth-century intellectual life would have been enough to secure one's academic credentials.

After studying mathematical physics with Marie Curie and Jean Perrin at the Sorbonne, Devereux was drawn to the anthropology then being taught at the Musée d'ethnographie du Trocadéro by Mauss, Lévy-Bruhl, and Rivet. By 1931 Devereux had earned a diploma from the Institut d'ethnologie and graduated from the École des langues orientales, where he studied Malay. He had, in effect, completed the three-year coursework required for these degrees in two years. What he remembered most about these years of grueling study was the Saturday afternoon seminars Mauss held on ethnology at the Collège de France. Devereux was one of several foreign-born students in Mauss's care. Others included Alfred Métraux, Georges Bataille's close friend and a specialist in the Indigenous cultures of South America, and Anatole Lewitsky, a specialist in Siberian shamanism who founded the resistance Groupe du musée de l'Homme during the Second World War (for which he was killed by firing squad in 1942).[12] Like the works of Métraux and Lewitsky (and Bataille, for that matter), Mauss's writings on sacrifice, animism, and potlatch had a profound influence on Devereux. If such archaic subjects were good enough for Mauss, they were good enough for him. In the summer of 1932 he graduated from the school of Durkheim and Mauss and earned a bachelor's degree from the Sorbonne for his study of ethnology, literature, and the history of religions.

Devereux's next big move was to the University of California, Berkeley, where Mauss and Rivet had arranged for him to study with the leading American authority on cultural anthropology, Alfred L. Kroeber. The dean of anthropology at Berkeley, Kroeber was a former student of Franz Boas and the author of *Handbook of the Indians of California* (1925). It was under Kroeber's direction that Devereux turned his attention from French Indochina to the American Southwest. After several extended field seasons among the Mohave in Parker, Arizona, Devereux was awarded a doctorate on December 20, 1935, for his "original research in anthropology." His dissertation, titled "Sexual Life of the Mohave Indians," was a groundbreaking study of the sexual attitudes and behaviors of a single Indigenous people. Thus, trained on two continents by two of the most eminent minds in anthropology, Devereux became a distinguished ethnographer in his own right. But his intellectual formation did not end there: In June 1939 he was appointed a research fellow in sociology at Harvard University, where he learned, from Parsons and Sorokin this time, how to root his social theories in hard empirical data. All the while, Devereux remained a Maussian. On November 7, 1938, he wrote to his former teacher: "You taught me much more than the facts. You taught me the art of drawing something from the facts . . . I earned my spurs under your excellent leadership."[13]

Given this illustrious intellectual training, a word needs to be said about the sense of homelessness that pervaded Devereux's life. Born in 1908, Devereux was a child of the century; he was also a man of exile—which, in the twentieth century, often amounted to the same thing. His life history is a story of vagabondage, of wandering from place to place without secure residence or employment. Rarely was he able to live and work in one place for very long. His personal letters suggest that he often felt like he didn't belong and wasn't appreciated; he believed forces were at work that prevented him from putting down roots, that gave him a sense of non-belonging. For example, because of the xenophobic legislation that followed the Alexandre Stavisky affair, Devereux couldn't find a post in France after he completed his PhD in 1935; so he was forced to remain in the United States, where he stayed for nearly thirty years. Displaced time and again, he was one of a myriad of uprooted people in the twentieth century. His first experience of displacement came when he was only ten years old. In 1919, with the demise of the Austro-Hungarian Empire after the First World War, he and his hometown abruptly became Romanian. Lugoj was ceded to the kingdom of Romania, and Devereux saw everything from street signs to history books suddenly change.

It has been written that "Georges Devereux went through two names, two religions, five disciplines, and many marriages."[14] But that doesn't capture the half of it. Wandering for years without a land to call his own, everything about Devereux's life was transient—a fact that helps explain the rigor of his weighty writings. It's true that along the way he became fluent in several languages, including Hungarian, Romanian, French, German, English, and Malay, and learned a smattering of Mohave. His experience as an émigré and with émigrés surely shaped his attention to social and cultural factors in mental health. First by necessity and then by choice, Devereux was a lifelong observer of cultures other than his own. His was the kind of life that is often called cosmopolitan. But that contemporary label misses the uncertainty and precarity and lack of belonging of those denied the right of rootedness. Not until Devereux returned to France in the last two decades of his life did he find secure employment and a permanent residence. Ever the uprooted émigré, Devereux described having spent "nearly forty years in outer limbo."[15]

There's a photograph that perfectly captures Devereux's vagabondage. In it, the French ethnographer is leaning against a large rock in California's Mojave Desert, reputedly the very core of desolation. Standing in some of the most arid country in the United States, Devereux doesn't look particularly robust; his bulging shirt pockets seem as if they might topple his wiry frame—at five feet ten inches, he weighed 130 pounds. He's got on the standard ethnographic attire: large hat, long-sleeved shirt (with those brimming pockets), Sam Browne belt, Norwegian calf boots, and a bandanna tied around his neck. It is an image of an ethnographer at the ready, to be sure. Yet it's also a snapshot of a life, not just an occupation. It tells the story of a social scientist searching for a place to call his own, and Devereux would have been the first to admit that rapid cultural changes often entail great psychological difficulties. Freud had got it wrong, Devereux argued—and not for the only time: Homeostasis and the desire for stability were not internal compulsions toward death; they were processes that perpetuated life.[16] It was only natural, then, that Devereux wanted to be among the autochthonous, that he sought out the one thing he never knew—a living community whose ancestors had inhabited a place since time immemorial.

My study of primitivism in postwar French thought thus turns to an intellectual whose extraordinary breadth was twofold: Devereux ranged across an unrivaled intellectual territory during a personal history of deracination. Only by examining the discrepancy between the solid-granite foundation of his intellect and the uncertain, uprooted realities of his life is it possible to understand Devereux's remarkable adventure in the archaic.

Sand, Sex, and Civilization: The Early Mohave Writings

Before the Colorado River bends upstream at Lake Mead, it passes through the Parker and Mohave Valleys. The Mohave, who have lived along the banks of the lower reaches of the Colorado since ancient times, are a people of the Yuman tribes. Never very large in number, the River Yumans—the Cocopa, Halchidhoma, Mohave, and Yuma—live in scattered small groups ranging over arid deserts and fertile river terraces. Surrounded by a vast desert, they have always depended on the river that Kroeber called "one of the great streams of the continent" and that today separates Arizona from California.[17] The shores of this Nile of the American Southwest are surrounded by high mesas, vast plateaus, barren mountains, and sand—lots of sand. The region's layered rock formations are enchanting and world-renowned: It is a special thrill to feel the touch of deep time in these geological marvels formed over durations too long to fathom. In this harsh and indifferent land, the petrified bedrock is dotted with cacti and traversed by paths that wind their way around sheer rock cliffs. Traveling these dry paths, you may discover an ancient pictograph hiding under a rocky outcropping, or you might look south to Yuma and see waves of sand rolling into the distance. This is the sense one gets in the region—that there is time enough and room enough. More often, though, what's most keenly felt is not painted deserts or infinite horizons, but the burning heat. From Parker to the jagged peaks of Needles, a vast desert scorches under a fierce sun.

But this wild corner of the American Southwest, which Simone de Beauvoir called "the very heart of hell," contains more than unbearable heat and deep-rooted cacti; it bears the stamp of a distinct civilization.[18] By training and by profession, Devereux was more concerned with living cultures than with timeless landscapes. Fortunately for the historian, Devereux's dogged Mohave orientation means that his imposing theories were rooted in a living *paysage*, however hardened by the sun. That the American Southwest had pride of place in Devereux's thought is made plain across his Mohave writings, the bulk of which were published between 1948 and 1951. It is too little recognized that Devereux's ethnopsychiatry, with its intricate web of theoretical associations, pulsated with the living warmth of real persons.[19] Everywhere in Devereux's ethnopsychiatry we see the robust, Rabelaisian shaman Hivsu Tupoma (Dan Lamont), dressed in denim with hat in hand. Attentive readers will find amid Devereux's writings the tall, intelligent interpreter Hama Utce (Agnes Savilla), wearing a long skirt, her hair parted down the middle.[20] Having come to Parker from Paris, Devereux was for them a piece of France. As for Devereux himself, he found in the Mohave a society driven by a different set of mores and morals than those he had found in Europe. Under a different, more colorful sky, he discovered the coexistence of the mercurial and the persistent, of generous excess and petrified stolidity.

Perplexingly, this vast desert was a congenial location for the existence of a generous society: "Generosity to the point of wastefulness is one of the cardinal virtues of Mohave culture." And again, Devereux observed, "Mohave custom requires the individual to be generous to the point of wastefulness."[21] The anthropologist's descriptions of reciprocal gift giving recalls another French ethnographer of expenditure, Devereux's mentor and the author of *The Gift*, Mauss. To mix freely and share generously were not just cultural preferences—they were an economic imperative in this luminous desert. But for Devereux, the Southwestern Indians' emphasis on reciprocal social relations was grounded in something just as primal as the individual's desire for self-preservation: the community's desire for cultural persistence. And ensuring cultural continuity was indeed "among the most fundamental values of Mohave culture."[22] In a place way off the beaten track, in a barren desert with few resources, you would expect to find a people preoccupied with material property. Yet, if anything, the reverse was true. The Mohave were entirely unmoved by currents of material progress. *Homo economicus* had no place deep in Mohave country: "This writer, for one, cannot see how the Mohave could be made money-conscious and avaricious, because it would destroy the very foundations of their culture."[23] Just as in the historic depths of the French Southwest, bourgeois acquisitiveness and possessive individualism were not to be found in this American *Sud-Ouest*. And the Mohave had a traditionally intense love for their ancestral homeland, "comparable to the fanatical love of European peasants for their acres." The peoples of these two Southwests were, in Devereux's words, "brothers under the skin."[24]

Mohave homes offer a telling example. They consist of four makeshift wooden poles arranged to make a rectangular frame of around twenty-five feet. In the middle of the home is a chimney, and outside, a ladder leading up to a flat, thatched roof made of arrowweed. Extending from one wall is a large lean-to shade, creating a covered porch where men, women, and children crowd to escape the sun's heat. The door to the house, which always faces south (not for cosmogonic reasons but to keep out the winds blowing from the north), opens onto a floor of soft sand. Houses are often grouped together in small settlements across the Parker and Mohave Valleys. To ensure cultural continuity and safeguard their traditional way of life, these homes were burned to the ground after their primary occupants died. In addition to cremating the deceased on a blazing pyre, Mohave funerary ceremonies included setting the deceased's home on fire and burning all their possessions with it. The Mohave even stripped themselves of garments associated with the deceased and threw these onto the blaze, too. Mohave mourning rites were typical of their attitude toward accumulation—a particularly poignant example of the relationship between cultural continuity and what Bataille called "unproductive expenditure." That these conflagrations ensured cultural survival was especially confounding to white America, where actions were habitually measured by how much profit they might yield. Yet, in the harshest of environments, the Mohave followed their time-honored strategy of survival: They instituted a disgust of material gain to safeguard against cultural loss.

Whether they were rooted in the prehistoric, the provincial, or the indigenous, primitivist critiques of postwar society employed some version of Ferdinand Tönnies's well-known gemeinschaft-gesellschaft distinction.[25] Societies of the gemeinschaft type consisted of extended families that were closely integrated and cohesive, whereas in gesellschaft-type societies the familial unit was conjugal, nuclear, and segregated from society at large. Devereux employed this famous distinction from German sociology throughout his Mohave writings. Occidental societies tended to minimize communal relationships and stress relations between men and the objects they accumulate, whereas so-called archaic societies like the Mohave devoted their affective energies to cultural passions and wider kinship relations. Socialization and secure belonging, in other words, were ingrained in Mohave society. The result was that the individual Mohave was "safely anchored to the bedrock of the social group," Devereux wrote. "In groups of the *gemeinschaft* type individuals do not rise and fall singly within the social structure, but participate in the varying fortunes of their kin, and of the tribe as a whole." The diffuse nature of Mohave socialization was learned early, often, and in "the workshop of daily interaction."[26] The Mohave's socialization was linked to the survival of their nation and the persistence of the culture they held dear. There were instances enough in which reciprocity solved many a Mohave social and cultural problem.

Devereux identified a high degree of socialization throughout Mohave culture, from etiquette to child-rearing. Mohave sociability manifested itself in a variety of ways: The Mohave were fairly unbuttoned, they lived "with a Gascon flourish," they burned the candle at both ends, and they tended to ignore outbursts of temper and to delight in unrestrained speech. Western culture was far less obstinate and frank, or so it seemed by comparison. Examining Mohave etiquette, Devereux observed that good manners were synonymous with communality. Guided by the principle of reciprocity, the Mohave were fond of spontaneous and excessive generosity. It was one reason, Kroeber noted, that the Mohave "were little interested in trade."[27] Their diffuse brand of socialization was also apparent in child-rearing. Early on the Mohave encouraged children to turn their attention outward and invest their energies in the social group rather than in themselves and their immediate family. Devereux called this early socialization of Mohave children a "singularly happy combination of home-rearing and nursery-rearing systems."[28] As you might expect, he hastened to compare the Mohave's distribution of the libido over the social body with the socialization typical of Western societies. *Égoïsme à deux* (when two people are bound tightly together because of mutual deprivation; in other words, when two people are alone together) and the inward-looking nuclear family amounted to an "infantile" failure to shift the libido position beyond the boundaries of one's immediate family. And while life among the Mohave was no libidinal utopia, the reason for their emphasis on socialization was clear—a Mohave child represented the tribe's future. Children, they knew, were the means by which the Mohave's cherished values would survive.[29]

The Mohave way of life, about which most of us know nothing, was of more than just academic interest. "Modern" society could learn a thing or two from the Mohave, the Maussian anthropologist insisted. The message runs like a thread through Devereux's writings after the Second World War.

Throughout the postwar period, he maintained that a thorough accounting of Mohave culture in action offered a wellspring of cultural insights. For those discontent with modern Western society, "archaic" cultures like the Mohave seemed an attractive alternative to their own culture of rampant production and consumption. Like his fellow would-be primitivist reformers, Devereux sought to reinvigorate Western society with a supposedly archaic culture. The Mohave, he suggested, exemplified the simple generosity, spontaneity, cohesion, and cultural continuity characteristic of a mature and healthy civilization. There was something more humane about Mohave mores, and so this dry corner of the American Southwest deserved a serious listen. To be sure. But didn't writers who assumed the right to speak for American Indians risk perpetuating the white man's entitlement to expropriate everyone and everything else? Can't enthusiastic identification and romantic idealization be as much of an insult as demonization?[30]

Not one to shy away from controversy, Devereux turned to Native sexuality. His Mohave writings remain one of the most comprehensive studies of Indigenous sexuality ever written. From his 1935 doctoral dissertation, "Sexual Life of the Mohave Indians," to his 1961 masterwork in primitive psychiatry, *Mohave Ethnopsychiatry*, Devereux recorded the sexual attitudes and practices of the desert tribe that straddled the lower reaches of the Colorado River. "It's safe to call Mr. Devereux the 'Indian Kinsey,'" the *Los Angeles Times* reported in 1950.[31] Sexuality permeated Mohave life, and it was an ever-present theme in Devereux's work. Since sexuality is intimately tied to morals and values, sexual mores are perhaps the single most important behavior patterned by any culture—as any simon-pure Freudian would argue. When it comes to sex, what is celebrated or curtailed depends not on psychological mechanisms, which are probably the same everywhere, but on what "crops the soil of culture produces."[32] Devereux approached Mohave sexuality from the point of view of the social sciences—more specifically, from the double vantage point of ethnography and psychoanalysis. Across the 1950s, he explained Mohave sexual behavior as a Freudian ethnopsychiatrist would, with reference to both psychoanalytic theory and local ways of life.

How did Devereux interpret Mohave sexual customs? Perhaps unsurprisingly, he declared Mohave sexuality guilt-free and nonaggressive. "In brief," Devereux concluded, "sex, to the Mohave, is something very natural, pleasant, not very important emotionally, easily obtainable and just a bit insipid."[33] At times all he could seem to talk about was the Mohave's sexual spontaneity. He spoke endlessly of how the young were urged to enjoy themselves, how sex was surrounded by levity instead of prohibitions, and how the open banks of the Colorado were a favorite trysting place. He was not the first to discover in a distant land an unfettered pleasure principle. In France, that honor goes to Denis Diderot, whose *Supplement to the Voyage of Bougainville* (1772) imagined the sexual activity of Tahitians as free from all guilt and aggression.[34] In any case, because of their easy attitude toward sex, the Mohave were notoriously uninhibited and outspoken about sexual desires, relations, and positions. In fact, this frankness was why Kroeber sent Devereux to study this searing corner of the American Southwest in the first place. With its sex-positive culture, the Colorado River Indian Reservation was an ideal setting to learn about Native sexual practices. For Devereux, that the Mohave spoke of sex freely, incessantly, and with levity was evidence of their sexual enlightenment. But wasn't this something more as well—namely, another instance of gemeinschaft-type community, of the reciprocal give-and-take of a mature society?

Decades earlier Kroeber had noted that "there seems to be no serious criticism of either men or women on the score of conduct dictated by sexual feeling."[35] The result, Devereux would come to add, was that Mohave sexuality was untrammeled by social constraint and the censorship of the superego. Only those blinded by puritanism or talk of "loose savages," he argued, would label the freedom and frequency of Mohave sexuality as overactive. Rather than diagnose Mohave sexuality with pseudoscientific terms such as "precocious" or "immoderate," Devereux emphasized the link between sexual behavior and sound ego development. The most remarkable example of this was Devereux's belief that the latency period—the lengthy period in childhood when sexuality is not yet developed or manifest—didn't exist among the Mohave. Because of their tolerant attitude toward infantile sexuality and because they did not forcibly repress the sexual feelings of the young, reaction formations against unconscious hostilities toward sex were "entirely unnecessary."[36] A passage from "Mohave Indian Autoerotic Behavior" (1950) illustrates just how radical Devereux's interpretation was on this score: "The data just presented cast additional doubt upon the validity of the more and more frequently challenged dogma that the latency period is a universal human phenomenon, and a natural stage in the psychosexual development of *Homo sapiens*. In light of anthropological data, it now seems legitimate to say that what stands in need of an explanation is not the absence, but the occurrence of a latency period."[37]

The Mohave used communal observances to encourage smooth sexual transitions. Devereux described how the tribe organized initiation ceremonies to publicly acknowledge an individual's new sexual status or orientation. A time and place were set, word was sent to various settlements, and people were invited to an early morning gathering. The ceremony itself did not initiate the change, obviously; the point of the gathering was to accustom everyone to the change. For example, a relaxed rite of passage might be arranged to initiate a recently transitioned transsexual into the community. During this ceremony, the transsexual "assumed a name befitting a person of the opposite sex." Naturally, they resented afterward being called by their former name or pronouns. As a society that had little or no objection to either homosexuality or transsexuality, the Mohave believed that public ceremonies such as these were an important social sanctioning of what was expected and inevitable. These communal observances were part of a culture of compassion and tolerance. And they were casual, for ritualism rested lightly on Mohave culture. In fact, one reason Devereux was attracted to the Mohave was that they tended to prune all anxiety and tension from their ceremonies. Mohave rites were much closer to festive games than to the religious rituals that Bataille imagined took place in the prehistoric depths of provincial France.[38]

Eventually, predictably, Devereux turned his study of Indigenous sexuality into a critique of Western societies. Comparing the generous give-and-take of Mohave sexuality to the intense object cathexis common in France and white America, Devereux concluded that Mohave sexual mores fostered healthier, more mature relationships. By "intense object cathexis" Devereux meant the highly individualized love characteristic of Western gesellschaft societies. Think of Stendhal's crystallizations, Gustave Flaubert's fixations, or the charged *égoïsme à deux* on full display in tales such as *Romeo and Juliet* or *Tristan and Isolde*—stories that, when Devereux told them around the fire, elicited visible disgust from his Mohave audience. That someone would carry out such amorous schemes or could have such an intense fixation on one other person, to the exclusion of all others, was incomprehensible; and that a culture would celebrate such stories and such asocial libidinal bonds was detestable. "An over-implementation of 'romantic love' is beyond the scope of Mohave patterns," Devereux remarked.[39] Likewise, sadism and masochism were so completely alien to the Mohave that after he explained what these words meant to his chief female informant, she replied, "We are not that civilized." Absent from Devereux's descriptions of Mohave sexuality is anything resembling the charged intensity Bataille had in mind when he spoke of sexual taboos and transgressions. Like Mohave rites, sex was more akin to a lighthearted dance than a grave sacrifice—although, given recent "progress" in the American Southwest, Aphrodite, who was conceived in sea-foam, had lost much of her levity.[40]

Devereux underscored two other long-kept customs of the Southwest antithetical to Western mores: The Mohave did not perform wedding ceremonies, and couples could separate whenever either partner was so inclined.

These unions and breakups did not have the humiliation of a moral Canossa. Because of this, the Mohave did not discriminate against unmarried mothers or illegitimate children as such. He went further and declared that the diffuse libidinal bonds inculcated by the Mohave avoided a host of affective disorders and complexes. There was thus a craftiness to Devereux's Mohave writings: Under the guise of obtaining ethnopsychiatric data from non-Western societies, he crafted a radical critique of French and American society. The importance of Mohave culture, it seems, extended from ethnopsychiatry to social criticism.

Devereux, who was himself as unashamed as a coyote, maintained that Mohave attitudes toward sex were the opposite of the sexual puritanism typical of Western societies. He spoke of puritanical societies with the same biting criticism Voltaire reserved for religion. Puritanical societies (Devereux had in mind the United States and, to a lesser extent, France) moralized sexuality and turned most sexual activity into a transgression of one kind or another. Such moral gravity led to feelings of guilt, anxiety, aggression, and abjection. As a consequence, where one should find intimacy and communion, one found instead aggression or abject submission, and often an admixture of the two. Devereux liked to point out how the Mohave described the way one's eyes sparkled after sex, whereas Westerners spoke of sadness and individuation after the sexual communion that Bataille called *la petite mort* (the little death). In light of his Mohave data, Devereux argued that it was not the human animal who saddens after sex, it was only the human animal in puritanical society who saddens after sex. *Post coitum omne animal triste* (all animals are sad after intercourse), as the Galenic saying goes, was a societal truth, not a universal one—a somewhat cynical but not inaccurate view of Western sexuality.

One example of this puritanical cocktail of aggression and abjection was adolescent female sexuality. In an article for *Les temps modernes*, Devereux reasoned that adolescent girls in puritanical societies didn't just learn how to vigilantly guard their sexual purity; they also learned that sex was a vehicle with which to offend moral sensibilities—in fact, the cultural lesson was that sex was *the* avenue through which to act out and assail social values. Therefore, adolescent girls in puritanical societies didn't take part in sexual activity primarily for enjoyment or intimacy. Most adolescent promiscuity, Devereux argued, wasn't actually about sex at all; it was a pattern of misconduct encouraged, ironically, by the sexual puritanism that condemned it. In short, sex was a "signal symptom." Devereux's point was that by surrounding sexual activity with so many prohibitions and condemnations, puritanical societies taught their children that sex was an occasion for expressing frustration, manifesting hostility, and feeling guilty. Nothing could be more degrading to human sexuality, he concluded, than overlaying it with an inflexible code of conduct. And nothing, he added, was more certain to turn sex into a neurotically motivated act.[41]

In this river enclave inside an ever-expanding puritanical society, Devereux found a culture that avoided many of the pathological disturbances that surrounded sex in the West. But he had not exhausted his comparative cultural criticism. Next, he brought the social value of Mohave sexuality into focus. Mohave sexual ethics were best described as noninterference. This Native culture's good-humored acceptance of a variety of instinctual gratifications meant that women, homosexuals, and transsexuals had far greater freedom than was usual in the West.[42] The Mohave permitted a range of sexualities, and not only in the dark groves of Corydon or the dim cabarets of Sappho. Through sexuality, the Mohave instilled not only a diffuse socialization, but the opportunity to practice tolerance toward others. This was because Mohave sexual ethics started and ended with intimations of the body. In the 1930s and '40s, Devereux discovered among the Mohave not a savage or simple-minded sexuality, but one that embraced the organic needs and desires of human beings. Mohave sexuality surely offended bourgeois tastes, but it didn't offend the body—and, in the long run, the psychological ramifications of offending the body are much graver than the social ramifications of a tarnished respectability. For Devereux, this was just one more piece of evidence that this Native community in the American Southwest was healthier and more mature than French or American society. An archaic island of tolerance and permissiveness, Mohave country maintained long-held customs that offered a viable alternative to an ever-encroaching sea of puritanism.[43]

A Dream Culture: The Late Mohave Writings

Mohave riches lay not in commodities but in dreams. Mohave material culture may have been simple, but its mental culture was well-developed. The Mohave didn't dream better or differently, obviously; but a preoccupation with dreams was the special foundation of their cultural life, so much so that Kroeber—who was as sensitive and careful a fieldworker as Devereux—had labeled the Mohave a "dream culture." "There is no people," he wrote, "whose activities and culture are more shaped by dreaming than the Mohave."[44] According to Mohave tradition, all knowledge, no matter how assiduously acquired, was barren until it was dreamed: "So as you dream, thus you are." Mohave customs were learned, of course—no one would deny that; but they were fully acquired only when dreamed. What was mastered in waking life must be actualized in dreams. Dream experience, in other words, validated lived experience. Compare this insistence on the significance of dreams with the Mohave's utter lack of regard for material culture, and you will see one reason this far-off corner of the American Southwest elicited praise from a postwar primitivist like Devereux. The restless pursuit of growth in postwar society confirmed Devereux's conviction that he had to look elsewhere for social alternatives. And the Mohave offered him a vision of the kind of human culture largely unexplored by Western societies: a society in which dream life, not things, was what mattered. Hunting for data on Indigenous sexuality, Devereux found what he could have only dreamed of: a Native culture that emphasized dreams, encouraged their narration, and had built up a great number of psychotherapeutic techniques around dream interpretation.

Where a culture values dreams, ethnopsychiatrists should keep their ears open. It was widely believed that of all the Southwestern Indians, the Mohave had the most appreciable insight into the nature and role of dreams. They believed that dreams were real adventures of the soul—so much so, in fact, that certain dreams were thought to cause illness or death. From a cultural point of view, this belief was unremarkable. What struck Devereux, however, was how thoroughly psychological processes had been integrated into Mohave society. Dreams, and the shamans who interpreted them, were the active distinctiveness of Mohave culture. In 1900 Freud had written in *The Interpretation of Dreams* that "the interpretation of dreams is the royal road to a knowledge of the unconscious activities of the mind." Modifying the psychoanalyst's memorable phrase a bit, Devereux stated that dream life was the royal road to unlocking the mysteries of Mohave culture. After several field seasons on the banks of the Colorado River, Devereux was convinced that Mohave dream culture was the finest, most valuable survival in that wild corner of the Southwest. And so he spent the next two decades helping his readers understand Mohave shamanism. We can only be thankful, he added, that despite the pauperizing effect of the American economy and the ongoing degradation of acculturation, the Mohave had successfully passed down their dream culture from generation to generation.

"Acculturation" is one term for the past and ongoing crimes against American Indians. Cultural contact is of course the rule of civilization, but acculturation refers to the breakup of a people's culture by the force of an alien dominant culture. "Human societies are sometimes negatively influenced by their neighbors" was the first and most understated line of Devereux's "Antagonistic Acculturation" (1943).[45] All along the river, communities that had once owned the Earth had fallen into the humiliating condition of hangers-on. Sufficiently Americanized to lose an intimate knowledge of ancient ways, the Mohave were in a crisis situation, as were the other River Yumans. New cultural elements had been added, while preexisting traditions were curtailed or eliminated altogether: "By the time this pressure is likely to relax—if, indeed, it will ever relax—most primitives will have become acculturated, and priceless and irreplaceable cultural material will have been lost."[46] There is no such thing as a pure, unadulterated culture, but there was resistance to rapid social and cultural change. Devereux, who was opposed to colonialism in all its guises, called this defense against annihilation "antagonistic acculturation." Antagonistic acculturation was a multifaceted means to maintain cultural continuity in the face of constant encroachment. Understandably, "each group has a jealous regard for its own ethnic distinctiveness and cultural autonomy, which is clearly reflected in resistance."[47] When isolation proved impossible (and, in the long run, it is always impossible), the Mohave responded by borrowing selectively, limiting knowledge to certain cultural items, reverting to traditions that existed before contact took place, and evolving new cultural patterns deliberately at odds with the intruding culture. As irrational as it may seem to the colonizer, to reject or severely distort seemingly innocuous new customs is vital to continued cultural patrimony. The solidarity of past and present is inscribed in the humblest of customs.

It would be an understatement to say that the study of myth was a significant feature of French thought after the Second World War. Not a few French intellectuals were fascinated by the timeless myths of so-called primitives. Intellectuals of a structuralist orientation brought an almost mathematical eye to examining the affinities between myth, exogamy, and exchange. Though not as brilliant a mythology as that of the Hopi, Mohave myths possess the kind of structural and literary qualities that would have appealed to many a mid-century French intellectual. Mohave myths like the one about the first god, Matavilya, contain an elaborate cosmogony about a primordial past. Despite their factual air, most of them contain no recollections of actual historic events or persons. Told in an "almost ritualized style," they have an amazing timelessness and universal validity; they bring about "the utter obliteration of time"—this, too, would have appealed to structuralists like Lévi-Strauss.[48] There was less in Mohave mythology, however, for those fond of the concrete and wary of the highly ritualized. The formal pattern of Mohave myths might have attracted more than a few of his former classmates at the Institut d'ethnologie, but for Devereux their lack of historical grounding and everyday experience was a sin of omission. So in 1948 he turned to a much less formal and far more historical branch of Mohave storytelling called Coyote tales.

More aligned with Devereux's passions were tales of Coyote, a catchall genre for a wide range of folkloric stories much closer to Mohave lifeways than myths. In one of Devereux's most suggestive articles, "Mohave Coyote

Tales" (1948), he proposed that if creation myths are to culture what early memories are to individuals, then Coyote tales are to culture what yesterday's dream is to the dreamer. That is to say, the truth of Coyote tales was the truth of dreams. Coyote tales seized on local occurrences in the same way dreams seize on what Freud called "the residue of the previous day." "It is probable," Devereux wrote, "that concrete incidents are transformed into myths or tales through a process resembling 'dream-work,' by means of which concrete events and basic drives are transmuted into dreams."[49] He would have found it easy to obtain evidence of Coyote tales, since they were often told casually at night around a low fire. Humorous and bellicose, Coyote tales were like nursery tales, but with a Mohave twist. The anthropomorphic animals of these tales had more than a touch of the obscene, and Coyote tales had enough sex talk to stifle most evening yawns. Full of foul language and Mohave customs, Coyote tales laid bare a carnal knowledge for Native and ethnographer alike. Or, as Devereux liked to put it, they were "an expression of id strivings untrammeled by the censorship of the superego."[50]

The more important point, I think, is that although there was a good deal of sex in Coyote tales, the Mohave didn't disguise or symbolize any of it. The sex in Coyote tales—as in life—was neither highly charged nor veiled by symbols. Eliade's understanding of primitive sexuality was not that of the Mohave. "It must be remembered that for man in archaic society, sexuality always conforms to a cosmological dimension," he wrote. "For such men, there is no 'pure' sexual life, free from symbolic implications."[51] Mohave sexuality, on the contrary, was transparent and expressed in only a "flimsy armor of fiction." In Coyote tales, "the latent sexual content of dreams and of folklore alike is barely disguised by a meager, obvious, and conventionalized set of symbols." Although sexuality often plays a large role in Coyote tales, it need not: "It is safe to say that the manifest content of Mohave folk tales, like the manifest content of song cycles and myths, does not revolve around sexuality in the traditional sense of the word." Societies that find it necessary to express sexuality chiefly with a highly elaborate camouflage—that is, societies that speak of sex incessantly but do so only through symbols and allusions—are societies that have a high level of sexual repression. Unrepressed things are rarely symbolized. "The tendency to assign an important role to eroticism and sexual symbolism," wrote Devereux, "provide us with a rough, though reasonably adequate, measure of the depth and intensity of sexual repression in a given culture."[52] To their credit, the Mohave were not very good at insinuating sexuality, an incompetence that Devereux attributed to their high degree of sexual freedom and tolerance. Modern Western societies, however, coated sexuality in symbolism—symbols were stacked upon allusions until they were piled high enough to match the depth of sexual repression.

But there was more to these fantastic tales than sex talk. Looser and less formal than the tribe's cosmogonic myths, Coyote tales were full of Native customs and historical events. Devereux found that Mohave cultural history—everything from shamanism and mourning to dietary habits and household routines—was sufficiently well-preserved in these amusing, anthropomorphic, and obscene stories. These tales were examples of cultural history avant la lettre, although their telling need not be letter-perfect: "The spirit was stable, but the letter was flexible."[53] To Devereux, the tales were essential to any broad understanding of Mohave culture. It often happened that Coyote tales absorbed Mohave history to such an extent that the ethnographer had a hard time differentiating between the folkloric telling and actual historical events. What better way for a dream culture to preserve its customs and history than in dreamlike tales? Thus, Coyote tales opened horizons onto Mohave mores and ethics. And Devereux was the first to see in Coyote tales a special window on the survival of long-held Native customs. The ultimate significance of Coyote tales rested in the way they encouraged cultural continuity and passed Native mores down from generation to generation.

To return to the main subject: According to Mohave custom, shamanic powers must be dreamed, as I have said. "All students of Mohave culture report that magical powers, and the knowledge of the myths, skills, and songs pertaining to them, are supposed to be acquired in dreams." And, as Kroeber wrote in 1948, "the Mohave validate what happens in their lives by referring it to their dreams."[54] If dreams pervaded Mohave cultural life, then their society was steeped in shamanism. Devereux saw at once that the vocation of shaman was reserved for atypical Mohave personalities. Shamans, who were never very numerous, were those called to dream vividly, interpret dreams frequently, and be intermediaries between spiritual and physical worlds. To be a shaman is an honor one seldom seeks but must accept.

With Mohave shamanism persisting well into the twentieth century, Devereux had the opportunity to discover the true significance of Mohave dream culture. Like everything else in this land far off the beaten path, the shaman's ability to heal was learned through a long apprenticeship, though it was believed to be acquired only in dreams. It's worth remembering that fascination with dreams was not limited to shamans alone; all Mohave were invested in their dream culture, and shamanism was a touchstone of tribal life.[55] Archaic cultures provided the climate for the shamanic style, yet it was shamans alone whose sacred domain was dream interpretation.

Thus, the trail again leads back to dreams, this time to the unusual dreams of the shaman. Shamans gained psychotherapeutic power in and through dreams. It often happened that a Mohave shaman used a combination of jimsonweed and song cycles originating in dreams to cure illnesses such as diarrhea, sadness, or snake bites. And it was widely believed (to great therapeutic effect, it should be said) that if a shaman dreamed it, it must be true. "A good many primitives do not differentiate too sharply between what was dreamed and what was thought or experienced," Devereux wrote.[56] But instead of drawing from this a determination about how rudimentary Mohave civilization was, he asked a series of more important questions: What did shamans typically dream? How did they interpret these dreams? And how did dream interpretation inform their psychiatric practice? For Devereux, it was Mohave cultural tenets that must be understood, not where this culture ranked in some presumed hierarchy.[57] Though often overlooked, Devereux's work on Mohave shamanism was crucial to the development of ethnopsychiatry. His Mohave writings set the stage for the discipline's most formative controversy: the postwar debate over the mental status of the Native shaman.

The problem of the shaman was one of the great intellectual controversies in the social sciences after 1945. Anthropologists, psychiatrists, and historians on both sides of the Atlantic argued about the mental health and social status of primitive healers. "The crux of all arguments over cultural relativism," Devereux pointed out, "is invariably the problem of the shaman: Is the shaman crazy, or is he not?"[58] Shamanism thus found itself in the middle of new debates about cultural difference and old debates about the relationship between religion and neurosis. Cultural relativists such as Erwin Ackerknecht and Ruth Benedict said that shamans could not be psychically abnormal, for their whole lives were altogether socially acceptable and prestigious. "We cannot any longer regard as abnormal a person only on the basis of certain fixed symptoms, disregarding the historical and cultural place of this person," wrote Ackerknecht. "We can only regard as abnormal a person whose character reactions hinder social integration in a given period or society."[59] To Devereux, however, the assertion that medicine men were normal was tantamount to saying that they were impostors—which they were not, as a rule. Shamans were often bona fide neurotics and sometimes even borderline psychotics, he continued. Or else they were in temporary remission, which means they were not cured in the medical sense and were likely to relapse. Not one to soft-pedal the evidence, Devereux concluded that shamans were therefore both highly esteemed and mentally deranged. "Primitive" peoples themselves thought as much. As more than one Mohave put it, "All medicine men are crazy." And in Mohave parlance, "crazy" (*ya amoom*) means what it means to us: insane.⁶⁰

At the heart of the problem was the fact that few anthropologists were qualified to make psychiatric evaluations. Since most anthropologists had at most an amateur's understanding of mental illness as a black-or-white category, they failed to see what the trained clinician saw: the gradations and dynamic fluidity of symptoms. Devereux, on the other hand, was a certified psychiatrist and an experienced ethnographer, so he didn't attach much importance to certificates of sanity issued by anthropologists. Every anthropologist, it seemed, knew a sane shaman. "So did I," Devereux responded, "until one day, when under the influence of alcohol, he [Hivsu Tupoma] confessed to witchcraft and to incest with the ghost of his bewitched cousin. Then he suddenly did not seem sane at all."⁶¹ Shamanic practices were symptoms, which must periodically increase in number and intensity to prevent a relapse. With this, Devereux arrived at Kroeber's position: The shaman is a neurotic who uses socially sanctioned defenses against internal psychic tension.⁶² In other words, shamans are crazy, but they are fortunate to be crazy in societies that provide them *socially sanctioned* defenses to cope with their mental problems. The contrast with Western societies, where those with mental problems are left to improvise their own *socially penalized* defenses, was clear.

There is, moreover, a broader cultural lesson to be drawn from this dream-oriented desert tribe. For those not blinded by Eurocentrism, Mohave shamanism contains a moral about how to treat the mentally ill. As Devereux saw it, the archaic institution of shamanism allowed budding shamans to channel their neuroses in ways that were both socially acceptable and prestigious. Characteristically, he interpreted a shaman's wholehearted embrace of his or her new social role as evidence of the health and maturity of Mohave society. If the Mohave shaman was more or less neurotic, wasn't that all the more reason to celebrate the humanity of this far-flung Indigenous culture? And if not for this diagnosis, the notorious shaman-as-neurotic diagnosis Devereux made in *Normal and Abnormal* (1956), then how could one celebrate the Mohave for their social solution to the problem of psychopathological suffering?⁶³ In a word, if the Mohave shaman was neurotic, all the more reason to champion this supposedly archaic culture of the American Southwest. After all, ethnopsychiatrists couldn't have it both ways: They couldn't declare shamans "sane" and at the same time praise Native cultures for their humane acceptance of their "insane" members—although this logical contradiction didn't stop some of them from doing precisely that. Shamans fulfilled a significant role in Mohave society, but that didn't prove they were normal; it proved that Mohave culture was mature and humane.

The Path to a Modern Ethnopsychiatry

At 592 pages and with eight chapters, ten plates, and 140 case histories, *Mohave Ethnopsychiatry and Suicide* (1961) stands as Devereux's crowning achievement, the result of nearly three decades spent studying the dream culture and folk psychiatry of the Mohave. Published by the Bureau of American Ethnology, the book bears a subtitle, *The Psychiatric Knowledge and the Psychic Disturbances of an Indian Tribe,* suggesting its subject: The theories, diagnoses, and therapeutic practices that a single tribe—the Mohave—had developed to treat mental illness. Devereux described his book as "the first systematic study of the psychiatric theories and practices of a primitive tribe." *Mohave Ethnopsychiatry* did the kind of work that forced readers to reimagine "archaic" psychotherapy. The book was exhaustive; it contained a thorough account of the Mohave's elaborate and often objectively valid evolution in the realm of psychiatry. With its wealth of case histories, Devereux's magnum opus was a trove of Mohave beliefs and practices related to mental illness. It may have been read by only a few specialists, but *Mohave Ethnopsychiatry* remains a permanent record of "one early system of psychiatry."[64]

The goal of *Mohave Ethnopsychiatry* was threefold: to describe an early but elaborate folk psychiatry from the viewpoint of Native culture; to demonstrate the extensive congruence between modern and Mohave psychiatry; and, through a process of defamiliarization, to show how Mohave shamanism provided insight into the future of ethnopsychiatry. These objectives Devereux accomplished with the help of Mohave informants, several of whom were shamans who specialized in the tribe's psychiatry. Shamans were the first practitioners of psychotherapy, and theirs was an exceptional vocation, reserved for a select few. Thus, at the center of *Mohave Ethnopsychiatry* were several Mohave shamans Devereux had known since his first visit to the Colorado River Indian Reservation in 1932. Most notable among them was Hivsu Tupoma (whose name, translated literally, means "burnt raw"). Tupoma, also known as Dan Lamont (fig. 3.2), was Devereux's friend and most trusted shaman informant. A shaman in his mid-fifties in 1932, Tupoma was "a truly Rabelaisian character."[65] Big, boisterous, and with a gargantuan appetite, he was also friendly, tolerant, and compassionate toward the mentally ill. Devereux was intent on writing him into the history of psychiatry, much as Henri Ellenberger would later do for the patient Anna O.[66] If it was information about Mohave mental illness you were after, a shaman like Tupoma was the person to whom you would turn: "Illness is the business of the shaman," Devereux wrote. "Even in our society doctors would provide better psychiatric case histories than lawyers or engineers."[67] *Mohave Ethnopsychiatry* was

FIGURE 3.2. The shaman stares back. Hivsu Tupoma, masterly psychologist and Mohave cultural leader. Photograph A, plate 9 of George Devereux's *Mohave Ethnopsychiatry and Suicide* (Smithsonian Institution Press, 1961). Courtesy of the Smithsonian Libraries and Archives.

therefore both an account of Mohave cultural patterns and a glimpse into Devereux's relationships with his shaman informants. So, while it is a difficult book full of anthropological and psychoanalytic terminology, *Mohave Ethnopsychiatry* rested, like the rest of Devereux's oeuvre, on the warmth of human relationships.[68]

Mohave Ethnopsychiatry is a veritable handbook of Mohave psychiatry. It contains a detailed description of the Mohave's elaborate folk psychiatry that "could actually serve as a textbook from which budding Mohave shamans, preparing to specialize in psychiatry, could learn their craft."[69] The book was not an ethnography à la Kroeber (although it contained a wealth of anthropological data), nor was it a psychoanalytic anthropology à la Róheim (it didn't map Mohave mental illness into Freudian nosology, although it did suggest possible connections). Rather, *Mohave Ethnopsychiatry* was first and foremost a study of Mohave psychiatric beliefs and practices in their specific sociocultural setting. Early on, Devereux made the critical decision to follow Native diagnostics and treatments. His masterwork thus spoke in an Indigenous vocabulary and was organized around Mohave etiological terms. He was the first to do so: "To the best of my knowledge," Devereux wrote, "the only work grappling systematically with the problem of primitive diagnostic science is my study of Mohave ethnopsychiatry."[70]

Among the Mohave, Devereux documented a shamanic style that had persisted since time immemorial. Much had changed, however, in the years between the ethnographer's first season of fieldwork in 1932 and his last in 1951. In the early 1930s, Mohave shamanism was still alive, despite American acculturation. By mid-century, however, the Mohave were in crisis, and the future of Mohave shamanism was in doubt. The first half of the American twentieth century had brought rapid, cataclysmic change—"World's end! World's end!"—and so he described his *Mohave Ethnopsychiatry* as a kind of "psychiatric archaeology." In its pages he excavated "beliefs and data antedating reservation conditions and surviving despite reservation life."[71] Salvaging what had survived—it's a perfect distillation of the paradox of the postwar primitivists: celebrating cultural persistence on the one hand while protecting against imminent loss on the other. *Mohave Ethnopsychiatry* was therefore at once a recovery of a stubborn cultural survival and a printed bulwark against a looming disappearance.

Mohave Ethnopsychiatry was remarkable, but it wasn't as singular as Devereux made it out to be. Rather, it was part of an ongoing reevaluation of the prehistory of dynamic psychiatry. It was anthropologists who first presented shamanism from the Native point of view and showed how "primitive" psychiatries such as those of the Apache, Mohave, and Navaho were more sophisticated than had previously been believed. While Devereux was living among the Mohave, Morris Opler articulated the wisdom of Apache shamanism. After spending two years among the Chiricahua and Mescalero, he wrote: "I have tried to see Apache shamanism from the point of view of a Native, in an attempt to determine what functions, therapeutic or otherwise, the shaman may perform." He concluded that Apache shamans were good judges, adroit and circumspect, who recognized mental disturbances, carefully prescribed remedies, and succeeded in curing everything from slight tics to suicidal manias. Devereux and Opler were not alone. Alexander and

Dorothea Leighton, specialists in Navaho psychotherapy, shared their heretical, primitivist, antiprogressive stance.[72] By 1970 the Swiss-Canadian historian of psychiatry Henri Ellenberger could write with confidence that when it came to archaic psychotherapy, "Today we have reached another, more positive evaluation."[73] They all agreed that shamanic healing rites were an ancient laboratory for understanding and treating mental affliction.

Together these revisionists showed that the ancestry of dynamic psychiatry was full of shockingly correct insights. A simplistic pitting of Native wisdom against white blindness? Not exactly. Once ethnopsychiatrists had proudly reassessed psychiatry's prehistory, they made clear the undeniable difference between the preludes of science and science itself. Primitive psychiatry referred to supernatural forces to explain mental illness and abnormal behavior; modern psychiatry didn't. Like modern psychiatrists, Mohave shamans attributed psychological meaning to events and illnesses often and with great care; but unlike most modern practitioners, they believed in supernaturalistic powers. It was no small difference. Soberingly, Devereux stated that shamans were specialists, but they were not scientists. As a consequence, shamans—who had explored the depths of the psyche for millennia—may have been the ancestors of modern psychiatrists, but the scientific investigation of the unconscious was a fairly recent development. Many primitive psychiatric views were similar to modern psychiatric theories, but shamans had not developed a truly naturalistic branch of medicine. Devereux didn't celebrate primitive psychiatry because it was scientific; he knew that shamans' insights were the fruit of culture, not science. Primitive healing was the result of a living tradition concerned with cultural continuity and quite impervious to the vicissitudes of empirical experience.[74]

But the tendency of Mohave shamans to speculate on the supernatural sources of phenomena did not prevent them from being accurate. It was possible, in other words, that a culture-bound psychiatry like the Mohave's could be objectively valid. Whether it was a dammed-up libido, early sibling rivalry, or the importance of dream life, the Mohave got a lot right. And they got things right not because they believed in sorcery or soul loss or evil spirits, but because they located the site of the mental afflictions in the patient's psyche. "Thus, in a very genuine sense," Devereux argued, "the Mohave view mental disease as essentially an intrapsychic happening."[75] This is how Mohave shamans could have a truly psychological point of view while still clinging to supernaturalistic explanations. It is why Devereux's shaman informant, Tupoma, could believe in souls and still be an almost clinical observer of neurotic behavior. Nothing seems more foreign to modern psychiatry than the idea of a lost soul. Yet, as Devereux and Ellenberger both noted, don't modern psychiatrists say that a patient is alienated or estranged from themselves and then attempt to recover and restore the patient's ego? Perhaps the Mohave shaman's great virtue was that she possessed two tools crucial to psychiatric research: the ability to empathize with patients and the faculties to organize insights into a larger body of theory.[76]

For example, in *Mohave Ethnopsychiatry* Devereux showed that the Mohave theory concerning hystero-epileptic convulsions anticipated modern dynamic psychiatry. The Mohave believed that masturbation and meaningless fornication were unable to effectively discharge sexual tension. A sexual libido too long dammed up, the Mohave thought, would suddenly flood in and produce convulsive seizures. When masturbation and fornication were only *physical* gratifications, they failed to "obtain release" of the individual's psychosexual tension, regardless of whether they culminated in orgasm, hence the eventual appearance of convulsions as orgasm substitutes—all of which "is in harmony with modern psychoanalytic thought," Devereux noted. "Since it is a well-established fact that neither masturbation nor mere fornication ever culminates in a real orgasm, because—as a Mohave might express it—in neither of these (predominantly physiological) activities is there also coitus between the *souls* of the partners."[77] This insight into the psychodynamics of various sexual activities is one example of the Mohave's early but elaborate folk psychiatry. Yet the Mohave's acuity was not the result of scientific observation. Rather, their insight may well have emerged from seeing in the periodic floods of the Colorado River an illustration of a dammed-up vitality suddenly bursting forth. Therefore, the Mohave theory about hystero-epileptic convulsions was essentially correct, even though it was rooted in local culture, not positive science.

Still, such an extensive overlap of Mohave folk psychiatry and modern dynamic psychiatry needed explaining. The source of the congruence lies in the distinctive traits of Mohave culture, in particular the Southwestern Indians' preoccupation with dreams. The Mohave tended to psychologize the universe and link everything from everyday actions and Coyote tales to the psychodynamics of dreams. Since dreams were intimately tied to life, they ought to be remembered and treated with care. Over time, the tribe's familiarity with the world of dreams developed into a vocation (shamanism) that specialized in dream interpretation. If Mohave psychiatry is psychological like ours, Roger Bastide wrote, it is because they are a dream civilization.[78] With their obstinate respect for dreams, Mohave shamans were less like blind hens pecking about in the dark than wide-eyed coyotes following familiar psychological paths, albeit under a supernatural moonlight. But Mohave dream culture was not the only reason their shamanism seemed so fine and coherent to the occidental observer. This desert tribe's humanity toward the mentally afflicted was another reason they had developed an elaborate psychiatry. The Mohave, Devereux observed, possessed a genuine empathy toward strangers, the sick, and the mentally ill: "The Mohave who are greatly interested in the human being, in dreams, and other deep psychological processes and who are, moreover, generous and kind, have developed a complex 'psychiatry'— both as regards theory and therapy—and treat the insane with great kindness and tolerance."[79] Therefore, it was no accident that modern and Mohave psychiatry were so strikingly similar. The source of the congruence lay in the Mohave's dream culture and their inclusive humanity.

Let anyone look at the literature of the eighteenth and nineteenth centuries and they will see shamans depicted as credulous dupes naively confident in their own powers of persuasion. *Customs of the American Indians Compared with the Customs of Primitive Times* (1724), by Joseph-François Lafitau is a prime example. In his account of the Huron, Iroquois, and Algonquin, Lafitau, who is considered the father of French ethnology, described North American shamanism as a superstitious vestige, not unlike the persistent paganism of Western antiquity. Missionaries such as Lafitau liked to present little vignettes about the violence and absurdity of Native medicine men. Shamans were mad, their techniques diabolical; theirs was "the work of the spirit of darkness as well as the blackest magic."[80] For two centuries shamanism was a scourge to be vigorously combated and confined to the past. By reducing the shamanic style to witch-doctoring nonsense, it was easier to declare modern psychiatry a clean break from the past.

But eventually, through the fog of dupery and darkness, some saw in shamanism a genuine psychosomatic medicine. In the early twentieth century it was beginning to be realized that something more profound lay beneath the shaman's supernatural grandiosity and esoteric rhetoric. Once again, the work of Hubert and Mauss marked a turning point. Their *General Theory of Magic* acknowledged the complexity and consistency of Native curing rites and located shamanism not in opposition to modern psychiatry, but in anticipation of it.[81] Shamanism was not psychiatric science, yet neither was it a baleful compendium of bad ideas. What most psychiatrists were unwilling to admit, and what ethnopsychiatrists such as Devereux and Ellenberger readily acknowledged, was that shamanism "offered a surprisingly high degree of insight into what are usually considered the most recent discoveries in the realm of the human mind." Shamans were psychosomaticians who often had "better insight into psychodynamics than we allow ourselves to have," Devereux wrote. Primitive psychiatric practice, he insisted, did not amount to an "entertaining anthropological or psychiatric curio."[82] The leading ethnopsychiatrists did not cling to nineteenth-century theories about the unidirectional evolution of ideas or the neat break between magico-religious and scientific worldviews advanced by the likes of Tylor and Frazer. It would take six decades to complete what Hubert and Mauss had started and transform shamanism from a temple of ignorance and vice into a field of appreciable psychological insight.

An intriguing aspect of *Mohave Ethnopsychiatry* concerns the matter of countertransference. It has happened, of course, that modern theories have been wrongly ascribed to earlier beliefs. Shakespeare's well-known remark in *Hamlet* that "though this be madness, yet there is method in it" doesn't resemble anything like the logic of the unconscious, but that hasn't stopped some from attributing to him a modern psychoanalytic theory. Had Devereux imputed modern postulates to archaic psychiatry? Had he credited "primitives" with more insight than they actually possess? Had he seen in Mohave shamanism more than was really there? Devereux—who wrote the book on countertransference, *From Anxiety to Method in the Behavioral Sciences* (1967)—thought not. Crucially, most of the data he collected on the Mohave, including the 140 case histories in *Mohave Ethnopsychiatry*, were collected during his first three field seasons on the Colorado River Indian Reservation. These stays in Mohave country occurred between 1932 and 1938. During that time Devereux was not only unanalytic—that is, ignorant of psychoanalysis—he was antianalytic, an aversion not uncommon among anthropologists then just as now. In the 1930s Devereux neither knew nor would have cared for the ethnopsychoanalytic inquiries of Freud and Róheim. Remember, Devereux didn't begin his formal psychoanalytic training until 1947. As a consequence, he declared that countertransference was thus impossible, for he "could not possibly have suggested to his Mohave informants their theory of convulsions for the simple reason that I did not even know at that time that there existed a similar psychoanalytic theory." "Thus," he added, "the congruence of my Mohave data with psychoanalysis is not the result of a preexisting bias."[83] In short, since the bulk of his Mohave field data was gathered before his psychoanalytic training, similarities between modern and Mohave psychiatry could not be explained away by countertransference.

Perhaps even more intriguing, though, is how this intimates that Devereux's initial psychoanalytic training took place not in Topeka but among the Mohave. As far as I can tell, Devereux's fieldwork was also a veritable apprenticeship in psychosomatic therapy. Day after day he listened in as shamans diagnosed patients and discussed their medico-magical treatment of psychic disturbances. The unwitting initiate even looked on as the shaman Hivsu Tupoma unraveled the meaning of Devereux's own dreams. In the

1930s Bataille wanted to be a shaman's apprentice; in those same years, it seems that Devereux was one. The Mohave "spoon-fed Freud to me," Devereux remembered. Thanks to the Mohave he eventually abandoned his antianalytic attitude and sought out formal psychoanalytic training with Karl Menninger in Topeka. In other words, it was the Mohave who led Devereux to Freudian psychoanalysis, and not the other way around: "Freud's patients converted him to psychoanalysis; I was converted by the Mohave Indians."[84] It was only after his time in Topeka that he realized how much Mohave shamanism shared with modern psychiatry. Devereux concluded that "having entered every possible caveat against overvaluing the realism of Mohave psychiatry, we must now take cognizance of the fact that, insofar as such matters can be judged impressionistically, the number of factual and theoretical congruences between modern and Mohave psychiatry is simply too great to be explainable in terms of any or all of the preceding considerations."[85] That Mohave folk psychiatry was in harmony with modern dynamic psychiatry was the result of neither chance nor countertransference. The reason for the extensive overlap rested squarely on the humane dream culture of the Mohave.

Thanks to its dream culture and compassion, Mohave shamanism was not some foul savagery but a stimulus to modern psychiatric thinking. Though supernaturalistic, Mohave psychiatry offered psychiatrists a new frame of reference in which to think through familiar psychiatric problems. It would not have been the first time that modern science advanced by making the familiar strange. It was precisely this estrangement effect that Devereux attributed to his development of a modern ethnopsychiatry: "While writing the present work I was forced to rethink all of psychiatry in startling unfamiliar ways which, in the end, appreciably deepened my understanding of the classical psychoanalytic frame of reference."[86] He concluded that Mohave shamanism resounded with real insight into the nature and treatment of mental illness and that these insights could lead to "a real shift in our way thinking." Over three decades later, Marc Augé, a French anthropologist and the author of *The War of Dreams* (1997), agreed: A humane dream culture like the Mohave could help today's psychiatrists reevaluate standard problems with a foreign frame.[87] As at the start of the second half of the twentieth century, so it was at the end: Modern psychiatrists had something to learn from the psychologically minded Mohave shaman.

At this stage, Devereux's primitivism welled up in an indictment of "the shibboleth of unilinear evolution." Because of their commitment to accelerated progress, the postwar societies Devereux knew best, France and the United States, were unable and unwilling to recognize the cultural survivals through which they might creatively readjust. Given this presentist state of affairs, Devereux declared in a memorable statement that "the frame of reference most likely to produce a real shift in our way of thinking would be one borrowed from an alien culture, such as that of the Mohave."[88] As a consequence, *Mohave Ethnopsychiatry* should be of interest not only to historians of psychiatry and psychologically attuned anthropologists, but also to practicing psychiatrists. Real science is never respectable, Devereux remarked; it is a wild child, a *sauvageonne*, "an unwashed urchin perpetually in rebellion against respectable shibboleths and forever questioning even the most firmly established scientific truths."[89] It was one thing to say that historians of psychiatry should take Native psychiatry seriously and quite another to argue, as Devereux did, that shamans had something to teach modern psychiatrists.

In most circles it was unwise to suggest that modern physicians might learn something from primitive peoples. For most physicians, Devereux's revival of psychiatry's deep past was a dangerous game, one that played fast and loose with the health of present-day patients. Others thought Devereux didn't go far enough, and they opposed his criticisms of culturally relativistic concepts of normality. For years Devereux and Ackerknecht wrangled over whether there was a universally valid standard of mental health. (Devereux thought there was; Ackerknecht didn't.) In 1963 Ackerknecht disparaged *Mohave Ethnopsychiatry* for its spotty data—an odd criticism for a book with 140 case histories obtained over five lengthy field seasons. Reading Ackerknecht's review today, it's hard not to see it as a spiteful outgrowth of their ongoing disagreement. Here's Ackerknecht's review, published in the *Bulletin of the History of Medicine* and quoted in full:

> Mr. Devereux visited the Mohave repeatedly in the 1930's. He collected from them data on their mental diseases and their opinions concerning mental disease. Since that time he has published more than sixty papers dealing with these materials, and he has now made a book out of them. It contains some interesting observations and ideas. Unfortunately it is very difficult to get at them, because the author has erected a voluminous "theoretical" structure on this thin factual foundation. Thus the book is rather clumsy and repetitious. The language is a mixture of "Psychanalyse" and "Anthropologese" with occasional admixtures of American slang.[90]

Dismissive detractors aside, what appeared when modern psychiatry was seen through the eyes of Mohave shamanism? Above all else, the Mohave taught Devereux the importance of social and cultural factors in psychotherapy. Would-be primitivist reformers like Devereux didn't need to resurrect psychosomatic techniques; that had already been done by the likes of

Charcot, Freud, and Pierre Janet during psychiatry's golden age at the fin de siècle. Rather, what postwar ethnopsychiatrists such as Devereux wanted was to integrate culture into psychiatric practice. Psychiatric phenomena were part and parcel of the cultures in which they were embedded.[91] Nothing was more important to the new field of ethnopsychiatry than understanding the role of sociocultural factors in patients' personalities and neuroses, which explains why Devereux revered the way the Mohave linked psychiatric therapy to cultural values. The lesson was simple yet revolutionary: To understand and treat mental illness required knowledge of the cultural milieu in which an illness evolved; Native cultural history was thus essential to psychiatric healing. It is the thesis of the present chapter that a supposedly archaic culture in and around Parker, Arizona was instrumental in the development of a modern social science. With *Mohave Ethnopsychiatry*, the path to integrating cultural diversity into psychiatric practice ran through this remote corner of the American Southwest. It sometimes happens that an arid desert path turns out to be a fertile royal road.

Mohave Ethnopsychiatry was a weighty contribution to modern ethnopsychiatry and a landmark in the revival of cultural survivals after the Second World War. Devereux was a formidable primitivist, a genuine proponent of age-old psychiatric customs: "Look out!" he wrote, "There is an opportunity to perfect savage devices."[92] Native inventions were more than precious; they were visionary. If only we took the trouble to reinstate them in our midst. But in his venture to revive primitive psychiatry, Devereux never renounced modern science. *Mohave Ethnopsychiatry* walked a fine line between declaring Native inventions visionary and remaining true to his conviction that the future of ethnopsychiatry must be naturalistic and scientific. By demonstrating the complexity and frequent accuracy of one supposedly archaic psychiatry, Devereux hoped to inaugurate a broad reappraisal of both modern and primitive psychiatry. But first psychiatrists had to acknowledge their long-standing prejudices against mad shamans and quack medicine men and lay to rest the ingrained idea that folk psychiatry was no more than an inconsequential survival. "On the whole," Sidney Axelrad wrote in *American Anthropologist*, "Devereux has made a signal contribution to anthropology and psychoanalysis. This may well be a seminal book."[93] It was and it wasn't. In a discipline that still struggles to integrate cultural diversity and local ways of life into practice, *Mohave Ethnopsychiatry* was not as seminal as some had hoped. Nevertheless, Devereux maintained that the systematic study of primitive psychiatry was the first step on the path to a modern ethnopsychiatry. Shamanism and psychiatry should be studied side by side, and not just by historians.[94]

From Parker to Paris and Back Again

In the summer of 1963, only a few months after Lascaux shuttered its doors for good, Devereux accepted a position on the faculty of the École pratique des hautes études (EPHE). At the invitation of Fernand Braudel, renowned historian and president of the EPHE's social sciences section, Devereux finally returned to Paris. His return to France was thanks in large part to the support of his fellow anthropologists Bastide and Lévi-Strauss. And while their combined influence went a long way toward bringing the ethnopsychiatrist back to France, Devereux knew he was benefiting from the vacancy left by Jacques Soustelle's forced departure from the EPHE. After serving as governor-general of Algeria at the start of the Algerian War, Soustelle—a former student of Mauss and an acclaimed ethnographer of indigenous Mexico—had joined the Organisation armée secrète and led the struggle to keep Algeria French. It was Soustelle's forced exile for these actions that eventually led to Devereux's appointment at the EPHE.[95] In any case, the next two decades were the most settled of Devereux's life. He taught a steady stream of courses in ethnography and psychiatry and established at the EPHE France's first program of ethnopsychiatry. "When I came to Paris, I thought I had a one year's job. I literally found out only late in May that I can have it for as long as I want," Devereux wrote in the summer of 1964. That same year he became an active member of the Société psychanalytique de Paris. For once, he had security, membership and a professorship, all of a permanent fashion.

Out of the terrible uncertainty of vagabondage and into a pace of life more befitting his personality, Devereux recovered his verve. In the winter of 1963–64, Devereux wrote to Daniel Silverman, his friend and colleague at Temple University, "I had to chuckle about your remark that you envy me for being in Paris. I actually live in a suburb and usually go to town once a week for two hours or so. Most of the time I am at home. It rests me and I enjoy very much the scientific work I am able to do once more. I see very little of Paris proper."[96] Away from the rat race of academic life in America, living southwest of Paris, Devereux had time to reflect and get down to the work of formulating a modern ethnopsychiatry. He was happy to go slow; it was a salubrious change from American hyperactivity and the principle that time is money. "Here," he wrote, "I get up when I wake up naturally, go to sleep when I am sleepy, nap during the day, take my time." After only two months in France, he described the situation a little more figuratively: "A curious fact, there is a story about a lighthouse keeper. The lighthouse had a warning canon, which fired automatically every fifteen minutes. The keeper slept right through it.

One night the mechanism broke down and the gun did not fire. The silence awakened the keeper with a start. I have been so nightmarishly overworked for years, I can hardly get accustomed to the fact that I can set my own pace." The situation was simple: Devereux now had the time to complete the work on ethnopsychiatry he had been planning for decades. With daring, he began fashioning a new social science.

Devereux had lived for so long on another continent that when he returned to France, he was something of a revenant. He soon found that even the most rigorous of intellectual programs runs up against the limits of status and prestige. So despite the support of some of the most distinguished social scientists in France, and despite having published half a dozen books and nearly two hundred articles, Devereux's work was met with silence or incomprehension.[97] He was arguably the founder of a discipline, yet he was practically unknown in his adopted country. "Despite the importance of your oeuvre you are not well-known. How do you explain this?" he was once asked by *Le Monde*. As late as 1970, Devereux wrote, "My thought has evolved amid a deafening silence, even the echo of my own voice comes back to me deformed." One of the reasons for his huge written output, he explained, was that "for all those years I had no one to talk to. So I wrote."[98]

But all that changed with Devereux's explosion into print in the early 1970s. With the publication of *Essais d'ethnopsychiatrie générale* (1970) and *Ethnopsychanalyse complémentariste* (1972), the ranking world authority on ethnopsychiatry was finally recognized as such. After years of being known only as an "intellectual's intellectual" to a small group of specialists, Devereux had at last become a wider property.[99] It would seem, then, that it required returning to Paris for a particularly rich and distinctly primitivist oeuvre like Devereux's to garner the attention it deserved. In the United States, he was like a preacher in the desert; transplanted to the soil of France, however, his ethnopsychiatry had finally found a favorable context in which to flower. "With a lateness of twenty or thirty years," Alain Besançon wrote in 1971, "we discover that Georges Devereux's solutions were always vigorous and alive, ready to serve."[100] The favorable reception is even more surprising given the context in which his work finally appeared: In the history of psychiatry in France, the early 1970s are remembered for the rise of the antipsychiatry movement. At the very moment when psychiatry was under siege, when Michel Foucault spoke of the death of man as an object of science, there was Devereux, speaking in a different voice. In these years when Devereux spoke of normality, sanity and mental hygiene, others evoked the terrible repression perpetuated by psychiatrists—a view punctuated by the publication of Gilles Deleuze and

Félix Guattari's *Anti-Oedipus: Capitalism and Schizophrenia* in 1972.[101] At the very moment when antipsychiatry was all the rage, Devereux's ethnopsychiatry was fated to appear for the first time.

At the same time as his intellectual star was rising, Devereux was awarded a doctorate in the human and social sciences from the Sorbonne. He defended his theses—which consisted of his two most important books, *Mohave Ethnopsychiatry and Suicide* (1961) and *Basic Problems of Ethnopsychiatry* (1970)—on Saturday, June 19, 1971, at the Académie de Paris. Bastide, Lévi-Strauss, and Otto Klineberg (a Canadian-born psychologist, a professor at the EPHE, and the author of *Race and Psychology*) adjudicated, and they unanimously agreed on the richness of Devereux's ethnopsychiatry. The Institut Mémoires de l'édition contemporaine has a fascinating three-page report on the illustrious jury's response to Devereux's theses. The jury noted that in addition to his research and writing, Devereux was a remarkable teacher who already had numerous disciples. It was true: In a few short years he had attracted and trained Besançon, François Laplantine, Tobie Nathan, and several other of the most original thinkers of a new generation of French social scientists. That same year Besançon, for example, had published a groundbreaking study of the role of countertransference in the writing of history, *History and Experience of the Self* (1971). "It is unanimously recognized," the jury concluded, "that Georges Devereux deserves the rank of Ph.D. with very honorable mention."[102]

Bastide, Klineberg, and Lévi-Strauss stressed that Devereux had struggled for decades to establish ethnopsychiatry as a new social science. In an almost boundless oeuvre, he had distinguished himself as an exemplar of the kind of creative interpretation characteristic of both Freudian psychoanalysis and Maussian ethnography. What's more, the jury declared that Devereux had an ethnographer's eye for what was most precious in human culture. Not only did he recognize precious cultural survivals when he saw them, but he had a rare competence for documenting them as well. Devereux's immersion into other cultures, his distinguished committee agreed, made him acutely aware of what was most valuable in their cultures and also his own. His social criticism was sharpened by the way ethnographic knowledge, and the cultural primitivism it engenders, upsets narrow prejudices. Devereux's exuberant appreciation of comparative cultural criticism, which turns received wisdom on its head, contested the status quo and presented social alternatives. Concerned, however, that all this praise might be seen as an endorsement of Devereux's ideas tout court, the jury added: "Certainly, certain members of the jury want it to be known that they do not systematically share the points of view or the positions taken up by Devereux, yet this in no way lowers the profound esteem that they have for his oeuvre."[103] It is a divergence worth remembering: For all Lévi-Strauss's championing of Native shamans, the French structuralist was no ethnopsychiatrist. And Devereux, the unapologetic ethnopsychiatrist, was no structuralist.

I have already described how *Mohave Ethnopsychiatry* shook psychiatry out of its ethnocentric, developmentalist slumber and permanently altered the way "primitive" psychiatric practice was perceived, at least for those who deigned to listen. A decade later, *Basic Problems of Ethnopsychiatry* had the same effect. Published by Gallimard in 1970, the collection of articles Devereux wrote between 1940 and 1965 soon became the most well received and widely reviewed of Devereux's books. *Basic Problems* makes three things about Devereux clear—each one familiar at this point: He formulated ethnopsychiatry as a multidisciplinary pursuit, not an interdisciplinary one; he believed that culturally relativistic concepts of normality were a dead end for ethnopsychiatry; and, finally, he was the sort of cultural pessimist who could make nostalgic dissatisfaction creative. Central to Devereux's ethnopsychiatry was a multidisciplinary approach he called "complementarity." He envisaged complementarity as a new epistemological foundation for the human and social sciences. Just as Niels Bohr had insisted on the complementarity of living matter, Devereux insisted on the complementarity of cultural and psychological phenomena. All human behavior was susceptible to at least two types of analysis, and, as its name implies, Devereux's ethnopsychiatry was built on a discrete double analysis of ethnography and psychiatry.[104] Ethnopsychiatrists must tack back and forth between ethnography and psychiatry, not mixing or diluting or synthesizing the disciplines but maintaining a rigorous complementarity. In this way, cultural history and psychiatric knowledge were mutually supportive but mutually exclusive disciplines. So, while Devereux consummated the marriage of ethnography and psychiatry, each slept in its own room, so to speak, and thereby maintained its intellectual integrity. The problem was that it was hard to find scholars qualified in both ethnography and psychiatry.[105] And so, while the principle of complementarity may have been unassailable, it seemed unlikely to be widely adopted.

Devereux also struggled to free ethnopsychiatry from culturally relativistic concepts of mental health. He believed that cultural relativism, which had been running riot in anthropology and psychiatry for decades, was a cul-de-sac for the nascent discipline. He strongly opposed those who used social adjustment as the basis for determining sanity, as many of the students of Boas and Malinowski did. In conversation with Roland Jaccard, Devereux declared, "I absolutely refuse to consider *adaptation* as a criterion of normality."[106] Don't confuse sanity with average or praised forms of behavior. The trap of culturalism was located in the problem of sick or dereistic societies.

Adjusting to a sick society—whether it be Hitlerian, Stalinist, or capitalist—was no mark of sanity, Devereux argued.[107] To internalize the norms of a dereistic society was to become sick in turn. One can become adjusted in a very sick way, after all; Devereux had in mind a German psychiatrist who had successfully adjusted a suffering patient to the norms of Nazi Germany. While North American culturalists refused to admit that there were sick societies, Devereux believed that there were indeed dereistic societies, and that the postwar West—turbulent, schizoid, and blind to the consequences of its feverish pace—was one of them.[108] Modern Western societies were shot through with belief in, as Devereux put it, "things that simply ain't so."

But if not social adjustment, then what? Normalcy, Devereux contended, was characterized above all by an individual's ability for creative readaptation. The ability to reorient oneself to a new social situation without losing the sense of one's personal and cultural continuity in time—that was the real criterion for sanity, the real signpost of mental health. Hence, the choice between cultural relativism, exceedingly popular in America, and ethnocentric universalism, a long-standing French custom, was a false choice. "Times have changed in the French university," Jean Ziegler wrote in an issue of *Jeune Afrique*. "Gaullist ethnocentrism—all powerful only about ten years ago—has been splintered. The proof: Georges Devereux's fine book, *Basic Problems of Ethnopsychiatry*." In many ways it was only by returning to France that Devereux got out from under the Boas-inspired cult of culturalism and conformity that pervaded North American social science.[109] Back in Paris, Devereux's alternative approach finally saw the light of day.

Finally, Devereux was indeed a cultural pessimist. His crystalline ideas were matched only by a deep skepticism about French and American society: on the one hand, a rigorous scientific realism; on the other, a vigorous cultural pessimism.[110] His pessimism was based on the belief that the rapid upheavals of the postwar period forced many to live beyond their means, psychologically speaking (although, for the ever-expanding precariat, the psyche wasn't the only thing stretched thin). *Les trente glorieuses* entailed great psychological difficulties. Devereux showed how the "economic miracle" that exploded after 1945 was matched by a sharp increase in cases of nervous illness. Isolation, schizophrenia, and hyperactivity were the by-products of hypermodernization after the Second World War. Economic growth wasn't just concentrating carbon dioxide in the atmosphere, it was injecting deluded perceptions into otherwise keen minds. As one commentator put it, Devereux's study of the social origins of schizophrenia "constitutes a terrible indictment of certain oppressive mechanisms particularly elevated in our Western society."[111]

Devereux memorably stated in 1971 that "only a fundamental revision of

Western culture and a radical restructuring of our society in conformity with human principles inspired by reason, patience, and good sense can avoid the coming catastrophe."[112] A decade later the writer and psychoanalyst Roland Jaccard recognized how deep Devereux's critique of postwar modernization ran; he wrote in *Le Monde*, "Pessimist Georges Devereux suggests that the growing percentage of serious ethnic psychoses, such as schizophrenia, constitutes one of the harbingers of a society's decline—and perhaps even a portent of its death." To a man, the postwar primitivists all demonstrate that nostalgic dissatisfaction can indeed be creative and that no one is as keen to preserve certain time-tested survivals as the cultural pessimist.[113]

But what sort of revisions and what kind of survivals was Devereux talking about? The most obvious place to turn if you are looking for the modern implications of a psychiatry informed by Devereux's analysis of the Mohave is to Paris, to Seine-Saint-Denis. There, you will find the Centre Georges Devereux, an ethnopsychiatric clinic that provides social aid and ethnically oriented therapy for immigrant families in France. Founded in 1993 by Tobie Nathan, a well-known French clinician and the self-described "favorite student" of Devereux, the Center treats patients according to their ethnic and cultural backgrounds. Therapy at the Center includes shamanic methods as well as group sessions, rather than each psychiatrist working with patients individually. But Nathan and the Center have been reproached for reifying cultural difference and contesting the very validity of psychiatry. It was no surprise, then, when in 1981 Devereux broke with Nathan, whose cultural relativism and general hostility toward science were not at all aligned with Devereux's teachings.[114]

The Center has its critics, but the problems it treats are problems Devereux knew all too well: the problem of disintegrating traditional cultures, on the one hand, and a modern culture that is affectively incomprehensible, on the other. Torn from habitual anchorages, the migrant families of France are awash in the capriciousness of our times. Yes, history means change, but there are varying rates of change; and since the start of the Great Acceleration the rate of change has been dizzying, hair-raising, and detrimental to psychological health. In societies such as these, Devereux maintained, psychological difficulties will persist until the customs and recurrent behavior patterns that enable man to cope with the environment and with himself have stabilized.[115] The ability to creatively readapt—Devereux's criterion for sanity—is not the same as being forced to *continually* readapt, which leads only to deindividuation. Nothing could be further from Devereux's thought than to deny the importance of long-established tradition and habit. Homeostasis is not synonymous with death; rather, it perpetuates life. Sometimes human inertia is as dynamically motivated as human spontaneity.

Devereux visited the Mohave for the last time in 1981, nearly a half century after the young ethnographer was first sent there by Kroeber. During his final stay on the banks of the Colorado, Devereux remembered how integral this particular tribe of the Colorado River Indian Tribes (CRIT) was to the formation of modern ethnopsychiatry. But the student of Mauss also remembered his personal friendships in this distant valley that he considered home. It was in Parker that he felt "inwardly at home" for the second time in his life: first Paris, then Parker.[116] It was during this final visit that he expressed his desire to receive a proper Mohave funeral. A primitivist, Devereux naturally wanted to end his life's journey by returning to the land where he remembered life most fondly: the old desire for paradise lost. Four years later, at the age of seventy-seven, Devereux died in a Paris hospital on May 29, 1985. As he wished, his remains were moved from Paris to Parker and dispersed according to Mohave funerary rites (fig. 3.3). Although Devereux had already been cremated in Paris, the funeral followed Mohave customs as closely as possible (fig. 3.4).

Starting at 6 p.m. on the evening of July 8, 1985, in the CRIT "cry house," Devereux received a traditional Mohave funeral. The ceremony inside the air-conditioned cry house (it was 108°F at 10 p.m.) lasted all night and ended at sunrise on July 9. Because of the Mohave's disdain for accumulation, there are no photographs or recordings of Devereux's funeral. But Charles A. Lamb, director of the CRIT Museum, did write a letter to Jane Wenning Devereux, Georges's widow in Paris, describing the ceremony in fine detail. He began, "The Mohave of this reservation hold cremation ceremonies in what is known as the cry house or big house. In times past this may have actually been the home of a leader of the tribe but today it is a large building next to an established cemetery ground. Grave sites were scattered throughout the valley and not marked in the past but today they are gathered in one location and some are marked."[117]

In the center of the cry house on a low table draped with a dark turquoise blanket were arranged some of Devereux's personal items: two photographs of the ethnographer in the field, a French newspaper clipping about his passing, and a canister containing his ashes. Some of these items were destined for the CRIT Museum and Library; the rest would be burned at dawn, according to Mohave custom. Pat Swick and Retha Romo were present, so were Lester and Lorraine White. Lester was the son of Hama Utce (Agnes Savilla), Devereux's principal interpreter and "one of the best and most loyal friends" the ethnopsychiatrist ever had. In addition to the funeral ceremony, there was a special exhibit at the CRIT Museum and Library, which hoped to make a new generation of Mohave aware of the French ethnopsychiatrist's work. The exhibit included photographs of Devereux teaching in Paris, several membership plaques to psychoanalytic societies, and many of his books and articles

FIGURE 3.3. A 1902 photograph of the Mohave Cry House, Parker, Arizona. Like the other River Yumans, the Mohave gathered at a cry house to mourn the loss of one of their own. Photograph by Charles C. Pierce, courtesy of the California Historical Society at the University of Southern California.

FIGURE 3.4. A characteristic conclusion to an individual life among an enduring people. "Mohave Cremation," plate 69 of A. L. Kroeber's *Handbook of the Indians of California* (Smithsonian Institution Press, 1925). Courtesy of the Smithsonian Libraries and Archives.

on Mohave culture. Anthony Drennan Sr., chair of the CRIT Tribal Council, described it succinctly: "We don't write so we appreciate his efforts. His books are in the library for our people. I am honored to be here to pay respect for what my elders taught, that things like this are to be."[118]

Standing vigil all night, the remembrance alternated, in the Mohave way, between singing and silence. Lamb reported that the playing of the gourd was mesmerizing and the whole scene cataclysmic. The desert heat had built into an apocalyptic thunderstorm: "Lightning bolts from the sky," he wrote; "it is hot and the wind blows as it always does before a storm." Hours later, the mourners emerged around 5 a.m. into the blue early morning light with Devereux's remains and personal belongings. Lamb continued: "Dawn's light is just appearing in the east rising behind Black Mountain (Avi-Saquilla). The ashes and belongings are arranged as it would be if the body and all worldly goods were here. Helen and John have continued singing the final songs leading the group from the cry house. Now we surround the cremation site and watch the men place the arrow weed and mesquite logs so that all will burn. The fire is lit, and all stay as it burns the ashes and the sun rises. The family stays until just embers remain."[119] This was Devereux's last journey, the end of an itinerant life. With his final resting place just outside Parker, he is one of a very few non-Indians buried in the CRIT Cemetery.

Devereux's funeral betrays his true sense of belonging. In the end, it was not in Hungary and certainly not in white America that the pioneering ethnopsychiatrist felt at home. Devereux's final act is evidence of both his own sense of belonging and of the Mohave's sense that he was one of their own. Devereux, then, was a double hyphenate: ethno-psychiatrist and Franco-Mohave. In death as in life, he joined the only two inner homes he had ever known.[120] In 1981 Thomas Stevens didn't hesitate when he said: "We honor Dr. Devereux as a Mohave with no regard to race or color. He came as a stranger but became acquainted and wrote many books with the help of his interpreter Agnes Savilla in 1931."[121] "Though he had traveled all over the world," the *Parker Pioneer* added, "this was one of the few places he had been happy."[122] If he had returned to Paris for professional and ideological reasons, the reasons for his posthumous return to Parker were personal and cultural. "Dr. Devereux," Lamb's letter ended, "is at home and at peace." You can still make the walk from the cry house to his burial marker outside Parker (though you might want to do so in the predawn light, not so much to recreate that morning in 1985 but to avoid the scorching sun). And you can still find a copy of his contribution to *Primitive Heritage* in the CRIT Library—dog-eared and tattered, as you might expect.

4

Mircea Eliade and Neopaganism as Postcolonial Critique

The Romanian historian of religion Mircea Eliade (1907–1986) needs little introduction. Born in Bucharest on March 13, 1907, Eliade's life as an émigré rehearses an all-too-familiar twentieth-century experience. But what led me to the problem of Eliade was not his life of exile or even his troubling interwar politics. Instead I was drawn to the peculiar, and peculiarly primitivist, combination of the neopagan and the postcolonial in his postwar oeuvre. This chapter tells a story—an intellectual history—about Eliade quite different from those that cast his writings after 1945 as disguised expressions of his sympathies before 1940. Eliade was no stereotypical political operator, and the fact remains—or rather, it is this fact that I have set out to prove—that his writings were guided by a new sensibility after 1945. Eliade found in an admixture of primitivism and anticolonialism a shining alternative to the marauding movement of modern history. He fought against every kind of Western exceptionalism. A neopagan postcolonialism, not a "spiritual nationalism," was at the core of his thinking after the Second World War. My intent is not to dispute his blemished interwar past (the evidence leaves little room for doubt on that score); rather, I shed light on Eliade's postwar oeuvre and argue that his masterworks in the history of religion are best understood not in the context of 1930s Romania but in the intellectual milieu in which they were written—in Paris, in the French social sciences, in the late 1940s and early 1950s.

Before starting at the beginning, perhaps it is best to begin at the end: On Monday, April 28, 1986, at Eliade's memorial service in Rockefeller Chapel on the campus of the University of Chicago, Charles Long told the overflowing crowd that from an early age his friend, colleague, and former teacher was driven by a desire "to understanding how the human species oriented itself and participated in the ordering of the world."[1] Mircea's intellectual curiosity was first piqued at the University of Bucharest, where the young historian studied literature and philosophy and was eventually awarded a degree for his thesis on mystical Platonic thinkers. In 1928, at the age of twenty-one, Eliade left his native Romania to study Indian religion under the philosopher Surendranath Das Gupta. Thanks to a grant from an Indian maharaja, he spent the next four years studying at the University of Calcutta. It was an Eastern education to complement his studies in Greek philosophy; it was also an education in the ways colonial regimes suppressed cultures they deemed inferior. When he wasn't at the University of Calcutta, Eliade could be found in Rishikesh, a world-renowned spiritual center and ashram devoted to worldly retreat and the ancient techniques of yoga. As Eliade remembered it, his sojourns in the Himalayan foothills were not a search for salvation in the exotic arts of the Orient but a means of reorienting himself toward European culture. Whatever the case may be, it was the closest he ever came to genuine fieldwork; like Bataille, Eliade was a gifted comparatist more than a faithful firsthand observer. In 1933 Eliade turned his experiences in South Asia into a doctoral dissertation on yoga and mysticism, "The Psychology of Indian Meditation."

When Eliade left India and returned to Romania to teach at the University of Bucharest, it was the start of a professorial career that would take him from Bucharest to Paris and eventually to Chicago. But first, Eliade was a cultural attaché and press officer in London and Lisbon during the Second World War. He fled Lisbon after the Soviet occupation of Romania in 1945 and arrived in Paris in September of that year. Like so many others, he was displaced, dispossessed, homeless, and broke. Exile was not a temporary condition but a permanent fate. He and his soon-to-be wife Christinel Cotescu scrambled to make ends meet and eke out a living in Paris. The thirty-eight-year-old historian earned a meager living with the occasional research stipend or paid lecture at the Sorbonne or the École pratique des hautes études. Nagged by uncertainty, Mircea and Christinel were caught up in what Eliade called "the terror of history"—shorthand for the wrenching realities of modern progress, including the bombings, massacres, forced migrations, and collective deportations of the recent past. The facts of Eliade's life between 1945 and 1975 can be compressed into a few familiar tropes: destitute refugee, wandering intellectual, permanent exile.[2] Yet Eliade was encouraged by what he found in his new milieu—he soon discovered the French tradition of studying religion and several kindred spirits among the intellectual elite of war-torn Paris.

Between 1945 and 1955, Eliade wrote his discipline-defining masterworks while living a precarious life of quiet desperation. His life in Paris was not an easy one. In 1947 the situation was so dire that he and Christinel nearly moved to Arizona so Eliade could earn a stable living teaching French at a preparatory school not far from Devereux's beloved Mohave Valley. To make matters worse, their apartment in Paris was robbed in 1949. Some relief came in December 1950 in the form of a grant-in-aid from the Bollingen Foundation, which provided Eliade a stipend of roughly $200 a month. Around the same time, he published the soon-to-be classic work *The Myth of the Eternal Return* (1949) and the underappreciated gem *Shamanism* (1951). It is significant that Eliade's greatest works, including *The Sacred and the Profane* (1957), were written in Paris, in French, and in the decade immediately after the Second World War. Eliade, who preferred Paris to Bucharest, proved to be a gifted armchair anthropologist in the tradition of Durkheim, Lévy-Bruhl, and Mauss. As with all of the postwar primitivists, his masterworks were marked by the French social sciences. The "Frenchness" of his thought was less a matter of language than it was the experience of the multidisciplinary milieu of the French sciences of man and society. If he couldn't turn himself into a Frenchman, Eliade wanted, like his countryman Emil Cioran, to at least be seen in a French light.

During his Paris years Eliade wrote prolifically and read voraciously in a staggering number of languages. He was determined to raise the history of religions to the standards that Durkheim and Mauss had set for sociology and anthropology.[3] It was the only way to make the sacred, that stubborn siren of French intellectuals, into an objective category of analysis. Eliade was committed to rigorous erudition, yet he moved comfortably between researching, writing fiction, and espousing a new humanism. Like Lefebvre's, his postwar writings are marked by a concern for human creativity and for nurturing the outdated mores necessary for such creativity. As for Eliade's own artistic endeavors, he eventually published more than eighty works of fiction, including fifteen novels and novellas. He was nominated for the Nobel Prize in Literature in 1957 and 1968. In the United States his fiction has gone largely unnoticed, but in France he has been called the Romanian Rimbaud—although that's a rather odd thing to call a middle-aged historian.[4] *The Forbidden Forest* (1955) is the best and most well-known of his fiction. Written in Paris between 1949 and 1954, when Eliade was at the height of his intellectual powers, the novel pits myth against bureaucracy, folklore against technology. I like to think of his fiction as Kafkaesque *à l'envers*: He wonderfully depicts the pleasures of falling into the burrows of ancient folklore instead of the anxieties of navigating the labyrinthine corridors of modern bureaucracy. In every genre, recovery and revival were at the center of Eliade's writerly life. Archaic modes of living were not to be underestimated, especially in an age hurtling toward cultural and ecological disaster.

In 1956 Eliade was hired by the University of Chicago. That first fall in Chicago's South Side, in his trademark white turtleneck and dark jacket,

Eliade must have swayed the hearts of his colleagues. After serving as visiting professor for a year, he was appointed Sewell L. Avery Professor of the History of Religions (fig. 4.1). With an endowed chair at the prestigious Midwestern university, Eliade secured a position he held for the next three decades. By 1971 he had become an American citizen, and his annual income was just over $33,000—not a fortune, but a far cry from the days of scraping by on a Bollingen allowance.[5] Although he loved and was widely admired at the university, with its Gothic architecture and half-tame squirrels, Eliade spent most summers in Paris on Montmartre's place Charles Dullin. In both locations he decorated his working cabinet with Paul Valéry's incisive phrase: "One need not debase man in order to understand him." But it was at the University of Chicago that Eliade finally reaped the harvest he had sown in France for the last decade. The book that had established his name in France, *The Myth of the Eternal Return*, sold more than 100,000 copies in the United States. As professor of the history of religions, editor of the journal *History of Religions*, and member of the Committee on Social Thought, the fidgety, pipe-digging Eliade transformed the academic study of religion in North America. Nearly fifty, with jacket cuffs that came down over his knuckles, Eliade, who never read newspapers and had no interest in politics, must have struck the casual observer as an unlikely pioneer.

Eliade's thought has been interpreted as either phenomenologist or fascist. I make the case for a third Eliade—a primitivist who after 1945 promoted a peculiar combination of neopaganism and postcolonialism. For a long time the received wisdom regarding Eliade, encouraged by Eliade himself, was that he was instrumental in bringing a phenomenological approach to the study of religion. Religion, he insisted, was irreducible. He popularized the view that religion was a primary not a secondary phenomenon, a reality sui generis (literally, "of its own kind") that needed to be understood on its own terms. As a consequence, the history of religions could only be properly understood by a method that didn't explain religion by going outside it, that avoided reducing religion to something else—say, a by-product of socioeconomic oppression or a projection of social experience or a symptom of wish-fulfilling delusion. At mid-century, phenomenology—a philosophy that suspended preexisting value judgments and relied on direct experience and objective knowledge—best fit the bill. The phenomenological perspective, which was the fashion in those days, seemed the most surefire way to remain an outsider, a nonbeliever, and still study religion from the inside. After the Second World War, Eliade's major works, including *The Myth of the Eternal Return* and *Shamanism*, had the audacity to advance *religious* explanations of *religious* phenomena.

FIGURE 4.1. One example of the rapt attention Mircea Eliade received on the campus of the University of Chicago. The subject of this day's lecture in the history of religions is unknown. Undated photograph, courtesy of the Hanna Holborn Gray Special Collections Research Center, University of Chicago Library.

Like phenomenology proper, Eliade's history of religions dwelled in the categories of space and time. Religion, Eliade argued, carved spatial and temporal centers out of the continuous onslaughts of space and time. "Any village anywhere is the 'center of the world,'" he wrote in *Images and Symbols* (1952).[6] A holy ground, a sacred moment, an *axis mundi*, a long-awaited rite: It was all too human to punctuate space with meaningful centers and break up time with significant moments. Thus we arrive at the sacred and the profane, the dichotomy at the heart of Eliade's conception of religion. In his lexicon such sanctified sites and seasonal rites were called "hierophanies"— times and places set apart, impregnated with magical or religious power, and qualitatively different from workaday life. A hierophany becomes something else while remaining itself: A charred oak is animated and charged, but it is still an oak. Hierophanies were meaning-laden ways of orienting oneself in an otherwise meaningless and indifferent universe: "the transformation of chaos into cosmos."[7] They offered a double escape: It was in these sacred times and localities that humanity was momentarily freed from the terror of time's passing and the disquiet of the vastness of space. Beginning with *Patterns in Comparative Religion* (1949) and *The Myth of the Eternal Return* (1949), the phenomenologically minded historian immortalized hierophanies in the history of religions. The real center of religion, he believed, was found in the desire to return to a sacred realm that transcended ordinary space and time.

Although Eliade's work is no longer in vogue, his name continues to spark debate. The debate revolves around the relationship between Eliade's unsavory interwar politics and his influential postwar histories. In the late 1930s Eliade was drawn to a far-right group in Bucharest called the Legion of the Archangel Michael—or, more colloquially, the Iron Guard, the interwar Romanian fascist party. Founded in 1927, the Iron Guard espoused ethnonationalist, xenophobic, anti-Semitic, and anticapitalist messages—a noxious but all-too-common cocktail across interwar Europe. Eliade's proximity to the Iron Guard owed much to his devotion to his mentor, Nae Ionescu, the charismatic Romanian philosopher whom Eliade assisted at the University of Bucharest and whose influence extended over a generation of young Romanian intellectuals between 1922 and 1940. Eliade was never a militant fascist, but for a time he was a sympathetic supporter of the Iron Guard. Because of this involvement with Romanian fascism, some argue that his masterworks in the history of religions were born out of the most violent political ideology of the twentieth century. By mid-century, however, Eliade's interwar politics were dead and buried. But someone so fixated on resurrection should have known that they would not stay that way forever.

In 1972 Theodor Lavi accused Eliade of having been an anti-Semite, a man of the extreme right, and a leading figure in the Iron Guard. The accusations appeared in the inaugural issue of *Toladot*, an obscure Romanian-language journal published in Israel.[8] Lavi maintained that one could not be associated with this virulent organization without being anti-Semitic. After reading Lavi's charge, Gershom Scholem, Eliade's friend and colleague, wrote from the Israel Academy of Sciences and Humanities: "I am turning to you in a matter which concerns both of us personally." How do you respond to these accusations? asked Scholem. Were you a Romanian nationalist? Did you express anti-Semitic views during the Hitler period? On July 3, 1972, Eliade replied in fourteen handwritten pages explaining that during the war he was a cultural attaché in Lisbon for the government of General Antonescu, which had broken violently with the Iron Guard several years earlier. Even before then, "I do not recall ever having written a single page of Legionnaire doctrine or propaganda." His association with the Iron Guard, he continued, came from his loyalty to Ionescu, who was an ideologue of the far right. But clearly his fidelity toward Ionescu only went so far, and in the end, he chose exile, he said, calling the whole affair "a stupid *malentendu*."[9]

In 1993, seven years after Eliade's death, the historian Daniel Dubuisson published *Twentieth-Century Mythologies*. The book caused quite a stir. The author, who had once praised Eliade (I've read among Eliade's papers several flattering notes from Dubuisson to Eliade), now condemned his former adviser as a lifelong bigot, charlatan, and fraud. Dubuisson wasn't the first to point to Eliade's early engagement with the Iron Guard, but he was the first to interpret every aspect of his oeuvre, both before and after the war, as camouflaged fascism. In this view—which seems to have gotten the last word in the matter—Eliade simply transposed his fascist prejudices into his histories of religion. In his preface to the English translation of *Mythologies du XXe siècle*, Dubuisson concludes: "After the war, in France and then in the United States, Eliade began the formidable task of rewriting his earlier work, at the end of which he succeeded in transposing his favorite ideas from the 1930s into his work as historian of religions."[10] Books like *The Myth of the Eternal Return* and *Shamanism* were thinly veiled messages of spiritual ethnonationalism, scholarly transcriptions of refrains once jubilantly sung by Romanian Legionnaires. When Eliade spoke of the sanctity of archaic societies, so the argument went, he was actually spewing the xenophobic passions of the Iron Guard. Old enthusiasms, new subterfuges. Dubuisson even went so far as to suggest—without evidence—that there must have been an "underground ideological complicity" between Eliade and the institutions that supported him like the University of Chicago and the Committee on Social Thought.

Eliade's political convictions ran so deep, Dubuisson argues, that it could not have been otherwise. Eliade was allegedly a master of translation and disguise, and his interwar politics are the master key to his thought. Dubuisson states this explicitly: "In Eliade's work this pagan apology for the archaic life and primitive man is nonetheless—and *nothing but*—an ideological fiction, built entirely with the help of the author's prejudices, the same prejudices, incidentally, that pushed him toward the Legionary movement in the 1930s."[11] But Dubuisson has got his own position wrong: As he sees it, there was nothing incidental about the link between Eliade's neopaganism after 1945 and his fascism in the 1930s. Everything Eliade wrote after 1945 he wrote with ulterior motives and a guilty conscience. As a consequence, it has been argued that Eliade, the unrepentant fascist, should be rejected wholesale and his books shelved for good. Predictably, justified criticisms of Eliade's Iron Guard episode were taken to insupportable extremes, such as when Steven Wasserstrom declared that Eliade's oeuvre "stands on a pile of corpses." A shadow fell over Eliade's writings, and a relative silence soon followed.[12]

Thirty years later the silence was broken by Bruce Lincoln. In *Secrets, Lies, and Consequences*, Lincoln reveals in fine detail the corrosive effects of Eliade's desperate efforts to conceal his shameful past—not on his postwar oeuvre, but on the lives of those he knew best after 1945. With an investigative eye, Lincoln exposes just how destructive the lingering residues of Eliade's morally repugnant past in Bucharest were on his relationships in postwar Chicago. "Ultimately, my judgment of Eliade's legionary involvement has shifted, becoming more critical and less defensive," writes Lincoln. "While I see no literal blood on Eliade's hands, the nature and goals of the Legion were abundantly clear. Hypernationalist, rabidly anti-Semitic, antidemocratic, antimodern, and anticommunist, it was a militantly aggressive movement, open to—often enough, eager for—violence."[13] *Secrets, Lies, and Consequences* is measured. Even when Eliade leaned to the right, Lincoln tells us, he tempered his language and hedged his bets. But there are moments when Lincoln, too, seems to suggest a wholesale rejection. After the war, Eliade's Legionnaire schema—the modern world is a malignant disaster whose only remedy is a spiritual reawakening and a new humanism—remained "more or less intact," he argues.[14]

Must we burn Eliade, then? Should his name remain on the list of those canceled in the West because of their putative fascist connections? Eliade, the student of Indian spiritualism, was attracted not to the Legion's bloodthirstiness but to its love of Romanian folklore and mysticism. It was the Legion's frankly unoriginal combination of agrarian culture and spiritual regeneration that drew Eliade in. Because of this, Saul Bellow, borrowing a baseball analogy, believed that if Louis-Ferdinand Céline was a true right fielder, then Eliade was at worst a substitute shortstop.[15] The point of this clarification is not to give Eliade a pass, but to show how for decades the epithet of fascism has been amended to any notion of belonging or rootedness and any valorization of the sacred. In the process, the mere invocation of an archaic past has become synonymous with fascism, as fascism is wielded like a gavel to settle the case against primitivism and for progress. Yet, we are in an aporetic predicament indeed when the impulse to recover and revive is relinquished to fascists, when the urge to rescue the remnant as something living is the privileged preserve of the far right. Like his fellow postwar primitivists, Eliade sought to redeem the archaic after 1945, freeing it (and perhaps himself in the process) from its negative association with fascism.

Eliade deserved the criticism and some of the scorn. Heavy-handed critics, however, have deemed no page innocent—an understandable response where Holocaust passions are involved. But the hyperbole and inflammatory rhetoric should raise one's antennae. Much of the criticism amounts to what the political philosopher Leo Strauss called *argumentum ad nazium* or *reductio ad Hitlerum*. My concern, however, is not whether Eliade cleaved to the fascist tendencies of the Iron Guard. Rather, what follows examines his postwar writings with more delicate senses and reveals the impress of the French social sciences, not the Romanian Iron Guard. In lieu of sterile discussions where people say "this is right" and "that is wrong," I turn to the relationship between his neopagan revivalism and his postwar postcolonialism. Again, the point is not to let Eliade off the hook, but to show that the politics of nostalgia is more complicated than his detractors recognize. Longing for days gone by—indeed, even longing for a paradise lost—was never the privileged preserve of any one political ideology, especially in the years of decolonization. I think there needs to be a harder distinction between Eliade's journalistic writings of the 1930s and his histories of religion after 1945, which contain countless examples of what today we would call a postcolonial critique of empire. In a decade when many hedged their bets, Eliade stood unreservedly on the side of non-Western societies. Time and again, he called for a veritable encounter with non-Western cultures. As I will show, it wasn't hard for a dyed-in-the-wool primitivist to become an anticipatory postcolonialist. Eliade brought neopaganism and postcolonialism if not into harmony, then at least into the same sacred circle. To dismiss the world's foremost historian of religions tout court, to cast suspicion on his every idea, is to miss too much.

It is important to capture the urgency in Eliade's belief that Western society was "dangerously close to provincializing itself." In 1952 he used the reflexive *se provincialiser* to indicate Europe's refusal to learn from "primitive" cultures and its unwillingness to see itself through the eyes of non-Westerners. Overcoming *le provincialisme* was fundamental to Eliade's postwar oeuvre.[16] Guided by this postcolonial perspective, it is little wonder Eliade spoke so often and in such glowing terms of so-called primitive cultures. The question then arises: Might neopaganism, a movement so often perceived as a handmaiden to fascism, be equally complementary with postcolonialism? To put the question differently: How was Eliade able to seamlessly reconcile his neopagan revivalism with his newfound postcolonialism after 1945? Some claim that the source of Eliade's anticolonialism and his distinctive weaving together of the archaic and the ethnographic was his four-year study in India in the late 1920s and early 1930s. And it is true that Eliade became politically aware not in Romania in the late 1930s, but when he witnessed the structural oppression of British colonialism. Although it falls outside my purview here, if this hypothesis could be proved, it would go a long way to rethinking the trajectory of Eliade's thought.

In any case, Eliade railed against everything narrowly Eurocentric in the 1950s and '60s, as a cursory reading of any of his books will show. After 1945 Eliade's hope for a new humanism was built on a dialogue with non-Westerners. This is why, for better or worse, ethnographic literature was such a mainstay of his histories of religion. Eliade was well aware that for some time the research of French ethnographers had revealed that although archaic societies lacked industrial progress and were "primitive" in the modern sense, they had nevertheless elaborated invaluable moral and economic systems. Most Western intellectuals, he wrote, "obstinately refuse to recognize any 'situation' except those of the man of the historical civilizations, in defiance of the experience of 'primitive' man, of man as a member of traditional societies."[17] Eliade's language will surely raise more than one eyebrow, but the idea behind "launching a dialogue" with "primitive others" resonates with today's unequivocal rejection of Eurocentrism. Charles Long confirmed Eliade's hatred of ethnocentrism in his eulogy for his friend and colleague: "Though he probably knew more than any living person, the various religious attitudes assumed by humankind, he never ... engaged in that kind of superior mode of the imperialism of knowledge so characteristic of many scholars in the West who have access to other cultures." In a decolonizing age, Eliade thought the history of religion was "a preeminent source of strength for a general cultural renewal."[18] He was not alone in thinking that the religious rituals of the non-Western world could revivify the West.

There was a postcolonial paradigm shift in the history of religions after 1945, and Eliade was in large part responsible for it. His histories of religions were built on the end of European empires; decolonization, not fascism, was the twentieth-century event that shaped his thinking. Thanks to decolonization, places that had once supplied the lifeless raw material for works on primitive culture now demanded to be treated as equals, with their own living and historical traditions. Thanks to decolonization, Europeans were finally beginning to "reckon with other ways of knowing and with scales of values other than their own."[19] With "the entrance of primitive peoples into history," in other words, came the end of Europe's perceived superiority. As grating as this phrase may sound to us now, the end of European empires had two significant meanings to Eliade—one liberatory, the other more equivocal. On the one hand, the influential critic of empire celebrated the fact that formerly colonized people were now "active subjects." The active presence of the third world had significant consequences not just for newly independent nations but for modern Europe as well.[20] On the other hand, "entering history" meant merging onto a busy one-way street; it meant entering the current of unidirectional time without regulating or reversing it. The unrelenting course of history, once anathema to archaic societies, now marked their modernity. To Eliade, however, being "outside of history" was in some respects a fertile source of disalienation. He thus turned the standard judgment of what it meant for a society to be historical on its head. All this is in the highest degree postcolonial. In those days it was difficult for Westerners to imagine a society that thwarted historical time and kept the terror of history at bay. But Eliade was intent on making the unimaginable a little less difficult to imagine.

Confronting the Terror of History

Walking the streets of Paris in January 1950, Eliade thought that the faces of the people he passed appeared yellow in the pale winter light. The historian was on his way to the Sorbonne, where he would deliver a lecture on the persistence of ancient myths in the modern world. He had been in Paris for five years now, and the City of Light had come to feel like home, even on a day like this, when he scarcely saw the sun. And now that his work was being seen in a French light, the Romanian émigré was confident it would shine. Given the recent reception of his *The Myth of the Eternal Return* (1949), he wasn't wrong. But for all that, he still lived a life of exile, without security or status, clinging only to his self-respect as a writer and scholar. That morning had been one of those frigid mornings when it was so cold that Eliade's hand nearly froze as he held his pen, a problem he'd taken to solving by pressing his fingers against a bottle of hot water to thaw his aching joints. Later that evening, Eliade assured his audience of immured apartment people, many of them Romanian, that it was still possible to find remnants of archaic religions floating about in our growth-addicted societies. Resistance to the rapid pace in which we were condemned to live and work, he argued, was not some simple "survival" but a constitutive part of what it meant to be human. How could he be sure? Well, the sallow-faced historian had the audacity to view postwar Europe through the eyes of non-Europeans. Eliade admitted how amazed he was at the overwhelming richness of primitive myths, rhythms, and symbols. His audience, though sympathetic, remained skeptical.

After the lecture, Eliade reemerged into the terrible din of the city. He feared that a cataclysm might descend at any moment (not an uncommon feeling for the lifelong exile, whose thoughts verged on catastrophism). "The air had become a kratophony," he remembered—an awe-inspiring manifestation of power. He knew the source of his alarm: Suddenly surrounded by a low-hanging sky and the incessant rumble of passing cars, the combined effect struck him as serious and terrible. You should know that in Eliade's novels, cars were always linked with death. And in 1950, in those first anxious days of *les trente glorieuses*, death by car accident seemed to him the only plausible conclusion. Like a novelist composing a scene, he paused to consider this morbid thought. Fortunately, Eliade had a sensibility that did not wither under the weight of cultural pessimism. As he returned home on the train, he reflected on his work in the history of religions and on the timeliness of his efforts to recover what was virtually timeless. That night Eliade stood for a long time at his apartment window gazing into the darkness and listening to the rustling of the trees in the yard next door. Overworked yet exuberant, he was fortified by the possibility of rejuvenating Western society through a cultural reawakening. "In a period of crisis such as we are in now," he thought, "it is not only useful but perhaps necessary to turn to primitive pathways."

Five years earlier, when Eliade began the French phase of his intellectual life in 1945, the Romanian-born exile started with a thorough reappraisal of the concept of cyclical time. Completed in the years immediately after the Second World War, *The Myth of the Eternal Return* appeared in French in 1949. The book, which earned Eliade acclaim in France and eventually widespread support in the United States, was his signal intellectual accomplishment: "I still consider this small book to be the most significant of all my books," he wrote in April 1964. But *The Myth of the Eternal Return* is no timeless masterpiece. Rather, it was a specific response to a particular postwar problem: What if modern societies did not regard historical progress as the measure of human life? Could the ritual repetitions of archaic religions cure the ills of societies wedded to a one-way future consisting only of growth? When will linear conceptions of time be associated with the world's ruination? *The Myth of the Eternal Return* argued that rediscovering cyclical conceptions of time could indeed revivify Western societies that had sacrificed the best part of their soul for industry and technology. Eliade knew that the modern West was an anomaly; consumed by an almost instinctive faith in a progress believed to be unstoppable and unending, the West was at odds with the vast majority of cultures throughout human history. Archaic or traditional societies feared history, rejected it, and found ways to thwart it. Part of a broad reappraisal of supposedly outdated cultures after 1945, Eliade's *Myth* contributed to the ongoing reevaluation of "primitive" cultures and the rituals that preserved cyclical conceptions of time.

The book's title, a misnomer really, caused much confusion. It led readers to believe that Eliade was concerned with Nietzsche's doctrine of eternal recurrence. Yet *The Myth of the Eternal Return* was chiefly concerned neither with Nietzsche nor with the Greek myth of eternal return. Most of the reviews that appeared in the summer of 1949 began precisely with this point: Readers, be warned—this book is not a study of Nietzsche.[21] Rather, Eliade's subject was the temporal customs and cultures of so-called primitive peoples. Roughly three-fourths of *The Myth of the Eternal Return* examines the cyclical rites of archaic societies, while the rest of the book concludes with an inquiry into historicist tendencies in the West over the last two hundred years. The book covers a long sweep of time, from the most archaic rites to the most modern developments. In addition to overflowing all the ages, *Myth* spans the globe and assembles evidence from around the world. The importance of ethnography is apparent on every page. Eliade was once asked: "You have been criticized on occasion for drawing your view of the nature of religion primarily from primitive religions rather than the full spectrum of religious traditions. How would you respond?" "I have insisted," he replied, "on the importance of primitive religions because they were more or less neglected by historians of religions in the past. The most important books on this problem were written by anthropologists and sociologists such as Frazer, Durkheim, Lévy-Bruhl, Wilhelm Schmidt, Robert Lowie, Malinowski, Paul Radin, and others."[22]

In the archaic world, human behavior was most meaningful when it re-enacted a primordial act. To demonstrate the importance of origins, Eliade never tired of employing the Latin phrases *ab origine* (at the beginning) and *in illo tempore* (once upon a time).[23] The book that thrust Eliade onto the Parisian intellectual scene provided example after example of religious rites that split time in two. Eliade showed that, for so-called primitive peoples, time, like space, is not homogeneous. In the archaic world, he observed, "There is a sacred time, eternally present because it is eternally repeatable, and profane time, the irreversible duration which implacably leads to death."[24] A revolt against history, against the unprecedented occurrence, against living life perpetually in time was the essential characteristic of archaic religions. Once upon a time, we learn, societies used a pattern of regularly repeated rituals to periodically escape the course of profane time. Eliade invested these archaic rites with all the mystery and enchantment that Bataille deposited in the depths of Lascaux. In *Myth*, archaic religion became an immemorial treasure, a durable trove of rites ripe for the taking. More than any other postwar primitivist, Eliade saw in pagan rites solutions to every modern problem born of "the terror of history."[25]

"The terror of history" was no empty phrase for Eliade. We are prey to history; we fall into the terror of its passing. He believed that after a half century of violent death and catastrophic upheaval, Western societies needed to change the way they approached time; they needed to relearn how to deprecate, not celebrate, historical progress. He was buoyed by the belief that "the modern world is, at present, not entirely converted to historicism." While historical societies celebrated progress, primitive societies "acknowledged no act, which has not been previously posited and lived by someone else."[26] Eliade transformed archaic rites from backward superstitions into timeless treasures. The archaic world possessed what modern societies lacked: a resolve to defend themselves against the terror of history. *The Myth of the*

Eternal Return thus revolves around a simple opposition between historical and ahistorical societies, between the Western world's violent historicism and the archaic world's compulsive conservatism. In effect, Eliade radically reimagined what it meant to be "outside of history" and turned the Hegelian assessment of ahistorical societies on its head. In this view, being outside history—something once deemed deeply alienating—might turn out to be a fertile source of disalienation.[27] Eliade first maintained that cyclical conceptions of time persisted in the cracks of modern society and then speculated on their prospective return. Survival and revival, in other words—the twin pillars of the postwar primitivists. A *sortie de temps*, a shelter from history: It was an awkward position to maintain in the age of decolonization, but Eliade maintained it nonetheless.

The historian then turned to the history of ideas. He believed that the seventeenth century marked the turning point from archaic to modern societies, from societies that repeat to societies that advance. It was then that linear progress began to truly assert itself in Europe. In science and religion, Francis Bacon and Blaise Pascal were representative of the new "faith in infinite progress."[28] In the nineteenth century that faith went mainstream and was eventually enshrined in the ideas of evolutionary biologists. When it came to his contemporaries, Eliade disdained how early techno-futurists such as Pierre Teilhard de Chardin cast humanity's coming voyage to the stars in a redemptive, theological light. As for existentialism, with its nausea and *amor fati*, it was the logical conclusion of the rise of historicism; it was what you got when you perceived man as a thoroughly historical being.

Eliade's big underlying assumption became clearer as the book wore on. What Eliade called history was unique and unidirectional and irreversible—and destructive. Abandoning cyclical conceptions of time had consequences. The loss of repetition and rootedness led to acceleration and catastrophe. For him, history equaled change—and change invariably was for the worse. History inevitably led to more and more suffering—a mid-twentieth-century view if ever there was one. Of all the postwar primitivists, Eliade fell victim to the worst excesses of cultural pessimism. If history is no more than a degenerative spectacle of suffering and violence, there is no room for the idea that historical events could have a liberating effect. When Eliade was at his most apocalyptic, he foresaw the catastrophic demise that would come from the busy hands of historical societies. Today he would be in good company. "Today, when time is filled with significant action and history gathers speed so rapidly that man is left behind, even though it is he who accelerates it, there is indeed an urgent need to analyze the basic conceptions of time and history prevalent in different cultures."[29] That's an Anthropocene statement if I ever heard one.

At this point in Eliade's exposition, Nietzsche finally stepped into the spotlight, much to the dismay of French reviewers. Nietzsche was an unrivaled critic of historicism and linear time, and his writings, Eliade observed, were "saturated with nostalgia for the myth of the eternal return."[30] With T. S. Eliot, James Joyce, Oswald Spengler, and Arnold Toynbee, Nietzsche had rediscovered the value of ritual repetition. Together these thinkers mark the start of a reaction against two hundred years of triumphalist progress. But these Western intellectuals weren't alone in keeping cyclical conceptions of time alive, Eliade hastened to add. Traditional and primitive societies, in Europe and in the third world, didn't perceive time as a direction, an arrow, or a river; they still clung to cyclical time: "This traditional conception of a defense against history, this way of tolerating historical events, continued to prevail in the world down to a time very close to our own; and that it still continues to console the agricultural (= traditional) societies of Europe, which obstinately adhere to an anhistorical position and are, by that fact, exposed to the violent attacks of all revolutionary ideologies." Later in *Myth* Eliade described this holding over of indispensable survivals more succinctly: "A very considerable fraction of the population of Europe, to say nothing of the other continents, still lives today by the light of the traditional, anti-'historicist' viewpoint."[31] As he saw it, cyclical time lived on in both the living fossils of archaic societies and in the writings of intellectuals like Nietzsche. Eliade didn't know it, but he and the leftist Lefebvre spoke with one voice.

With the first edition of *The Myth of the Eternal Return* came another confusing intellectual association. Any student of Eliade must immediately consider Carl Jung's influence on the Romanian historian. From the beginning, Eliade's use of the word "archetype" in *The Myth of the Eternal Return* was a source of confusion. If the book's title made readers think of Nietzsche's doctrine of eternal recurrence, then its subtitle, *Archetypes and Repetition*, conjured images of Jung's theory of archetypes. No wonder people spoke for years to come of Eliade's Jungian vision. As Eliade's notoriety grew, it put him in the crosshairs of the outspoken anti-Jungian crowd in France. Even Devereux described the historian of religion's books as plagued by an "overly Jungian optic."[32] But Eliade's masterwork had even less to do with depth psychology than it did with Nietzsche's eternal return. In 1958 Eliade finally admitted that his repeated use of archetypes in *The Myth of the Eternal Return* had been "a regrettable error." "In using the term 'archetypes,' I neglected to specify that I was not referring to the archetypes described by Professor C. G.

Jung," Eliade wrote. "For to use, in an entirely different meaning, a term that plays a role of primary importance in Jung's psychology could lead to confusion."[33] Yes, it could—and it did.

Despite the author's protestations, the path to understanding what Eliade meant by archetypes must begin with the Eranos circle. Its name taken from a Greek word meaning "banquet," Eranos was an annual symposium in Ascona, a charming little Swiss town on the shores of Lake Maggiore. Each summer Eranos brought together twelve scholars from a range of disciplines to discuss religious symbols. Jung was the symposium's *spiritus rector*, the guiding spirit of Eranos. Between 1933 and 1952 the illustrious psychologist took part in every meeting, often determining the specific symbol that would be the focus of that year's gathering. In a letter dated January 22, 1955, Eliade admitted to Jung that reading him had been "the greatest discovery of my spiritual maturity."[34] And in "A Meeting with Jung," Eliade describes a discussion he had with Jung one August afternoon in 1952 on the terrace of Casa Eranos (fig. 4.2). The discussion, which Eliade published in the French journal *Combat*, makes plain the two men's shared aim: to deliver modern man from his spiritual vacuity

FIGURE 4.2. Photograph by Margarethe Fellerer, the official photographer of the Eranos Conferences, showing Eliade, Jung, and Erich Neumann at the famed round table in Ascona, Switzerland, August 1950. Eliade's admiring gaze only underscores his attraction to Jungian views. Neumann was an Israeli analytical psychologist and one of Jung's favorite students. Reproduced by permission of the Eranos Foundation.

by recuperating the rich religious reservoir of human history. Jung may have called it "psychical integrity" and Eliade "spiritual integration," but both believed it catastrophically naive to think that modern Western societies could continue on their current course.[35]

Nevertheless, in the gradual adjustment of his thought over the 1950s, Eliade moved away from archetypes, employing instead paradigmatic behaviors or cultural patterns. In later editions of *Myth*, Eliade struck through every archetype and replaced it with unwieldy phrases like "exemplary models of significant activities." (The proofs of these later editions and translations indicate that Eliade's handwritten excision of every archetype verged on the obsessive.) As the years passed, he was emphatic that the archetypes he described had nothing to do with the collective unconscious. Nowhere, he insisted, "do I touch upon the problems of depth psychology, nor do I use the concept of the collective unconscious."[36] And he was right: *Myth's* archetypes were not Jungian; they were the living fossils of ritual repetitions that once dominated primitive cultures. This was Eliade's essential idea: the ritual repetition of cosmogonic acts that abolish time's passing.

Eliade was once asked, "How would you evaluate Carl Jung's contribution to our understanding of religion? Has his work had any significant influence on your own work?" Eliade's answer is enlightening in its blanket dismissal: "I do not recognize the influence of Jung's ideas on my work."[37] But the Eliade-Jung connection was more complicated than that. Eliade's Jungian peregrinations began in the 1940s, when he first read Jung's work on archaic religions. There he found something akin to survivals and living fossils. It is no surprise, then, that Eliade vacillated when it came to Jung. In "Religions" (1977), he wrote, "Jung proposed many definitions of archetypes, one of the last being 'patterns of behavior.'" So, in essence, so many years and so many edits later, Eliade's emphasis on cultural patterns was right back in the fold of Jungian psychoanalysis. In moments of self-reflective clarity, Eliade admitted that archaic cultural patterns "exhibited astonishing similarities with the structures of the unconscious," to the extent that an interpreter could do worse than see Eliade's paradigmatic rites as an outgrowth of Jung's controversial concept.[38] In the end, there was at least one similarity between the structures of the Jungian collective unconscious and the rites of Eliadean archaic societies: the former was forgotten in the depths of the collective unconscious, while the latter was relegated to the attics of time.

We can therefore assume that Eliade knew very well the proximity of his ideas to Jung's—a fact that became clear when I discovered in Eliade's archives that the same year *Myth* appeared, Eliade taught applied psychology for a working group, the Groupe de travail pour la psychologie de C. G. Jung, dedicated to spreading the ideas of the famous Zurich psychologist. On Monday, March 28, 1949, at the Hôtel des sociétés savantes near Odéon, Eliade gave a two-hour lecture on the initiation rites of primitive societies under the telling title "Archetypes and the Collective Unconscious." It was part of a week of seminars dedicated to studying the main points of Jung's doctrine. In short, Eliade used Jungian terminology when it suited him and distanced himself from Jung when it was in his best interest to do so. Bellow, Eliade's University of Chicago colleague, said it best: Eliade was "not exactly a follower of Jung—but not exactly *not* a Jungian."[39]

Jungian or not, the ritual repetitions of archaic societies possessed two principal powers: They preserved culture and valorized life. The rites that filled the pages of *Myth* were a way, Eliade liked to say, of *preserving what was timeless*.[40] Like so much else in the arsenal of the postwar primitivists, archaic rites were both persistent and precarious. Eliade's repeated insistence that these rites were both transhistorical and on the verge of disappearing made for one the baldest expressions of the postwar primitivists' paradox. Yet he didn't shy away from but in fact testified to the conservative desires of archaic societies. Repulsed by rapid change, archaic societies tended toward equilibrium and rest. Seasonal rites repelled the passage of time, and the festivals that punctuated the religious calendar were the antithesis of "history."[41] At the same time, Eliade bore witness to the transformative power of a certain cultural continuity. He went to great lengths to show that long-held customs were not only conservative but creative. Where does creativity come from? Repeating primordial acts is "the paradigmatic model for every creation, for every kind of doing." In other words, out of a certain nostalgia, creativity—it was just as Lefebvre had said.[42] For Eliade, a long-standing seasonal rite that abolished the passing of time was the creative act par excellence. Repetition revitalized a community's flagging energies and transfigured life by living in the sacred, even if only provisionally. Yes, primitive cultures cared about preservation, but they also instituted a certain repetition to endow life with some semblance of the sacred. Repetition need not be a vicious circle, in other words, rather it could be a source of periodic regeneration. The archaic rites of *Myth* were thus a way to preserve a particular style of life and a means to affirm life itself.[43]

In September 1953, four years after the publication of *Myth*, a concerned and somewhat cynical Eliade turned to the subject of anxiety. The eighth annual symposium of Rencontres Internationales in Geneva gave him the opportunity to assert a link between historical change and heightened anguish.[44] Anxiety, naturally, was not unique to the modern world, but a certain type of unshakable anxiety might have been. Suggestively, speculatively, Eliade posited that anxiety of the kind experienced in the West was the product of historicity. For the author of *The Myth of the Eternal Return*, the anxiety he saw floating all around him was linked to historical consciousness. Since Western societies led the way in swift historical change, it only followed that they ranked first in nervous illnesses as well. If his diagnosis of *les trente glorieuses* was correct, then the therapeutic for this malady was not more history-making but a return to the rites that encouraged repetition and cultural continuity. With its rapid march forward, postwar France had overcome material difficulties only to exacerbate mental ones. Again, we confront the question: What were the hidden costs of all that growth?

Eliade's revolt against modern history's endless departures turned on the distinction between *Homo faber* and *Homo religiosus*. Eliade sided with the noble *Homo religiosus* over the utilitarian *Homo faber*. This surprised no one. His distinction underscored the difference between historical demands to "make it new" and religious rites that returned to what was "made long ago." With the image of *Homo religiosus*, Eliade's transhistorical anthropology jumps off the page: Every human being, archaic or modern, is essentially and inescapably religious. This was no provisional formulation, but the unqualified foundation of Eliade's thought. *Homo religiosus* was constitutive of humankind itself, even in our so-called secular age. "Modern man," he wrote, "has not yet succeeded in abolishing the *Homo religiosus* that is in him: he has only done away with the *christianus*. That means that he is left with being 'pagan,' without knowing it." So long as there are humans, they will long to live in the sacred and long for days gone by.[45]

And yet—and yet—is it not all too typical of the postwar primitivists that Eliade lamented the loss of these eternal longings? Here the paradox of their primitivist sensibility takes on an almost crystalline expression. But why did these wedded desires for immersion in the sacred and for paradise lost persist? To demonstrate how deep-seated these desires were, Eliade liked to tell the story of a group of prisoners in a Soviet gulag. An eccentric old woman was interned in a dormitory in a Siberian concentration camp. Each evening, after the day's backbreaking labor, she liked to tell fascinating mythical tales. The prisoners of her dormitory recognized the importance of her nightly mythmaking—so much so, in fact, that they sacrificed a share of their meager rations to keep the old woman alive. While it was common in other dormitories for a dozen people to die each week, in this dormitory—the one that listened to stories of paradise lost each evening—only one or two of its members succumbed to the grueling labor over an entire month. The point is, some stories help us survive, and myths help us do things that history can't. Stories like this aside, Eliade took great pains to salvage the politics of nostalgia. He insisted that nostalgia is both a noble sentiment and a practical endeavor to reestablish some kind of connection with a past that can no longer be easily reconciled with the present.

Behind every page of *The Myth of the Eternal Return* lurked Eliade's hope for a world "less haunted by the terror of history." To the postwar primitivist, the solution boiled down to one fact: "Tens of millions of men were able, for century after century, to endure great historical pressures without despairing, without committing suicide or falling into that spiritual aridity that always brings with it a relativistic or nihilistic view of history."[46] Predictably, he tacked back and forth between lamenting desacralization and praising the vestiges of archaic societies. Redemption, for Eliade, was found neither in history-making nor in freeing oneself from all transhistorical meaning. In the late 1940s there was still reason to believe that as existence became more and more precarious, the valorization of what we call historical progress would lose its shine. The last thing humanity needed, Eliade warned, was more history. As with the other thinkers analyzed in this book, Eliade's revivalist streak was not only a reaction to the wrenching upheaval of the recent past but an imperative for the immediate future.

"As the terror of history grows worse," Eliade warned his French readers, a renewed interest in traditional cultures is likely to emerge. "It is not inadmissible to think of an epoch, and an epoch not too far distant, when humanity, to ensure its survival, will find itself reduced to desisting from any further 'making' of history." Eliade envisaged a future in which we cheerfully confine ourselves to repeating "prescribed archetypal gestures."[47] We already possess, we have long possessed, the ethos and the practices needed to secure a livable future. So, *abstain from more history-making*, the otherwise reserved historian proclaimed. There were two smoldering, transhistorical desires that could stave off the terror of time's passing: the desire to live in the sacred and the desire to rediscover paradise lost. These "universal thirsts" were two sides of the same nostalgic coin.[48] Apparently a renewed revolt against historical time and another dramatic breakthrough of the sacred were upon us. And Eliade believed that the French social sciences offered the first signs of just such a breakthrough. Survival was still possible, he insisted, if only we rediscovered a different conception of time. Thus, it was incumbent on historians such as Eliade to keep alive a certain primitivism. Nothing less than humanity's survival was at stake. At no time between 1945 and 1975 did he ever think otherwise.

Different Shamanism, Same Sensibility

After the appearance of *The Myth of the Eternal Return*, Eliade's position in Paris became a bit more secure. With support from the Bollingen Foundation and the Centre national de la recherche scientifique, Eliade soon completed his next major work, *Shamanism and the Archaic Techniques of Ecstasy* (1951). Between March 1946 and March 1951 Eliade devoted himself to shamanism—a controversial subject to which he, like Devereux, would return time and again in the 1950s and '60s. Eliade wasn't the first foreign-born scholar in France to take an interest in shamanism (that honor goes to the heroic Lewitsky), but he was the first to finish a full-length study of it.[49] For nearly two decades after 1945, amid all the hypermodernization and decolonization, intellectuals across the French social sciences argued passionately about shamanism. It may have been hard "to imagine what such a shamanism can represent for an archaic society," but it is not hard to see why shamans suddenly received so much scholarly attention, nor why the subject was so hotly contested.[50] As the world was remade around them, scholars like Eliade believed that a more accurate understanding of "primitive" cultures was needed before it was too late. And, in many instances, the person of the shaman was at the heart of so-called primitive cultures. Eliade wasn't embroiled in an arcane dispute about archaic rites; he was in search of an education in shamanic cultural traditions. That education may have been romanticized, but it was far from sentimental.

Written in French and published in 1951, Eliade dedicated *Shamanism* to his "French teachers and colleagues." In the first pages we find a ready acknowledgment of Eliade's debt to the French social sciences: "We have taken the liberty of dedicating this book to our French teachers and colleagues, as a modest testimony of gratitude for the encouragement that they have never ceased to lavish on us since our arrival in France."[51] His French colleagues, it seems, were eager to reciprocate. Such was the intellectual atmosphere of the French social sciences in the early 1950s. Reviewers heaped praise on Eliade's new book, declaring it remarkable, prodigious, and indispensable to any understanding of the subject. In a November 1952 review for *Diogène*, the leading expert on Siberian shamanism, Éveline Lot-Falck (the same Lot-Falck whom Bataille was so fond of quoting), described Eliade's latest book as "a work of immense erudition." Marcelle Bouteiller, a student of Mauss and the author of *Shamanism and Magical Healing* (1950), called Eliade's *Shamanism* considerable and authoritative. "For the first time in the history of religion, we have a clear idea of what shamanism is," the French ethnologist Maurice Leenhardt added. "We can only be grateful that he [Eliade] has chosen our language to make his history of religion known."[52] The chorus of applause, however, should not mislead us. *Shamanism* was a strange, unorthodox book. Eliade approached shamanism not from the usual perspectives of ethnology or psychology, but as a perennial subject in the history of religion. Despite being widely recognized as a religious phenomenon, shamanism had up to that point never been interpreted in the framework of the history of religions.[53]

If Eliade succeeded in educating his readers in the secrets of shamanism, it was because he started by defining it simply: *A shaman is a healer who has ecstatic experiences for the benefit of the community.* He insisted that ecstasy was the defining characteristic of shamanism. Shamanism was unthinkable without ecstasy and its cousins, possession and trance. Eliade's thesis was not hard to find; it was clearly stated in the second part of the book's title, *Archaic Techniques of Ecstasy*. In a very French way, Eliade described the shaman's ecstatic states as *a rupture with the real*. But he also insisted that, despite its dissociative states, shamanism was a calling and a vocation, an expertise learned over a long apprenticeship. This view of the shaman as a professional was a necessary corrective to the prevailing view of shamans as mentally deranged savages eager to spout quack cures. Eliade's shamans struck a different chord. Naturally, then, not everyone could become a shaman; it required a certain constitution and a long training. No doubt Eliade made the shaman a most contradictory figure in the history of religions—a possessed personage dancing, leaping, and in the throes of ecstasy as well as a trained specialist, a keeper of age-old traditions, and a devotee of the "fire of intelligence," as Eliade liked to say.

Eliade didn't avoid the fraught subject of ecstasy, as many academic interpreters did. Instead, he showed how even something so paroxysmal as ecstasy could be neatly categorized into different types of journeys. Shamans were able to "leave" their bodies, not at will but ritually. Ecstatic rites allowed the shaman to transcend time and space and enter into the sacred. Like Devereux, Eliade turned to the American Southwest: Among the Mohave, he wrote, "shamanic power comes from the mythical beings who transmitted it to shamans at the beginning of the world."[54] Skilled in ecstatic voyages, shamans were specialists in the sacred. Ecstatic voyages went by a whole slew of names in *Shamanism*: archaic odysseys, spiritual adventures, magical flights, celestial ascensions, and infernal descents. Each stood for the moment when the shaman crossed the threshold that separates the sacred from the profane. Eliade knew how such phrases as "magical flight" and "soul travel" sounded to his colleagues. But he insisted that the shaman's ecstatic experiences were an example of "the eternal return of an atemporal moment."[55] And just like the rites of eternal return, the meaning of shamanism was twofold: to preserve precious cultural patterns and to valorize life. With this, Eliade joined his *Shamanism* to the thesis of his *Myth of the Eternal Return*. He set out to prove that shamanic techniques were not just extraordinary—they were archaic cultural patterns crafted over millennia. It is for this reason that *Shamanism* dealt primarily with initiation, apprenticeship, and mastery; Eliade's shamanism had little to do with the pseudo-ecstasies of drugs and drunkenness and everything to do with consecrating time and space.

In addition to ecstasy, there was a transhistorical element to shamanism that was not reducible to history—a view that was characteristic of Eliade's thought. The author of *Shamanism* wanted his readers to understand that the shaman's temporary altering of consciousness was not as exotic or esoteric as it might first appear. The desire to transcend profane life was not merely the whim of Paleolithic hunters; it was a universal human desire, found "in primitive man as in all human beings," Eliade wrote.[56] He knew his French colleagues would be wary of admitting to soul travel, but he thought that everyone would recognize the shamanic motifs of ascension into the sky and descent into the underworld. While shamans were specialists in ecstatic experience, their continued existence reminds us not only of the various ways human beings have tried to temporarily alter consciousness, but also of the universal desire to do so. Such ecstatic experiences "belong to man as such." The shaman's specialty, ritual ecstasy, was thus an archetypal and virtually timeless experience, Eliade wrote a few years earlier. "It is found everywhere, and it forms an integral part of the human condition." Just like anxiety or dreams, "*ecstasy* is a constitutive experience of man," he concluded.[57]

Then, in a striking similarity with Bataille, Eliade attested to shamanism's origins in the hunting cultures of the Upper Paleolithic. Shamanism, it turns out, was much older than had previously been thought. It was the Paleolithic *Urkultur*. By the 1950s it was clear that shamanism had a prehistoric provenance and that the shaman's ecstasies were part and parcel of the prehistoric hunting cultures that decorated the walls of Lascaux. The proof, Eliade argued, was right there in luminous polychrome. The famous Well Scene of Lascaux, for example, depicts a bird-headed man in a shamanic trance next to a bird perched atop a post, which symbolizes shamanic ascension. Traces of the most ancient shamanism could still be observed in these representations of the bird, the tutelary spirit, and the ecstatic. "At any rate," Eliade declared in 1961, "the antiquity of 'shamanic' rituals and symbols seems to be settled."[58] The oldest forms of shamanism in Western Europe, it was generally agreed, dated to the age of Lascaux. Like Bataille, Eliade drew on the work of French prehistorians to support his thesis. Today, I should add, the situation is reversed. Prominent prehistorians such as Jean Clottes and David Lewis-Williams rely on Eliade's *Shamanism* to bolster their shamanistic interpretations of parietal art.[59]

Underneath the extraordinary economic growth of the Great Acceleration, there remained not a few nagging reminders that the postwar period was also the (second) golden age of the archaic. And no remainder nagged more than Lascaux. Eliade spoke of a "shamanistic rupture" in prehistory, of a definitive but difficult-to-date break between a magic bent on accumulating and the appearance of sacred-seeking shamans. As I have shown, Bataille pointed to the exact same rupture in *Lascaux or the Birth of Art*. Not for the first time, Eliade's account meshed with Bataille's. Ruptures aside, it is clear that Eliade turned archaic societies into a grand cultural unity, which stretched from the painted halls of Lascaux to the newly independent nations of the third world.[60] This, too, he shared with Bataille. Eliade oriented his thought by the same Lascaux–Siberia–indigenous North America triangulation we saw in Bataille. The same magico-religious complexes, Eliade wrote, dominate "the paleolithic cultures in Europe, where bear-ceremonialism and shamanism seem to occur (Lascaux), and the present Siberian and North American civilizations." "As the Siberian and North American shamans still do" was not an uncommon phrase in Eliade's writings in the 1950s.[61]

Shamanism leaves no doubt about Eliade's preference for synthesis. This, too, he shared with Bataille. Eliade was as committed to the comparative method as he was to the *longue durée*; he cobbled together an enormous amount of data from across the world to achieve a total picture. The word "shaman" comes from Siberia, but shamanism was not limited to North Asia. As in *The Myth of the Eternal Return*, *Shamanism* dipped in and out of several branches of the French social sciences, including ethnography, psychology, and sociology. Eliade was especially familiar with work on shamanism in Siberia and North America, and he appreciated Alfred Métraux's studies of South American shamanism. Eliade might have imagined himself as a specialist in the sacred, but he was mainly a comparatist. And his synthetic works impressed the literary critic Northrop Frye. In a letter to Eliade dated April 12, 1960, Frye wrote that he had been reading Eliade "in the full pride of possession": "I never expected to meet any writer who could fill me with the same sense of fresh discovery that Frazer did in my early student days, but I reckoned without M. Eliade." Frye was amazed by Eliade's almost uncanny ability to bring so many different facets of archaic religions into a unified pattern.[62]

Well and fine, but we know the shaman debates revolved around the mental status of the shaman. Did Eliade think shamans were neurotics? Right at the beginning of *Shamanism*, Eliade stated that it was "unacceptable to assimilate shamanism to any kind of mental illness." "One cannot," he affirmed elsewhere, "in every case, explain the shamanic phenomenon by some nervous disequilibrium."[63] Shamanism was religious, not psychopathological, and Eliade hoped the days were over when the former was thought to be only a symptom of the latter. The historian was arguing against those such as

Róheim, the Hungarian ethnologist and psychoanalyst, who couldn't resist explaining the shaman's "magical flights" in Freudian terms of delusion and derangement.[64] To regard shamanism as a mental malady was to condemn a near-universal cultural pattern of Indigenous and archaic societies. In Eliade's view, a shaman is above all "a sick man who has been cured, who has succeeded in curing himself."[65] When budding shamans mastered their vocation, they mastered their nervous illness. It would be wrong, then, to equate the adept shaman's ecstasies with epilepsy, schizophrenia, Arctic hysteria, or any other nervous disorder. To reduce ecstatic rites to mental derangements was to make a pathetic caricature out of primitive cultures, and hadn't missionaries and colonial administrators been doing just that for centuries?

Devereux, it won't surprise you, thought Eliade's *Shamanism* too Jungian, too obsessed with archetypes and ecstasy. For his part, Eliade thought that Devereux's shamanism was too Freudian, too inclined to equate anything religious with psychopathology. The rub was in what the leading scholars of shamanism thought happened after the budding shaman's *maladie initiatique*.[66] From the perspective of the history of religion, the shaman is a mystical healer who has passed through a spiritual crisis. In an unpublished manuscript found among Eliade's papers at the University of Chicago, Eliade wrote: "A generation ago shamanism was considered to be either a psychopathic phenomenon, a primitive healing practice or an archaic type of black magic, but contemporary scholarship has convincingly demonstrated the complexity, the rigor, and the rich spiritual meaning of shamanistic initiation and practices."[67] The demands of shamanism were just too great and its rituals far too complex for a neurotic to grasp. (Devereux disagreed, as I showed in the previous chapter.) Thus, Eliade's championing of shamanism in the 1950s had nothing to do with the celebration of "madness" that would mark the antipsychiatry movement of the late 1960s and '70s. Eliade was unequivocal: The shaman's ecstasies were rites of communal significance, not signs of individual illness. As for why they couldn't be both, Eliade was less plainspoken.

Carlos Castaneda's writings on shamanism offer another instructive counterpoint to Eliade's work. Castaneda's fourteen-year off-and-on apprenticeship with a Yaqui shaman began when he was a graduate student in the anthropology department at the University of California, Los Angeles. The Yaqui are an Indigenous people in the Mexican state of Sonora, southeast of where the Mohave live along the Colorado River. There he found an old, outcast Yaqui shaman named don Juan Matus, who reluctantly agreed to teach him how to lead the life of a Yaqui shaman. Castaneda, who had arrived in Sonora to classify hallucinogenic plants, soon admitted that he wanted nothing more than to immerse himself in don Juan's shamanism. Published by the University of California Press, *The Teachings of Don Juan: A Yaqui Way of Knowledge* details Castaneda's use of psychotropic drugs such as datura, jimsonweed, and *Psilocybe mexicana*.[68] *Teachings* tells a story of existential anxiety and the interdependence of all things rather than ritual ecstasy and the distinct manifestations of the sacred that Eliade called "hierophanies." Castaneda celebrated cosmic flux in a way that will remind intellectual historians of the ever-pulsating energies of D. H. Lawrence or the fluctuating lines of flight of Gilles Deleuze. "What don Juan Matus had offered me was a total cognitive revolution," Castaneda wrote. "We must voluntarily acquiesce to the infinite."[69] If Castaneda's *Teachings* was your only exposure to shamanism, I wouldn't blame you for thinking that shamanism was all about existential anguish and drug-induced discoveries of the self. Needless to say, Castaneda's psychotropic trips and his cult of the self were well suited to the late 1960s counterculture then in full bloom in France and the United States.

In 1968 Castaneda wrote to Eliade just before leaving for another stint of fieldwork in the Sonora Desert. In a letter dated September 12 of that year, Castaneda mailed Eliade a copy of *The Teachings of Don Juan* and asked him if he would comment on it. "I would like to ask for your criticism," he ended the typed letter. "In such matters [as shamanism], your opinion is invaluable to me."[70] I don't know whether Eliade replied. But I do know that Eliade never endorsed Castaneda's don Juan series. How could he? Castaneda's voguish adventure in the archaic failed to meet the standards of the French social sciences. The historian of religion saw in shamanism well-established cultural patterns, not existential trials; he concentrated on consecrated times and places rather than cosmic flux. What was important to Eliade was not the preparation and partaking of such and such a drug, but the way that particular times and places were made sacred by the ritual reenactment of ancestral events. There were "survivals" that needed to be recovered, and Eliade didn't think pseudo-philosophical musings about the merits of drug use were the best way to accomplish that. But Eliade was fascinated by Castaneda's soaring popularity. In a ten-page manuscript titled "Shamanism, Hallucinogens, Initiation," he stated that the rediscovery of shamanism after 1945 was "a fascinating episode in the history of ideas." "Only thirty years ago," he added, "shamanism had a rather limited interest even for specialists—i.e., anthropologists and historians of religions." Eliade optimistically opined that regardless of Castaneda's merits (or lack thereof), his literary fortunes were proof of a swelling interest in archaic religions in general and shamanism in particular. Castaneda's books, Eliade noted, "not only became best-sellers, but created a para-shamanistic underground movement, especially in California."[71]

At any rate, the shaman's contributions to the communities that supported them were far from modest. *A shaman, you will remember, is a healer who has ecstatic experiences for the benefit of the community*. Devereux and Eliade agreed that shamans played an essential role in the defense of the psychic integrity of the community.[72] This explains why shamans enjoyed such a high status in archaic societies. Able to cure certain illnesses, shamans were amateur physicians as much as they were artists. "There is always a cure, a control, an equilibrium brought about by the actual practice of shamanism," Eliade wrote. Their firsthand knowledge of psychotherapy and homeopathy allowed them to cure others: "For if they have cured themselves and are able to cure others, it is, among other things, because they know the mechanism, or rather, the *theory* of illness."[73] In other words, shamans cured illnesses, they were not victims of them. But Eliade was not content with this reevaluation. He believed there was an even deeper meaning to the enigmatic practices of shamans. More than anyone else, shamans internalized the cosmologies and customs of their communities—they were living fossils, so to speak, cultural patrimony in the flesh. The shaman's very existence confirmed, preserved, and reinforced the long-established traditions of the societies they served. If shamans played a vital role in defending the psychic integrity of the community, they played an equally essential role in cultural transmission. Unsurprisingly, Eliade contrasted this conservative aspect of the shamanic vocation with postwar progress and its growing indifference toward continuities of all kinds. Europe had, in his estimation, "sacrificed the best part of its soul" to conquer nature, produce, accumulate, and voraciously consume. With his usual malice toward such matters, he declared that faith in unending progress and the certainty of its empire could not be reconciled with time.

By the mid-1950s Eliade had pushed his interpretation of shamanism one step further. Ten years after the end of the Second World War and in the midst of Europe's great imperial unraveling, Eliade thought that historians, prehistorians, sociologists, and ethnographers had finally begun to speak of shamanism and primitive cultures in "just and unprejudiced terms." With rising feeling, he declared in *The Forge and the Crucible* (1956) that the perceived cultural superiority and the "polemically partisan spirit characteristic of the eighteenth and nineteenth centuries" was finally over.[74] It is in moments like these that you realize the sincere optimism that accompanied the cultural pessimism of the postwar primitivists. Pessimism of the intellect, optimism of the will, the saying goes. In any event, after the first half of the twentieth century, all the old arguments for the superiority of modern European civilization were rapidly rendered out of date. This was a rapid change the postwar primitivists could get behind. Between the time Eliade published *Shamanism* in 1951 and when he returned to the subject in *The Forge and the Crucible* in 1956 people had begun to realize that Western-style progress was not the only, nor even the most desirable, path possible. A few years later Frantz Fanon distilled the revelation: "Come, comrades, the European game is finally over, we must look for something else. We can do anything today provided we do not ape Europe, provided we are not obsessed with catching up with Europe. Europe has gained such a mad and reckless momentum that it has lost control and reason and is heading at dizzying speed toward the brink from which we would be advised to remove ourselves as quickly as possible."[75]

Thus, with catastrophic fears on one side and emancipatory hopes on the other, Eliade was resolute that the history of religions was ideally suited to facilitate the coming rapprochement. By identifying humanity's shared desires and its common cultural bedrock, the history of religions could help reestablish harmonious relations between former colonizers and the formerly colonized. Among Eliade papers there's an undated, untitled manuscript in which the historian reaffirms his postcolonial perspective. It is worth quoting at length:

> As I have repeated on many occasions, the most significant event of our century is not the "proletarian revolution," but the active presence in history of Asia and the "primitive world" (the third world). In the perspective of cultural history—the only one that interests us here—the discovery of Asiatic and archaic spiritual traditions already bears significant consequences and will affect considerably more in the future. The mystique of the proletarian liberation is of a Judeo-Christian origin, and interests primarily the Western world. The discovery (or rediscovery) of the value and significance of non-Western spiritualities represents a *cultural innovation*, for it launches a dialogue and an interrelationship with *the others*, that is, the representatives of Asiatic and archaic traditions.[76]

The University of Chicago and Eliade's Pagan Ideal

In 1956 Eliade moved from Paris to the University of Chicago, where he soon emerged as a leading figure in the history of religions. From Paris, where the history of religions was associated with the social sciences, he brought the French tradition of the scientific study of religion. No single scholar was perhaps more influential in shaping the history of religion into an academic discipline that studied religious sentiments and practices in comparative and historical perspective.[77] But Eliade thought the history of religions was more than a new social science; it was an intellectual response to a profound spiritual crisis.

After settling in the Midwest, Eliade grew more and more convinced that the ills of postwar society were spiritual and that a deeper knowledge of archaic religions could help alleviate them. *Desacralization*—the supplanting of spiritual values by economic growth and political machinations, a process that he considered more pervasive and pernicious than secularization—quickly became Eliade's principal concern. Having no collective spiritual life of their own, the middle classes in modern Western societies worshipped material growth—with disastrous consequences, naturally. As Eliade saw it, this kind of desacralization was one of "the immense problems of today." But when asked in an interview with *L'express* if he believed desacralization was irreversible, he replied quickly, "Ah! No." Fortunately for desacralized societies, primitive religion remained a meaning-laden way of making sense of the world and compelling action. Eliade believed that "to whatever degree he may have desacralized the world, the man who has made his choice in favor of a profane life never succeeds in completely doing away with religious behavior."[78] The problem of desacralization was therefore the problem of a cipher—historians of archaic religions needed to decipher the old sacred elements that persisted in a newly desacralized world, albeit in degraded, caricatured, and camouflaged forms. With one eye on the deep past and the other on a coming cultural reawakening, Eliade encouraged encounters with archaic cultures and with those nations newly unshackled from colonial rule. At the University of Chicago he encouraged a dialogue between past and present, between East and West, and, in his words, between "archaic man" and "modern man." The hope was that such encounters would spark the rebirth of modern man.[79] And so it was that Eliade's pagan ideal went transatlantic.

In the fall of 1956 Eliade accepted a position as visiting professor in the Divinity School at the University of Chicago. In addition to teaching, Eliade delivered the Haskell Lectures, a lecture series held over six Wednesdays in October and November. Not surprisingly, Eliade lectured on initiation rites, secret societies, and shamanism. As you would expect, he described these archaic traditions from a global perspective, with examples from Australia, Africa, Asia, Oceania, and the Americas. In the last two lectures of the series, Eliade argued that the rites of so-called primitive religions had, in one way or another, persisted in modern society. He thought it didn't take a trained archaeologist to unearth archaic cultural patterns in today's practices and "higher religions." That first fall term his emphasis on primitive religions, the rites of Paleolithic hunters, the folkways of Neolithic agriculturalists, and the cultural patterns of so-called ethnographic peoples flew in the face of convention. But he must have impressed his colleagues. Less than a year later Eliade was named Sewell L. Avery Professor and chair of the History of Religions in the Divinity School. It was only a few years later that he founded a new journal, *History of Religion*—a patent transplant of the *Revue de l'histoire des religions*, founded in France in 1880, which he knew well. Eliade's pagan ideal had crossed the Atlantic, and his primitivism found a new home in the halls of the University of Chicago.

In those early days at Chicago it was not unusual to find lecture halls overflowing with students and colleagues eager to hear from Eliade. In print and on campus, the historian's appeal was considerable. Not infrequently, hundreds gathered to hear him speak. *Criterion*, the campus paper, remarked that "the Commons Room of Swift Hall was overflowing on Saturday morning as Professor Mircea Eliade of the Divinity School delivered the final lecture of the conference."[80] It may surprise us today, but Eliade was quite popular. Some went so far as to say that he was "the Frazer of our generation"—referring, of course, to the great comparatist and author of *The Golden Bough*.[81] "If Frazer's research influenced men so dissimilar as Sigmund Freud and T. S. Eliot, Eliade's findings will almost certainly be echoed by great voices in the future," *The New York Times* added in 1964. Here is what one of the Eliade's former students had to say about his influence: "He probably did more than anyone else to get undergraduates who were believers and non-believers, who were Christians or of other faiths, to get curricularly interested in what religion has to tell about the human story."[82] Outside Hyde Park Eliade found a wide readership, just as he had a decade earlier in France. By 1964 nearly every one of his books had appeared in English translation, and many of them sold quite well. In a short time, the history of religions had become a credible academic field. Eliade flourished on foreign soil, and not for the first time.

Searching for the same kind of multidisciplinary community he had known in France, Eliade discovered the Committee on Social Thought. Unlike the Jung-Institut that Eliade knew so well in Zurich, the Committee on Social Thought at the University of Chicago was not devoted to any one worldview. Instead, it crossed disciplinary frontiers and unified the arts, sciences, and humanities. Founded in 1941 by the historian John U. Nef, the economist Frank Knight, and the anthropologist Robert Redfield, the Committee brought together scholars of art, literature, philosophy, history, society, politics, and religion (fig. 4.3). Notable members of the Committee have included Hannah Arendt, Saul Bellow, Allan Bloom, J. M. Coetzee, François Furet, Friedrich Hayek, and Paul Ricoeur. Its program of study dispensed with textbooks and rapid generalizations. The Committee insisted that the essence

FIGURE 4.3. Two skeptics of yet more history-making: Mircea Eliade and John Nef. One in a series of photographs of Eliade and Nef, cofounder of the University of Chicago's Committee on Social Thought and author of *War and Human Progress: An Essay on the Rise of Industrial Civilization* (1950). Undated photograph, courtesy of the Hanna Holborn Gray Special Collections Research Center, University of Chicago Library.

of learned inquiry was studying ancient and modern texts in their pristine state and in an interdisciplinary setting. On January 3, 1964, *Time* magazine called the Committee on Social Thought "the oddest graduate school in the United States." It is no surprise, then, that in addition to his duties at the Divinity School, Eliade became a member of the Committee on Social Thought. He described the Committee as striving for "a richer life of the mind and a more serious concern with the life of the spirit." The Committee was daring, but a big part of its daring was that it didn't claim to be novel. Its program of study was "odd" only by virtue of the age in which it appeared.[83]

What first attracted Eliade to the Committee on Social Thought was its opposition to the "excessive atomization of learning."[84] Eliade knew from his years in Paris that large swaths of academia were rapidly becoming training grounds for technicians and technocrats. What need was there for the life of the mind and the history of ideas when higher education was no more than a measured step on the way to vocational expertise? The question, so often heard on campuses today, was not unfamiliar in the early 1960s, even in the hallowed halls of an institution like the University of Chicago. But the Committee abhorred narrow specialization—which didn't mean, Eliade hastened to add, that scholars shouldn't start out as specialists.[85] This lakeside corner of the Midwest rejected highfalutin jargon and disciplinary enclosure in favor of a more unified vision. Since the Committee opposed both the pigeonholed expert and the dilettante, it was not short of enemies. Unsurprisingly, resistance to Eliade was particularly pronounced in the positivistic social sciences. But Eliade, ever the postcolonialist, recognized that the source of the mounting criticisms was not academic parochialism but "a growing cultural parochialism."[86]

Reading Eliade on the Committee on Social Thought reveals many of the historian's own views on scholarship, creativity, and cultural rejuvenation. Like Eliade, the Committee turned out bold synthetic works. In an age when it was increasingly in bad taste to admit to being a humanist, the Committee strove for a broad, humanistic approach. The Committee, moreover, also aligned with Eliade's own long-standing opposition to cultural parochialism. As I have shown, Eliade's postwar writings were saturated with the belief that Europe needed to rediscover the great diversity of human cultures. Finally, the Committee's search for enduring values mirrored the historian's own reasons for contradicting his time and building up the past. A collective search in the attics of time was critical to the Committee's "creative spirit." Here Eliade's project of recovery and revival found institutional shelter. The Committee encouraged him to ponder how to salvage the creative spirit from the halls of higher education. Together, the aims of Eliade and the Committee were grander than merely diagnosing "the closing of the American mind." They wanted to preserve cultural creativity and renew modern society in the process.

It was not uncommon to hear Committee members talk of saving Western civilization from itself. Like Eliade, Committee members such as Arendt and Bellow lamented the sterility of modern life and complained about the moral bankruptcy of Western societies. It seems many members shared Eliade's concern for saving "modern man" from the spiritual and cultural vacuity that was his lot. And the Committee's general disdain for modern industrial life was matched by its own revivalist proclivities. In the first decades of the Committee, then, we find this book's central thesis: the restoration of earlier, more meaningful, and more creative cultures as an antidote to modern life. There is a big difference between repeating what has been done and doing something new. The former is religious and, in Eliade's estimation, creative; the latter is historical and anxiety-inducing. "Cultural creativity," Eliade wrote, "was perhaps the most cherished concern of the Committee." The historian's pessimism, however, was just around the corner. "One dares not be too optimistic," he wrote. "We know now that the menace of a final destruction through a thermo-nuclear war is only one aspect of the profound crisis of our times. No less dangerous, though not so spectacular, is the increasing spiritual sterility resulting from the atomization of knowledge. And we also know that, in the domain of spirit, prolonged sterility leads ineluctably to spiritual death."[87]

Eliade settled into his new post at the University of Chicago and on the Committee on Social Thought during the decades of decolonization. It was a world-historical moment that "forced us into confrontations that we could not even have imagined fifty years ago."[88] The historian had two engagements in mind: Decolonization demanded intellectuals confront their hypermodernized, desacralized societies; liberation also demanded a more meaningful encounter with cultures that until recently had been suppressed by European empires. These were the key contexts in which Eliade situated his postwar oeuvre. And it is no coincidence that as the number of newly independent nations rose out of the ashes of European empires, so too did the number of religious studies departments on campuses across the United States. While it would be foolhardy to argue for any direct causal link, their contemporaneity is surely more than coincidental. By 1986, when death took the seventy-nine-year-old scholar, there were some 450 religious studies departments in tax-supported universities and colleges across America.

Because of decolonization, Eliade was certain that the history of religions would play an important role in contemporary cultural life. "For as we know," Eliade wrote in the summer of 1961, formerly colonized, non-European cultures are "still nourished by a rich religious soil." But these so-called archaic religions apparently still required translation. And so, intellectuals like Eliade made primitive cultures—still in the throes of *Homo religiosus*, evidently—intelligible to the minds of modern men. This, Eliade declared, was the cultural mission of the new social science he helped establish in the United States: "Whatever its role has been in the past, the comparative study of religions is destined to assume a cultural role of the first importance in the near future." Again, Eliade emerges as a dyed-in-the-wool primitivist turned anticipatory postcolonialist; he celebrated non-European cultures and encouraged his students to heed the call of the third world. In this, he envisaged the history of religions as leading the way in breaking the West out of its "cultural provincialism."[89]

When Eliade arrived in Chicago in 1956, the idea that primitive cultures were nothing but bizarre curios and superstitious survivals was largely over. Gone were the days—in the academic study of religions, at least—when monstrous mosaics of primitive violence were assembled in books such as Tylor's *Primitive Culture* and Frazer's *Golden Bough*. Tylor was "one of the best living ethnologists of his day," but his naive evolutionary schema of historical succession, his escalator philosophy of progress, was no longer acceptable. *The Golden Bough* remained a landmark of modern European intellectual history, but its thesis that science would one day supplant religion just as religion had supplanted magic was untenable.[90] What distinguished Eliade's approach from theirs? First, Eliade insisted that religion must be examined and explained "on its own terms." In their battle against religion earlier in the century, comparatists such as Tylor and Frazer had used a notion of survivals to show the sociological and psychological reasons that primitive superstitions persisted in the so-called higher religions. Further, Eliade's immersion in the French human and social sciences distinguished him from his English forerunners. As Eliade told it, it took the ascendancy of the French social sciences to make the scientific study of religion a reality.[91]

In time, Eliade shaped the history of religions in the United States. But what shape did his *Religionswissenschaft* take? The scientific study of religions took religious experience out of the realm of revelation and into the domain of the social sciences. The history of religion was no longer the property of faith traditions that spoke of true and false religions. Durkheim had taken the first step: In *The Elementary Forms of Religious Life* (1912), the founder of the French sociological school had identified religion with society and concluded that sacredness and the social were one and the same. It may have been a reduction, but it was a reduction that thrust religion into the purview of the social sciences. "I have great respect for theologians and theological methods of inquiry," Eliade wrote. "But I am a historian of religions, and see myself as doing something very different."[92] If the English anthropologist E. E. Evans-Pritchard could integrate primitive religions into the larger history of religions in 1965 in *Theories of Primitive Religion*, it was because scholars like Durkheim, Mauss, and Eliade had succeeded in wresting what was pagan from the viselike grip of theology. Thanks to the French tradition of studying religion, the history of religions had come a long way from Freud's *Totem and Taboo*, and even further from David Hume's insistence in *Dialogues Concerning Natural Religion* (1779) that religion was either "a sick man's dream" or "the playsome whimsy of monkeys in human shape." But all was not new: The new *Religionswissenschaft*, like the comparatists of old, often folded time into space. Eliade and his ilk often compared Franco-Cantabrian hunting cultures to the cultures of present-day "primitives," just as Bataille had done a decade earlier in France. There wasn't much that stopped Eliade from leaping across time and illuminating the obscure links between various ethnographic and prehistoric provinces: "Would a naturalist who has studied an elephant only under the microscope really have an adequate conception of that animal?"[93] Not exactly—or rather, only exactly. And so, he compared "primitive" cultures whenever he felt like it, even though he knew doing so risked "assimilating current ethnographic peoples and cultures to the peoples and cultures of prehistory."[94]

By tacking back and forth between local manifestations and transhistorical meanings, Eliade avoided the two big pitfalls in the history of religions. The first was forgetting that every symbol, be it a spiral or a sun, has its own unique cultural and historical context. Religion, like everything else, was historically conditioned. "There is no such thing as a 'pure' religious fact," Eliade wrote in 1963. "Such a fact is always *also* a historical, sociological, cultural, and psychological fact, to name only the most important contexts." Hence, a rigorous *Religionswissenschaft* required historical interpretations. Eliade believed that what was most striking in the history of religions was not the universal presence of certain rituals, myths, and symbols, "but the fact that their significance is never *exactly* the same."[95] But there was a second pitfall, which Eliade called the "problem of historicism." It was wrong to think that because religious data always have a specific context, cross-cultural comparisons were leaps of faith. In good universalist fashion, Eliade argued that every culture had a similar religious structure.[96] This allowed him to apply the language of autonomy and sovereignty to archaic religions in the decades of decolonization. The way Eliade told it, ever since the publication of *The Myth of the Eternal Return* in 1949, every religion presents the same essential story, told from a slightly different point of view.[97] The solution to these two extremes was quite simple: Show that religious phenomena such as ritual repetitions or ecstatic experiences were virtually timeless *and* historically situated.

There were few things Eliade spoke of with greater assurance than "the human spirit." He argued that the desire for sanctity and the desire for paradise lost—the transhistorical desires that defined *Homo religiosus*—were permanent features of the human spirit. Religious sentiments, then, were not in the main by-products of social inequality (Marx) or psychic need (Freud). Religion was inextricably entwined with what it meant to be human.[98] By the time Eliade arrived in the Midwest, he had known for at least a decade that it took the light of the *longue durée* to reveal transhistorical meanings and desires. Honestly but not sheepishly, Eliade admitted, "Personally, but it's a very personal opinion and I cannot prove it, I think the sacred is the structure of human consciousness and I don't think that it is possible to live without the sacred." As long as there are human beings, he continued, there will be a thirst for "something basic, meaningful, and absolutely true."[99] And thus we find once again Eliade's assertion that religion is *irreducible* to any social, psychological, or economic factor. Religion was and remains "an experience *sui generis*, incited by man's encounter with the sacred." Elsewhere he repeated that though "religion is obviously a very complex phenomenon," it is first of all "an experience *sui generis* that is incited by man's encounter with the sacred."[100]

After untangling the sacred from a web of degradation and caricature, Eliade emphasized the continued importance of archaic spiritualities. In his hands, the history of religions became an avenue to unearthing cultural survivals and challenging the destructive dynamism of capitalist progress. Much like Lovejoy in *Primitivism and Related Ideas in Antiquity* (1935), a book Eliade knew and cited, the twice-transplanted historian was always on the lookout for documents of the sacred that had survived the ravages of time. And it was not for aesthetic reasons that Eliade returned to the symbols and rites of archaic societies; for him, liberation was found in the rediscovery of archaic cultural patterns, not in freeing oneself from all primitive mystifications.[101] Archaic religions may be mystifying, but their mystifications offered the refuge of ritual repetition, the adventure of ecstatic experience, and the durability of what was time-tested. The trick, then, was to explain archaic religions without demythologize them. There was more to age-old myths and symbols and cycles than the instant need to demystify.

But there is a final twist in this tale of Eliade at the University of Chicago, beyond the aforementioned revelations about his noxious political life in the 1930s. We know Eliade hoped to breathe new life into pagan cultures, but some believed that his oeuvre secreted something akin to religious conversion. And it's true that pure disinterestedness found no place in Eliade's writings. A certain covert evangelism runs through his postwar writings—if by "evangelism" we mean an ardent advocacy of archaic religions, not the spreading of the Christian gospel. The onetime follower of Jung often described himself as "sympathetic" to religious beliefs of all kinds.[102] Although Eliade was always cautious about anything that veered into the territory of modern religiosity, time and again he acknowledged his role as a valet of archaic forms of religiosity.

First in Paris and then in Chicago, Eliade preserved the living remnants of archaic societies against the spiritual exodus of the postwar period. To him, simple vestiges turned out not to be so simple after all. Not uncontroversially, he believed that living in accordance with archaic religion was the best way to live authentically in the world. Such were the redemptive aspirations of Eliade's pagan ideal. The recovery and revival he sought was possible; the deep past could once again by possessed; demise was not inevitable. Redemption was not found in Cioran's melancholic defeat, nor in rejecting all convention, as other foreign-born French writers such as Eugène Ionesco did.[103] For Eliade, there was a natural link between resurrection and human happiness. Indeed, if we remember Stendhal's *The Red and the Black* for *la promesse de bonheur*, then we should remember Eliade as a defender of *la promesse de résurrection*. More than any other postwar primitivist, Eliade's ideal was torn between a buried past and a reawakened future. No tombs, no resurrections. If only his contemporaries could see through the accelerated cadence of modern life and rediscover the patterns of archaic religion.

EPILOGUE

Primitivism in Our Time

> All manner of alternative futures are now being imagined, and many of them invoke the wilderness, and moments of our distant past, envisioning futures that from the viewpoint of the industrial model look "primitive."
> KIM STANLEY ROBINSON, *Future Primitive*

Four intellectuals with ties to the French social sciences found in so-called primitive cultures time-tested alternatives to the frenetic pace of modernization in the 1950s and '60s. The preceding chapters tell the story of how Georges Bataille, a specialist in prehistory; Henri Lefebvre, a philosopher turned rural sociologist; Georges Devereux, an ethnographer and psychiatrist; and Mircea Eliade, a historian of religion, took it upon themselves to keep primitivism alive, lest we forget about archaic religions, our animal origins, and much else. Their work marks an especially rich episode in the history of modern primitivism. Today, we tend to think of primitivism as an escape into the exotic or bizarre. We think of the artist Paul Gauguin, that first modern "primitive," or we recall his more subversive successor, André Breton. But primitivism hasn't always been an aesthetic project of aggrandizing the placid or the paroxysmal. In the years after the Second World War, primitivism emerged in certain French social scientific circles not as a modernist crutch or a surrealist headdress to be thrown aside at any moment, but as a weighty response to capitalism's growth imperative. The postwar primitivists demonstrate how radical the championing of survivals can be in an era that celebrates ceaseless change.

To counter the dispossession of an immemorial world, four men of letters sought to resurrect older ways of living in and with the world. Their work demonstrates that if you know where to look, proof abounds that the remnants of noncapitalist societies are not gone but still living. They were exemplars of how to think of the past not as a foreign country but as a familiar place of possibility. If the postwar primitivists seem didactic, it is because they were. They were adamant that it was not humanity that was the problem—it was that acquisitive, economical, machine-minded automaton *Homo economicus*. Although they were several steps from grappling with the intricacies of the Anthropocene, their oeuvres are a testament to what the deep past still has to teach us. As I've said, their work was marked by an antipathy to modernization and a fascination with what they called "survivals"—archaic pathways that they believed could provide a living link to more sustainable styles of life. It was these survivals that fueled the postwar primitivists' stubborn optimism, the sunny counterpart to their cultural pessimism. In the tradition of Rousseau and Mauss, they contemplated the present with the eyes of a remote age.

Adventures in the Archaic has uncovered one intellectual strand of primitivism that flourished in the French social sciences in the first years of the Great Acceleration. Now several new primitivist winds are blowing. One has been called bourgeois primitivism, and it is far removed from the primitivism in the pages of this book. Another is anarcho-primitivism, which is bourgeois primitivism's opposite. And then there is the degrowth movement, one of the most unexpected developments in the first quarter of the twenty-first century. At any rate, sensibilities are slowly changing, and so the varieties of present-day primitivism are well worth looking at.

Bourgeois primitivism targets upscale individuals who want to transform their consumption patterns and improve their personal well-being.[1] A lifestyle approach to the Anthropocene available to a privileged few, bourgeois primitivism is packed with the language of self-improvement. Shop farmers' markets, buy organic vegetables, run without shoes, and talk incessantly about quality of life—bourgeois primitivism has effectively tapped into the growing environmental zeitgeist among progressive consumers. And well-being is exactly the kind of thing you would expect affluent moderns to go into raptures over. At its core, bourgeois primitivism is postwar consumer culture rebranded. "The magic act of bourgeois primitivist thought," writes the geographer David Correia, "has been to fashion forms of consumption that reduce environmental impact without requiring any sacrifice of class-based luxuries."[2] Is this rebranding of capitalist consumption even primitivism? If primitivism is no more than French people buying African-inspired clothes at mid-century or Americans talking about paleo diets in the twenty-first century, then the unit-idea is surely lost.

Bourgeois primitivism not only reinforces the status quo, it offers capital the veneer of sustainability it so desperately craves. True, there is much to admire in it: Bourgeois primitivists practice voluntary simplicity; they opt for the minimum to fulfill their needs; they tend to care more about quality than quantity; and they are skeptical of the view that techno-fixes will save us. Get outdoors, walk around, use your body, have sex, look at fire, live in small groups, coordinate yourself in time and space. Simple. But bourgeois primitivists ignore matters of production and distribution, preferring to focus on individual patterns of consumption rather than political economy. The historian William Cronon criticized this kind of well-intentioned bourgeois environmentalism decades ago in "The Trouble with Wilderness: Or, Getting Back to the Wrong Nature."[3] It is a response to anthropogenic global warming located only in the sphere of consumption. There is a difference between the societal preoccupations of the postwar primitivists and the personal choices of bourgeois primitivists. The latter is a fad for well-being, a fashion for flaunting how one can afford to live with less. There's nothing inherently wrong with well-being, of course. The postwar primitivists, too, spoke of an infectious joie de vivre. But individuals making better, healthier consumption choices is no solution to the problem of cultural degradation, no path toward an ecologically viable society. Bourgeois primitivism shifts the blame onto consumers, spreading the disastrous illusion that if only more people committed to living better, healthier lives, today's ecological concerns would disappear. What bourgeois primitivism lacks is a political ecology determined to bring society back in line with the natural world.

At the opposite extreme stands anarcho-primitivism. If bourgeois primitivism has gone mainstream, anarcho-primitivism remains decidedly marginal. Anarcho-primitivists like John Zerzan, the movement's best-known ideologue, think that civilization qua civilization is to blame for alienation, conquest, conformity, domination, hierarchy, patriarchy, genocide, and ecocide. Not capitalism, not even industrial modernity, but the civilizing process itself is responsible for the demise of humanity and the planet. Zerzan is intent on subverting the entire project of civilization and eliminating absolutely all power relations. The intriguing thing about Zerzan's anarcho-primitivism—what makes it worth mentioning—is that it assails not only civil society but also culture. Articulated language and symbolic culture, we learn, are two of the main weapons in the arsenal of civilization, bringing instinct, sexuality, women, and wildness all into line. "We have taken a monstrously wrong turn with symbolic culture," Zerzan (on whom irony is apparently lost) writes. What other primitivists see as the very stuff of life—culture, the arts, rites of passage, sacred times and sacred places—are for Zerzan the dark origins of domination. "Primitivists like John Zerzan, who in trying to whittle away what seems to divide us from pure, unmediated experience, end up whittling away absolutely everything," writes David Graeber. Lascaux is a prime example. According to Zerzan, the cultural outpouring of the Upper Paleolithic was "an early turning away from a life of openness and communion with nature."[4] The shamanic rites at Lascaux were a concerted effort to domesticate man and manipulate nature. This is precisely the opposite of what Bataille read on the painted rock face. Zerzan's Lascaux is not a dark reprieve from the daily weight of relentless accumulation; it is a prison house of calculation and coercion.

Granted, anarcho-primitivism is easily dismissed. Of all today's primitivisms, it is the most openly anti-civilization, the most overtly anti-tech, and the most akin to "going back to the caves." It's hard not to think of (and slightly tweak) Voltaire's anti-Rousseauian quip: "I have read your manifesto against civilization, and thank you for it. One longs, after reading you, to walk on all fours. But as I have lost that habit long ago, I feel unhappily the impossibility of resuming it." But there is another strain of anarcho-primitivism, more subtle and scholarly. In the last two decades scholars such as Graeber, Sahlins, James C. Scott, and David Wengrow have used primitivist themes to overturn the Hobbesian image of the primitive past as a precivilized state of deprivation, brutality, and ignorance. "Life outside the state—life as a 'barbarian'—may often have been materially easier, freer, and healthier than life within it," writes Scott in *Against the Grain* (2017).[5] The anarcho-primitivism in Scott's work is more sophisticated than Zerzan's, as you would expect from a trained political scientist. Civilization need not lead ineluctably to domestication, bondage, and violence. Where Zerzan conflates, Scott distinguishes. The latter rejects the identification of civilization with the state and the identification of power with coercion. Nonstate societies—which are chock-full of symbolic culture—offer an alternative to the state's ferocious demands for labor and growth.

The word "degrowth" is the most recent idea to appear in the primitivist firmament. When it appeared in February 2002 in *Revue silence*, it was designed to "expose the mystification of the ideology of sustainable development."[6] The very idea of growth, degrowth theorists believe, is a trap. As for the phrase "sustainable growth," well, it's a contradiction in terms. The only sensible response to the climate crisis is for affluent nations to scale back. Degrowth soon became an activist slogan in France and Spain, and by 2008 the primitivist resurgence that unfolded in France had come to the attention of Americans. Critics of the mad, headlong rush into growth finally came together in Paris in April 2008. This first international conference (it has been held every other year since) was called the Conference on Economic Degrowth for Ecological Sustainability and Social Equity. That it took place in 2008 should strike no one as strange. In such a climate of financial corruption and crisis, there was an appetite for alternatives to societies that promoted advertising, automobiles, urban sprawl, subprime mortgages, venture capitalists, Black Fridays, Ponzi schemes, and widening economic inequality. Every year the degrowth movement has more and more to say to those who realize that what's needed is less and less. Produce less, buy less, consume less, pollute less—the reality is simple; getting there is not.[7]

The degrowth movement thinks that we need to downshift, to slow down life's pace, to stop picturing the future as a kind of growth and start rediscovering life outside what Eliade called "historical time." Stagnation is not a dirty word but a pristine aim. Deceleration and leveling down are the movement's chief tenets.[8] Part of this leveling down comes from individuals practicing voluntary simplicity. We live better when we choose to live with less, as all the data attest. This degrowth shares with bourgeois primitivism. But unlike bourgeois primitivism, the degrowth movement has its roots in twentieth-century French thought. The movement routinely recognizes three French forerunners, two of whom will be quite familiar at this point. Gift economies remain popular among degrowth advocates, and Mauss's plea for a moral economy that has limits in *The Gift* remains a shining example of one way to escape the spirit of capitalism and the confines of *Homo economicus*. The give-and-take of obligatory reciprocity is intrinsic to maintaining a sense of balance and equilibrium. Bataille, too, exerts a strong pull on degrowth theorists. His *The Accursed Share* proposed Marshall Plan–type expenditures to redistribute the social surplus of decades of carbon burning, similar to what the affluent states of the Global North promised the Global South in the Paris Agreement. But it is the philosopher André Gorz who coined the term *décroissance*. In *Ecology as Politics* (1975), he argued for the return of worker self-management and a focus on use-values rather than exchange-values. Since then, this Lefebvre-inspired intellectual has inspired a host of degrowth thinkers, including Serge Latouche.[9]

An anthropologist and economist, Latouche is the most renowned French proponent of degrowth today. He cofounded the Research & Degrowth network, an academic collective dedicated to finally bidding adieu to growth. He is the author of *Farewell to Growth* (2010), probably his most well-known book in the United States.[10] He is a self-identified "growth objector" and a frequent contributor to Alain Caillé's *Revue du MAUSS*, a journal that sparked an anti-utilitarian revival in the French social sciences. As Latouche sees it, Euro-American societies don't just have growth economies—they are growth societies. "Growth for growth's sake" has become the primary objective of the modern economy, and the industrial values of utility and efficiency have become the sine qua non of modern life. Full on the idea of growth, everybody is in on the act.[11] Like the most compelling primitivisms, Latouche's vision of degrowth is based in the social sciences. He calls for an equitable downsizing of production and consumption, which will increase human happiness and enhance ecological conditions in the short run and the long run alike. In fact, he proposes a threefold program: Reduce overall growth and rewild much of the Earth while expanding clean-energy infrastructure.[12] That is the way to a global economy considerably smaller in material terms and to societies that care about quality and cooperation, not quantity and competition.

But, as the preceding chapters have shown, critics of advanced industrial society did not wait for the concentration of carbon dioxide in the Earth's atmosphere to reach 370 parts per million (as it did early in the twenty-first century). Already in the early 1950s there was a sense in some circles that the "economic miracle" was a grave mistake. The word *décroissance* may have appeared in France in the early 1970s, but the idea of degrowth, which entails a certain primitivism, emerged in the French social sciences two decades earlier.

An older generation of French intellectuals, four middle-aged men in particular, were troubled by the degradations the boom years had wrought not just on nature but on culture. They responded to the perpetual growth machine by leaning on the social sciences and turning to prehistoric paintings, rustic terrains, and so-called primitive cultures. Whether it was the rites of Paleolithic hunters, the folkways of Neolithic agriculturalists, or the patterns of Indigenous peoples, these reformers-to-be used the archaic to challenge the era's emphasis on unabated growth. But they were exceptional. For most people, it was not age-old cultures but technological progress that had a reassuring aura of inevitability about it. The postwar primitivists, however, took steps to drag the monuments of growth and technocracy down from their glimmering pedestals. They were unaware, of course, of the true consequences of fossil capitalism. But they knew the fantasies that fueled it well enough to understand that it heralded cultural and ecological devastation. Untimely in the 1950s, their particular strand of primitivism seems to suit the current climate. "Green" ideas and practices ought to matter to intellectual historians, and one claim of this book is that often there are no greener ideas or practices than archaic ones.[13] That's a big part of the intellectual appeal of deep history. Survivals are windows into sustainable styles of life—what is radical, by definition, has roots. Come what may, the postwar primitivists had seen the writing on the wall.

When Kim Stanley Robinson observes in *Future Primitive* (1994) that "all manner of alternative futures are now being imagined, and many of them invoke the wilderness, and moments of our distant past, envisioning futures that from the viewpoint of the industrial model look 'primitive,'" I am reminded of the postwar primitivists' conviction that we need to look backward in order to move forward. Primitivism demands dexterity. And the postwar primitivists saw in fine detail a future that combined elements of the archaic past with select advantages of the technological present. They proposed an amalgamation of the best of the present with the best of the past. That was the promise of a certain primitivism. "We are in a race to invent and practice a sustainable mode of life before catastrophes strike us," Robinson adds. Thankfully, we need not start from scratch. Many of these practices will be derived from the kind of biosphere-sustaining habits that were once deemed veritably archaic. Continuing with the first-person plural, Robinson concludes, "We might for very good reasons choose to live in ways that resemble in part the ways of our ancestors and of the primitives that still inhabit corners of our planet."[14] The revival of precious survivals therefore represents a great deal more than a reactionary impulse. The environmental movement, deep ecology, steady-state economics, ecofeminism, ecosocialism, degrowth initiatives, ecosocialist degrowth, bioregionalism, return-to-the-land collectives, and the Vía Campesina network all harvest the fruits of archaic ways to build greener, more sustainable societies with virtually no carbon footprint. So-called primitive cultures knew a thing or two about our relationship to the world that we forget at our own peril, which explains why peasant movements and Indigenous communities are at the forefront of responsible social and ecological change.

Unfortunately, the apocalyptic seductions of the Anthropocene are great. Dire warnings and ominous predictions often accompany discussions of man-made climate change. Rising seas, forests ablaze, glaciers disappearing—today's ecological degradations, we are told, will bring tomorrow's civilizational collapse. Confronted with the possibility of an end-of-days +4°C of warming, responses can vary from a desire to run away to a feeling that since demise is inevitable, why bother changing course now? It is easy to feel caught between self-indulgent detachment and the cynical desire to blow everything up. The future isn't what it used to be, so doomsaying is everywhere these days, as any cursory look at the literature will prove. "It is worse, much worse, than you think" is how David Wallace-Wells opens *The Uninhabitable Earth* (2019). "Words such as symbiosis, harmony, agreement, accord, all those ideas of deep ecology smack of an earlier, less benighted time," writes Bruno Latour. "Since then, everything has taken a turn for the worse."[15] It seems the funeral pyre is already lit. In the words of Cioran, Eliade's Franco-Romanian friend, "Trees are massacred, houses go up—faces, faces everywhere. Man is *spreading*. Man is the cancer of the earth."[16] Hasn't humanity been unambiguously bad for the planet and for pretty much every other living creature on it? No more "brightsiding" the Anthropocene. Alarmists never tire of affixing *ir-* to the beginning of words—irrevocable, irredeemable, irreversible—much like the postwar primitivists and their preferred prefix *re-*. The literary critic

Fredric Jameson captured this widespread belief in the planet's irreversible decline with the quip, "It is easier to imagine the end of the world than the end of capitalism." It is telling that this bon mot is the most repeated observation in all the literature on the Anthropocene.

A big reason the Anthropocene tends toward misanthropy is that "the age of man" attributes to all of human history developments that are actually the product of recent history. The root *anthropos* blames an entire species for what has been the work of relatively few men.[17] Neither human enterprise per se nor civilization as such is the source of anthropogenic climate change. Rather, today's crises are the outgrowth of a particular kind of human enterprise and a specific way of organizing human life that has dominated the Earth only very recently. The problem with an all-encompassing Anthropocene is that it misses all those people who came before who lived in better harmony with nature. What currently counts as civilization is a historical aberration, an anomaly at odds with nearly the whole of the human past. Thus, we need a more precise term. It is not man as such but the rapacious logic of capital that is to blame. We live on a planet, after all, that for the last seventy years has been more or less dominated by fossil capitalism. The ruination that we attribute to the Anthropocene is in fact the perturbations of late capitalism. Rightly understood, the Anthropocene is a capitalist crisis, the flash point of decades of capitalist production and consumption. Instead of "the age of man," we ought to say "the age of capital." We arrive, then, at the Capitalocene—an ugly name for an even uglier reality.[18]

And yet, a starry-eyed techno-optimism defines us starkly now. For in addition to being inaccurately named, the Anthropocene has a technological bias aligned with the interests of entrenched wealth. By reducing human history to a series of technological innovations, the Anthropocene essentially argues that the future, like the past, will be determined by technological progress—a Whiggish view of what's to come if there ever was one. Apparently, the most reliable solution to the crises created by the conjunction of capital and technology is more capital and more technology, more tech start-ups and more start-up nations. Technocrats assert that whatever problems exist today, including dire ecological ones, will one day be engineered away. Therefore, we must continue to fuel economic growth and technological innovation. What's needed is more of the dazzling tech and mastery of nature that fueled the crisis in the first place. The only way out is to push forward: advance, scale, advance, scale, advance, scale—until we gain enough speed to blow past the stars. In short, have faith, tech will provide. Quick techno-fixes offer tremendous hope and comforting reassurance that we are on the right path. But they also extend the postwar fantasy that growth can indeed be unending. In case it isn't clear already, techno-futurism is an outgrowth of fast capitalism, which further entrenches the markets, institutions, and culture that gave us the climate crisis in the first place.[19]

Meanwhile, the thing to remember is not to be confused by these competing responses to the Anthropocene, as if one were right and the other wrong. Soured on contemporary human existence, the first response is a kind of curdled romanticism, the second a tech-charged science fiction.[20] The postwar primitivists were neither catastrophists nor capitalists. Abject despair and misanthropy were to them distasteful dead ends. There is a big difference between being against the species as such and opposing the capitalist world system. What the postwar primitivists criticized was the modern Western rapine of the archaic and natural worlds—the invisible hand that everywhere reached for more. Unlike catastrophists, they channeled their discontent into the recovery of survivals. In the end, their efforts were not dismal but creative. Their reverence for age and tradition was not a rustic dream or a wistful melancholy, but a humanistic response to relentless change. If nothing else, they are models of how to resist the worst seductions of the Anthropocene. As for the techno-futurists and their image of man as a Promethean superspecies, they advance the same apotheosis of *Homo economicus* that got us into this mess in the first place. A technocratic space opera, all piercing coloratura and no sotto voce. But the blessed isle of another planet is a lie; there is no planet B; we are bound, earthbound. Do we really need more delusions of planetary mastery and superlative control? The reproach recalls Eliade's remark, made in 1949, when the fires of the Great Acceleration were barely lit: "It is not inadmissible to think of an epoch, and an epoch not too far distant, when humanity, to ensure its survival, will find itself reduced to desisting from any further 'making' of history."[21]

In the decades to come, ecological degradation will force us to take a hard look at the fantasy of limitless growth and the culture of voracious consumption embraced by Western societies in the wake of the Second World War. It is already beginning to be realized that the societies that emerged after 1945, with their sharp rise in carbon emissions, are not models of sane development but examples of pathological dysfunction.[22] As the years of warming wear on, the coming sea change will surely have cultural as well as ecological dimensions. It's possible that societies once disparaged as prehistoric, provincial, and primitive will suddenly be seen in a new light. It is important to remember that history is our handiest counterfactual, and it is full of societies that lived satisfying, meaning-laden lives within their ecological means—which explains the aura of prestige that once again surrounds what is ancestral and indigenous. At any rate, the cultural transformation that will accompany the climate crisis is set to be one of the most gripping stories of the century, in much the same way as the freedom of formerly colonized peoples transformed certain corners of Western culture in the last century. In this book I have examined the cultural degradations of the postwar period more than its ecological ones. After all, it wasn't just the natural world that was rapidly transformed: The Great Acceleration threatened the very existence of customs that had survived for millennia. With greater hindsight, we see that one of the most pernicious symptoms of postwar modernization was that it broke up as many perennial cultural patterns as environmental ones. We've burned far too many fossil fuels to go on living as we have, but as a species we've forgotten how to live well without them.[23]

It was the forces of modernization and the cultures of the formerly colonized unchained after the Second World War that spurred Bataille, Lefebvre, Devereux, and Eliade to champion the archaic. They did not look for solutions in greater technological mastery; salvation was not located in the domain that had triggered the Great Acceleration in the first place. There was also no going back to some state of nature, whatever that might mean. If solutions to postwar problems were to be found anywhere, they argued, they would be found in the survivals and the sacred times and places that appear with some frequency in this book. More specifically, they believed that the archaic offered a wealth of time-tested alternatives: cyclical rhythms, local resilience, durable communities, rustic hospitality, collective expenditure, no-growth economies, diffuse libidinal energies, cooperative control of production, a commitment to quality over quantity, and a devotion to social solidarity more than individual profit. At the same time, the postwar primitivists recognized that the deep past, like the onrushing present, was a mixed bag. They were not infatuated with primitive culture whole cloth. If primitive cultures were to be revived, they needed to be selectively revived. Therefore, they promoted *certain* archaic arts of living by judiciously picking through tradition, choosing what they thought best and discarding the rest.

By the same token, only in the last decade or so have we come to realize that our future might lie precisely in the remains of yesterday. But how can we draw on prehistoric, provincial, or primitive folkways in an increasingly inhospitable age? What's needed, some primitivists argue, is a kind of triple action: Resurrect older ways of living; create cleaner, decarbonized technologies; and eliminate capitalism's entrenched wealth. Climate work—be it land stewardship; wind and solar farms; energy storage and distribution; altered diets and redesigned cities; habitat restoration and rewilding large swaths of the Earth; or the study of forests, glaciers, permafrost, the atmosphere and the oceans—will be the main business of this century. But alongside this essential work we need to relearn how to live on a vital minimum. Nearly a century ago, Lovejoy reminded us that "a life far simpler and less sophisticated in some or in all respects is a more desirable life."[24]

Collective amnesia about the archaic has no place in our anthropogenic age. It's as I've been saying all along: Somewhere between indiscriminately celebrating progress and obstinately clinging to the past there remains the promise of a certain primitivism. As the planet we know changes all around us, it's possible there will be another great cultural shift built on another broad reinterpretation of the past. Naturally, this next adventure in the archaic will not be the same as the one described here, but neither will it be altogether different. Seventy years ago, Georges Bataille, Henri Lefebvre, Georges Devereux, and Mircea Eliade reevaluated the relationship between tradition and disalienation, repetition and beauty, and sustainability and happiness. The survivals they celebrated weren't new; they would just be new to us.

Acknowledgments

A number of mentors, colleagues, and friends have contributed to this book, which I have been working on since 2018. Tamara Chaplin, Jean-Philippe Mathy, Mark Micale, and Behrooz Ghamari-Tabrizi read early versions of each chapter and offered far-reaching suggestions. Peter Thompson, who has guided me around many pitfalls, helped me to revise the introduction and epilogue. Paul Cheney plotted a course of final revisions with a trained eye. For over ten years Choi Chatterjee has read nearly everything I have written; the search for alternative ways of living in these pages owes much to her example.

The ideas in this book were first expressed in "Resurrecting the Archaic," *Modern Intellectual History* 18 (2021): 474–96. Thank you to Darrin McMahon for supporting its publication and for including this book in the series Life of Ideas. My wholehearted thanks to Fabiola Enríquez Flores, Dylan Montanari, and Adriana Smith, who guided the manuscript through to publication; to Barbara Norton, who provided thorough copyediting; to Shannon Li for her detailed work on the index; and to Kristen Raddatz and all those affiliated with the University of Chicago Press. Prompt, incisive, considerate, and thorough—Dylan has been everything a writer hopes an editor will be. Two anonymous reviewers for the press read the manuscript with care and offered valuable advice. Thanks to them for their perspicacity and candor.

Special thanks to Eileen Ielmini and the Special Collections Research Center at the University of Chicago for giving me welcome funds for research and writing. I am grateful to the Graduate College at the University of Illinois, Urbana-Champaign, for the same. I thank the archivists and librarians at the Bibliothèque Médicale Henri Ey, the Colorado River Indian Tribes Library and Archives, the Bibliothèque nationale de France, the Institut Mémoires de l'édition contemporaine, the Pitt Rivers Museum, and the Rare Book and Manuscript Library at Columbia University.

I am beholden to my university and its commitment to the life of the mind. I must thank my colleagues for their conviviality and penetrating insight into all manner of social and political thought. Thank you, Paul Cheney, Isaac Hand, Phillip Henry, Omar Kutty, Laura Martin, Pamela Nogales, Sunit Singh, Jennifer Spruill, James Vaughn, Joy Wang, and Nicole Whalen. Julia Brown made the last mile of editing an unexpected delight, contributing her exceptional sense and penchant for clarity. In the course of writing this book, I have been able to test out ideas in the making in the classroom. My deepest appreciation to all the students who have pointed me in the right direction more times than they could imagine and in more ways than I can record.

Over the years David Anderson, Allen Brown, Virginia Christman, Angie Estes, Melyssa Gonzalez, Vince Leporini, Brittany and Kevin Lindsey, Natasha Lueras, Kristy and Paul Mason, Alison Masyr, Taylor McKillop, Joel Murphy, Terry Russo, Eric and Nicole Sorenson, Peter Thompson, and Carla Vellutini have contributed the crucial qualities of mind and spirit necessary to sustain an adventure such as this. Thanks for your unremitting friendship.

I dedicate this book to my parents, Steve and Jan, and sister, Bri. Thank you for your loving patience.

Notes

Introduction

1. J. M. Coetzee, *Diary of a Bad Year* (Viking, 2007), 77.

2. Such as the exceptionally good Daniel J. Sherman, *French Primitivism and the Ends of Empire, 1945–1975* (University of Chicago Press, 2011).

3. Here's Lefebvre: "Archaism, did you say? So culture is one big job lot, take it or leave it? Does it come down to us as a single bequest?" It doesn't, and it is possible to be for progress in one segment of life and cling to the past in other segments. Such temporal flexibility could ensure continuity and stability, without crippling needed development. Henri Lefebvre, *Introduction to Modernity: Twelve Preludes, September 1959–May 1961*, trans. John Moore (Verso, 1995), 373.

4. What Marshall Sahlins calls "the planetary juggernaut of western capitalism," in *How "Natives" Think: About Captain Cook, for Example* (University of Chicago Press, 1995), 13.

5. Émile Durkheim, *The Division of Labor in Society*, trans. W D. Halls (Free Press, 1984), 279; Marcel Mauss, *The Gift: The Form and Reason for Exchange in Archaic Societies*, trans. W. D. Halls (W. W. Norton, 1990), 69.

6. Durkheim, *Division of Labor*, 318, 269.

7. Mauss, *Gift*, 65, 69.

8. Arthur O. Lovejoy and George Boas, *Primitivism and Related Ideas in Antiquity* (Johns Hopkins University Press, 1935). On unit-ideas as a way to identify similarities and differences over time, see Daniel Wickberg, "In the Environment of Ideas: Arthur Lovejoy and the History of Ideas as a Form of Cultural History," *Modern Intellectual History* 11, no. 2 (2014): 439–64.

9. "The nostalgia of civilized man for a return to a primitive or pre-civilized condition is as old it seems as his civilized capacity for self-reflection." Michael Bell, *Primitivism* (Methuen, 1972), 2.

10. Lovejoy and Boas, *Primitivism and Related Ideas*, 16.

11. Robert J. Goldwater, *Primitivism in Modern Painting* (Harper & Brothers, 1938).

12. "The primitive condition of mankind, or the life of 'savage' peoples, has usually been extolled because it has been supposed to constitute 'the state of nature.'" Lovejoy and Boas, *Primitivism and Related Ideas*, 12.

13. Arthur O. Lovejoy, "'Nature' as Aesthetic Norm," *Modern Language Notes* 42, no. 7 (1927): 444–50.

14. Lovejoy and Boas, *Primitivism and Related Ideas*, 9; Stanley Diamond, *In Search of the Primitive: A Critique of Civilization* (Transaction Books, 1974), xiii.

15. John Patrick Diggins, "Arthur O. Lovejoy and the Challenge of Intellectual History," *Journal of the History of Ideas* 67, no. 1 (2006): 181–208.

16. Lovejoy and Boas, *Primitivism and Related Ideas*, 17.

17. Pascal Bruckner, *The Tears of the White Man: Compassion as Contempt*, trans. William R. Beer (Free Press, 1986), 5.

18. "From existentialism to deconstructionism, all of modern thought can be reduced to a mechanical denunciation of the West, emphasizing the latter's hypocrisy, violence, and abomination." Pascal Bruckner, *The Tyranny of Guilt: An Essay on Western Masochism*, trans. Steven Rendall (Princeton University Press, 2010), 2.

19. Johannes Fabian, *Time and the Other: How Anthropology Makes Its Object* (Columbia University Press, 1983). Among those that disparaged primitivism after Fabian, Marianna Torgovnick is the most representative. Torgovnick's *Gone Primitive* is denigrating, but not devastatingly so. It is worth wrestling with for its explanation of how the primitive was made to do precisely what its Western authors wanted it to do. Marianna Torgovnick, *Gone Primitive: Savage Intellects, Modern Lives* (University of Chicago Press, 1990).

20. "Distances in space and time and, in fact, a different Time are made prerequisites not only for certain ways of doing anthropology but for its very existence." Fabian, *Time and the Other*, 68.

21. Provocatively, Fabian calls the French anthropologist Claude Lévi-Strauss an "actual contributor to ideologies apt to sustain the new, vast, anonymous, but terribly effective regime of absentee colonialism." But the point of Lévi-Strauss's *Race and History* (1952), which Fabian neither analyzes nor cites, was precisely to argue for the coevality of societies the world over. Fabian, *Time and the Other*, 69.

22. "To tell other stories, local histories of cultural survival and emergence, we need to resist deep-seated habits of mind and systems of authenticity." James Clifford, *The Predicament of Culture: Twentieth-Century Ethnography, Literature, and Art* (Harvard University Press, 1988), 246.

23. Gary Edward Holcomb, review of *Literary Primitivism*, by Ben Etherington, *Modern Philology* 117, no. 3 (2019): 203–6.

24. Michel Serres, *The Natural Contract*, trans. Elizabeth MacArthur and William Paulson (University of Michigan Press, 1995), 101.

25. Victor Li, *The Neo-Primitivist Turn: Critical Reflections on Alterity, Culture, and Modernity* (University of Toronto Press, 2006). See also Marianna Torgovnick, "On Victor Li's *The Neo-Primitivist Turn*," *Criticism* 49, no. 4 (2007): 545–50. That French social scientists were not handmaidens of colonialism after 1945 is also the view expressed in Alice L. Conklin, *In the Museum of Man: Race, Anthropology, and Empire in France, 1850–1950* (Cornell University Press, 2013).

26. Ben Etherington, *Literary Primitivism* (Stanford University Press, 2018), 75; Etherington, "The New Primitives," *Los Angeles Review of Books*, May 24, 2018.

27. "The eclipse of primitiveness has created a potentially problematic situation for the human sciences, since the cross-cultural mode of critique cultivated through this myth risks being neglected in a post-'primitive' age." Fuyuki Kurasawa, "A Requiem for the 'Primitive,'" *History of the Human Sciences* 15, no. 3 (2002): 3.

28. Arthur O. Lovejoy, "Reflections on the History of Ideas," *Journal of the History of Ideas* 1, no. 1 (1940): 21.

29. For the present as a state of restless transformation, refer to Reinhart Koselleck, *Futures Past: On the Semantics of Historical Time*, trans. Keith Tribe (MIT Press, 1990). Presentism is

what François Hartog calls this temporal regime of uncertainty and unpredictability. More recently, the French historian has asked if man-made climate change has thrust us into a new, post-presentist time regime. François Hartog, *Regimes of Historicity: Presentism and Experiences of Time*, trans. Saskia Brown (Columbia University Press, 2015); Hartog, *Chronos: The West Confronts Time*, trans. S. R. Gilbert (Columbia University Press, 2024).

30. Three books published since 2020 insist that the human and social sciences were integral to French thought in and immediately after the boom years that the French call *les trente glorieuses*. The historians Jacob Collins, Camille Robcis, and Ian Merkel have turned away from French theory and philosophy proper and toward the fertile fields of anthropology, psychiatry, and sociology. In what can only be a coincidence full of meaning, each new history consists of the intellectual biographies of four men who shaped and were shaped by the French social sciences. In *The Anthropological Turn*, Collins shows how ideas that originated in French anthropology came to permeate political rhetoric in France after 1968. The most striking thing about Collins's book is its suggestion that in the second half of the twentieth century the political needed to be anchored in the primitive. Robcis is equally concerned with the political import of a single social science. Her history of French institutional psychotherapy, *Disalienation*, is less a story of French psychiatry *and* politics than a history of French psychiatry *as* politics. Robcis shows how psychiatrists changed institutional psychotherapy from an apolitical asylum into a beacon of political engagement. Merkel's *Terms of Exchange* takes a slightly different tack, arguing for an intellectual exchange *à l'envers*. The book consists of two crossings—one across the Atlantic, the other across the social sciences. The intellectual life of Brazil was marked by French thought, as has been so often observed, but Merkel reveals that the reverse was also true. Jacob Collins, *The Anthropological Turn: French Political Thought After 1968* (University of Pennsylvania Press, 2020); Camille Robcis, *Disalienation: Politics, Philosophy, and Radical Psychiatry in Postwar France* (University of Chicago Press, 2021); Ian Merkel, *Terms of Exchange: Brazilian Intellectuals and the French Social Sciences* (University of Chicago Press, 2022).

31. H. Stuart Hughes, *Consciousness and Society: The Reorientation of European Social Thought, 1890–1930* (Vintage Books, 1958), 10. See also Hughes, "The Historian and the Social Scientist," *American Historical Review* 66, no. 1 (1960): 20–46; Hughes, *The Obstructed Path: French Social Thought in the Years of Desperation, 1930–1960* (Harper & Row, 1966); Paul A. Robinson, ed., *Social Thought in America and Europe: Readings in Comparative Intellectual History* (Little, Brown, 1970); Robinson, "H. Stuart Hughes and Intellectual History: Reflections on the State of the Discipline," *Intellectual History Newsletter* 9 (1987): 29–35; and Eugene Lunn, "European Social Thought in the Twentieth Century," *Massachusetts Review* 16, no. 1 (1975): 98–108. For a critique of Hughes's approach, see Michael S. Roth, "Narrative as Enclosure: The Contextual Histories of H. Stuart Hughes," *Journal of the History of Ideas* 51, no. 3 (1990): 505–15.

32. For historians' ambivalent relationship to biography, see Antoine Lilti, "Does Intellectual History Exist in France? The Chronicle of a Renaissance Foretold," in *Rethinking Modern European Intellectual History*, ed. Darrin M. McMahon and Samuel Moyn (Oxford University Press, 2014), 56–73.

33. Robert Darnton, "In Search of the Enlightenment: Recent Attempts to Create a Social History of Ideas," *Journal of Modern History* 43, no. 1 (1971): 132. See, by way of comparison, Peter Gay, *The Party of Humanity: Essays in the French Enlightenment* (Knopf, 1964); and Gay, "The Social History of Ideas: Ernst Cassirer and After," in *The Critical Spirit: Essays in Honor of Herbert Marcuse*, ed. Kurt H. Wolff and Barrington Moore, Jr. (Beacon Press, 1967), 106–20.

34. Unfortunately, there's no companion piece to Lovejoy and Boas's classic *Primitivism and Related Ideas in Antiquity*, no gold-standard study of primitivism and related ideas in modernity.

And the last good compilation of primary sources on the subject was *Primitive Heritage*, edited by Margaret Mead and published in 1953. Margaret Mead and Nicolas Calas, eds., *Primitive Heritage: An Anthropological Anthology* (Random House, 1953). On intellectual history and the *longue durée*, see Darrin M. McMahon, "Afterword: Why Big, Why Now?," *New Literary History* 48, no. 4 (2017): 783–87; and Suzanne Marchand, "Intellectual History Confronts the *Longue Durée*," *History and Theory* 59, no. 3 (2020): 485.

35. Georges Bataille, "Lecture, January 18, 1955," in *The Cradle of Humanity: Prehistoric Art and Culture*, trans. Michelle Kendall and Stuart Kendall (Zone Books, 2009), 87.

36. David Wallace-Wells, "Beyond Catastrophe: A New Climate Reality Is Coming into View," *New York Times Magazine*, October 26, 2022.

Chapter One

1. Michel Surya, *Georges Bataille: An Intellectual Biography*, trans. Krzysztof Fijalkowski and Michael Richardson (Verso, 2002), 451.

2. Philippe Sollers, "La société de Bataille," *Le Monde*, April 30, 1999. On the relationship between transgression and sexual violence in *Story of the Eye*, see Judith Surkis, "No Fun and Games Until Someone Loses an Eye: Transgression and Masculinity in Bataille and Foucault," *Diacritics* 26, no. 2 (1996): 19.

3. "I have made a very archaic religion the subject of my research," Durkheim wrote in *The Elementary Forms of Religious Life*, "because it seems better suited than any other to help us comprehend the religious nature of man, that is, to reveal a fundamental and permanent aspect of humanity." Émile Durkheim, *The Elementary Forms of Religious Life*, trans. Karen E. Fields (Free Press, 1995), 1. On what Bataille owed to Mauss, see Michèle H. Richman, *Reading Georges Bataille: Beyond the Gift* (Johns Hopkins University Press, 1982). For the place of political economy and the history of religions in Bataille's oeuvre, refer to Shannon Winnubst, ed., *Reading Bataille Now* (Indiana University Press, 2007).

4. Georges Bataille, "Autobiographical Note," *October* 36 (1986): 106–10.

5. Martin Jay, "Two Cheers for Paraphrase: The Confessions of a Synoptic Intellectual Historian," in *Fin-de-Siècle Socialism and Other Essays* (Routledge, 1988), 38–48.

6. James Clifford, *The Predicament of Culture: Twentieth-Century Ethnography, Literature, and Art* (Harvard University Press, 1988).

7. For the lectures given at the Collège by Bataille and others, see Denis Hollier, ed., *The College of Sociology* (University of Minnesota Press, 1988). Two good treatments of the Collège are Michèle H. Richman, *Sacred Revolution: Durkheim and the Collège de Sociologie* (University of Minnesota Press, 2002); and Simonetta Falasca-Zamponi, *Rethinking the Political: The Sacred, Aesthetic Politics, and the Collège de Sociologie* (McGill–Queen's University Press, 2011). It is worth noting, but only noting, that some exploit Bataille's analyses of fascism to allege that he himself was fascist. For such accusations, see Bernard Henri-Lévy, *Adventures on the Freedom Road: French Intellectuals in the Twentieth Century*, trans. Richard Veasey (Harvill Press, 1995); and Richard Wolin, *The Seduction of Unreason: The Intellectual Romance with Fascism from Nietzsche to Postmodernism* (Princeton University Press, 2006).

8. On the concept of creative illness, see Henri Ellenberger, "The Concept of 'Maladie Créatrice,'" in *Beyond the Unconscious: Essays in the History of Psychiatry*, ed. Mark S. Micale (Princeton University Press, 1993), 328–40; originally published as "La notion de maladie créatrice," *Dialogue: Canadian Philosophical Review* 3 (1964): 25–41.

9. Georges Bataille, *The Accursed Share: An Essay on General Economy*, trans. Robert Hurley (Zone Books, 1991), 129; originally published as *La part maudit: Essai d'économie générale* (Éditions de Minuit, 1949). See also Bataille's plans and draft essays for *The Accursed Share*, which are now available in print and in English in Georges Bataille, *The Limit of the Useful*, ed. and trans. Cory Austin Knudson and Tomas Elliott (MIT Press, 2023).

10. Alfred Métraux, "Rencontre avec les ethnologues," *Critique* 195–96 (1963): 677–78; Michel Leiris, "De Bataille l'impossible à l'impossible *Documents*," *Critique* 195–96 (1963): 685–93. See also Michel Leiris, "Le donjuanisme de Georges Bataille," *La ciguë* 1 (1958): 37–38.

11. Georges Bataille, "Les peintures politiques de Picasso," in *Actualité*, ed. Georges Bataille (Calmann Lévy, 1946). See also Bataille, *Oeuvres complètes*, vol. 11 (Gallimard, 1988), 24–25. On the relationship between Bataille's general economy and today's discourse of sustainability, see Allan Stoekl, *Bataille's Peak: Energy, Religion, and Postsustainability* (University of Minnesota Press, 2007); and Serge Zenkine, "Paysage après Bataille," *Critique* 761 (2010): 839–50.

12. The French demographer Alfred Sauvy coined the term the "third world" in August 1952 in "Trois mondes, une planète," *L'observateur* 118 (1952): 14.

13. A significant feature of Bataille's postwar primitivism was that his criticisms were situated beyond the concerns commonly shaped by contemporary politics. For better or worse, Bataille was an outsider to all political parties of his time. He only occasionally peppered his anthropological picture of early man with political implications, and not the other way around. Georges Bataille, "Nietzsche est-il fasciste?," *Combat*, October 20, 1944, 2. See also Bataille, *Oeuvres complètes*, 11:9–11. On uses of French anthropology for expressly political ends, refer to Camille Robcis, *The Law of Kinship: Anthropology, Psychoanalysis, and the Family in France* (Cornell University Press, 2013); and Jacob Collins, *The Anthropological Turn: French Political Thought After 1968* (University of Pennsylvania Press, 2020).

14. Jeffrey Kosky, "Georges Bataille's Religion Without Religion," *Journal of Religion* 84, no. 1 (2004): 78–87; Mark Taylor, Amy Hollywood, Jeremy Biles, and Kent L. Brintnall, eds., *Negative Ecstasies: Georges Bataille and the Study of Religion* (Fordham University Press, 2015).

15. Georges Bataille, *Theory of Religion*, trans. Robert Hurley (Zone Books, 1992), 110; originally published as *Théorie de la religion* (Gallimard, 1973).

16. Bataille, *Theory of Religion*, 57.

17. "For me, the feelings that we call noble . . . are all archaic feelings, feelings that connect us to the earliest humanity." Georges Bataille, *The Cradle of Humanity: Prehistoric Art and Culture*, trans. Michelle Kendall and Stuart Kendall (Zone Books, 2009), 54.

18. Bataille, *Theory of Religion*, 9; Denis Hollier, *Against Architecture: The Writings of Georges Bataille*, trans. Betsy Wing (MIT Press, 1990). On Bataille's association with poststructuralists such as Jacques Derrida, Julia Kristeva, Jacques Lacan, and Michel Foucault, see, among others, Carolyn J. Dean, *The Self and Its Pleasures: Bataille, Lacan, and the History of the Decentered Subject* (Cornell University Press, 1992); Eleanor Kaufman, *The Delirium of Praise: Bataille, Blanchot, Deleuze, Foucault, Klossowski* (Johns Hopkins University Press, 2001); and Amy Hollywood, *Sensible Ecstasy: Mysticism, Sexual Difference, and the Demands of History* (University of Chicago Press, 2002).

19. Marianne Esposito, "Une passion en commun: Extase et politique chez Georges Bataille et Simone Weil," *Lignes* 17 (2005): 172–92. See also box 4, folder 90, Georges Bataille Papers, Département des Manuscrits, Bibliothèque nationale de France.

20. Simone Weil, *The Need for Roots: Prelude to a Declaration of Duties Towards Mankind*, trans. Arthur Wills (New York: Routledge, 2002), 61; originally published as *L'enracinement*

(Gallimard, 1949). On Weil's lasting influence on Camus, see John M. Dunaway, "Estrangement and the Need for Roots: Prophetic Visions of the Human Condition in Albert Camus and Simone Weil," *Religion and Literature* 17, no. 2 (1985): 35–42.

21. Georges Bataille, "La notion de dépense," *La critique sociale* 7 (1933): 7–15. See Simone Pétrement's early portrait of Weil in "La vie et la pensée de Simone Weil," *Critique* 28 (1948): 793–805 and her full-length biography: Simone Pétrement, *La vie de Simone Weil* (Fayard, 1973). See also Bataille's review of Pétrement's *Le dualisme dans l'histoire de la philosophie et des religions* (Gallimard, 1946) in "Du rapport entre le divin et le mal," *Critique* 10 (1947): 227–34.

22. Georges Bataille, "La victoire militaire et la banqueroute de la morale qui maudit," *Critique* 40 (1949): 789–803. On Weil's life and prose, see, for example, Susan Sontag, review of *Selected Essays, 1934–1943*, by Simone Weil, *New York Review of Books*, February 1, 1963.

23. Bataille, *Oeuvres complètes*, 11:537.

24. Bataille, *Oeuvres complètes*, 11:540. Compare with Alexander Irwin, *Saints of the Impossible: Bataille, Weil, and the Politics of the Sacred* (University of Minnesota Press, 2002); and Christy Wampole, *Rootedness: The Ramifications of a Metaphor* (University of Chicago Press, 2016).

25. Georges Bataille, "Schéma d'une histoire des religions," in Bataille, *Oeuvres complètes*, vol. 7 (Gallimard, 1976), 406–42. See also "Schéma d'une histoire des religions" in box 12, folder E, Bataille Papers.

26. Box 12, folder E, Bataille Papers.

27. Mircea Eliade, *Journal I, 1945–1955*, trans. Mac Linscott Ricketts (University of Chicago Press, 1990), 84; originally published as *Fragments d'un journal I* (Gallimard, 1973).

28. Bataille, *Theory of Religion*, 119. Eliade's contributions to *Critique* are Mircea Eliade, "Science, idéalisme et phénomènes paranormaux," *Critique* 23 (1948): 315–23; "La mythologie primitive," *Critique* 27 (1948): 708–17; "Origines et diffusion de la civilisation," *Critique* 29 (1948): 897–908; "La souveraineté et la religion Indo-Européennes," *Critique* 35 (1949): 342–49; "Phénoménologie de la religion et sociologie religieuse," *Critique* 39 (1949): 713–20; "Actualité de la mythologie," *Critique* 43 (1949): 236–43; and "Symbolisme et histoire des religions," *Critique* 83 (1954): 323–57.

29. Bataille's project in the first volume of *The Accursed Share*—to resuscitate archaic modes of unproductive expenditure—was so anathema to the age in which it appeared that the book sold no more than fifty copies, which all but ensured that the two subsequent volumes would not be published in Bataille's lifetime. Today things have changed. On Bataille's increasingly influential political economy, see John Armitage, "Economies of Excess," *Parallax* 7, no. 1 (2001): 1–2; and Linsey McGoey, "Bataille and the Sociology of Abundance: Reassessing Gifts, Debt, and Economic Excess," *Theory, Culture, and Society* 35, nos. 4–5 (2018): 69–91. On the newfound importance of *The Accursed Share* for postcolonial theory, refer to Timothy Brennan, *Borrowed Light*, vol. 1, *Vico, Hegel, and the Colonies* (Stanford University Press, 2014).

30. On the remarkable forms of expenditure practiced by the Haida, Kwakiutl, Tlingit, and Tsimshian in the American Northwest, see, of course, Marcel Mauss, "Essai sur le don, forme archaïque de l'échange," *L'année sociologique*, n.s., 1 (1923–1924): 30–126.

31. Bataille, *Oeuvres complètes*, 7:440–41.

32. See, for example, the twenty-five-page annotated bibliography "Notes sur la préhistoire," box 10, Bataille Papers.

33. Henri Breuil, "Cérémonie: Organisée au Musée de l'homme, le 25 juin 1957; En l'honneur des quatre-vingts ans de Breuil," *Bulletin de la Société préhistorique de France* 54, no. 9 (1957): 482–92.

34. In a session held on May 24, 1928, French prehistorians asserted the pluri-disciplinary nature of their program. Paul Rivet, "Séance du 24 mai 1928," *Bulletin de la Société préhistorique française* 25, no. 5 (1928): 241–51.

35. Georges Bataille, "Le passage de l'animal à l'homme et la naissance de l'art," *Critique* 71 (1953): 312–30; Bataille, "Au rendez-vous de Lascaux, l'homme civilisé se retrouve homme de désir," *Arts* 423 (1953): 1, 6.

36. On the history of such controversies, see Daniel J. Sherman, *Sensations* (University of Chicago Press, 2025), with its deliciously apt subtitle: *French Archaeology Between Science and Spectacle, 1890–1940*.

37. Adrien Dax was a signatory to Breton's manifesto, "Surrealism and Anarchism," *Le libertaire*, October 12, 1951, which announced a new age "liberated from all hierarchy and constraint."

38. See *Arts* 372 (1952).

39. Part of the campaign against Pech-Merle involved publishing two photographs of one of its prehistoric paintings—one photograph taken in 1923, a year after the cave was discovered, and the other in 1951, a year before the affair. Placed side by side, the photos appear to show alterations to the painting. "This is not the first time photographs have been used against the authenticity of prehistoric paintings," Breuil observed. But, he hastened to add, it is not the painting but the photograph that has been altered. See, among others, *France-Dimanche*, August 17–23, 1952, 9; *Franc-Tireur*, September 1, 1952; *Combat*, November 14–15, 1953; *Figaro*, November 14–15, 1953; *France-Soir*, November 15–16, 1953; and *Le Monde*, November 15–16, 1953, 6.

40. Hélène Tournaire and Hervé Magny, "Le scandale de la grotte préhistorique de Cabrerets," *Arts* 373 (1952).

41. *Franc-Tireur*, November 10, 1953.

42. *Bulletin de la Société préhistorique française* 49, no. 10 (1952): 465.

43. *Le Monde*, November 20, 1953. Cf. "Procès contre André Breton à propos de l'incident de Cabrerets," *Bulletin de la Société préhistorique de France* 50, no. 11 (1953): 577–79.

44. Georges Bataille, *Oeuvres complètes*, vol. 9 (Gallimard, 1979), 93, 423–28.

45. Georges Bataille, "Le surréalisme au jour le jour," in Bataille, *Oeuvres complètes*, vol. 8 (Gallimard, 1976), 167–84. The chapter was first published posthumously in *Change* 7 (1970): 84–98. Georges Bataille, "Les problèmes du surréalisme," in Bataille, *Oeuvres complètes*, 7:457, which likely dates from 1949. See also Bataille, review of *La lampe dans l'horloge*, by André Breton, *Critique* 33 (1949): 175–78. "Surrealism, by establishing as a fundamental principle that 'poetry must be made by all,' definitively broke the stranglehold of individualism, but in a way that was still tentative," says Michael Richardson in his commentary on Bataille, published in 1994. "The failure of surrealism, according to Bataille, was to have been unable to take this very tentative step any further." Georges Bataille, *The Absence of Myth: Writings on Surrealism*, trans. Michael Richardson (Verson, 1994), 24.

46. Georges Bataille, "L'art primitif," *Documents* 7 (1930): 389–97. See also Bataille, *Oeuvres complètes*, vol. 1 (Gallimard, 1970), 247–54.

47. When formlessness did appear in the 1950s, it smacked of an ingrained reflex more than a committed position. One big reason for thinking the opposite is the tendency among interpreters to read Bataille's interwar ambitions and ideas into his postwar work. For a detailed study that takes Bataille's break with Breton in an entirely different direction, see Jeremy Biles, *Ecce Monstrum: Georges Bataille and the Sacrifice of Form* (Fordham University Press, 2007). Although Biles thinks that Bataille was a dyed-in-the-wool primitivist, he argues that when Bataille moved away from Breton, he moved deeper into surrealism. By appropriating Breton's language,

Bataille fashioned his own "sinister" surrealism. Bataille's Lascaux writings, too, were part and parcel of this extreme surrealism. To argue that there was an avoidance of form in Lascaux that "must have seduced Bataille's eye," Biles says this: *Lascaux* was an uncharacteristic book, but it was not a renunciation of Bataille's interwar writings, rather it was "consonant" with them. Biles here (but not everywhere) confuses long-standing constraints for formlessness, creation for monstrous destruction, and therefore endeavors to prove that Bataille's interwar writings on primitive art hold the key to unlocking the meaning of his postwar writings on Lascaux.

48. Bataille, "Le passage," 312.

49. Henri Breuil, *Quatre cents siècles d'art pariétal: Les cavernes ornées de l'âge du renne*, ed. Fernand Windels (Centre d'études et de documentation préhistoriques, 1952). "The Abbé Breuil has spent more time face to face with European cave art than any man alive," M. H. Levine wrote in a review of *Four Hundred Centuries of Cave Art* in *American Anthropologist* 59, no. 1 (1957): 142. See also Jean Clottes and David Lewis-Williams, *Les chamanes de la préhistoire: Transe et magie dans les grottes ornées* (Éditions du Seuil, 1996), 78.

50. In 1952 Bataille indicated the direction his work on Lascaux would take when he criticized socialist realism for reducing all art to productive ends. Georges Bataille, "L'utilité de l'art," *Critique* 60 (1952): 464–66. See, by way of comparison, John Berger, "Why Look at Animals?," in *About Looking* (Vintage, 1980), 4.

51. Bataille published two articles on prehistoric cave art in 1953: "Le passage," a review of Breuil's *Quatre cents siècles d'art pariétal*; and "Au rendez-vous de Lascaux, l'homme civilisé se retrouve homme de désir," *Arts* 423 (1953): 1, 6.

52. On the fortuitous discovery of Lascaux, see Henri Breuil, "Séance du 24 avril 1941," *Bulletin de la Société préhistorique de France* 38, no. 4 (1941): 58–67. On opening the cave to the general public, refer to Henri Breuil, "Lascaux," *Bulletin de la Société préhistorique de France* 47, nos. 6–8 (1950): 355–63.

53. Georges Bataille, *Lascaux or the Birth of Art*, trans. Austryn Wainhouse (Skira, 1955), 34; originally published as *Lascaux ou la naissance de l'art* (Skira, 1955). On the theme of returning to "the old human house," see Maurice Blanchot, "Naissance de l'art," *Nouvelle revue française* 35 (1955): 923–33.

54. Georges Bataille, *The Tears of Eros*, trans. Peter Connor (City Lights Books, 1989) 50–51; originally published as *Les larmes d'Eros* (Jacques Pauvert, 1961).

55. "Dissatisfied with your present state for reasons that herald even greater dissatisfactions for your unhappy posterity, perhaps you would want to be able to go backward. And this sentiment must serve as the praise of your earliest ancestors, the criticism of your contemporaries, and the terror of those who will have the misfortune to live after you." Jean-Jacques Rousseau, *The Major Political Writings of Jean-Jacques Rousseau: The Two "Discourses" and the "Social Contract"* (University of Chicago Press, 2012), 63.

56. Bataille, *Tears of Eros*, 28.

57. Bataille, *Lascaux*, 50.

58. Bataille, *Lascaux*, 129.

59. In April 1963 André Malraux, the minister of cultural affairs, was forced to close the cave because of the invasive micro-algae eating away at the paintings. The layer of crystal calcite grown over millennia proved no match for the sudden injection of carbon dioxide.

60. Bataille, *Lascaux*, 33–34. See also Bataille, *Tears of Eros*, 46–47. "To consider man as primarily a tool-using animal is to overlook the main chapters of human prehistory." Lewis Mumford, "Technics and the Nature of Man," *Technology and Culture* 7, no. 3 (1966): 308.

61. When Bataille spoke of prehistoric art, he spoke of the most evident facts and of material specialists considered seriously. This is what made *Lascaux* accessible, reserved, and scholarly. Bataille, *Cradle of Humanity*, 80.

62. Bataille, *Lascaux*, 62–63.

63. Bataille, *Lascaux*, 57. Stoekl captures this correction eloquently: "The hunter hunts to live so that he can practice the rite; he does not practice the rite only so that he can survive." Stoekl, *Bataille's Peak*, 175.

64. Bataille, *Lascaux*, 129; Henri Lefebvre, *The Production of Space*, trans. Donald Nicholson-Smith (Blackwell, 1991), 52.

65. Bataille, *Lascaux*, 37–39. See also Bataille, *Cradle of Humanity*, 98: "In one sense, we, in the middle of the twentieth century, are poor, we are very poor, we are incapable of undertaking an important job if it has no return."

66. Bataille, *Lascaux*, 105.

67. There is a long line of scholars who read signatures of Bataille's ethnographic surrealism of the 1930s into his work of the 1950s. Steven Ungar emphasizes the elisions, elusiveness, and "semantic instability" of Bataille's Lascaux writings. Like Ungar, Suzanne Guerlac thinks that Heidegger and Foucault help us understand Bataille's alleged focus of formlessness. In the 2018 Mellon Lectures in the Fine Arts, Hal Foster spoke of the instability and brutality (not intimacy) of Bataille's *Lascaux*. Following James Clifford and Denis Hollier, these scholars understand Bataille to be an anti-architectural thinker who repudiated all certainty and advanced play and pure transgression (whatever that may mean). But as I've said, neither modernism nor postmodernism adequately captures what Bataille was up to after 1945. Primitivism can, though—which is what makes it all the more disappointing when Douglas Smith, who is good on the cultural context of Bataille's Lascaux writings, writes that *Lascaux* did not lead Bataille into a "new primitivism" rooted in prehistory and the social sciences. Rather, the book was a scholarly "parenthesis" in an oeuvre that, Smith predictably adds, continued to refuse all stable ground, preferring instead to dance over the abyss. Smith has, in effect, confused the text with the context. Steven Ungar, "Phantom Lascaux: Origin of the Work of Art," *Yale French Studies* 78 (1990): 246–62; Suzanne Guerlac, "Bataille in Theory: Afterimages (Lascaux)," *Diacritics* 26, no. 2 (1996): 6–17; Hal Foster, "Positive Barbarism: Brutal Aesthetics in the Postwar Period," A. W. Mellon Lectures in the Fine Arts (April 22, 2018); Douglas Smith, "Beyond the Cave: Lascaux and the Prehistoric in Postwar French Culture," *French Studies* 58, no. 2 (2004): 219–32. A noteworthy exception to the tendency to transport the formlessness of the 1930s into the 1950s is Maria Stavrinaki, "Prehistory and Posthistory: Apes, Caves, Bombs, and Time in Georges Bataille," in *Power and Time: Temporalities in Conflict and the Making of History*, ed. Dan Edelstein, Stefanos Geroulanos, and Natasha Wheatley (University of Chicago Press, 2020), 201–19. In multiple texts after 1945, she writes, Bataille completely opposed his earlier vision. Stavrinaki interprets this shift in Bataille's thought through the lens of a Hegelian end of history, however.

68. In *Les chamanes de la préhistoire*, Clottes and Lewis-Williams link the painting of prehistoric cave art to states of altered consciousness. Clottes, the former director of prehistory for the Midi-Pyrénées, and Lewis-Williams, a South African archaeologist, use ethnographic comparisons and neuroscience to argue that paintings such as those at Lascaux were drawn by shamans having trancelike visions brought on by drugs, solitude, darkness, fasting, and other prolonged privations. Shamanism, they write, corresponds "better than any other interpretation to the particularities of the art found deep in the caves." Not incidentally, they draw on the work of Mircea Eliade, who was in France during the Lascaux moment, to bring out the shamanic elements in

the religion of Paleolithic hunters. But intoxicating trances fail to explain the rule-bound style and un-hallucinatory fidelity to nature one finds in the caves. The problem is resolved, I think, when we are more clear-eyed about what shamanism actually was.

69. Judith Thurman, "First Impressions: What Does the World's Oldest Art Say About Us?," *New Yorker*, June 23, 2008.

70. Bataille, *Lascaux*, 115.

71. "This new born world held animal nature as divine." Georges Bataille, *Erotism: Death and Sensuality*, trans. Mary Dalwood (City Lights Books, 1986), 84; originally published as *L'erotisme* (Éditions de Minuit, 1957). Man, on the other hand, is a kind of deviation: "Man is more sick, uncertain, changeable, indeterminate than any other animal, there is no doubt of that—he is *the* sick animal." Friedrich Nietzsche, *On the Genealogy of Morals*, trans. Walter Kaufmann and R. J. Hollingdale (Vintage, 1989), 121. Compare with George Boas's other study in the history of primitivism, *The Happy Beast in French Thought of the Seventeenth Century* (Johns Hopkins University Press, 1933); and, more recently, Christine M. Korsgaard, *Fellow Creatures: Our Obligations to the Other Animals* (Oxford University Press, 2018), 52: "In one way, we might think that they [nonhuman animals] are lucky. Because they do not experience themselves as living in an indifferent world of mechanical forces, they are more at home in the world than we are, even if it is not always a very happy home."

72. J. M. Coetzee, *The Lives of Animals* (Princeton University Press, 1999), 52.

73. Bataille, *Lascaux*, 125–27. Cf. Bataille, *Cradle of Humanity*, 160. It remains an open question whether the remnants of Pleistocene hunter-gatherers are in fact comparable to the practices anthropologists observe in the field. Breuil and Bataille thought so. But all that was about to change. Beginning in the 1960s, structuralist approaches to parietal art rejected analogies between ethnography and prehistory. It was impossible, prehistorians such as André Leroi-Gourhan and Annette Laming-Emperaire argued, to prove anything (including the presence of shamanism in the caves) by referring to the present. They preferred instead to apply statistical techniques to the paintings themselves to understand their composition and combinatorial arrangement. See Annette Laming-Emperaire, *La signification de l'art rupestre paléolithique* (Éditions A. & J. Picard, 1962); André Leroi-Gourhan, *Préhistoire de l'art occidental* (Éditions d'Art Lucien Mazenod, 1965); and Jean-Paul Demoule, "Images préhistoriques, rêves du préhistoriens," *Critique* 606 (1997): 853–70.

74. Bataille, *Lascaux*, 51; Berger, *About Looking*, 6.

75. Éveline Lot-Falck, *Les rites de chasse chez les peuples sibériens* (Gallimard, 1953). For the view that shamanism corresponds better than any other interpretation to the particulars of Paleolithic cave art, see Clottes and Lewis-Williams, *Les chamanes de la préhistoire*, 10. On the shamanic theme of permeability, see Alfred Métraux's review of *Les rites*, by Lot-Falck, in *American Anthropologist* 56, no. 5 (1954): 915; and Jacques Faublée, "Éveline Lot-Falck (1918–1974)," *L'année sociologique* 24 (1973): 9–10. Compare with Mircea Eliade, *Shamanism: Archaic Techniques of Ecstasy*, trans. Willard R. Trask (Princeton University Press, 1964), 51. For a different view on where Bataille stands on the shamanism-in-the-caves theory advanced by Eliade and by Clottes and Lewis-Williams, see Stefanos Geroulanos, *The Invention of Prehistory: Empire, Violence, and Our Obsession with Human Origins* (Liveright, 2024), 447. Geroulanos notes that Bataille argued that the caves did not testify to some shamanic ritual, though he neither explains nor cites how he arrived at this conclusion. For an extreme example of how transformational it can be to embrace uncomfortable models of communion, see the French anthropologist Nastassja Martin's

account of her animal encounter in Siberia, *In the Eyes of the Wild*, trans. Sophie R. Lewis (New York Review of Books, 2021).

76. "The ethnographic literature is full of examples of anomalous beings—human or otherwise—who are treated simultaneously as exalted and profoundly dangerous, or who alternate between the two." David Wengrow and David Graeber, "Farewell to the 'Childhood of Man': Ritual, Seasonality, and the Origins of Inequality," *Journal of the Royal Anthropological Institute* 21 (2015): 605.

77. Bataille, *Lascaux*, 116. Cf. Bataille, *Cradle of Humanity*, 172: "The bird face reminds us of the bird costumes of the shamans of Siberia. This kind of bird signifies the shaman's voyage into the beyond." Eliade agreed. The historian of religion noted that Lascaux's bird-headed man and bird perched on a stick were "frequent symbols in shamanic circles." Eliade, *Shamanism*, 481. Ever the comparatist, Bataille was repeating the German anthropologist Hörst Kirchner's views on the ecstatic rites of Yakut shamans. Hörst Kirchner, "An Archaeological Contribution to the Early History of Shamanism," *Anthropos* 47 (1952): 244–86.

78. Bataille, *Erotism*, 74–75.

79. Bataille, *Tears of Eros*, 37.

80. On Lascaux as an intellectual Rorschach test, see Jean-Paul Demoule, "La préhistoire et ses mythes," *Annales E.S.C.* 37, nos. 5–6 (1982): 741–59. Prehistoric sites like Lascaux, he writes, are "pure, empty forms that can be filled with whatever concepts, emotions, or symbols we like."

81. In 1958 Bataille said as much himself: "My recent work in the history of art, *Lascaux ou la naissance de l'art* and *Manet*, means a lot to me and explains the most important aspects of my thought, especially the former." Bataille, "Notice autobiographique," in *Oeuvres complètes*, 7:615. On the importance of Lascaux in Bataille's life and thought between 1948 and 1962, see Daniel Fabre, *Bataille à Lascaux: Comment l'art préhistorique apparut aux enfants* (L'Échoppe, 2014).

82. Such histories, spanning a range from human origins to potential disasters, remain popular today. Consider Yuval Noah Harari, *Sapiens: A Brief History of Humankind* (Harper, 2015); James C. Scott, *Against the Grain: A Deep History of the Earliest States* (Yale University Press, 2017); and David Graeber and David Wengrow, *The Dawn of Everything: A New History of Humankind* (Farrar, Straus & Giroux, 2021).

83. Georges Bataille, "Qu'est-ce que l'histoire universelle?," *Critique* 111–12 (1956): 748–68. See also Bataille, *Oeuvres complètes*, vol. 12 (Gallimard, 1988), 414–36. The occasion for Bataille's article was the publication of *Histoire universelle*, vol. 1, *Des origines à l'Islam*, ed. René Grousset and Émile Léonard (Gallimard, 1956).

84. Box 10, folder G, Bataille Papers. For Bataille's one-page handwritten outline, see Bataille, *Oeuvres complètes*, 9:485. Dated July 27, 1959, Bataille's plan for a universal history in four chapters was written immediately before he published his essay on prehistoric religion; Bataille, "La religion préhistorique," *Critique* 147–48 (August 1959): 765–84. See also "Notes pour le projet d'histoire universelle," box 10, folder H, Bataille Papers; and Bataille, "La bouteille à la mer, ou l'histoire universelle, des origines à la veille d'un désastre éventuel," in *Oeuvres complètes*, 12:642–45. For a fine collection of recent essays on these materials, see Laurent Ferri and Christophe Gauthier, eds., *L'histoire-Bataille: L'écriture de l'histoire dans l'oeuvre de Georges Bataille* (École des chartes, 2006). The École nationale des chartes was Bataille's alma mater.

85. Bataille, *Oeuvres complètes*, 7:615; box 10, folder H, Bataille Papers.

86. Bataille, "Religion préhistorique."

87. Bataille, *Oeuvres complètes*, 12:417, 420. "Prehistory is at once the domain that systematically exceeds knowledge sensu stricto and yet also the one most necessary to sustain theoretical work." Stefanos Geroulanos and Maria Stavrinaki, "Writing Prehistory," *Res* 69–70 (2018): 2.

88. Georges Bataille, "Le berceau de l'humanité: La Vallée de la Vézère," in *Oeuvres complètes*, 9:353–76.

89. Like the other postwar primitivists, Bataille was not indifferent to politics; it just wasn't his primary concern. "Apart from wars, the consequences of politics are of the utmost interest," he wrote in 1949. "We cannot be sure that they will save us from disaster; but they are our only chance." Bataille, *Accursed Share*, 186.

90. The preceding image as well as the phrase "weaving themselves together for the winter to come" comes from Kim Stanley Robinson's fictional account of a shaman-apprentice's first trip inside a painted cave in *Shaman* (Orbit Books, 2013), 180–195. On the communal nature of Bataille's understanding of sacrifice, see Maurice Blanchot, *The Unavowable Community*, trans. Pierre Joris (Station Hill Press, 1988); and Jean-Luc Nancy, *Inoperative Community*, trans. Peter Connor, Lisa Garbus, Michael Holland, and Simona Sawhney (University of Minnesota Press, 1991). See also Patrick ffrench, *After Bataille: Sacrifice, Exposure, Community* (Legenda, 2007); and Wolfgang Palaver, "Sacrificial Cults as 'the Mysterious Center of Every Religion,'" in *Sacrifice and Modern Thought*, ed. Julia Meszaros and Johannes Zachhuber (Oxford University Press, 2013).

91. Marcel Mauss, *A General Theory of Magic*, trans. Robert Brain (W. W. Norton, 1972), 7. Of course, "the sacrificial animal does not share the spectators' ideas about sacrifice, but one has never let it have its say." Friedrich Nietzsche, *The Gay Science*, trans. Walter Kaufmann (Vintage, 1974), 210.

92. Bataille, *Erotism*, 85.

93. Bataille, *Erotism*, 18.

94. "A proto-ecological drama about humans' separation from nature" is what Geroulanos calls this Paleolithic nostalgia for a time when humans still possessed an animal's intimacy with the natural world in his book *The Invention of Prehistory*. I was pleasantly surprised to read the following about Lascaux in a book whose thesis is that the deep past isn't worth our time and should be set aside for good: "Who can fail to be moved by this terrible elegance that refuses meaning, by the scenes the paintings conjure, by how they force us to think about centuries of human descent, by the way the animals in the paintings now play against the backdrop of a century of modern art, nuclear threat, and ecological catastrophe?" Geroulanos, *Invention of Prehistory*, 303, 308. Bataille and Lascaux, and Bataille at Lascaux, I argue, are worthy of our attention precisely because they help us think about the ever-pressing issues of intimacy, sacrifice, rootedness, and our compound (animal) being in the age of anthropogenic climate change.

95. Steven Pinker, *The Better Angels of Our Nature: The Decline of Violence in History and Its Causes* (Viking, 2011). See, by way of comparison, Philip Dwyer and Mark Micale, eds., *The Darker Angels of Our Nature: Refuting the Pinker Theory of History and Violence* (Bloomsbury, 2021).

96. Bataille's five apocalyptic pieces are "Notes pour un film," in *Oeuvres complètes*, 9:319–24; "À propos de récits d'habitants d'Hiroshima," *Critique* 8–9 (1947): 126–40; "Ce monde où nous mourons," *Critique* 123–24 (1957): 675–84; "Le planète encombrée," *La ciguë* 1 (1958): 47–49; and "Terre invivable?," *United States Lines, Paris Review* (Summer 1960).

97. Bataille, *Cradle of Humanity*, 59, 176.

98. Bataille, *Accursed Share*, 168.

99. Box 10, folder H, Bataille Papers.

100. Compare with Knudson and Elliott's introduction to Bataille, *Limit of the Useful*, xli.

101. Bataille, "À propos de récits d'habitants d'Hiroshima," 187. See also Bataille, *Cradle of Humanity*, 178.

Chapter Two

1. On the diktat of acceleration, see Adrian Grama, "Antidotes to Alienation? The Social Philosophy of Hartmut Rosa," *New Left Review* 131 (2021): 99–118. As for disalienation—an unbecoming but important word in the Marxist lexicon—Lefebvre thought it no less than a pivot, denoting a shift from alienating lifestyles to regenerating styles of life: "Authentic Marxist thought has a *style*: the style of the intensification and broadening of life." Henri Lefebvre, *Introduction to Modernity: Twelve Preludes, September 1959–May 1961*, trans. John Moore (Verso, 1995), 140.

2. Lefebvre's yearning for the life peasants once lived anticipated the affective attachment to the countryside that, Sarah Farmer argues, became an "abiding characteristic" in France in the late 1970s. Sarah Farmer, *Rural Inventions: The French Countryside after 1945* (Oxford University Press, 2020), 5. See also Susan Carol Rogers, "Good to Think: The 'Peasant' in Contemporary France," *Anthropological Quarterly* 60, no. 2 (1987): 56–63.

3. "The more extensive literature on Lefebvre has yet to make anything of his association with Delbo." Michael Rothberg, "Between Auschwitz and Algeria: Multidirectional Memory and the Counterpublic Witness," *Critical Inquiry* 33 (2006): 163. See also Rothberg, *Multidirectional Memory: Remembering the Holocaust in the Age of Decolonization* (Stanford University Press, 2009), 203–4.

4. Lefebvre, *Introduction to Modernity*, 374–75. For an intimate look at how life in a village in the South of France fundamentally changed after 1945, refer to Laurence Wylie, *Village in the Vaucluse* (Harvard University Press, 1957).

5. Here is how Lefebvre described his youth: "Born in 1901, to a family belonging to the middle class. A strongly religious (Catholic) education. Youth tormented, rebellious, anarchistic." Henri Lefebvre, "Connaissance et critique sociale," in *L'activité philosophique contemporaine en France et aux États-Unis*, vol. 2, *La philosophie française*, ed. Marvin Farber (Presses universitaires de France, 1950), 298. Compare with the fine portrait of Lefebvre in Maurice Blanchot, "Lentes funérailles," in *L'amitié* (Gallimard, 1971), 98–108.

6. Norbert Guterman and Henri Lefebvre, *Morceaux choisis de Karl Marx* (Gallimard, 1934). The best study of Lefebvre's early intellectual development is Bud Burkhard, *French Marxism Between the Wars: Henri Lefebvre and the "Philosophies"* (Humanity Books, 2000).

7. Henri Lefebvre, *Les communautés paysannes pyrénéennes: Thèse soutenue à la Sorbonne, 1954* (Société Ramond, 2014), 109.

8. Readers familiar with Lefebvre's urban writings are beginning to recognize the importance of his rural sociology. "The Anglophone tendency to privilege the urban in its reading of Lefebvre's work misses both his intention of approaching urban and rural sociology together and of seeing the process of transformation at stake in the production and organization of state space." Stuart Elden and Adam David Morton, "From the Rural to the Urban and the Production of Space," in Henri Lefebvre, *On the Rural: Economy, Sociology, Geography*, trans. Robert Bononno, Matthew Dennis, and Sîan Rosa Hunter Dodsworth (University of Minnesota Press, 2022), xvii. See also Stuart Elden and Adam David Morton, "Thinking Past Henri Lefebvre," *Antipode* 48, no. 1 (2016): 57–66.

9. Lefebvre deemed existentialism and surrealism degenerative offshoots of nineteenth-century Romanticism. But that hasn't stopped scholars from understanding the French sociologist through these fashionable twentieth-century movements. Readings that emphasize Lefebvre's proximity to existentialism include George Lichtheim, *Marxism in Modern France* (Columbia University Press, 1966); Mark Poster, *Existential Marxism in Postwar France: From Sartre to Althusser* (Princeton University Press, 1975); Michael Kelly, *Modern French Marxism* (Johns Hopkins University Press, 1982); and Edward Baring, "Humanist Pretensions: Catholics, Communists, and Sartre's Struggle for Existentialism in Postwar France," *Modern Intellectual History* 7, no. 3 (2010): 581–609. Notable among surrealist interpretations are Rémi Hess, *Henri Lefebvre et l'aventure du siècle* (A. M. Métailié, 1988); Martin Jay, *Marxism and Totality: The Adventures of a Concept from Lukács to Habermas* (University of California Press, 1984); Jay, *Downcast Eyes: The Denigration of Vision in Twentieth-Century French Thought* (University of California Press, 1993); Richard Wolin, *The Wind from the East: French Intellectuals, the Cultural Revolution, and the Legacy of the 1960s* (Princeton University Press, 2010); and Stefanos Geroulanos, *Transparency in Postwar France: A Critical History of the Present* (Stanford University Press, 2017).

10. The historian Mark Poster, who falsified Lefebvre's trajectory in the interest of a certain existentialism, maintained that "having rejected philosophy, Lefebvre scanned the European intellectual traditions for signs of a new direction. Conscious of the inadequacies of Marx, he looked primarily to the existentialists, to Nietzsche, Heidegger, and especially Sartre." Poster, *Existential Marxism*, 240.

11. Lefebvre, *Introduction to Modernity*, 141. "What unites all of his work—from his first to his most mature works—is his deeply humanistic interest in alienation." Rob Shields, *Lefebvre, Love and Struggle: Spatial Dialectics* (Routledge, 1999), 2.

12. Henri Lefebvre, *Dialectical Materialism*, trans. John Sturrock (University of Minnesota Press, 2009). *Dialectical Materialism* was "the first outright presentation in France of Marx as a theorist of alienation," Tony Judt writes in *Marxism and the French Left: Studies in Labor and Politics in France, 1830–1981* (Clarendon Press, 1986), 180. For Western Marxism, see Maurice Merleau-Ponty, *Adventures of the Dialectic*, trans. Joseph J. Bien (Northwestern University Press, 1973); Jay, *Marxism and Totality*; and Cary Nelson and Lawrence Grossberg, eds., *Marxism and the Interpretation of Culture* (University of Illinois Press, 1988).

13. Henri Lefebvre, *La somme et le reste* (La Nef, 1959), 474. "Lefebvre looked at the similarities and differences between Marx and Nietzsche, and suggested that each can supplement and advance the thought of the other." Stuart Elden, "Some Are Born Posthumously: The French Afterlife of Henri Lefebvre," *Historical Materialism* 14, no. 4 (2006): 190.

14. "By searching the past, Nietzsche believed he had found the secret of human aspirations and regrets." Henri Lefebvre, *Nietzsche* (Éditions Sociales Internationales, 1939), 63.

15. Henri Lefebvre, *L'existentialisme* (Éditions du Sagittaire, 1946), 151; Henri Lefebvre and Michel Trebitsch, "Le renouveau philosophique avorté des années trente: Entretien avec Henri Lefebvre," *Europe: Revue littéraire mensuelle* 683 (1986): 38–39. See also Henri Lefebvre, "Nietzsche et le fascisme hitlérien," *Commune* 7 (1939): 229–34. Cf. George S. Williamson, *The Longing for Myth in Germany: Religion and Aesthetic Culture from Romanticism to Nietzsche* (University of Chicago Press, 2004).

16. For Lefebvre's history of how Narbonne, Navarre, and other "archaic states" in the Pyrenees resisted the crippling demands of national homage, see Henri Lefebvre, *Le nationalisme contre les nations* (Éditions Sociales Internationales, 1937), 112–13. The "coldest of cold monsters"

comes from Friedrich Nietzsche, "The New Idol," in *Thus Spoke Zarathustra*, trans. Walter Kaufmann (Modern Library, 1995), 49.

17. Lefebvre, *Nietzsche*, 160. "Uprootedness uproots everything except the need for roots." Christopher Lasch, *The True and Only Heaven: Progress and Its Critics* (W. W. Norton, 1991).

18. Henri Lefebvre, *Critique of Everyday Life: The One-Volume Edition*, trans. John Moore and Gregory Elliott (Verso, 2014), 352, 609–10.

19. "How are we to understand a world we have lost or, rather, a world we have just lost? How are we to study phenomena that, even though close to us in time, bear witness to a paradoxical distance? With this end in mind, we would clearly do well to pay particular attention to what is no longer current." Alain Corbin, *Village Bells: Sound and Meaning in the Nineteenth-Century French Countryside*, trans. Martin Thom (Columbia University Press, 1998), xviii.

20. Henri Lefebvre, "Toward a Leftist Cultural Politics: Remarks Occasioned by the Centenary of Marx's Death," in Nelson and Grossberg, *Marxism and the Interpretation of Culture*, 87.

21. Lefebvre, *Critique of Everyday Life*, 228. On the history of the commons in the Pyrenees, see Marc Bloch, *Les caractères originaux de l'histoire rurale française* (Les Belles lettres, 1931).

22. Lefebvre spoke of the Basque and the Béarnais not across a gulf of wishful thinking, but from a place of personal knowledge. A writer who is a rural sociologist is apt to actually know some actual country folk, and this is a significant advantage. To earlier primitivists, who flourished primarily in literature and the arts, Lefebvre's scientific pretensions would have seemed in league with modern progress itself. Moreover, by taking up the peasant problem, Lefebvre avoided the standard trajectory of French sociologists described by Eugen Weber: "French sociologists seem to have progressed straight from their early studies of primitive societies to the study of urban and industrial ones, dismissing the peasant realities around or just behind them." Eugen Weber, *Peasants into Frenchmen: The Modernization of Rural France, 1870–1914* (Stanford University Press, 1976), 8.

23. Lefebvre, *Introduction to Modernity*, 376.

24. Stendhal, *Love*, trans. Gilbert and Suzanne Sale (Penguin, 1975), 183. It would be remiss of me not to note that Lefebvre once wrote, "Frankly, I get rather irritated when people start accusing me of primitivism." But not all primitivisms are the same; and it seems clear that Lefebvre was referring to Roupnel's brand of frozen-in-time, pure-nature primitivism. See Lefebvre, *Introduction to Modernity*, 367. And see, by way of comparison, Henri Lefebvre, "Problèmes de sociologie rurale: La communauté paysanne et ses problèmes historico-sociologiques," *Cahiers internationaux de sociologie* 6 (1949): 94; and Lefebvre, "Perspectives de la sociologie rurale," *Cahiers internationaux de sociologie* 14 (1953): 132.

25. I am paraphrasing Aimé Césaire, *Discourse on Colonialism*, trans. Joan Pinkham (Monthly Review Press, 1972), 51–52.

26. On how peasants became the repository of everything that was good about France during the Vichy regime, see James R. Lehning, *Peasant and French: Cultural Contact in Rural France During the Nineteenth Century* (Cambridge University Press, 1995), 2.

27. Henri Lefebvre, *La vallée de Campan: Étude de sociologie rurale* (Presses universitaires de France, 1963), 116. See also Lefebvre's vivid descriptions of his native land in *Pyrénées* (Éditions Rencontre, 1965).

28. The Anthropocene is not the age to abandon the love of place. It is the time to lean into a sense of place, to remain in place. Yet affection for and fidelity to a particular place, such as Lefebvre attested to in his theses, are often dismissed on the left as "parochial localism." See, for example, Marcelo Lopes de Souza, "From the 'Right to the City' to the Right to the *Planet*:

Reinterpreting Our Contemporary Challenges for Socio-Spatial Development," *City* 19, no. 4 (2015): 408–33.

29. Microfiche FOL-LN27-72054, July 1953, "Protestation de M. Henri Lefebvre contre la fin de son détachement au Centre national de la recherche scientifique," Bibliothèque nationale de France.

30. "Protestation de M. Henri Lefebvre."

31. Henri Lefebvre, "La communauté villageoise," *La pensée* 66 (1956): 38.

32. "For a long while now I have been looking at this city, at its villas and pleasure gardens and the far-flung periphery of its inhabited heights and slopes. In the end I must say: I see faces that belong to past generations; this region is studded with the images of bold and autocratic human beings. They have *lived* and wished to live on: that is what they are telling me with their houses, built and adorned to last for centuries and not for a fleeting hour; they were well-disposed toward life, however ill-disposed they often may have been toward themselves." Friedrich Nietzsche, *The Gay Science*, trans. Walter Kaufmann (Vintage, 1974), 233.

33. Henri Lefebvre, "Accumulation et progrès," *Cahiers de l'institut de science économique appliquée: Recherches et dialogues philosophiques et économiques* 110 (1961): 53; Henri Lefebvre, *The Sociology of Marx*, trans. Norbert Guterman (Columbia University Press, 1968), 72; and Lefebvre, *Critique of Everyday Life*, 854: "The collecting of archaisms and the study of their uses is a task for anthropology and sociology."

34. On the history of labeling Pyreneans "Indians," see Jean-François Soulet, *Les Pyrénées au XIXe siècle* (Éché, 1987). For how these mountain regions resisted assimilation and shaped their own identities, see Peter Sahlins, *Boundaries: The Making of France and Spain in the Pyrenees* (University of California Press, 1989).

35. "Isn't it weird that people so often refer to *la France profonde* in connection with backward city centers, out-of-the-way villages, and small towns frozen in archaism? This Frenchness is obsolete, antiquated; yet it is exalted on television and in the press. Are not some harsh truths being masked under manipulative ideologies here?" Lefebvre, *Critique of Everyday Life*, 733.

36. Lefebvre, *Introduction to Modernity*, 146; Lefebvre, *Critique of Everyday Life*, 222.

37. Such is Timothy Bewes's view of nostalgia in his review of Svetlana Boym's *The Future of Nostalgia* in *New Left Review* 14 (2002): 167–72.

38. For a cogent analysis of nostalgia, see Peter Fritzsche, "Specters of History: On Nostalgia, Exile, and Modernity," *American Historical Review* 106, no. 5 (2001): 1591. On Lefebvre's nostalgia, see Joe Moran, "History, Memory and the Everyday," *Rethinking History* 8, no. 1 (2004): 56.

39. Edward B. Tylor, *Primitive Culture: Researches into the Development of Mythology, Philosophy, Religion, Language, Art, and Custom* (John Murray, 1871), 70. Tylor had first used the term "survivals" two years earlier in "On the Survival of Savage Thought in Modern Civilization," *Notices of the Proceedings at the Meetings of the Royal Institution of Great Britain* 5 (April 23, 1869): 522–35. See also Margaret T. Hodgen, "The Doctrine of Survivals: The History of an Idea," *American Anthropologist* 33, no. 3 (1931): 307–24; and Hodgen, "Survivals and Social Origins: The Pioneers," *American Journal of Sociology* 38, no. 4 (1933): 583–94.

40. Tylor, *Primitive Culture*, 453. One of the survivals on which Tylor obsessively sought information was the Pyrenean practice of *faire la couvade*, the "bizarre custom" of a peasant father taking to his bed during the birth of his child, as if he himself were physically affected by the pains of labor. To Tylor, the belief that the vicarious suffering of the malingering father would alleviate the actual suffering of the mother was an example of a harmful religious superstition unbecoming of modern man. See Tylor's correspondence with Jean Réville in box 13, Tylor Papers, Pitt Rivers Museum, University of Oxford.

41. Gerald Vizenor, "The Ruins of Representation: Shadow Survivance and the Literature of Dominance," *American Indian Quarterly* 17, no. 1 (1993): 7–30; Vizenor, *Manifest Manners: Narratives of Postindian Survivance* (University of Nebraska Press, 1999); Vizenor, "Aesthetics of Survivance," in *Survivance: Narratives of Native Presence*, ed. Gerald Vizenor (University of Nebraska Press, 2008), 1–24; Vizenor, *Native Liberty: Natural Reason and Cultural Survivance* (University of Nebraska Press, 2009).

42. On Georges Candilis, another disciple of Le Corbusier, and his lifeless Mirail neighborhood outside Toulouse, see Rosemary Wakeman, *Modernizing the Provincial City: Toulouse, 1945–1975* (Harvard University Press, 1997), 133.

43. On the city as the machinery and the hero of modernity, refer to Michel de Certeau, *The Practice of Everyday Life* (University of California Press, 1984), 95.

44. Henri Lefebvre, "Mourenx: Ville nouvelle," in *Quinze jours en France*, ed. Jacqueline Eichart (La documentation française, 1965), 206–25; Roland Barthes, "The New Citroën," in *Mythologies*, trans. Annette Lavers (Hill and Wang, 1972), 88–90. See also Paulette Girard, "Mourenx: De la ville nouvelle à 'la ville de banlieue'?," *Société française d'histoire urbaine* 3, no. 17 (2006): 99–108.

45. "The greatest event of the twentieth century incontestably remains the disappearance of agricultural activity at the helm of human life." Michel Serres, *The Natural Contract*, trans. Elizabeth MacArthur and William Paulson (University of Michigan Press, 1995), 28. There has been considerable debate on the exact date of the demise of the French peasantry and the peasant way of life. The debate revolves around two books: Henri Mendras, *La fin des paysans* (Sédéis, 1967), which locates the collapse in the decades after 1945; and Weber, *Peasants into Frenchmen*, which dates the decline earlier in the fin de siècle.

46. Henri Lefebvre, "Les nouveaux ensembles urbains: Un cas concret, Lacq-Mourenx et les problèmes urbains de la nouvelle classe ouvrière," *Revue française de sociologie* 1, no. 2 (1960): 196–98.

47. Although it has come to be used to refer to time, the term "nostalgia" was originally coined to refer to the agony of being separated from home. On the historical link between homesickness and nostalgia, see Thomas Dodman, *What Nostalgia Was: War, Empire, and the Time of a Deadly Emotion* (University of Chicago Press, 2018). On climate change and the homesickness we now feel at home, see the Australian philosopher Glenn A. Albrecht, *Earth Emotions: New Words for a New World* (Cornell University Press, 2019); and Paul Bogard, ed., *Solastalgia: An Anthology of Emotions in a Disappearing World* (University of Virginia Press, 2023).

48. "We witness thousands upon thousands of buildings constructed or under construction which have no tenants, which could never be paid for under capitalist conditions, whose very existence cannot be justified by any market standards." Fredric Jameson, "Future City," *New Left Review* 21 (2003): 66.

49. Henri Lefebvre, "Utopie expérimentale: Pour un nouvel urbanisme," *Revue française de la sociologie* 2, no. 3 (1961): 191–98.

50. It must be remembered that modernization theory—that is, the program for abandoning tradition and reaching modernity—was the key idea of the era in and beyond the social sciences. Between 1945 and 1960 social scientists rarely contradicted the urgent need for more cars, more refrigerators, more housing, more investment, higher incomes, and fuller integration into global markets.

51. Henri Lefebvre, "Notes sur la ville nouvelle," in *Introduction à la modernité* (Éditions de Minuit, 1962), 121–30.

52. Lefebvre, "Utopie expérimentale," 192.

53. The historian Michael Bess describes how the sudden arrival of the farm tractor "ineluctably entailed a new way of living on the land, a new way of seeing the soil, the crops, one's family, one's future." Michael Bess, *The Light-Green Society: Ecology and Technological Modernity in France, 1960–2000* (University of Chicago Press, 2003), 43.

54. Henri Lefebvre, "Structures familiales comparées," in *Villes et campagnes: Civilisation urbaine et civilisation rurale en France*, ed. Georges Friedmann (Armand Colin, 1953), 327.

55. Lefebvre, "Problèmes de sociologie rurale," 100.

56. A big reason capitalism lays waste to the nonhuman nature on which it feeds is that the rhythms of nature are completely different from the accelerated speeds of capitalist production. But it is important to remember that "the 'pure' nature that some writers applaud is in fact this peasant life at a highly evolved stage." Lefebvre, *Critique of Everyday Life*, 227. Drawing on the writings of Mircea Eliade, the historian Patrick Joyce describes how peasants protect themselves from the changes capitalism brings by "the attentive living of a conception of time which is cyclical and repetitive, like the labor they perform." Patrick Joyce, *Remembering Peasants: A Personal History of a Vanished World* (Scribner, 2024), 63.

57. Folder 4-COL-208-65, Charlotte Delbo Papers, Département des Arts du spectacle, Bibliothèque nationale de France.

58. Their fertile collaboration lasted until 1978, when Lefebvre, swayed by a new love interest, declared his support for the French Communist Party (PCF). It was a shocking reversal. Lefebvre had been a staunch critic of the PCF ever since his expulsion from the Party in 1958. Immediately after his abrupt change of heart, he and Delbo met, argued, and never spoke again. Seven years later Lefebvre came to Delbo's funeral in tears.

59. Ghislaine Dunant, *Charlotte Delbo: A Life Reclaimed*, trans. Kathryn M. Lachman (University of Massachusetts Press, 2021), 392.

60. Rosette C. Lamont, "The Triple Courage of Charlotte Delbo," *Massachusetts Review* 41, no. 4 (2000–2001): 483–97.

61. Folder 4-COL-208-49, Delbo Papers.

62. Charlotte Delbo, *Revue française de sociologie* 3, no. 4 (1962): 453. See also folder 4-COL-208-50, Delbo Papers.

63. Dunant, *Charlotte Delbo*, 187.

64. Charlotte Delbo, "February," *Massachusetts Review* 60, no. 1 (2019): 23.

65. Henri Lefebvre, "Qu'est-ce que le passé historique?," *Les temps modernes* 161 (1959): 159–69. The essay was ostensibly a review of Albert Soboul's *Les sans-culottes Parisiens en l'An II* (Librairie Clavreuil, 1958). For Soboul's own interest in the French countryside, see Soboul, "The French Rural Countryside in the Eighteenth and Nineteenth Centuries," *Past and Present* 10 (1956): 78–95.

66. Henri Lefebvre, "What Is the Historical Past?" *New Left Review* 90 (1975): 34.

67. Charlotte Delbo, *Auschwitz and After*, trans. Rosette C. Lamont (Yale University Press, 1995), 264.

68. Delbo, *Auschwitz and After*, 255–58.

69. Folder 4-COL-208-52, Delbo Papers.

70. Folder 4-COL-208-52, Delbo Papers.

71. Lefebvre, "Toward a Leftist Cultural Politics," 79. "The hidden hallmark of western Marxism as a whole is that it is a product of defeat." Perry Anderson, *Considerations on Western Marxism* (Verso, 1979), 42.

72. The phrase is actually Walter Benjamin's. It might be splitting hairs, but melancholia, which is a feeling of pensive sadness *with no obvious cause*, is not the same as mourning or

nostalgia. For Marxism and melancholy, see Enzo Traverso, *Left-Wing Melancholia: Marxism, History, and Memory* (Columbia University Press, 2016), 22.

73. Lefebvre, "Toward a Leftist Cultural Politics," 77. Even the detractor Tony Judt, who made a living excoriating Western Marxists, singled Lefebvre out for his legitimate interest in what remained alive in Marx's thought. Tony Judt, *Past Imperfect: French Intellectuals, 1944–1956* (University of California Press, 1992), 158.

74. Folder 4-COL-208-255, Delbo Papers. On the importance of the symbol of the crucified sun in Lefebvre's thought, see Ryan L. Allen, "Resurrecting the Archaic: Symbols and Recurrence in Henri Lefebvre's Revolutionary Romanticism," *Modern Intellectual History* 18 (2021): 474–96.

75. Folder 4-COL-208-49, Delbo Papers.

76. Delbo's influence shows the triviality of the view adopted by those who claim Lefebvre's sociology was derived from his debts to surrealism and its surrogate, situationism. Michael Gardiner, for example, remarks that Lefebvre was "directly influenced" by the writings of André Breton, and that he "drew heavily" on the surrealists with whom he consorted in the 1920s. Michael Gardiner, "Utopia and Everyday Life in French Social Thought," *Utopia Studies* 6, no. 2 (1995): 93, 97. It is worth noting that, with more insight, Delbo herself warned Lefebvre not to make too much of the schemes of the situationists. Folder 4-COL-208-52, Delbo Papers.

77. For more on Lefebvre's influential phrase "the right to the city," which is shorthand for the rights of urban dwellers to control and enjoy the material and cultural riches concentrated in city centers, see Henri Lefebvre, *Le droit à la ville* (Anthropos, 1968).

78. Henri Lefebvre, The *Survival of Capitalism: Reproduction of the Relations of Production*, trans. Frank Bryant (St. Martin's Press, 1976), 118.

79. For contemporary theories of the metabolic rift Lefebvre observed during *les trente glorieuses*, see John Bellamy Foster, *Marx's Ecology: Materialism and Nature* (Monthly Review Press, 2000); John Bellamy Foster, Brett Clark, and Richard York, *The Ecological Rift: Capitalism's War on the Earth* (Monthly Review Press, 2010); and Jason W. Moore, *Capitalism in the Web of Life: Ecology and the Accumulation of Capital* (Verso, 2015).

80. Lefebvre, *Survival*, 111.

81. French *dirigisme*, from the Latin *dirigere* (to direct), combined state bureaucracy and corporate capitalism. On this fundamental partnership, see Georges Gurvitch, *Industrialisation et technocratie* (Armand Colin, 1949); Jean Meynaud, *Technocratie et politique* (R. Bellanger, 1960); Georges Perec, *Things: A Story of the Sixties*, trans. David Bellos (Verba Mundi, 1990); and Gabrielle Hecht, *The Radiance of France: Nuclear Power and National Identity After World War II* (MIT Press, 1998).

82. Lefebvre, *Survival*, 163.

83. Lefebvre, *Survival*, 117. "True, nature is resistant and infinite in depth, but it has been defeated, and now waits only for its ultimate voidance and destruction." Henri Lefebvre, *The Production of Space*, trans. Donald Nicholson-Smith (Blackwell, 1991), 31. See also Lefebvre's manuscript "Plan" in the Norbert Guterman Papers, Butler Library, Columbia University.

84. "Peasants are among the closest of humankind to nature, knowing intimately and with great depth what nature is, even though their idea of nature is assuredly not ours. Perhaps we might even learn something from them, something about the 'nature' we think we know, and something about what we call progress has done to nature." Joyce, *Remembering Peasants*, xii.

85. On the differences between Lefebvre and Marcuse, see Delbo's extraordinary *La théorie et la pratique: Dialogue imaginaire mais non tout à fait apocryphe entre Herbert Marcuse et Henri Lefebvre* (Anthropos, 1969).

86. Lefebvre, *Survival*, 105.

87. Lefebvre, *Introduction to Modernity*, 133–34.

88. Compare with Michael Löwy, *Morning Star: Surrealism, Marxism, Anarchism, Situationism, Utopia* (University of Texas Press, 2009), 100.

89. Lefebvre, *Survival*, 118.

90. Farmer, *Rural Inventions*, 5. John Berger, *Into Their Labours* (Granta Books, 1992), xxvii.

91. Kohei Saito, *Marx in the Anthropocene: Towards the Idea of Degrowth Communism* (Cambridge University Press, 2022), 194. Marx's turn from a progressive view of history and a Promethean vision of production to non-Western and precapitalist societies has been well-documented by Saito, Löwy, and Kevin B. Anderson, *Marx at the Margins: On Nationalism, Ethnicity, and Non-Western Societies* (University of Chicago Press, 2016).

92. Kohei Saito, *Slow Down: The Degrowth Manifesto*, trans. Brian Bergstrom (Astra House, 2024), 117.

93. Lefebvre, *Introduction to Modernity*, 355.

94. "In default of a viable present, we've come to valorize the past as never before." Gustaf Sobin, *Luminous Debris: Reflecting on Vestige in Provence and Languedoc* (University of California Press, 1999), 4.

95. "Alongside the modern evils," Marx wrote in 1867, "we are oppressed by a whole series of inherited evils, arising from the passive survival of archaic and outmoded modes of production, with their accompanying train of anachronistic social and political relations. We suffer not only from the living, but from the dead. *Le mort saisit le vif!*" Karl Marx, *Capital*, vol. 1, *A Critique of Political Economy*, trans. Ben Fowkes (Penguin, 1976), 91.

96. Lefebvre, *Survival*, 120.

97. Lefebvre, *Survival*, 124. On how green language became an object of commercialization in France, see Bess, *Light-Green Society*, 5. For how the Pyrenees were transformed from an agropastoral territory into a hotly contested ecological green zone, see Martin Lyons, *The Pyrenees in the Modern Era: Reinvention of a Landscape, 1775–2012* (Bloomsbury Academic, 2018).

98. Henri Lefebvre, *Hegel, Marx, Nietzsche, or, The Realm of Shadows*, trans. David Fernbach (Verso, 2020), 112.

99. Nancy Fraser, "Behind Marx's Hidden Abode: For an Expanded Conception of Capitalism," *New Left Review* 86 (2014): 58. See also Fraser, *Cannibal Capitalism: How Our System Is Devouring Democracy, Care, and the Planet—and What We Can Do About It* (Verso, 2022).

100. Fraser, "Behind Marx's Hidden Abode," 58.

101. Lefebvre, *Hegel, Marx, Nietzsche*, 113.

Chapter Three

1. "But man is not built so as to do the reasonable thing just because it is reasonable. It is far easier for him to do an irrational thing because it has always been done." Robert H. Lowie, *Are We Civilized? Human Culture in Perspective* (Harcourt, Brace and Company, 1929), 68.

2. Lawrence J. Friedman, *Menninger: The Family and the Clinic* (Knopf, 1990), 173.

3. On how Freudian psychoanalysis altered the human and social sciences after 1945, see Dagmar Herzog, *Cold War Freud: Psychoanalysis in an Age of Catastrophes* (Cambridge University Press, 2017).

4. Box 7, folder 8, Georges Devereux Papers, Institut Mémoires de l'édition contemporaine. On Devereux's role in shaping a postcolonial ethnopsychiatry, see François Laplantine, "Pour

une ethnopsychiatrie critique," *Vie sociale et traitements* 73 (2002): 28–33; and Richard C. Keller, *Colonial Madness: Psychiatry in French North Africa* (University of Chicago Press, 2007), 215.

5. Box 93, Devereux Papers. Thanks to Devereux's mentor, Marcel Mauss, intensive fieldwork was now required of all young French anthropologists. This new demand led Claude Lévi-Strauss to describe Mauss, an armchair anthropologist himself, as "like Moses leading his people to a promised land whose splendor he would never contemplate." Claude Lévi-Strauss, *Introduction to the Work of Marcel Mauss*, trans. Felicity Baker (Routledge, 1987), 45.

6. C. N. Rudkin, *Los Angeles Corral* 62 (1962). Perhaps Devereux said it better: "We have a great deal of trouble in ascertaining just what we do mean by 'primitive' and by 'non-primitive,' what we mean by pre-historic and what we mean by contemporary." Box 147, Devereux Papers.

7. Georges Devereux, *Mohave Ethnopsychiatry and Suicide: The Psychiatric Knowledge and Psychic Disturbances of an Indian Tribe* (Smithsonian Institution Press, 1961), 501.

8. Simone Valentin, *International Dictionary of Psychoanalysis* (Macmillan, 2005).

9. "You asked whether I have turned existentialist. Me—never," Devereux wrote years later. "As an adolescent I read this Hegelian gem: Being is not-being; not-being is being. That did the trick, forever." Box 7, folder 8, Devereux Papers.

10. Box 7, folder 5, Devereux Papers.

11. Box 7, folder 15, Devereux Papers.

12. Alice L. Conklin, *In the Museum of Man: Race, Anthropology, and Empire in France, 1850–1950* (Cornell University Press, 2013), 243.

13. Thirty years later, Devereux dedicated his *Essais d'ethnopsychiatrie générale* (Éditions Gallimard, 1970) to "the memory of my teacher Marcel Mauss." Refer to Marcel Fournier, *Marcel Mauss: A Biography* (Princeton University Press, 2006), 405.

14. "George Devereux: In Memoriam," in *The Psychoanalytic Study of Society*, vol. 12, ed. George Devereux, L. Bryce Boyer, and Simon A. Grolnick (Analytic Press, 1988).

15. Each of the "founders" of ethnopsychiatry—Devereux, Ellenberger, and Eric Wittkower—experienced the dispossession and distorting effects of rapid sociocultural change. George D. Spindler, ed., *The Making of Psychoanalytic Anthropology* (University of California Press, 1978), 360. In 1953 Devereux nearly accepted a three-year position as a research professor in medical psychology at the University of São Paulo. He went so far as to obtain a Brazilian visa, but his crippling financial debt kept him in the United States. On the bond between Brazilian intellectual life and the French social sciences, see Ian Merkel, *Terms of Exchange: Brazilian Intellectuals and the French Social Sciences* (University of Chicago Press, 2022).

16. "Possibly the least contested ideas of the last half-century were assertions that confrontations with change and difference begat psychological disturbance." Anne E. Becker and Arthur Kleinman, "The History of Cultural Psychiatry in the Last Half-Century," in *Psychiatry: Past, Present, and Prospect*, ed. Sidney Bloch, Stephen A. Green, and Jeremy Holmes (Oxford University Press, 2014), 80. As Devereux put it: "So-called homeostasis processes should be called *heterostatic* processes, because they do not promote absolute *stability*, but, on the contrary, seek to perpetuate the organism's capacity for continued and continuous change, by keeping these changes between *safe limits*—i.e., between moderate extremes from which a spontaneous return to, and further limited departures from, an *ideal* 'point of origin' or 'point of maximum stability' are still possible." This was just one aspect of Devereux's creative reworking of Freud, whom he obstinately defended. Box 122, folder 10, Devereux Papers.

17. Alfred L. Kroeber, *Handbook of the Indians of California* (Smithsonian Institution Press, 1925), 726. Today the future of this "great stream" hangs in the balance because of drought, rising temperatures, and over-allocation to millions across the Southwest.

18. Simone de Beauvoir, *America Day by Day*, trans. Carol Cosman (University of California Press, 1999), 158.

19. What little has been written about Devereux tends to focus on his epistemology and his status as the "father" of ethnopsychiatry. See Alessandra Cerea, "Culture and Psychism: The Ethnopsychoanalysis of Georges Devereux," *History of Psychiatry* 29 (2018): 297–314; and Cerea, "Georges Devereux et l'ethnopsychiatrie: Fonder sa science et assurer sa consécration," *Revue d'histoire des sciences humaines* 37 (2020): 193–208.

20. Hama Utce was thirty-two when Devereux first visited the Mohave in 1932. She was extremely intelligent and the best educated of all the Mohave. From the start, she was Devereux's principal interpreter and one of his most loyal friends. He described their first meeting: "When I told her what topic I had come to study [Mohave sexuality], she seemed a little taken aback; hesitant though not hostile. Then I told her the circumstances which made it imperative for me to succeed—and what had led up to it. She looked at me for a moment and said: 'You need help and you ask us to help you.' I said: 'Yes.' She smiled briefly, stood up, shook hands with me and said: 'We'll begin tomorrow morning.' That was my first experience of the boundless generosity of the Mohave and the first of my close Mohave friendships; it lasted half a century." Box 94, Devereux Papers.

21. George Devereux, "The Social and Cultural Implications of Incest Among the Mohave Indians," *Psychoanalytic Quarterly* 8 (1939): 529; George Devereux, "Mohave Culture and Personality," *Character and Personality* 8 (1939): 104. "I met the Mohave Indians for the first time in 1932. It was for me a kind of earthly paradise, because I had never known a human group so good and generous." Georges Devereux, interview with Emile Malet, *Le quotidien*, August 5, 1980.

22. George Devereux, "Mohave Indian Infanticide," *Psychoanalytic Review* 35 (1948): 126.

23. Box 127, Devereux Papers.

24. Box 94, Devereux Papers; box 142, Devereux Papers.

25. "One word," Harry Liebersohn explains, "captured much of the sociologists' discontent with the social division of their day: *gemeinschaft*." Harry Liebersohn, *Fate and Utopia in German Sociology, 1870–1923* (MIT Press, 1988), 7.

26. George Devereux, "Social Structure and the Economy of Affective Bonds," *Psychoanalytic Review* (1942): 311, 307; George Devereux, "Status, Socialization, and Interpersonal Relations of Mohave Children," *Psychiatry* (1950): 492. The same diffusion extended to politics: Mohave chieftains were essentially servants who held little personal power, even in times of crisis. George Devereux, "Mohave Chieftainship in Action: A Narrative of the First Contacts of the Mohave Indians with the United States," *Plateau* 23, no. 3 (1951): 33–43.

27. Box 92, Devereux Papers; Georges Devereux, "Mohave Etiquette," *Masterkey: Southwest Museum Leaflets* 22, no. 4 (1948): 119–27. The Mohave, Kroeber observed, are "as far different from the usual California native as Frenchmen and Englishmen stand apart." Kroeber, *Handbook*, 727, 731.

28. Devereux, "Mohave Children," 501. "The libidinal mass of the child, as well as his aggressions, are distributed over a great number of individuals, representing a fair section of the body social in a not too large tribe." Devereux, "Mohave Culture," 99.

29. Devereux, "Mohave Children," 491. See also George Devereux, "Notes on the Developmental Patterns and Organic Needs of Mohave Indian Children," *Transactions of the Kansas Academy of Science* 53, no. 2 (1950): 178–85.

30. "To speak for those who have been silenced is one thing; to co-opt their voice or drown it out with yours is another. This wrong was done for so long that maybe no amount of honest

goodwill and good work can entirely clear the White novelist (or memoirist, or anthropologist) writing about Indians of the suspicion of expropriation. Guilt is there in the whole history of Indian-White relations, unavoidable." Ursula K. Le Guin, "Getting It Right: Charles L. McNichols's *Crazy Weather*," in *Words Are My Matter: Writings on Life and Books* (Mariner Books, 2019), 143–44. See also the review by the anthropologist Alfred Kroeber—Le Guin's father and Devereux's mentor—of *Crazy Weather*, by Charles L. McNichols, *American Anthropology* 46, no. 3 (1944): 394.

31. *Los Angeles Times*, March 12, 1950, 164. Most anthropologists avoided speaking frankly about sexuality and insanity. Not Devereux. He spoke of the charged subjects in a tone that the historian Dagmar Herzog describes as ranging from "neutral-documentary" to "intrigued-by-fascinating-ethnographic-detail." Dagmar Herzog, "All Is Not Sexuality That Looks Like It," *Modern Intellectual History* 17, no. 1 (2020): 246. On the homophobia in Devereux's frank talk, see Todd Shepard, "More than a Stage: Decolonization, Anal Sex, and the Dirty Erotics of Power in Deleuze, Guattari, Devereux, and Herzog," *Modern Intellectual History* 17, no. 1 (2020): 233–38. Here's an example: "For my part," Devereux said, "I consider myself to have poorly conducted an analysis if an anxious homosexual patient becomes a content homosexual; the analysis has only succeeded if he becomes a content heterosexual." Devereux in conversation with Geneiève Delaisi, "Georges Devereux ethnopsychiatre," *Le Monde*, May 19, 1980.

32. Devereux, "Mohave Culture," 106.

33. Devereux, "Mohave Culture," 97.

34. Denis Diderot, "The Supplément au Voyage de Bougainville," in *Political Writings*, trans. John Hope Mason and Robert Wokler (Cambridge University Press, 1992), 31–75. Devereux was more circumspect. You should not assume, he cautioned, that outside Western culture "all will be out in the open." He knew full well that primitive cultures were not paradises of unmodified instinct. George Devereux, "Primitive Genital Mutilations in a Neurotic Dream," *Journal of the American Psychoanalytic Association* 2, no. 3 (July 1954): 484.

35. Kroeber, *Handbook*, 747.

36. George Devereux, "Mohave Pregnancy," *Acta Americana* 6, nos. 1–2 (1948): 115. See also George Devereux, "The Primal Scene and Juvenile Heterosexuality in Mohave Society," in *Psychoanalysis and Culture: Essays in Honor of Géza Róheim* (International Universities Press, 1951), 90–107.

37. George Devereux, "Mohave Indian Autoerotic Behavior," *Psychoanalytic Review* 37, no. 3 (1950): 203.

38. George Devereux, "Institutionalized Homosexuality of the Mohave Indians," *Human Biology* 9, no. 4 (1937): 509–11. See also George Devereux, "Post-Partum Parental Observances of the Mohave Indians," *Transactions of the Kansas Academy of Science* 52, no. 4 (1949): 458–65; and Devereux, "The Psychology of Feminine Genital Bleeding: An Analysis of Mohave Indian Puberty and Menstrual Rites," *International Journal of Psycho-Analysis* 31 (1950): 237–57.

39. George Devereux, "Mohave Beliefs Concerning Twins," *American Anthropologist* 43, no. 4 (1941): 589. See also Devereux, "Implications of Incest," 510–33.

40. Box 95, Devereux Papers. "Sex, as practiced nearly everywhere, is at once biologically degraded, psychologically hollow, and socially 'uncivilized.'" Box 109, folder 4, Devereux Papers.

41. Georges Devereux, "La délinquance sexuelle des jeunes filles dans une société 'puritaine,'" *Les temps modernes* 221 (1964): 621–59. "I have the impression that the Mohave Indians, for example, think that it is the refusal of sexual relations that requires explanation, and not the inverse as among us." Devereux, *Le Monde*, May 19, 1980.

42. Important to note: There was one exception, however, to the Mohave's good-humored acceptance of the endless variety of things human beings can do with one another's bodies. The Mohave leveled serious criticism at a kind of conspicuously promiscuous woman whom they called *kamalo*. *Kamatluuch* were essentially parasites, and what the Mohave took issue with was not these women's sexual relationships but their overbearing and acquisitional natures. The Mohave were highly contemptuous of anyone who transformed the human body into a commodity, none more so than the despised *kamalo*. Devereux, "The Mohave Indian Kamalo:y," *Journal of Clinical Psychopathology* 9, no. 3 (1948): 444.

43. "To the vast white America, either in our generation or in the time of our children or grandchildren, will come some fearful convulsion. Some terrible convulsion will take place among the millions of this country, sooner or later.... So, let us try to adjust ourselves again to the Indian outlook, to take up an old dark thread from their vision, and see again as they see, without forgetting we are ourselves. For it is a new era we have now got to cross into. And our own electric light won't show us over the gulf. We have to feel our way by the dark thread of the old vision. Before it lapses, let us take it up." D. H. Lawrence, "Certain Americans and an Englishman," in *Phoenix II* (Viking Press, 1959), 243.

44. Kroeber, *Handbook*, 754–55.

45. George Devereux and Edwin M. Loeb, "Antagonistic Acculturation," *American Sociological Review* (1943): 133–47. On antagonistic acculturation in a psychoanalytic context, refer to Georges Devereux, "La renonciation à l'identité: Defense contre l'anéantissement," *Revue française de psychanalyse* 31, no. 1 (1967): 101–42.

46. Box 134, Devereux Papers. After criticizing acculturation, Devereux added, "I am not trying to save the Indian from adjustment to our social system and do not wish to make a museum piece out of human beings." Box 142, folder 27, Devereux Papers.

47. Devereux and Loeb, "Antagonistic Acculturation," 135.

48. A. L. Kroeber, "Seven Mohave Myths," *Anthropological Records* 11, no. 1 (1948): 1, 3. See also Kroeber, "A Mohave Historical Epic," *Anthropological Records* 11, no. 2 (1951): 71–176.

49. George Devereux, "Mohave Coyote Tales," *Journal of American Folklore* 241 (1948): 236–37.

50. Devereux, " Implications of Incest," 515.

51. Mircea Eliade, "Chasteté, sexualité et vie mystique chez les primitifs," *Extrait des Études carmélitaines, Mystique et continence* (1952): 49–50.

52. Devereux, "Coyote Tales," 234–35. "The scantiness and indeed barrenness of Mohave sex-symbolism contrasts sharply with the wealth of Occidental sex-symbolism." Box 109, folder 4, Devereux Papers.

53. Box 93, Devereux Papers.

54. George Devereux, "Dream Learning and Individual Ritual Differences in Mohave Shamanism," *American Anthropologist* 59, no. 6 (1957): 1036; Kroeber, "Seven Mohave Myths," 1.

55. Box 94, Devereux Papers. See also George Devereux, "Mohave Soul Concepts," *American Anthropologist* 39, no. 3 (1937): 417.

56. Devereux, "Dream Learning," 1037.

57. On how Parisian institutions such as the Musée de l'Homme and UNESCO led the way in moving away from scientific racism and the hierarchical ranking of human cultures, see Conklin, *In the Museum of Man*.

58. Box 115, Devereux Papers.

59. Erwin H. Ackerknecht, "Psychopathology, Primitive Medicine and Primitive Culture," *Bulletin of the History of Medicine* 14, no. 1 (1943): 30–67.

60. Box 142, Devereux Papers. "Among the Mohave both the madman and the shaman are called 'mad.'" Box 109, folder 4, Devereux Papers.

61. Box 142, Devereux Papers. "Respect for aboriginals is one matter," Weston La Barre noted, "but some persons have the air of defending shamans against gross charges in being called mentally unstable or neurotic, an excess of cultural courtesy that recognizes neither what neurosis is nor its prevalence." Weston La Barre, *The Ghost Dance: Origins of Religion* (Crescent Moon, 1970), 325.

62. This explains why the shaman is *less* disturbed by abrupt social and cultural change than the non-shaman. Cloistered in the confines of an anachronistic shelter, the shaman is relatively safe. "The shaman can still derive, from the previously stable but now disappearing aboriginal ethos of his tribe, the 'solution' for his neurotic conflicts," whereas the nonshaman no longer has access to age-old customs and is, from a psychological point of view, adrift. George Devereux, *Basic Problems of Ethnopsychiatry*, trans. Basia Miller Gulati and George Devereux (University of Chicago Press, 1980), 26; A. L. Kroeber, "Psychotic Factors in Shamanism," *Character and Personality* 8 (1940): 204–15; A. L. Kroeber, "Psychosis or Social Sanction," in *The Nature of Culture* (University of Chicago Press, 1952), 310–19.

63. George Devereux, *Normal and Abnormal: The Key Problem of Psychiatric Anthropology* (University of California Press, 1956). See also Devereux, "The Origin of Shamanistic Powers as Reflected in Neurosis," *Revue internationale d'ethnopsychologie normale et pathologique* 1 (1945): 19–28.

64. Devereux, *Mohave Ethnopsychiatry*, 1–2.

65. "I imagine Socrates and Aristophanes to have been persons much like my friend Hivsu Tupoma." Box 142, Devereux Papers.

66. Henri Ellenberger, "The Story of 'Anna O.': A Critical Review with New Data," *Journal of the History of the Behavioral Sciences* 8, no. 3 (1972): 267–79. See also Mark S. Micale, ed., *Beyond the Unconscious: Essays of Henri F. Ellenberger in the History of Psychiatry* (Princeton University Press, 1993), 18.

67. This quotation is from a six-page unpublished manuscript Devereux wrote in preparation for George Devereux, "Rejoinder to Parsons and to Wintrob," *Transcultural Psychiatric Research* 1, no. 2 (1964): 167–69. Refer to box 110, folder 10, Devereux Papers.

68. Devereux is a difficult author, but not for the normal reasons: no willed convolution, no confusing obscurity with profundity. One reason reading him can be a challenge is that, despite his youthful literary pursuits, his ethnopsychiatry bore no relationship to literature. This lack of literary aspiration sets him apart from the other postwar primitivists and from many of his fellow French anthropologists. On the specifically French combination of anthropology and literature, see Vincent Debaene, *Far Afield: French Anthropology between Science and Literature*, trans. Justin Izzo (University of Chicago Press, 2014).

69. Devereux, *Mohave Ethnopsychiatry*, 371.

70. George Devereux, "Primitive Psychiatric Diagnosis: A General Theory of the Diagnostic Process," in *Man's Image in Medicine and Anthropology*, ed. Iago Galdston (International Universities Press, 1963), 337–38.

71. Box 110, folder 10, Devereux Papers.

72. Morris E. Opler, "Some Points of Comparison and Contrast between the Treatment of Functional Disorders by Apache Shamans and Modern Psychiatric Practice," *American Journal*

of Psychiatry 92, no. 5 (1936): 1371–87; Alexander H. Leighton and Dorothea C. Leighton, "Elements of Psychotherapy in Navaho Religion," Psychiatry 4 (1941): 515–23.

73. Henri F. Ellenberger, *The Discovery of the Unconscious: The History and Evolution of Dynamic Psychiatry* (Basic Books, 1970), 3. "The remote source of modern dynamic psychiatry is to be found in 'primitive' medicine, which is still an almost illimited source of insights and suggestions" is the opening line of Ellenberger's early notes for *The Discovery of the Unconscious*. See E13.15, Ellenberger Papers, Bibliothèque Médicale Henri Ey de l'Hôpital Sainte-Anne.

74. Devereux demonstrated how culture shaped modern psychiatry as well. It was characteristic of Devereux to turn criticisms of the shamanic style against psychiatric science itself. See George Devereux, "Cultural Thought Models in Primitive and Modern Psychiatric Theories," Psychiatry 21, no. 4 (1958): 363–64, 371.

75. Devereux, *Mohave Ethnopsychiatry*, 497.

76. Devereux, "Cultural Thought Models," 361.

77. Devereux, *Mohave Ethnopsychiatry*, 75–76, 491.

78. Roger Bastide, review of *Mohave Ethnopsychiatry and Suicide*, by George Devereux, L'année sociologique (1962): 299–301.

79. Box 115, Devereux Papers.

80. Joseph-François Lafitau, *Customs of the American Indians Compared with the Customs of Primitive Tribes* (Champlain Society, 1974), 241. On Lafitau's place in the history of French ethnography, see Alfred Métraux, "Les précurseurs de l'ethnologie en France du XVIe au XVIIIe siècle," Cahiers d'histoire mondiale 7, no. 3 (1963): 721–38.

81. Henri Hubert and Marcel Mauss, "Esquisse d'une théorie générale de la magie," L'année sociologique 7 (1902–3): 1–146. "It must be accepted that the sorcerer sincerely, though willingly, believes his gestures to be a reality and the beginnings of an action to be complete surgical operations. The ritual preliminaries, the gravity of each move, the intensity of the dangers undergone, and the seriousness of the whole performance reveals a genuine will to believe in it," Mauss wrote. "This treasury of ideas, amassed by magic, was a capital store which science for a long time exploited. Magic served science and magicians served scholars. In primitive societies, sorcerers are the only people who have the leisure to make observations on nature, to reflect and dream about these matters. They do so as part of their profession." Marcel Mauss, *A General Theory of Magic*, trans. Robert Brain (W. W. Norton, 1972), 94, 143–44.

82. Ellenberger, *Discovery*, 3; box 127, Devereux Papers; box 122, Devereux Papers. See the illuminating discussion of the relationship between Devereux and Ellenberger's development of ethnopsychiatry and their treatment of American Indians in Emmanuel Delille, "On the History of Cultural Psychiatry: Georges Devereux, Henri Ellenberger, and the Psychological Treatment of Native Americans," Transcultural Psychiatry 53, no. 3 (2016): 392–411.

83. Devereux, *Mohave Ethnopsychiatry*, 3.

84. Box 161, folder 4, Devereux Papers. See also Catherine Clément, Le matin, May 20, 1980, 34.

85. Devereux, *Mohave Ethnopsychiatry*, 490.

86. Devereux, *Mohave Ethnopsychiatry*, 504.

87. See Marc Augé, "Vies de rêve des indiens mohaves," Critique 603–4 (1997): 584–90, for Augé's review of Françoise Bouillot's French translation of *Mohave Ethnopsychiatry*, *Ethnopsychiatrie des Indiens Mohave* (Éditions Synthélabo, 1996). "Primitive psychiatric knowledge," Devereux wrote, "ranges from deep psychological insight to purely ritual notions. The modern

psychiatrist has something to learn from the psychologically minded Mohave shaman; the ritually oriented Sedang healer can teach him nothing." Box 115, Devereux Papers.

88. Devereux, *Mohave Ethnopsychiatry*, 499, 504. Compare with Ellenberger, who wrote in *The Discovery of the Unconscious*: "The study of primitive healing thus is of interest not only to anthropologists and historians but is also of great theoretical importance to the study of psychiatry as the basis of a new science of comparative psychotherapy." Ellenberger, *Discovery*, 3.

89. Devereux, "Cultural Thought Models," 374.

90. Erwin H. Ackerknecht, review of *Mohave Ethnopsychiatry and Suicide*, by George Devereux, *Bulletin of the History of Medicine* 37, no. 4 (1963): 385–86.

91. "To a degree unparalleled in bodily disease, the experience, understanding, and treatment of mental disorders are deeply inflected by culture." Alice Bullard, "The Critical Impact of Frantz Fanon and Henri Collomb: Race, Gender, and Personality Testing of North and West Africans," *Journal of the History of the Behavioral Sciences* 41, no. 3 (2005): 226.

92. Box 119, Devereux Papers.

93. Sidney Axelrad, review of *Mohave Ethnopsychiatry and Suicide*, by George Devereux, *American Anthropologist* 65, no. 6 (1963): 1395.

94. Devereux, "Mohave Pregnancy," 90.

95. Box 7, folder 14, Devereux Papers.

96. Box 7, folder 9, Devereux Papers.

97. Roger Bastide, "Un puritain de la pensée," *La quinzaine littéraire* 150 (1972): 21–22. See also François Laplantine, *L'ethnopsychiatrie* (Éditions universitaires, 1973), 13.

98. Geneviève Delassi, "Georges Devereux ethnopsychiatre," *Le Monde*, May 18, 1980; Devereux, quoted in Ariane Deluz, "George Devereux: A Portrait," in *Fantasy and Symbol: Studies in Anthropological Interpretation; Essays in Honour of George Devereux*, ed. R. H. Hook (Academic Press, 1979), 15. This woefully mistitled festschrift includes contributions by Weston La Barre, Claude Lévi-Strauss, and Margaret Mead. See also Suzette Heald and Ariane Deluz, eds., *Anthropology and Psychoanalysis: An Encounter Through Culture* (Routledge, 1994).

99. Georges Devereux, *Essais d'ethnopsychiatrie générale* (Gallimard, 1970); Georges Devereux, *Ethnopsychanalyse complémentariste* (Flammarion, 1972). On the belated recognition of Devereux's oeuvre, see Weston La Barre, review of *Basic Problems of Ethnopsychiatry*, by George Devereux, *Journal of Psychoanalytic Anthropology* 4, no. 2 (1981): 258.

100. Alain Besançon, "Un méconnu: Devereux," *La quinzaine littéraire* 110 (1971): 25–26.

101. Gilles Deleuze and Félix Guattari, *Anti-Oedipus: Capitalism and Schizophrenia*, trans. Robert Hurley, Mark Seem, and Helen R. Lane (Penguin Books, 1977). On insanity as a repressive label, see, among others, Thomas S. Szasz, *The Myth of Mental Illness* (Dell, 1961); Szasz, *The Manufacture of Madness: A Comparative Study of the Inquisition and the Mental Health Movement* (Harper & Row, 1970); and Erving Goffman, *Asylums: Essays on the Social Situation of Mental Patients and Other Inmates* (Doubleday, 1961).

102. Box 1, folder 8, Devereux Papers. See Alain Besançon, *Histoire et expérience du Moi* (Flammarion, 1971); and Georges Devereux, "À l'écoute psychanalytique de l'histoire," review of *Histoire et expérience du Moi*, by Alain Besançon, *La quinzaine littéraire* 145 (1972): 19–20. For Besançon's review of Devereux's *Essais d'ethnopsychiatrie générale*, see Alain Besançon, "Un méconnu: Devereux," *La quinzaine littéraire* 110 (1971): 25–26.

103. Box 1, folder 8, Devereux Papers. Without naming the dean of structural anthropology, criticisms of Lévi-Strauss can be found in Devereux's papers: "We have too many people

who write about the mind of 'The Savage,' and no one to write about the psychological 'set' of a tribe. One cannot begin the house by putting a roof in the air." Box 147, Devereux Papers. See, by way of comparison, Georges Balandier, "Devereux et Bastide, deux frontaliers des savoirs," *Le Monde*, April 10, 1998, vii–viii.

104. See George Devereux, "Psychoanalysis as Anthropological Fieldwork: Data and Theoretical Implications," *Transactions of the New York Academy of Sciences* 19, no. 5 (1957): 457–72; and Alain Besançon, review of *Ethnopsychanalyse complémentariste*, by Georges Devereux, in *Annales: Histoire, sciences sociales* 28, no. 5 (1973): 1311–13.

105. In the words of Margaret Mead, Devereux was the "rare individual who actually includes—in his own person—two fully comprehended disciplines, psychoanalytic psychotherapy and anthropology." Margaret Mead, preface to George Devereux, *Reality and Dreams*, 2nd ed. (New York University Press, 1969).

106. Georges Devereux, interview with Roland Jaccard, *Gazette de Lausanne*, April 24–25, 1971.

107. "No one will deny that a person who, in the current sense of the word, was well-adjusted to a totalitarian system, is and must be a neurotic." Box 109, folder 6, Devereux Papers.

108. "The complexity of the world in which we live has come to exceed our powers to grasp it. This produces a generalized sense of disorientation, which can culminate in schizophrenia." Box 115, folder 13, Devereux Papers.

109. Jean Ziegler, "La culture cannibale," *Jeune Afrique*, April 6, 1971, 12. "The central conception of psychoanalysis, psychiatry, American sociology, and even of America tout court is the problem of 'normality,' the problem of conformity, of the adaptation of man to his milieu, his 'adjustment.' It's more than a problem—it is an obsession." Georges Devereux, "Quelques aspects de la psychanalyse aux États-Unis," *Les temps modernes* 11–12 (1946): 303.

110. A brief story to illustrate Devereux's penchant for clarity. It comes from François Laplantine, one of Devereux's best students. He recalls that Jacques Lacan, a French psychoanalyst well-known for his deliberate obscurantism, "constituted for Devereux the approach par excellence by which psychoanalysis became completely misguided. Each time I met with Devereux in his Châtenay-Malabry apartment, he warned me to avoid drugs, religious passion, political fanaticism (for him the three major forms of psychotic delirium) . . . and Lacan's *Écrits*." Laplantine, "Pour une ethnopsychiatrie critique," 33.

111. Jean Ziegler, "Deux génies en marge," *Jeune Afrique*, January 29, 1972, 58.

112. Georges Devereux, interview with Roland Jaccard, *Gazette de Lausanne*, April 24–25, 1971.

113. Roland Jaccard, *Le Monde*, November 18, 1983, 30. On the difference between what anthropologists call cultural lag, which should be abolished, and what sociologists call survivals, which should be selectively preserved, see Georges Devereux, "Cultural Lag and Survivals: The Dynamics of Social Misevaluations," *Journal of Psychoanalytic Anthropology* 7, no. 2 (1984): 119–40.

114. On Nathan's controversial treatment of immigrants, see Didier Fassin and Richard Rechtman, "An Anthropological Hybrid: The Pragmatic Arrangement of Universalism and Culturalism in French Mental Health," *Transcultural Psychiatry* 42, no. 3 (2005): 347–66; and Fassin, "Ethnopsychiatry and the Postcolonial Encounter: A French Psychopolitics of Otherness," in *Unconscious Dominions: Psychoanalysis, Global Trauma, and Global Sovereignties*, ed. Warwick Anderson, Deborah Jenson and Richard C. Keller (Duke University Press, 2011), 223–46. See also Paul Freeman, "Ethnopsychiatry in France," *Transcultural Psychiatry* 34, no. 3 (1997): 313–19;

NOTES TO PAGES 137–145   219

and Virginie Bloch-Lainé, "Tobie Nathan: Totem sans tabou," *Liberation*, September 1, 2015. For the gist of Nathan's response to his critics, see Nathan, "Psychothérapie et politique," *Genèses* 38 (2000): 136–59.

115. "The total disorganization that some advocate as the very essence of freedom is also a technique of enslavement, for the technique that deprives man of all organization is the first condition of his slavehood." Devereux, *Basic Problems*, 320.

116. "Now, a topic seldom discussed by anthropologists, who take pride in their lack of ethnocentricity, is the fact that even they do not feel equally at home in all cultures they investigate or read about." George Devereux, "A Heuristic Measure of Cultural Affinity," *Anthropological Quarterly* 35, no. 1 (1962): 26. Box 94, Devereux Papers.

117. Box 164, Devereux Papers.

118. Box 164, Devereux Papers.

119. Box 164, Devereux Papers.

120. "I felt closer to France in Parker than in New York, as I feel closer to Parker in Paris than I did in Chicago." Box 94, Devereux Papers.

121. Box 164, Devereux Papers.

122. Sheryl Drew, "Anthropologist Georges Devereux's Ashes Buried in Mohave Ritual," *Parker Pioneer*, July 17, 1985, 1–2.

Chapter Four

1. Box 163, folder 10, Mircea Eliade Papers, Special Collections Research Center, University of Chicago Library. Long, a student of Eliade's and a preeminent scholar of American and Black religions, contributed to Eliade's festschrift, *Myths and Symbols: Studies in Honor of Mircea Eliade*, ed. Joseph M. Kitagawa and Charles H. Long with the collaboration of Jerald C. Brauer and Marshall G. S. Hodgson (University of Chicago Press, 1969). Other contributors included Joseph Campbell, Emil Cioran, Georges Dumézil, Ernst Jünger, Paul Ricoeur, and Gershom Scholem.

2. Although the Romanian émigré thought modern history a comprehensive disaster, he remained hopeful about the future. His optimism made an impression on those he met. In a letter dated January 9, 1962, the French cultural theorist Denis de Rougemont asked Eliade to contribute to a collected volume on how refugees had shaped the history of ideas. Rougemont turned to Eliade because, as he wrote, "you have lived and continue to live the refugee life in a positive manner that overcomes the challenges of being uprooted." Box 87, folder 34, Eliade Papers.

3. For a detailed discussion of what Eliade thought of his French forerunners, see Mircea Eliade, "The History of Religions in Retrospect: 1912–1962," *Journal of Bible and Religion* 31, no. 2 (1963): 98–109.

4. Claude-Henri Rocques, *L'autre monde* 28 (1981): 19–22.

5. Box 163, folder 7, Eliade Papers. On the Bollingen Foundation and the Bollingen book series published by Princeton University Press, see William McGuire, *Bollingen: An Adventure in Collecting the Past* (Princeton University Press, 1982).

6. Mircea Eliade, *Images and Symbols: Studies in Religious Symbolism*, trans. Philip Mairet (Sheed & Ward, 1961), 120; originally published as *Images et symboles* (Gallimard, 1952). Take the Pyrenean town of Lourdes, for example: "A fountain in Gaul, regarded as sacred ever since prehistoric times, but sanctified by the presence of a divine local or regional figure, became sacred *for Christianity as a whole* after its consecration to the Virgin Mary." Eliade, *Images and Symbols*, 174.

7. Mircea Eliade, *The Sacred and the Profane: The Nature of Religion*, trans. Willard R. Trask (Harcourt, 1959), 31.

8. Theodor Lavi, "Dosarul Mircea Eliade," *Toladot* 1 (1972): 21–27.

9. Box 88, folder 2, Eliade Papers.

10. Daniel Dubuisson, *Twentieth Century Mythologies: Dumézil, Lévi-Strauss, Eliade*, trans. Martha Cunningham (Equinox, 2006), xvii. In letters to Eliade, Dubuisson expressed his admiration and respect as late as March 18, 1978. Box 143, folder 13, Eliade Papers. Dubuisson, *Mythologies du XXe siècle: Dumézil, Lévi-Strauss, Eliade* (Presses Universitaires de Lille, 1993). See also Dubuisson, *Impostures et pseudo-science: L'oeuvre de Mircea Eliade* (Presses Universitaires de Lille, 2005). Among Eliade's French critics are Alexandra Laignel-Lavastine, *Cioran, Eliade, Ionesco: L'oubli du fascisme* (Presses Universitaires de France, 2002); and Florin Turcanu, *Mircea Eliade: Le prisonnier de l'histoire* (Éditions de la Découverte, 2003). Ivan Strenski, *Four Theories of Myth in Twentieth-Century History: Cassirer, Eliade, Lévi-Strauss, and Malinowski* (University of Iowa Press, 1987), was the first book in English to emphasize Eliade's interwar politics.

11. Dubuisson, *Twentieth Century Mythologies*, 222, emphasis added.

12. Steven M. Wasserstrom, *Religion After Religion: Gershom Scholem, Mircea Eliade, and Henry Corbin at Eranos* (Princeton University Press, 1999), 213. Notable exceptions to the silence in English-language scholarship include Bryan Rennie, *Changing Religious Worlds: The Meaning and End of Mircea Eliade* (State University of New York Press, 2000); Marta Petreu, *An Infamous Past: E. M. Cioran and the Rise of Fascism in Romania* (Ivan R. Dee, 2005); Carlo Ginzburg, "Mircea Eliade's Ambivalent Legacy," in *Hermeneutics, Politics, and the History of Religions: The Contested Legacies of Joachim Wach and Mircea Eliade*, ed. Christian K. Wedemeyer and Wendy Doniger (Oxford University Press, 2010), 307–23; and Moshe Idel, *Mircea Eliade: From Magic to Myth* (Peter Lang, 2014).

13. This is the conclusion of Lincoln, whose analysis of Eliade's legionnaire articles and their effects in Bruce Lincoln, *Secrets, Lies, and Consequences: A Great Scholar's Hidden Past and His Protégé's Unsolved Murder* (Oxford University Press, 2024), 132, I have followed closely.

14. Lincoln, *Secrets*, 34.

15. Saul Bellow, *Ravelstein* (Penguin Books, 2000), 203. Cf. Philip Ó. Ceallaigh, "'The Terror of History': On Saul Bellow and Mircea Eliade," *Los Angeles Review of Books*, August 11, 2018. "It is necessary to take into account not only the nationalistic and decidedly anti-Semitic aspects of the Iron Guard, but also the side that marked by asceticism, Christian mysticism, and Romanian folklore—after all, the Guard had taken the Archangel Michael as its symbol," writes Hans Thomas Hakl in *Eranos: An Alternative Intellectual History of the Twentieth Century* (McGill-Queen's University Press, 2013), 175.

16. "Nothing is more disturbing than the provincialism of great cultures" is the first line of Mircea Eliade, "L'Europe et les rideaux," *Comprendre* (May 1952): 115–22. See, by way of comparison, Jacques Brosse, "Mircea Eliade: Sortir du provincialisme culturel," *Les nouvelles littéraires* 295 (September 17, 1971): 8; and Dipesh Chakrabarty, *Provincializing Europe: Postcolonial Thought and Historical Difference* (Princeton University Press, 2000).

17. Mircea Eliade, *The Myth of the Eternal Return: Cosmos and History*, trans. Willard R. Trask (Princeton University Press, 1954), xii; originally published as *Le mythe de l'étérnel retour: Archétypes et répétition* (Gallimard, 1949). Cf. Eliade, *The Forge and the Crucible*, trans. Stephen Corrin (Rider, 1962), 12, originally published as *Forgerons et alchimistes* (Flammarion, 1956).

18. Box 163, folder 10, Eliade Papers. See also Hakl, *Eranos*, 185; and Eliade, *The Forge and the Crucible*, 12. In another telling example, Eliade wrote in his journal: "I am continuing my

discussion with Tom Altizer. To his objection that I'm not writing a book in which I hold a dialogue with the representatives of modern consciousness (Nietzsche, Freud, Marx, et al.), I reply: All these famous authors that Tom admires so are *westerners*. That is, they attacked problems and crises belonging to modern Western spirituality. Personally, I think that these cultural horizons are provincial. The crises and problematic issues of a Freud, Nietzsche, Marx, et al., have been left behind or resolved. As for me, I'm trying to open windows onto other worlds for westerners—even if some of these worlds foundered tens of thousands of years ago. My dialogue had other interlocutors than those of Freud or James Joyce: I'm trying to understand a Paleolithic hunter, a yogi or a shaman, a peasant from Indonesia, an African, et al., and to communicate with each one." Mircea Eliade, *Journal II, 1957-1969* (University of Chicago Press, 1989), 179.

19. Eliade, *Images and Symbols*, 10–11.

20. Box 38, folder 2, Eliade Papers.

21. See, for example, *Figaro littéraire*, July 9, 1949. Eliade's *Myth of the Eternal Return* was not a study of Nietzsche; it was "an exploration of archaic man's relation to time," writes Tomoko Masuzawa. Masuzawa goes on to point out that the book's original title, *Cosmos and History*, referred to the fundamental difference between the cyclical (cosmic) rhythms of archaic societies and the linear (historical) progress of modern societies. Tomoko Masuzawa, *In Search of Dreamtime: The Quest for the Origin of Religion* (University of Chicago Press, 1993), 26–27.

22. Refer to Eliade's 1976 interview for *Parabola*, box 53, folder 1, Eliade Papers.

23. Eliade continued to use Latin phrases even though the editors at Harper & Row pleaded with him to "guard against any impression of pedantry which an American or British reader might be tempted to feel." Box 74, folder 10, Eliade Papers.

24. Mircea Eliade, "History and the Cyclical View of Time," *Perspectives* 5 (1960): 11. For a French challenge to Eliade's dichotomy between sacred and profane time, see Paul Ricoeur, "The History of Religions and the Phenomenology of Time Consciousness," in *The History of Religions: Retrospect and Prospect*, ed. Joseph M. Kitagawa (MacMillan, 1985), 13–30.

25. Eliade's desire to banish history and replace it with selected elements of an imagined past, Harry Harootunian writes, was textbook fascism. Harry Harootunian, *Archaism and Actuality: Japan and the Global Fascist Imaginary* (Duke University Press, 2023), xiv, 91.

26. Eliade, *Myth of the Eternal Return*, 141, 5. "The crucial difference between the man of the archaic civilizations and modern, historical man lies in the increasing value the latter gives to historical events, that is, to the 'novelties' that, for traditional man, represented either meaningless conjunctures or infractions of norms." Eliade, *Myth of the Eternal Return*, 154.

27. "A need for what transcends time, or is mysteriously spared by time, is built into the very nature of the human mind and imagination." John Berger, "Go Ask the Time," *Granta*, March 1, 1985, 201.

28. Eliade, *Myth of the Eternal Return*, 145.

29. Box 88, folder 28, Eliade Papers. Compare with Louis Ménard, review of *Traité d'histoire des religions* and *Le mythe de l'éternel retour*, by Mircea Eliade, *Les temps modernes* 50 (1949): 1139–41; and Maxime Rodinson, "Chronique d'histoire des religions," *La pensée* 38 (1951): 127–30.

30. Eliade, "History and the Cyclical View," 14.

31. Eliade, *Myth of the Eternal Return*, 142, 152. "Modern man is free to despise mythologies and theologies, but that will not prevent his continuing to feed upon decayed myths and degraded images." Eliade, *Images and Symbols*, 19. On the often-overlooked overlap between the Marxian Left and the anticapitalist Right, see Harootunian, *Archaism and Actuality*, 108–9.

32. Box 115, folder 14, Georges Devereux Papers, Institut Mémoires de l'édition contemporaine.

33. Eliade, *Myth of the Eternal Return*, viii.

34. The admiration was mutual. "I just finished your book on shamanism, a reading which I enjoyed enormously," Jung wrote to Eliade on June 20, 1952. "The richness of your data is extraordinary and of the greatest interest." Box 84, folder 20, Eliade Papers. See also Eliade's unpublished manuscript "Le 'miracle' d'Ascona," in box 40, folder 5, Eliade Papers. It is worth noting that after 1956 the Bollingen Foundation paid Eliade roughly $1200 each year to cover his travel expenses to the annual Eranos symposium.

35. Mircea Eliade, "Rencontre avec Jung," *Combat*, October 9, 1952; Mircea Eliade, "Rencontres à Ascona," in *À propos des conférences Eranos* (1960): 23. Eliade shared another fascinating similarity with Jung: each attracted eccentrics in search of a spiritual leader. Thomas Altizer, professor at Stony Brook University, for example, believed there was a hidden theology in Eliade's work, which he was eager to follow. "YOU ARE THE SHAMAN AT THE CENTER OF THIS MAELSTROM," he wrote to Eliade in all caps. You alone have resurrected "COSMIC SACRALITY," and you are "THE LAST ONE IN OUR WORLD WHO KNOWS THE IDENTITY OF HELL." Box 79, folder 6, Eliade Papers.

36. Mircea Eliade, *Myth of the Eternal Return*, ix. In addition, Eliade replaced every "primitive mentality" with "for traditional societies" in later editions and translations of this book.

37. See Eliade's 1976 interview for *Parabola*, box 53, folder 1, Eliade Papers.

38. Mircea Eliade, "Religions," *International Social Science Journal* 29, no. 4 (1977): 621; Eliade, "Archaic Myth and Historical Man," *McCormick Quarterly* (January 1965): 35–36.

39. Bellow, *Ravelstein*, 105. The literary critic Northrop Frye expressed a similar ambivalence: "Mr. Eliade is very far from being a Jungian disciple, but he shows a similar desire to oversimplify our present situation into a dilemma." Northrop Frye, "World Enough Without Time," *Hudson Review* 12, no. 3 (1959): 431. The British anthropologist Edmund Leach, however, did not equivocate. He accused Eliade of spreading a "Christian-Jungian faith" in books sponsored by the Bollingen Foundation, "always a stalwart patron of Jungian psychology." Edmund Leach, "Sermons by a Man on a Ladder," *New York Review of Books*, October 20, 1966.

40. Mircea Eliade, "Rituals and Symbols of Time Reborn," *UNESCO Courier* 12 (1955): 7, 32. This special issue of the *Courrier de l'UNESCO* also included contributions by Éveline Lot-Falck, Alfred Métraux, and Claude Lévi-Strauss.

41. Eliade, *Myth of the Eternal Return*, 155.

42. Eliade, *Myth of the Eternal Return*, xi; Eliade, *The Sacred and the Profane*, 81. "One of the most arrogant features of the new," Lefebvre wrote, "is that on both an emotional and intellectual level it manages in some obscure way to give the impression of being synonymous with creativity." Henri Lefebvre, *Introduction to Modernity: Twelve Preludes, September 1959–May 1961*, trans. John Moore (Verso, 1995), 185.

43. Masuzawa sees a blatant contradiction in Eliade's thinking here: The ritual repetitions of archaic religions can't both resist change and be creative. "What exactly is the nature of 'religious creativity,'" she asks, "when 'creativity,' as opposed to stagnation, means development and change in some sense?" The question shows how hard it is to decouple cultural creativity from novelty and progress. Masuzawa, *Dreamtime*, 168.

44. Mircea Eliade, "Le symbolisme religieux et la valorisation de l'angoisse," in *L'angoisse du temps présent et les devoirs de l'esprit*, ed. Raymond de Saussure, Paul Ricoeur, Mircea Eliade, et al. (Éditions La Baconnière, 1954), 55–71. See also Microfiche 8-R-51235 (8), Bibliothèque nationale de France; and Daniel Christoff, review of *L'angoisse du temps présent et les devoirs de l'esprit*, *Revue de théologie et de philosophie* 3, no. 4 (1953): 270–73.

45. Mircea Eliade, *No Souvenirs: Journal, 1957–1969* (Harper & Row, 1977), 18. Terry Eagleton uses different words to make the same point: "As far as religious conviction is concerned, one does not jettison history's most formidably successful symbolic system overnight." Terry Eagleton, *Culture and the Death of God* (Yale University Press, 2014), 196.

46. Eliade, *Myth of the Eternal Return*, 160, 152.

47. Eliade, *Myth of the Eternal Return*, 153–54.

48. Box 34, folder 7, Eliade Papers.

49. Mircea Eliade, *Shamanism: Archaic Techniques of Ecstasy*, trans. Willard R. Trask (Princeton University Press, 1964); originally published as *Le chamanisme et les techniques archaïques de l'extase* (Payot, 1951). For Eliade's revisions and corrections to his original 1951 text, see box 33, Eliade Papers.

50. Mircea Eliade, "Recent Works on Shamanism: A Review Article," *History of Religions* 1, no. 1 (1961): 184. His first article on the subject dates from 1946: Eliade, "Le problème du chamanisme," *Revue de l'histoire des religions* 131 (1946): 5–52.

51. Eliade, *Shamanism*, xxi.

52. Evidence of the attention and praise *Shamanism* garnered was everywhere: Albert-Marie Schmidt, review of *Le chamanisme et les techniques archaïques de l'extase*, by Mircea Eliade, *Reforme*, October 13, 1951; Marcelle Bouteiller, review of *Le chamanisme et les techniques archaïques de l'extase*, by Mircea Eliade, *Revue philosophique* (October–December 1952): 568–70; M. Dambruyant, review of *Le chamanisme et les techniques archaïques de l'extase*, by Mircea Eliade, *Journal de psychologie* (September 1952): 367–69; Éveline Falck, review of *Le chamanisme et les techniques archaïques de l'extase*, by Mircea Eliade, *Diogène* (November 1952): 128–34; Maurice Leenhardt, review of *Le chamanisme et les techniques archaïques de l'extase*, by Mircea Eliade, *Le monde non-chrétien* 22 (1952): 229–33; Gonzague Truc, review of *Le chamanisme et les techniques archaïques de l'extase*, by Mircea Eliade, *L'école*, November 24, 1951; A. Bombieri, "Confrontations des mystiques de l'orient et de l'occident," review of *Le chamanisme et les techniques archaïques de l'extase*, by Mircea Eliade, *La croix*, May 3, 1952; Georges Buraud, review of *Le chamanisme et les techniques archaïques de l'extase*, by Mircea Eliade, *Psyché* (January 1952): 73–77; Michel Carrouges, review of *Le chamanisme et les techniques archaïques de l'extase*, by Mircea Eliade, *Monde nouveau-paru* 51–52 (1951): 228–29; Albert Vincent, review of *Le chamanisme et les techniques archaïques de l'extase*, by Mircea Eliade, *Revue des sciences religieuses* (January 1953): 66–68. "Many thanks for your *Shamanism*," Paul Radin wrote to Eliade on September 17, 1954. "I don't have to tell you what an excellent presentation of the subject it gives. There are certainly aspects of the subject I would like to discuss with you, particularly data about the American Indians and Polynesians." Box 87, folder 20, Eliade Papers.

53. On February 27, 1947, Eliade wrote in his journal: "G. Dumézil tells me that 'Le problème du chamanisme' is a milestone in the history of religions. Listening to him, I blush. But I believe there is some truth in what he says; with all its imperfections, my study has the merit of presenting for the first time the phenomenon of shamanism in the only perspective in which it becomes intelligible, that of the history of religions." Eliade, *Journal I*, 50.

54. Eliade, *Shamanism*, 32, 103.

55. Eliade, *Shamanism*, xvi–xvii.

56. Eliade, *Shamanism*, 23. "There is always a kernel that remains refractory to explanation, and this indefinable, irreducible element perhaps reveals the real situation of man in the cosmos, a situation that, we shall never tire of repeating, is not solely 'historical.'" Eliade, *Shamanism*, xiv.

57. Eliade, "Recent Works," 159–160.

58. Eliade, "Recent Works," 184. Like Bataille, Eliade cited Hörst Kirchner, "An Archaeological Contribution to the Early History of Shamanism," *Anthropos* 47 (1952): 244–86. "The oldest religion of which we have any secure knowledge is the shamanism of the late Old Stone Age, as we have seen it depicted in the caves of southern France and northern Spain," wrote Devereux's friend and frequent correspondent Weston La Barre in "Shamanic Origins of Religion and Medicine," *Journal of Psychedelic Drugs* 11 (1979): 8.

59. See Jean Clottes and David Lewis-Williams, *Les chamanes de la préhistoire: Transe et magie dans les grottes ornées* (Éditions du Seuil, 1996).

60. See Mircea Eliade, "Le dieu lointain dans les religions primitives," *Témoignages* 28 (1951): 22.

61. Eliade, "Recent Works," 183. "I'm trying to understand a Paleolithic hunter, a yogi or a shaman, a peasant from Indonesia." Eliade, *No Souvenirs*, 179. See also Mircea Eliade, "Smiths, Shamans and Mystagogues," *East and West* 6, no. 3 (1955): 207.

62. "Mr. Eliade," Frye observed, "clearly feels that, his own interest being in comparative religion, it is possible to revert to nineteenth-century comparative methods." Frye, "World Enough," 426.

63. Eliade, *Shamanism*, xi–xii; Eliade, "Chasteté, sexualité et vie mystique chez les primitifs," *Extrait des Études carmélitaines, Mystique et continence* (1952): 35.

64. Eliade, "Recent Works," 171.

65. Eliade, *Shamanism*, 27. See also Mircea Eliade, "Foreword," in *The Jonah Complex*, ed. André Lacocque and Pierre-Emmanuel Lacocque (John Knox Press, 1981), xii.

66. Eliade drew on the French ethnographer Alfred Métraux, who "saw the crux of the problem better when he wrote, in regard to South American shamans, that temperamentally neuropathic or religious individuals feel drawn to a kind of life that gives them intimate contact with the supernatural world and allows them to expend their nervous force freely." See Alfred Métraux, "Le shamanisme chez les Indiens l'Amérique du sud tropicale," *Acta Americana* 2 (1944): 200.

67. Box 38, folder 2, Eliade Papers.

68. Carlos Castaneda, *The Teachings of Don Juan: A Yaqui Way of Knowledge* (University of California Press, 1968). Cf. Henri Desroche, review of *Voir: Les enseignements d'un sorcier Yaqui*, by Carlos Castaneda, *Archives des sciences sociales des religions* 39 (1975): 209–10.

69. Castaneda, *The Teachings of Don Juan*, xix. For a perspective on the relationship between North American shamanism and psychotropic drugs quite different from Castaneda's, see La Barre, "Shamanic Origins," 7–11.

70. This letter is found in box 81, folder 1, Eliade Papers. "Thank you for your letter of September 12, and the copy of your book on shamanism," Eliade replied one month later. "As soon as I get things organized after my return from Europe, I will read your book and write you in more detail about it." If this letter exists, I haven't seen it. Box 81, folder 1, Eliade Papers.

71. Box 38, folder 2, Eliade Papers. Going a step further, Devereux emphasized the remunerative rewards that came from Castaneda's conjuring of a fictitious don Juan Matus. Refer to box 115, folder 13, Devereux Papers.

72. Eliade, "Recent Works," 184.

73. Eliade, *Shamanism*, 29, 31.

74. Eliade, *The Forge and the Crucible*, 11–13. See also Eliade, "Smiths, Shamans and Mystagogues," 206–15; and Henri Desroche, review of *Forgerons et alchimistes*, by Mircea Eliade, *Archives de sociologie des religions* 3 (1957): 178–79.

75. Frantz Fanon, *The Wretched of the Earth*, trans. Richard Philcox (Grove Press, 2004), 236.
76. Box 38, folder 2, Eliade Papers.
77. "Religion was the last of the controversial, passion-inspiring human pursuits—such as politics, economics, and ethics—to be accorded its own academic discipline in the neutral setting of research, debate, and free thinking that characterizes the university." Rita M. Gross, *Feminism and Religion* (Beacon Press, 1996), 6.
78. Mircea Eliade, interview in *L'express*, August 31, 1979. "It should be said at once that the completely profane world, the wholly desacralized cosmos, is a recent discovery in the history of the human spirit." Eliade, *The Sacred and the Profane*, 13.
79. Mircea Eliade, "Myths for Moderns," *Times Literary Supplement*, February 10, 1966.
80. *Criterion* 17, no. 2 (1978): 27.
81. "Ancient Man Is In Us Still," *New York Times Book Review*, July 12, 1964, 24–25.
82. Box 53, folder 9, Eliade Papers.
83. Mircea Eliade, "The Oddest Graduate School in the United States," *University of Chicago Magazine* (January 1965): 18–23.
84. Additional institutional support was also attractive, of course. In 1962 John Nef, chair of the committee, declared that "to facilitate the important work that Mr. Eliade does, he should have the assurances that he will be given the year 1962–63 under the auspices of the Committee on Social Thought with complete freedom to carry on his research." Box 85, folder 23, Eliade Papers.
85. Eliade, "Graduate School," 21. See also Mircea Eliade, "The Quest for the 'Origins' of Religions," *History of Religions* 4, no. 1 (1964): 154–69.
86. Eliade, "Graduate School," 21. For Leach's critique of Eliade's armchair ethnography, see Leach, "Sermons by a Man on a Ladder."
87. Eliade, "Graduate School," 19.
88. Mircea Eliade, "History of Religions and a New Humanism," *History of Religions* 1, no. 1 (1961): 2.
89. Eliade, "History of Religions and a New Humanism," 2–3.
90. Compare with Theodor H. Gaster, foreword to James George Frazer, *The New Golden Bough* (Criterion Books, 1959). According to Frazer, "everything thought, imagined or desired by man in archaic societies, all his myths and rites, all his gods and religious experiences, are nothing but a monstrous accumulation of madnesses, cruelties, and superstitions now happily abolished by the progress of mankind." Eliade, *Images and Symbols*, 30. For more on Tylor and Frazer, see Eliade's lecture notes for a course on primitive religion in box 54, folder 6, Eliade Papers.
91. Eliade, "Religions," 622.
92. Box 81, folder 7, Eliade Papers. On religious traditions as phenomena to be observed rather than creeds to be followed, see Eric J. Sharpe, *Comparative Religion: A History* (Open Court, 1986).
93. In fact, Eliade quoted Georges Dumézil, who had quoted Henri Poincaré in his preface to Mircea Eliade, *Patterns in Comparative Religion* (Sheed and Ward, 1958).
94. See Microfiche 8-G-4541, Bibliothèque nationale de France, for Mircea Eliade's preface to Pia Laviosa Zambotti, *Les origines et la diffusion de la civilisation: Introduction à l'histoire universelle* (Payot, 1949).
95. Eliade, "History of Religions in Retrospect," 100–1; Eliade, *Jonah Complex*, ix.
96. Eliade, "Le symbolisme religieux," 57. On these pitfalls, see box 31, folder 4, Eliade Papers.
97. Box 54, folder 6, Eliade Papers.

98. Eliade, "History of Religions and a New Humanism," 1–8. Compare with Henri Desroche, *Marxisme et religion* (Presses Universitaires de France, 1962).

99. Box 38, folder 17, Eliade Papers.

100. Eliade, "History of Religions in Retrospect," 103–6; Eliade, "Religions," 618. See also Mircea Eliade, "Methodological Remarks on the Study of Religious Symbolism," in *The History of Religions: Essays in Methodology*, ed. Mircea Eliade and J. M. Kitagawa (University of Chicago Press, 1959), 86–107.

101. People today, Eliade thought, "are not only grasping the importance of symbolism in archaic thinking, they are seeing its intrinsic coherence, validity, speculative audacity, and nobility." Eliade, *Images and Symbols*, 11. See Eliade's opening reference to Lovejoy in "Le mythe du bon sauvage ou les prestiges de l'origine," *Nouvelle revue française* 32 (1955): 229–49.

102. Box 38, folder 17, Eliade Papers.

103. In *The Fall into Time* (1964), Emil Cioran, Eliade's friend and fellow Franco-Romanian writer, declared that "vestiges of humanity are still to be found among the people who, outdistanced by history, are in no hurry to catch up." This sounds very much like Eliade, but Cioran comes to a different conclusion: "Certainly they are *backwards*, and would gladly persevere in their stagnation if they had the means to do so. But this they are not allowed." Emil Cioran, *The Fall into Time*, trans. Richard Howard (Quadrangle Books, 1970), 60.

Epilogue

1. And improve their social standing while they're at it: We are well aware that individual tastes—what one likes, buys, eats, drives, hangs on the wall, etc.—are acts of distinction that reinforce socioeconomic divisions. Pierre Bourdieu, *Distinction: A Social Critique of the Judgement of Taste*, trans. Richard Nice (Harvard University Press, 1987).

2. David Correia, "Degrowth, American Style: *No Impact Man* and Bourgeois Primitivism," *Capitalism Nature Socialism* 23, no. 1 (2012): 113. On bourgeois primitivism in France after 1945, see Daniel J. Sherman, *French Primitivism and the Ends of Empire, 1945–1975* (University of Chicago Press, 2011).

3. William Cronon, "The Trouble with Wilderness: Or, Getting Back to the Wrong Nature," *Environmental History* 1, no. 1 (1996): 7–28.

4. David Graeber, *Fragments of an Anarchist Anthropology* (Prickly Paradigm Press, 2004), 75; John Zerzan, *Future Primitive* (Autonomedia, 1994), 8. See, by way of comparison, Chamsy el-Ojeili and Dylan Taylor, "'The Future in the Past': Anarcho-Primitivism and the Critique of Civilization Today," *Rethinking Marxism* 32, no. 2 (2020): 168–86.

5. James C. Scott, *Against the Grain: A Deep History of the Earliest States* (Yale University Press, 2017), 26–27. See also Marshall Sahlins, *Stone Age Economics* (Aldine, 1972).

6. Bruno Clémentin and Vincent Cheynet, "La décroissance soutenable," *Revue silence* 280–281 (2002).

7. The degrowth movement's search for a prosperous way down faces three significant but not insurmountable challenges: How can the movement pull people out of poverty and raise living standards across the world when the global economy is shrinking? How can a national economy decelerate and scale down while at the same time encouraging growth in areas such as clean, renewable energy? And finally, how can a degrowth agenda of buying less, using public transport, abstaining from eating meat, and giving up a carbon-intensive lifestyle be anything other than politically disastrous in a country such as the United States? The 2010 Degrowth

Declaration ends with the following lines: "A process of degrowth of the world economy is inevitable and will ultimately benefit the environment, but the challenge is how to manage the process so that it is socially equitable at national and global scales. This is the challenge of the Degrowth movement, originating in rich countries in Europe and elsewhere, where the change must start from." Refer to Federico Demaria, François Schneider, Filka Sekulova, and Joan Martinez-Alier, "What Is Degrowth? From an Activist Slogan to a Social Movement," *Research & Degrowth*.

8. "Deceleration is the natural enemy of capitalism, which can only function by accelerating." Kohei Saito, *Slow Down: The Degrowth Manifesto*, trans. Brian Bergstrom (Astra House, 2024), 189. See also Giorgos Kallis, "Socialism Without Growth," *Capitalism Nature Socialism* 30, no. 2 (2019): 189–206.

9. André Gorz, *Ecology as Politics*, trans. Patsy Vigderman and Jonathan Cloud (South End Press, 1980). On how Gorz aligned himself with Lefebvre, often in opposition to fellow Marxists such as Herbert Marcuse, see Willy Gianinazzi, *André Gorz: A Life*, trans. Chris Turner (University of Chicago Press, 2022), 107.

10. Serge Latouche, *Farewell to Growth* (Polity, 2009). See also Latouche, *Le pari de la décroissance* (Fayard, 2006); Latouche, "Is a Degrowth Society Desirable?" *Revue juridique de l'environnement* 2 (2015): 208–10; and Latouche, "Communs, bien commun et décroissance," *Revue du MAUSS* 61, no. 1 (2023): 155–66.

11. Pascal Bruckner, that long-suffering critic of primitivism, is incensed by Latouche's assertion that the West exported an unbridled passion for growth to the rest of the world. Bruckner, *The Tyranny of Guilt: An Essay on Western Masochism*, trans. Steven Rendall (Princeton University Press, 2010), 8.

12. Serge Latouche, "Pour une société de décroissance," *Le monde diplomatique*, December 2003. Compare Latouche's threefold program with Michael Löwy's: "Some productions—for example, fossil energies, pesticides, nuclear submarines, and advertising—should not be merely reduced, but *suppressed*. Others, such as private cars, meat, and airplanes, should be *substantially reduced*. Still others, such as organic food, public means of transport, and carbon neutral housing, should be *developed*. Löwy, "Nine Theses on Ecosocialist Degrowth," *Monthly Review* 75, no. 3 (2023): 156–57.

13. On green ideas and intellectual history, see Paul S. Sutter, "Putting the Intellectual Back in Environmental History," *Modern Intellectual History* 18, no. 2 (2021): 596–605.

14. Kim Stanley Robinson, *Future Primitive: The New Ecotopias* (Tor Books, 1994), 11. Robinson completed his Ph.D. in English in 1982 at the University of California, San Diego under the guidance of the literary critic Fredric Jameson and the novelist Ursula K. Le Guin. Like Le Guin, he is a native of California and an eco-leftist who writes in the style of William Morris and John Ruskin. While his book on shamanism, *Shaman* (2013), is infused with a primitivist sensibility, Robinson most clearly outlines his views in *Future Primitive*.

15. David Wallace-Wells, *The Uninhabitable Earth: Life After Warming* (Tim Duggan Books, 2019), 3; Bruno Latour, "Agency at the Time of the Anthropocene," *New Literary History* 45, no. 1 (2014): 6.

16. E. M. Cioran, *The Trouble with Being Born*, trans. Richard Howard (Arcade Publishing, 1976), 172.

17. "Why should one include the poor of the world—whose carbon footprint is small anyway—by use of such all-inclusive terms as *species* or *mankind* when the blame for the current crisis should be squarely laid at the door of the rich nations in the first place and of the richer classes in the poorer ones?" Dipesh Chakrabarty, "The Climate of History: Four Theses," *Critical Inquiry* 35, no. 2 (2009): 216.

18. Jason W. Moore, ed., *Anthropocene or Capitalocene? Nature, History, and the Crisis of Capitalism* (PM Press, 2016).

19. "There is no solution to the ecological crisis within the framework of capitalism, a system entirely devoted to productivism, consumerism, and the ferocious struggle for market share." Löwy, "Nine Theses," 155.

20. This is the point Adam Kirsch makes in his interesting book *The Revolt Against Humanity: Imagining a Future Without Us* (Columbia Global Reports, 2023).

21. Mircea Eliade, *The Myth of the Eternal Return: Cosmos and History*, trans. Willard R. Trask (Princeton University Press, 1954), 153.

22. For the regular symptoms of that pathological dysfunction, see Amitav Ghosh, *The Great Derangement: Climate Change and the Unthinkable* (University of Chicago Press, 2017).

23. On living well by doing less with less, which Heinrich Heine called a spirit of vigorous repose, see Tracie Matysik, *When Spinoza Met Marx: Experiments in Nonhumanist Activity* (University of Chicago Press, 2022).

24. Arthur O. Lovejoy and George Boas, *Primitivism and Related Ideas in Antiquity* (Johns Hopkins University Press, 1935), 7.

Archives Consulted

In addition to published sources, this book has also drawn on archival materials. The archives I consulted are listed below.

Bibliothèque Médicale Henri Ey de l'Hôpital Sainte-Anne, Paris, France
Colorado River Indian Tribes Library and Archives, Parker, Arizona, United States
Département des Arts du Spectacle, Bibliothèque Nationale de France, Paris, France
Département des Manuscrits, Bibliothèque Nationale de France, Paris, France
Institut Mémoires de l'Édition Contemporaine, Saint-Germain-la-Blanche-Herbe, France
Pitt Rivers Museum, University of Oxford, Oxford, United Kingdom
Rare Book and Manuscript Library, Columbia University, New York, New York, United States
Special Collections Research Center, University of Chicago Library, Chicago, Illinois, United States

Index

Page numbers in italics refer to figures.

acculturation, 116–17, 124
Ackerknecht, Erwin, 120, 130
alienation, 63
Altamira cave, 29, 30
Altizer, Tom, 221n18, 222n35
anarcho-primitivism, 180–81
animals: anthropomorphic, 118; as cave painting motif, Bataille's interpretation, 40, 43–46, 48–51; as cave painting motif, Breuil's interpretation, 36–38; Lascaux depictions, *41, 44, 47, 50*; sacrifice of, 26, 54; totemic, 26
Anthropocene, ix, 184–85
anthropology: Devereux's training in, 104, 105; fieldwork requirements, 211n5
anti-Semitism, 146–48
anxiety, and historical change, 158–59
Apache shamanism, 124
archaic, as term, 1. *See also* primitivism
archetypes, 155–58
architectural futurism, 74–77, *75*
Arendt, Hannah, 170, 172
art, prehistoric. *See* cave paintings
artistic primitivism, 8
Arts (journal), 33
Augé, Marc, 129
authenticity and forgery, of prehistoric art, 31–35
Axelrad, Sidney, 131

Bachelard, Gaston, 33
Barthes, Roland, 76
Basque culture, 66, 70, 81. *See also* Pyrenean peasant communities
Bastide, Roger, 126, 132, 134

Bataille, Georges, 20, *41*; and Breuil, 36, 43; career overview, 18–22; and Eliade, 26–27, 163, 164; on eroticism, 17–18, 50; on expenditure, 22, 25, 27–28, 35, 43, 45–46, 50, 54, 57–58, 97, 109; on formlessness, 35–36, 47, 197n47, 199n67; and Frazer, 26, 52, 55; and Freud, 26; generational experience of the twentieth century, 2; on intimacy of religion, 22–23; on Lascaux, aesthetic tradition views, 47; Lascaux, early fascination with, 39–42; on Lascaux, sacred interpretation of, 38, 42–46, 48–51; and Lefebvre, 71, 94, 96, 97, 98; and macrohistory, 51–53, 54–58; and Nietzsche, 19, 21, 55; on noble feelings, 195n17; and Pech-Merle affair, 30–31, 34–35; political views, 194n7, 195n13, 202n89; on sacrifice, 25–26, 27–28, 54, 55; on sexual taboos and transgressions, 17–18, 113, 114; and surrealism, 18, 19, 35, 197n45, 197n47; on survival/persistence of the archaic, 51, 53, 58; turn to prehistory, 29, 30; and Tylor, 26; and Weil, 23–25
Bataille, Georges, works: *The Accursed Share*, 21, 28, 30, 56, 182, 196n29; *Atheological Summa*, 19; *Blue of Noon*, 24; *Eroticism*, 49; *Lascaux or the Birth of Art*, 34–35, 43; "Military Victory and the Moral Bankruptcy That Confounds It," 24; "The Notion of Expenditure," 24; "On Eliade's Question," 26; "Outline for a History of Religions," 25; "Prehistoric Religion," 53; "Primitive Art," 35; *Story of the Eye*, 18; "Surrealism Day by Day," 35; *The Tears of Eros*, 50; *Theory of Religion*, 19–20, 22–23, 27
Baudrillard, Jean, 12, 84
Béarnais culture, 66, 70, 81. *See also* Pyrenean peasant communities

Beauvoir, Simone de, 108
Bégouën, Henri, 29
Bellow, Saul, 148, 158, 170, 172
Benedict, Ruth, 120
Benjamin, Walter, 19, 208n72
Berger, John, 48, 95, 221n27
Besançon, Alain, 133, 134
Bess, Michael, 208n53
Bessac, Abel, 33
Biles, Jeremy, 197n47
bird imagery, 49, 50, 163, 201n77
bison imagery, 46, 47, 47, 49–50, 50
Bloom, Allan, 170
Boas, Franz, 105
Boas, George, 7, 191n12, 200n71
Bohr, Niels, 135
Bordes, François, 34
bourgeois primitivism, 179–80
Bouteiller, Marcelle, 161
Braudel, Fernand, 132
Breton, André, 17, 30–35, 178, 209n76
Breuil, Henri, 37; *Four Hundred Centuries of Cave Art*, 35, 36–37; influence on prehistory field, 29–30; interpretation of cave paintings, 36–38, 43; Lascaux oversight, 39; and Pech-Merle affair, 32, 33–34, 197n39
Bruckner, Pascal, 10, 11, 192n18, 227n11
Brunschvicg, Léon, 61
bull imagery, 41, 43–44, 44, 45
Bullard, Alice, 217n91

Cabrerets affair, 30–35, 197n39
Cahiers internationaux de sociologie (journal), 69
Caillé, Alain, 182
Caillois, Roger, 19
Camus, Albert, 22, 24, 33
capitalism and industrialism: avoidance of, for emergence of socialist societies, 69–70; and "Capitalocene," 185; vs. communal production and distribution, 95–96; environmental destruction caused by, 92–93; and Great Acceleration, 2, 59–60; postwar reconstruction, 73–74 (*see also* Mourenx, France); rise of, as world-historical shift, 55–56; and uneven development, 65
Capitalocene, 185
Castaneda, Carlos, 165–66
cave paintings: and aesthetic tradition, 47–48; and Bataille's formlessness views, 35–36, 47, 199n67; Bataille's sacred interpretation of, 38, 42–46, 48–51; Breuil's hunting-magic interpretation of, 36–38, 43; Pech-Merle affair, 30–35, 197n39; and shamanism, 48–49, 163, 199n68, 201n77; structuralist approaches to, 200n73
Céline, Louis-Ferdinand, 148
Centre Georges Devereux, Paris, 137

Centre national de la recherche scientifique (CNRS), 68–69, 82–83
Centre Pompidou, prehistory exhibition, 29
Cercle communiste démocratique, 24
Césaire, Aimé, 11, 12
Chakrabarty, Dipesh, 227n17
Charcot, Jean-Martin, 103, 131
child-rearing, Mohave, 110
Cioran, Emil, 24, 143, 184, 226n103
Clifford, James, 11, 19, 192n22, 199n67
climate change and ecological crisis, ix, 2, 11–12, 72, 92–93, 184–85
Clottes, Jean, 163, 199n68
CNRS (Centre national de la recherche scientifique), 68–69, 82–83
Coetzee, J. M., 1, 170
collective unconscious, 157
Collège de sociologie, 11, 19
Collins, Jacob, 193n30
colonialism: and acculturation, 116–17, 124; and artistic primitivism, 8; and decolonization, 67, 150, 173; and end of archaic age, 55
Colorado River Indian Tribes (CRIT) Museum and Library, 138–40
Combat (journal), 32, 156
Committee on Social Thought, University of Chicago, 170–73
community: and communal production, 70–71, 95–97; and creativity, 63, 158; and cultural continuity, 68, 79–80, 108, 158, 167; cyclical rhythms to foster, 81–82, 98; and democracy, 79–80; and expenditure, 25, 54, 71–72; gemeinschaft-gesellschaft distinction, 101, 109–10; and gift economy, 6, 70–71, 97, 108, 110, 182; modern cities as lacking, 76–79; and nature, 71; shamans as essential to, 167
complementarity, 135
Conklin, Alice L., 192n25
cooperatives, worker-owned, 70, 71, 96–97
Corbin, Alain, 205n19
Correia, David, 179
Cotescu, Christinel, 142
countertransference, 128
Coyote tales, 117–19
creativity: and community, 63, 158; and cultural pessimism, 4, 23, 88–89, 137, 172, 186
CRIT (Colorado River Indian Tribes) Museum and Library, 138–40
Critique (journal), 19, 20–21, 27
Cronon, William, 180
Crossed Bison, Lascaux, 46, 47
cultural continuity, and community, 79–80, 108, 158, 167
cultural pessimism: creative potential of, 4, 23, 88–89, 137, 172, 186; of postwar primitivists, overview, 4–5, 7

cultural relativism, 130, 135–36
Curie, Marie, 104, 105
cyclical time and rhythms, 46, 80, 81–82, 98, 152, 154, 155, 158

Damas, Léon-Gontran, 12
Darnton, Robert, 14
Das Gupta, Surendranath, 142
Dax, Adrien, 31, 197n37
Debord, Guy, 89
decolonization, 67, 150, 173
deconstructionism, 23
degrowth movement, 92, 94–95, 182–83, 226n7
Delbo, Charlotte, *84*; as assistant and editor for Lefebvre, 82–85; *Auschwitz and After*, 87; "February," 86; as Holocaust survivor, 85; influence on Lefebvre, overview, 60; influence on Lefebvre's reorientation from rural to urban sociology, 89–90; influence on Lefebvre's thought on Marx, 87–88; influence on Lefebvre's thought on time, 86–87; urban sociology approach, 85–86
Deleuze, Gilles, 166; *Anti-Oedipus* (with Guattari), 133–34
democracy, and community, 79–80
dereistic societies, 103, 135–36
Derrida, Jacques, 23
desacralization, 169
Devereux, Georges, *102*; on complementarity, 135; cultural background and intellectual training, 103–5; displacement experience, 106–7; and Eliade, 165; ethnopsychiatry, establishment of field, 100–101, 132–34; on expenditure, 108–9; generational experience of the twentieth century, 2; on homeostasis, 107, 211n16; and Mauss, 104, 105, 108; on the Mohave, Coyote tales, 117–19; on the Mohave, cultural continuity of, 108–9; on the Mohave, as gemeinschaft, 109–10; on the Mohave, threat of acculturation, 116–17; on the Mohave, sexuality of, 111–15, 118–19, 126, 214n42; Mohave funeral for, 138–40, *139*; on Mohave shamanism, potential contribution to modern psychiatric practice, 129–31; on Mohave shamanism, reevaluation of, 101–3, 122–24, 131; on Mohave shamanism, similarity to modern psychiatry, 125–29; postwar modernization, critique of, 136–37; psychoanalytic training, 100, 128–29
Devereux, Georges, works: "Antagonistic Acculturation," 116–17; *Basic Problems of Ethnopsychiatry*, 134, 135; *Essais d'ethnopsychiatrie générale*, 133; *Ethnopsychanalyse complémentariste*, 133; *From Anxiety to Method in the Behavioral Sciences*, 128; "Mohave Coyote Tales," 117–18; *Mohave Ethnopsychiatry and Suicide*, 103, 111, 122–31, 134; "Mohave Indian Autoerotic Behavior," 112; *Normal and Abnormal*, 121; "Sexual Life of the Mohave Indians," 111
Devereux, Jane Wenning, 138
Diderot, Denis, 62; *Supplement to the Voyage of Bougainville*, 112
disalienation, 150, 154, 203n1
Documents (journal), 11, 18
dream culture, Mohave, 115–16, 118, 119–20, 126
Drennan, Anthony, Sr., 140
Dubuisson, Daniel, *Twentieth-Century Mythologies*, 146–47
Dudach, Georges, 85
Dumézil, Georges, 223n53, 225n93
Dunant, Ghislaine, 83
Durkheim, Émile, 5–6, 18, 22, 54, 143, 153, 194n3; *The Division of Labor in Society*, 6; *The Elementary Forms of Religious Life*, 174

Eagleton, Terry, 223n45
École pratique des hautes études (EPHE), 132
ecological crisis and climate change, ix, 2, 11–12, 72, 92–93, 184–85
ecstatic experiences, 49, 162–63
Elden, Stuart, 203n8, 204n13
Eliade, Mircea, *145*, *156*, *171*; and Bataille, 26–27, 163, 164; career overview, 141–44; and Castenada, 166; as comparatist, 142, 164, 173, 174–75, 224n62; on cyclical time and ritual repetition, 152, 154, 155, 157, 158; on desacralization, 169; and Devereux, 165; ethnocentrism, critique of, 149–50, 153, 167–68, 221n18; generational experience of the twentieth century, 2; interwar politics, 146–47; and Jung, 155–58, 222n34, 222n39; and Lascaux painting interpretations, 163, 199n68, 201n77; and Lefebvre, 155; and Nietzsche, 152, 155; as phenomenologist, 144–45; on religion as essential to humanity, 159, 175–76; on sacred time and space, 145–46, 153, 158; on sexuality, 118; on shamanism, and mental illness, 164–65; on shamanism, cultural unity of, 164; on shamanism, ecstatic experience of, 162–63; on "terror of history," 142, 153–55, 158–59, 160; on totemism, 26; at University of Chicago, 143–44, 168–73
Eliade, Mircea, works: *The Forbidden Forest*, 143; *The Forge and the Crucible*, 167; *Images and Symbols*, 145; *The Myth of the Eternal Return*, 27, 143, 144, 145, 147, 151–55, 157–60, 221n21; *Patterns in Comparative Religion*, 145; "Religions," 157; *The Sacred and the Profane*, 143; "Shamanism, Hallucinogens, Initiation," 166; *Shamanism and the Archaic Techniques of Ecstasy*, 143, 144, 147, 161–62
Eliot, T. S., 155, 170
Ellenberger, Henri, 100, 122, 125, 211n15, 216n73, 217n88

environmental crisis and climate change, ix, 2, 11–12, 72, 92–93, 184–85
EPHE (École pratique des hautes études), 132
equilibrium between production and expenditure, 45–46
Eranos Conferences, 156, *156*
eroticism, 17–18, 50
Etherington, Ben, 12
ethnocentrism, 149–50, 153, 167–68, 221n18
ethnographic romanticism, 67
ethnographic surrealism, 11, 19
ethnopsychiatry: and complementarity, 135; and countertransference, 128; establishment as field, 100–101, 132–34; Indigenous shamanism's similarity to modern psychiatry, 124–29; potential contribution of Mohave shamanism to modern psychiatric practice, 129–31
Eurocentrism, 149–50, 153, 167–68, 221n18
Evans-Pritchard, E. E., 174
existentialism, 62, 154, 204n9, 204n10
expenditure: Bataille on, 22, 25, 27–28, 35, 43, 45–46, 50, 54, 57–58, 97, 109; Devereux on, 108–9; Lefebvre on, 71–72, 96, 97–98

Fabian, Johannes, 10–11, 192nn20–21
Fanon, Frantz, 12, 168
Farmer, Sarah, 95, 203n2
fascism, 146–48, 194n7, 221n25
festivals, 71–72, 82
Figaro littéraire (journal), 32
Flaubert, Gustave, 113
Font-de-Gaume cave, 29
forgery and authenticity, of prehistoric art, 31–35
formlessness, 35–36, 47, 197n47, 199n67
Foster, Hal, 199n67
Foucault, Michel, 133, 199n67
France-Soir (newspaper), 32
France-Tireur (newspaper), 33
Fraser, Nancy, 97
Frazer, James G., 26, 52, 55, 153, 164; *The Golden Bough*, 36, 170, 174, 225n90
French Communist Party (PCF), 87, 208n58
Freud, Sigmund, 103, 129, 131, 165, 170; *The Interpretation of Dreams*, 116; *Totem and Taboo*, 26, 100, 174
Friedman, Lawrence, 100
Frye, Northrop, 164, 222n39, 224n62
funerary rites, Mohave, 109, 138–40, *139*
Furet, François, 170

Gardiner, Michael, 209n76
Gauguin, Paul, 178
gemeinschaft-gesellschaft distinction, 101, 109–10
generosity and reciprocity, of the Mohave, 108, 110
Geroulanos, Stefanos, 200n75, 202n94
gift economy, 6, 70–71, 97, 108, 110, 182

gilets jaunes (yellow vest movement), x–xi
Goldwater, Robert, *Primitivism in Modern Painting*, 8
Gorz, André, 182
Graeber, David, 180, 181
Great Acceleration, overview, 2, 59–60
Gross, Rita M., 225n77
growth, critique of, overview, 2–3
Guattari, Félix, *Anti-Oedipus* (with Deleuze), 133–34
Guerlac, Suzanne, 199n67
Gurvitch, Georges, 69
Guterman, Norbert, 61, 62

Hakl, Hans Thomas, 220n15
Hall of Bulls, Lascaux, 39, 40, *41*, 45
hallucinogenics, 165–66
Harootunian, Harry, 221n25
Hartog, François, 193n29
Hayek, Friedrich, 170
Heidegger, Martin, 199n67
Heine, Heinrich, 228n23
Herzog, Dagmar, 213n31
hierophanies, 145–46, 166
historicism, 153, 154, 155, 175
historicity, 159
History of Religion (journal), 170
history of religions: Bataille's approach to, overview, 22–28; Eliade's transformation of field, 168–70, 173–74
Hollier, Denis, 199n67
homeostasis, 107, 211n16
Homo economicus, 5, 56, 108, 178, 186
Homo religiosus, 43, 53, 159, 175
homosexuality, 113, 115, 213n31
Hubert, Henri, 18, 53–54, 127; *General Theory of Magic* (with Mauss), 127
Hughes, H. Stuart, 13
Hume, David, *Dialogues Concerning Natural Religion*, 174
hunting magic, 36–38, 43–44

ibex imagery, 36, 47
imitative magic, 36–38, 43–44
imperialism. *See* colonialism
Indigenous cultures: and acculturation, 116–17, 124; Basque and Béarnais disparaged as, 70; Marx's study of, 95; Paleolithic comparisons, 48–49; shamanism, 49, 124–25, 127, 164, 165–66. *See also* Apache shamanism; Mohave; Mohave shamans and shamanism; Navaho; Yaqui shamanism
industrialization. *See* capitalism and industrialism
intimacy: with animal/natural world, 38, 46, 50–51, 54, 202n94; as essence of religion, 22–23; and sacrifice, 22, 25, 54

INDEX 235

Ionesco, Eugène, 177
Ionescu, Nae, 146
Iron Guard, 146–48, 220n15

Jaccard, Roland, 135, 137
Jameson, Fredric, 184–85, 227n14
Janet, Pierre, 131
Joyce, James, 155
Joyce, Patrick, 208n56, 209n84
Judt, Tony, 209n73
Jung, Carl, 155–58, *156*, 222n34, 222n39

Kirchner, Hörst, 201n77
Klineberg, Otto, 134
Klossowski, Pierre, 19
Knight, Frank, 170
Kroeber, Alfred, 104, 105, 107, 110, 112, 115, 119
Kurasawa, Fuyuki, 192n27

La Barre, Weston, 215n61, 224n58
La critique sociale (journal), 24
Lacan, Jacques, 218n110
Lacq industrial complex, 73–74, *74*, 76, *78*. See also Mourenx, France
Lafitau, Joseph-François, *Customs of the American Indians Compared with the Customs of Primitive Times*, 127
Lamb, Charles A., 138, 140
Laming-Emperaire, Annette, 200n73
Laplantine, François, 134, 218n110
Lascaux cave, 20, 37, 41, 44, 47, 50; and aesthetic tradition, 47–48; Bataille's early fascination with, 39–42; Bataille's sacred interpretation of, 38, 42–46, 48–51; degradation and closure of, 42, 58, 198n59; discovery of, 38–39; and shamanism, 48–49, 163, 199–200n68, 201n77
Latouche, Serge, 181–82
Latour, Bruno, 184
Lavi, Theodor, 146
Lawrence, D. H., 12, 166, 214n43
Le Corbusier, 74
Le Guin, Ursula K., 212–13n30, 227n14
Le Monde (newspaper), 32, 34, 133, 137
Leach, Edmund, 222n39
Leenhardt, Maurice, 161
Lefebvre, Henri, 62; on alienation, 63; and Bataille, 71, 94, 96, 97, 98; career overview, 61–65; at CNRS, 68–69, 82–83; on communal production, 70–71, 95–97; on cyclical rhythms of community formation, 81–82, 98; Delbo as editor for, 83–85; Delbo's influence on approach to Marx, 87–88; Delbo's influence on approach to time, 86–87; Delbo's influence on reorientation from rural to urban sociology, 89–90; on destructive nature of capitalism, 92–93; on differential spaces, 45; and Eliade, 155; and existentialism, 62, 204n9, 204n10; on expenditure, 71–72, 96, 97–98; generational experience of the twentieth century, 2; growth ideologies, critique of, 91–92; Mourenx, critique of, 76–79, 90–91; and Nietzsche, 64–65, 204n13; on nostalgia for nature, 93–94; PCF association, 87, 208n58; on primitivism, 205n24; Pyrenean communities, early fascination with, 66–68, 205n22; revivalist thought, 66, 81, 86; and situationism, 89, 209n76; on spring festivals, 71–72; and surrealism, 62, 204n9, 209n76; on survivals, as underliving, 65–66; upbringing, 61, 203n5; urban sociology, turn to, 79–81, 90

Lefebvre, Henri, works: *Critique of Everyday Life*, 66; *Dialectical Materialism*, 63–64; *The Explosion*, 68; *Introduction to Modernity*, 95; *La somme et le reste*, 64; *L'existentialisme*, 64; *Metaphilosophy*, 83–84; "Nature and Nature Conquered," 93; *Nietzsche*, 64; "Notes on the New Town," 80; "Notes Written One Sunday in the French Countryside," 66; *The Production of Space*, 45, 84; *The Survival of Capitalism*, 96; "What Is the Historical Past?," 86
Leighton, Alexander and Dorothea, 124–25
Leiris, Michel, 11, 18, 19, 21
Leroi-Gourhan, André, 200n73
Les temps modernes (journal), 86, 114
Lévi-Strauss, Claude, 19, 33, 117, 132, 134–35, 192n21, 211n5, 217–18n103
Lévy-Bruhl, Henri, 69
Lévy-Bruhl, Lucien, 104, 105, 153
Lewis-Williams, David, 163, 199n68
Lewitsky, Anatole, 19, 48, 105, 161
Li, Victor, 12
"like produces like" principle, 36, 37, 44
Lincoln, Bruce, *Secrets, Lies, and Consequences*, 147–48
Long, Charles, 141–42, 150
Lot-Falck, Éveline, 48–49, 161
Lovejoy, Arthur O., 7, 8–9, 188, 191n12; *Primitivism and Related Ideas in Antiquity*, 7, 176
Lowie, Robert, 104, 153
Löwy, Michael, 210n91, 227n12, 228n19
Luquet, Georges-Henri, *Primitive Art*, 35

macrohistory, 51–53, 54–58
Macron, Emmanuel, xi
magic, sympathetic, 36–38, 43–44
Malinowski, Bronisław, 104, 135, 153
Malraux, André, 33, 198n59
Maneval, Jean-Benjamin, 74
Mann, Thomas, 104
Marcuse, Herbert, 93
Marshall Plan (1948), 54
Marx, Karl, and Marxism: on alienation, 63; *Capital*, 95, 96, 210n95; on communal production,

Marx, Karl, and Marxism (*cont.*) 95; *Economic and Philosophical Manuscripts*, 61; Lefebvre's augmentation of, with Nietzsche, 64–65, 204n13; Lefebvre's early interest in, 61; on nature, 71; postwar relevance of, 87–88; on transformation of rural communities to socialist societies, 69–70; on uneven development, 65

Masson, André, 17

Masuzawa, Tomoko, 221n21, 222n43

Mauriac, François, 33

Mauss, Marcel: and anthropology fieldwork requirements, 211n5; and Bataille, 18; and Devereux, 104, 105, 108; *General Theory of Magic* (with Hubert), 127; *The Gift*, 6, 182; as progenitor of postwar primitivists, 2, 5–6, 14; on sacrifice, 53–54; on shamanism, 127, 216n81

Mead, Margaret, 194n34, 218n105

memory, and remembrances, 87

Mendras, Henri, 207n45

Menninger, Karl A., 100, 104, 129

Menninger Clinic, Topeka, Kansas, 100

mental illness: and culturally relativistic concepts of normality, 130, 135–36; and empathy in caring for the mentally ill, 121, 127; and postwar modernization, 136–37, 158–59; of shamans, 120–21, 164–65

Merkel, Ian, 193n30

Merleau-Ponty, Maurice, 63

Métraux, Alfred, 18, 19, 21, 105, 164, 224n66

millenarianism, 92

modernization theory, 207n50

Mohave: Coyote tales, 117–19; cultural continuity of, 108–9; dream culture of, 115–16, 118, 119–20, 126; funerary rites, 109, 138–40, *139*; as gemeinschaft, 109–10; generosity of, 108, 110; homeland, 107–8; inclusive humanity of, 113, 115, 121, 127; mythology, 117; photographs as taboo, 99–100; sexuality of, 111–15, 118–19, 126, 214n42; wealth and accumulation, opposition to, 99, 100, 109

Mohave shamans and shamanism: Devereux's reevaluation of, overview, 101–3, 122–24, 131; and dream interpretation, 119–20, 126; ecstatic experience of, 162; mental illness of, 120–21; potential contribution to modern psychiatric practice, 129–31; similarity to modern psychiatry, 125–29

Mourenx, France, 75, 78; establishment, 73–75; Lefebvre's critique of, 75–79, 90–91; postwar reconstruction, 75–76; as social laboratory, 80–81; standard of living in, 79

Mumford, Lewis, 198n60; *The City in History*, 86

mythical tales, primitive desire for, 159

mythology, Mohave, 117

Nathan, Tobie, 134, 137

nationalism, 146–48

nature: and communal solidarity, 71; desire for intimacy with, 38, 46, 50–51, 54, 202n94; and naturalizing the historical, 67; primitivist return to, 8–9. *See also* animals

Navaho: animals in culture of, 49; psychotherapy, 124–25

Navarrenx, France, 61, 73, 76, 80

Nef, John U., 170, *171*, 225n84

Neumann, Erich, 156

Niaux cave, 29, 36, 45

Nietzsche, Friedrich: and Bataille, 19, 21, 55; *Genealogy of Morals*, 55; and Eliade, 152, 155; and Lefebvre, 64–65, 204n13; nostalgic ruminations, 206n32

normality, culturally relativistic concepts of, 130, 135–36

nostalgia: and creative potential of cultural pessimism, 4, 23, 88–89, 137, 172, 186; critique of, 72; and homesickness, 77, 207n47; and mourning, 88; for nature, 93–94; and survival, 159–60

obscurantism, 5

Opler, Morris, 124

Paleolithic art. *See* cave paintings

paradox of disappearance and persistence, 5, 58, 70, 81, 124, 158, 159, 205n19

Parsons, Talcott, 104, 105

past: modern cities without, 77, 90–91; perennial vs. withering, 87; realization of possibilities of, in the present, 86

Paulhan, Jean, 33, 104

PCF (French Communist Party), 87, 208n58

peasant experience. *See* Pyrenean peasant communities

Pech-Merle cave, 29, 30–35, 197n39

Perrin, Jean, 105

persistence-disappearance paradox, 5, 58, 70, 81, 124, 158, 159, 205n19

pessimism. *See* cultural pessimism

phenomenology, 144–45

Picasso, Pablo, 39

Pinker, Steven, 55

Poincaré, Henri, 225n93

postcolonialism, 141, 144, 149–50, 168, 172

Poster, Mark, 204n10

poststructuralism and structuralism, 11, 53, 200n73

postwar primitivism, as term, x, 7

prehistory: Bataille's turn to, 29, 30; as cornerstone of human history, 53; establishment as field in France, 29–30

presentism, 192–93n29

primitive, as term, 1

primitivism: as concept, x, 7–10; critique of, 10–11; modern resurgence of, 11–12, 179–84; and persistence-disappearance paradox, 5, 58, 70, 81,

124, 158, 159, 205n19; and selective revival, x, 4, 7, 60, 66, 70, 80, 187. *See also* cultural pessimism
production: and alienation, 63; and expenditure, 43, 45–46
profane/sacred dichotomy, 51, 52, 71, 145, 153, 158
provincial France. *See* Pyrenean peasant communities
psychoanalysis, Jungian, 155–58
psychoanalytic anthropology. *See* ethnopsychiatry
psychological health. *See* mental illness
puritanical societies, 114–15
Pyrenean peasant communities: cyclical rhythms of, 81–82; demise of, in postwar modernization, 80, 81; Lefebvre's early fascination with, 66–68, 205n22; spring festivals, 71–72; worker-owned cooperatives and gift economy in, 70–71

Queneau, Raymond, 33

Radin, Paul, 153, 223n52
reciprocity and generosity, of the Mohave, 108, 110
Redfield, Robert, 170
religious history. *See* history of religions
remembrances, 87
repetition, ritual, 152, 153, 155, 157, 158
repression, sexual, 118–19
revival, selective, x, 4, 7, 60, 66, 70, 80, 187
Revue de l'histoire des religions (journal), 170
Revue du MAUSS (journal), 182
Revue française de sociologie (journal), 85, 86
Richardson, Michael, 197n45
Ricoeur, Paul, 170
ritual repetition, 152, 153, 155, 157, 158
Rivet, Paul, 33, 104, 105
Robcis, Camille, 193n30
Robinson, Kim Stanley, 183–84, 202n90, 227n14
Rodinson, Maxime, 69–70
Róheim, Géza, *Psychoanalysis and the Social Sciences*, 100–101, 165
Romanian Iron Guard, 146–48, 220n15
Romo, Retha, 138
rootedness, 25
Rothberg, Michael, 60, 203n3
Rougemont, Denis de, 219n2
Roupnel, Gaston, 67, 205n24
Rousseau, Jean-Jacques, 62, 179, 198n55
Rudkin, C. N., 102
rural France. *See* Pyrenean peasant communities
rural sociology: and Lefebvre's position at CNRS, 68–69; rethinking survivals as analytical framework, 67–68, 73; urban sociology rooted in lessons of, 79–81, 90. *See also* urban sociology

sacred/profane dichotomy, 51, 52, 71, 145, 153, 158
sacrifice: of animals, 26, 54; collective, 25, 54; as duty of individuals, 24, 25; as fundamental rite of archaic religions, 53–54; and intimacy, 22, 25, 54; and violence, 55
Sahlins, Marshall, 12, 181, 191n4
Saito, Kohei, 95, 210n91, 227n8
schizophrenia, 136, 137, 165, 218n108
Schmidt, Wilhelm, 153
Scholem, Gershom, 146
Schorske, Carl, 13
Scott, James C., 181
selective revival, x, 4, 7, 60, 66, 70, 80, 187
Senghor, Léopold Sédar, 12
Serres, Michel, 12
sexuality: and eroticism, 17–18, 50; Mohave, 111–15, 118–19, 126, 214n42; in puritanical societies, 114–15; taboos and transgressions, 17–18, 113, 114
shamanism: and animality, 48–49; communal role of, 167; cultural unity of, 164; ecstatic experience of, 49, 162–63; and hallucinogenics, 165–66; and Lascaux painting interpretation, 48–49, 163, 199–200n68, 201n77; and mental illness, 120–21, 164–65; prejudice against, 101–2, 120, 127, 131. *See also* Mohave shamans and shamanism
Siberian shamanism, 48–49, 164, 201n77
Silverman, Daniel, 132
situationism, 89, 209n76
Skira, Albert, 43
slavery, 54–55
Smith, Douglas, 199n67
SNPA (Société nationale des pétroles d'Aquitaine), 73–74
Sobin, Gustaf, 210n94
social surplus, 97. *See also* expenditure
social thought, defined, 13
socialism. *See* Marx, Karl, and Marxism
Société nationale des pétroles d'Aquitaine (SNPA), 73–74
Société préhistorique française, 29
sociology. *See* rural sociology; urban sociology
Sollers, Philippe, 18
Sorokin, Pitirim, 104, 105
Soustelle, Jacques, 132
Souvarine, Boris, 24
Souvestre, Émile, 70
Spengler, Oswald, 155; *The Decline of the West*, 86
spring festivals, 71–72
standards of living, 79
Stavisky, Alexandre, 106
Stavrinaki, Maria, 199n67
Stendhal, 67, 113, 177
Stevens, Thomas, 140
Stoekl, Allan, 199n63
Stoetzel, Jean, 83, 85
Strauss, Leo, 148
structuralism and poststructuralism, 11, 53, 200n73
supernaturalism, 125

surrealism: and Bataille, 18, 19, 35, 197n47, 197n45; ethnographic, 11, 19; and Lefebvre, 62, 204n9, 209n76; vs. social sciences, 34, 35
survivals: Bataille on, 58; as concept, x; Lefebvre on, 65–66, 67–68, 73; modern imperative to analyze, 72–73; of Mohave culture, 109–10, 124
survivances, as term, 65
Surya, Michel, 18
Swick, Pat, 138
symbolism: and community formation, 81–82; as historically situated, 175; sexual, 118–19
sympathetic magic, 36–38, 43–44

techno-futurism, 185–86
Teilhard de Chardin, Pierre, 94, 154
terror of history, 142, 153–55, 158–59, 160
time: and cultural continuity, 68, 79–80, 108, 158, 167; cyclical, 46, 80, 81–82, 98, 152, 154, 155, 158; in ecstatic experience, 163; modern cities without a past, 77, 90–91; perennial vs. withering past, 87; in postwar primitivism, overview, 3; realization of past possibilities in the present, 86; religious phenomena as both timeless and historically situated, 175; sacred vs. profane, 145, 153, 158; and the "terror of history," 142, 153–55, 158–59, 160
Toladot (journal), 146
Tönnies, Ferdinand, 109
Topeka Psychoanalytic Society, 100
Torgovnick, Marianna, 192n19
totemism, 26
tower block architecture, 74–77, *75*
Toynbee, Arnold, 155
transsexuality, 113, 115
Traverso, Enzo, 88
Trois Frères cave, 29
Tupoma, Hivsu (Dan Lamont), 101, 103, 108, 121, 122, *123*, 125, 128

Tylor, Edward Burnett, 26, 72–73, 206n39, 206n40; *Primitive Culture*, 174
Tzara, Tristan, 89

underliving, 65–66
uneven development, 65, 72
Ungar, Steven, 199n67
Unicorn, the, Lascaux, 43–44, *44*
University of Chicago, 143–44, 168–73
urban sociology: Delbo-Lefebvre collaboration, 89–90; Delbo's, 85–86; Lefebvre's turn to, 79–81, 90. *See also* rural sociology
Utce, Hama (Agnes Savilla), 100, 108, 138, 212n20
utopian thinking, 66, 72, 80, 82

Valéry, Paul, 144
Vézelay commune, 19
Vézère Valley. *See* Lascaux cave
violence, and sacrifice, 55
Vizenor, Gerald, 73

Wahl, Jean, 25, 33
Wallace-Wells, David, 16, 184
Wasserstrom, Steven, 147
Weber, Eugen, 205n22, 207n45
Weil, Simone, 22, 23–25; *The Need for Roots*, 23–25
Well Scene, Lascaux, 49–50, *50*
Wengrow, David, 181
White, Lester, 138
White, Lorraine, 138
Windels, Fernand, 36
Wittkower, Eric, 211n15
worker-owned cooperatives, 70, 71, 96–97

Yaqui shamanism, 165–66
yellow vest movement (*gilets jaunes*), x–xi

Zerzan, John, 180–81
Ziegler, Jean, 136, 218n109

www.ingramcontent.com/pod-product-compliance
Lightning Source LLC
Chambersburg PA
CBHW022049290426
44109CB00014B/1035